BURGOYNE
and the Saratoga Campaign

Eighteenth-century engraving of
Lieutenant General John Burgoyne,
by Swaine, c. 1780–86. *Author's collection.*

BURGOYNE
and the Saratoga Campaign
HIS PAPERS

By
Douglas R. Cubbison

UNIVERSITY OF OKLAHOMA PRESS
Norman, Oklahoma

Also by Douglas R. Cubbison

"The Artillery never gained more Honour": The British Artillery in the 1776 Valcour Island and 1777 Saratoga Campaigns (Fleischmanns, N.Y., 2007)

The American Northern Theater Army in 1776: The Ruin and Reconstruction of the Continental Force (Jefferson, N.C., 2010)

The British Defeat of the French in Pennsylvania, 1758: A Military History of the Forbes Campaign against Fort Duquesne (Jefferson, N.C., 2010)

Library of Congress Cataloging-in-Publication Data

Burgoyne, John, 1722–1792.

Burgoyne and the Saratoga Campaign : his papers / by Douglas R. Cubbison. — 1st ed.

p. cm.

Includes bibliographical references and index.

ISBN 978-0-87062-409-4 (cloth)

ISBN 978-0-8061-4461-0 (paper)

1. Saratoga Campaign, N.Y., 1777—Personal narratives, British. 2. Burgoyne, John, 1722–1792—Military leadership. 3. Burgoyne, John, 1722–1792—Correspondence. 4. Dorchester, Guy Carleton, Baron, 1724–1808—Correspondence. 5. Generals—Great Britain—Correspondence. 6. Generals—Great Britain—Biography. I. Cubbison, Douglas. II. Title.

E241.S2B87 2012

973.3'41—dc23

2011046118

The paper in this book meets the guidelines for permanence and durability of the Committee on Production Guidelines for Book Longevity of the Council on Library Resources, Inc. ∞

To Clio, the Muse that I serve

Contents

Illustrations

Maps

Prepared by Michael F. Beard,
SunSyne Graphics, Johnson City, Tennessee

Acknowledgments

I wish to thank Wendy Newell and the staff of the Fort Drum Library, Fort Drum, New York, and Heather Turner and other members of the Reference Department of the Combined Arms Research Library, Fort Leavenworth, Kansas, for their generous and always uncomplaining assistance. This book could not have been prepared without the numerous, otherwise unobtainable references and sources that they were able to locate. Katherine Ludwig, librarian, Greg Johnson, and the other members of the David Library of the American Revolution, Washington Crossing, Pennsylvania, provided me with considerable assistance on numerous occasions, and I deeply appreciate their always friendly aid. Assistance with the letter of Burgoyne regarding the Battle of Bunker Hill was provided by Susan Lintelmann, manuscripts curator at Jefferson Hall, the library of the U.S. Military Academy at West Point. Dr. Brenda J. Buchanan, author of *Gunpowder, Explosives, and the State: A Technological History*, generously assisted me with information regarding British Board of Ordnance gunpowder barrel weights.

A professional colleague at the U.S. Army Combat Studies Institute, Fort Leavenworth, Kansas, John Magrath, generously assisted me with the French translation of one letter. Chris Fox, curator at the Fort Ticonderoga Museum, provided considerable assistance with numerous photographs of items in the Fort Ticonderoga Museum's collections.

I also wish to acknowledge my old comrade in His Majesty's 64th Regiment of Foot, Dr. Gregory J. W. Urwin of Temple University, for his assistance in preparing this manuscript for publication.

My good friends Gavin Watt and Christian Cameron of Ontario, Canada, assisted me with identifying the existence of these letters and obtaining copies from the United Kingdom. For readers interested in the St. Leger Campaign, Gavin has written the finest campaign history of that column: Gavin K. Watt, *Rebellion in the Mohawk Valley: The St. Leger Expedition of 1777* (Toronto: Dundurn Press, 2002).

Permission to publish the letter of John Burgoyne to General Gates, [Dovegot House,] October 9, 1777, Sol Feinstone Collection, David Library of the American Revolution (on deposit at the American Philosophical Society), Washington Crossing, Pennsylvania, was generously provided courtesy of the library.

Permission to publish the letters of Lieutenant General John Burgoyne (dated July 7, 1776; November 7, 1776; and March 2, 1777) from the Sir Henry Clinton Papers and the mezzotint of George Germain, Lord Sackville, was generously provided courtesy of the William L. Clements Library, University of Michigan, Ann Arbor.

Photographs of items from the collections of the Fort Ticonderoga Museum, Ticonderoga, New York, were generously provided through the assistance of Christopher Fox, curator; permission to use these photographs was generously provided by Beth Hill, executive director of the museum.

The maps were prepared by my good friend and professional associate for many years, Michael Beard of SunSyne Graphics, Johnson City, Tennessee.

The author's photograph was taken by another good friend and professional associate, Jennifer Almquist Butkus, of Jennifer Butkus Photography.

Editorial Procedures

Throughout the transcription, every effort was made to retain the original documents without alteration. Capitalization, punctuation, sentence structure, and spelling have not been altered in this transcription. Within the original documents, emphasis was often indicated by underlining, which has been retained. Any editorial comments deemed appropriate for insertion are incorporated within square brackets. All other editorial comments are provided as footnotes. It should be noted that, as per eighteenth-century usage, capitalization, punctuation, and sentence structure were not formalized and thus vary widely across the documents. In fact, these elements frequently vary within a single document. Interestingly enough, Burgoyne's spelling tended to be relatively consistent.[1] Finally, the file numbers used throughout this book are as assigned by the Parliamentary Archives, House of Parliament (unless otherwise noted).

[1]*Dr. Samuel Johnson's Dictionary*, the first true English-language dictionary, had only been released in 1755. McAdam and Milne, eds., *Johnson's Dictionary: A Modern Selection.*

Introduction

The papers presented in this book, most of which are previously unpublished in either the United States or the United Kingdom, were gathered by Lieutenant General John Burgoyne in support of his intended defense during the 1779 parliamentary investigations into his conduct of the Saratoga Campaign of 1777. The originals are located in the Parliamentary Archives, Houses of Parliament, London. Although historians have cited a number of these letters, the documents have never been placed within their proper context or published in their entirety.

An early Burgoyne letter, written in June 1775 after the Battle of Bunker Hill, has also been included. This letter is critical to understanding Burgoyne's approach to the Saratoga Campaign, as his observations of the engagement on Bunker Hill strongly influenced his subsequent tactics and strategy. The copy included here is a handwritten version from the U.S. Military Academy Special Collections and Archives. The Massachusetts Historical Society has a reprinted version of this letter that is nearly identical. Some additional Burgoyne letters located in various papers at the William L. Clements Library, University of Michigan, have also been transcribed in their entirety and added to supplement the 1779 Parliamentary Papers. These few letters were identified as critical to comprehending the formulation of the campaign or were originally attachments to some of the documents included in the Parliamentary Papers but were later separated. In addition, three letters Burgoyne wrote at the culmination of the campaign from Cambridge, Massachusetts, were located in the Sir Frederick Haldimand Papers, and their transcriptions were added to this collection. The original Haldimand Papers are deposited in the British Library, and copies are available on microfilm at the David Library of the American Revolution, Washington Crossing, Pennsylvania, and at the University of Toronto Library.

Twelve of these papers were previously published as supporting documents in Burgoyne's *State of the Expedition from Canada* (London:

J. Almon, 1780; reprint, New York: The New York Times & Arno Press, 1969). This book presented the British public with the defense of the Saratoga Campaign that Burgoyne had been denied before Parliament. The twelve documents that Burgoyne published in his book were extracted from these papers that would eventually be placed into the Archives of Parliament. Perhaps these papers' most important revelation is contained within the twelve documents previously published by Burgoyne. When the original documents are compared with the versions that Burgoyne had printed, they reveal that he did not materially alter, delete, or otherwise change any of the papers. All twelve papers that Burgoyne utilized are reproduced herein in their entirety and display no modifications except minor variations in punctuation and capitalization, which may well have been the work of the printer and not Burgoyne. Whatever may have been his faults, Burgoyne was publishing the truth of the campaign not only as he saw it but also as the official records documented.

These papers in the present volume provide hitherto unpublished accounts of the campaign, particularly as regards its planning, preparations, and logistics. Some of these letters are familiar to, and have been used by, other historians, but they have never previously benefited from a full transcription and publication. General Sir William Howe's role in the campaign is clearly revealed by these papers. Additionally, valuable new British army accounts of the engagements at Oriskany, Fort Stanwix, and Bennington are contained within these papers. It is intended that making these primary source documents available to historians and students of the American War of Independence will facilitate future study and research related to Burgoyne's 1777 Saratoga Campaign and provide another invaluable addition to the relatively limited number of British army primary source documents for this campaign.

The three Burgoyne letters from the Haldimand Papers reveal the challenges faced by the surrendered British army as it wintered in Cambridge, Massachusetts. It is hoped their inclusion here will make some small contribution to the comprehension of the saga of the Convention Army.

The three principal actors in these papers are Lieutenant General John Burgoyne; the Governor of Canada, General Guy Carleton; and British Secretary of State for North America Lord George Germain.

Lieutenant General Burgoyne was, at the outbreak of the American War of Independence, a highly experienced professional officer with superlative political connections.[1] Born in London in 1723, he was allegedly the illegitimate son of the wealthy Lord Bingley, a self-made English gentleman who was well placed at the Royal Court. As a youth Burgoyne had attended school at Westminster, an institution that stressed Latin and English composition, and from which many Englishmen prominent in civic affairs would graduate. Burgoyne purchased his first commission in 1737, at the age of fifteen, in the elite Horse Guards, thus validating his eminent patronage. Burgoyne went on to serve with distinction in Europe. During the War of the Austrian Succession, he fought with the 1st Royal Dragoons in Flanders, then returned to England to help defend London during the 1745 Jacobite Rebellion. Burgoyne was not present at the Battle of Culloden in April 1746, where the Duke of Cumberland, the son of George II, crushed the Jacobite pretender to the throne. By the start of the Seven Years' War (1756–1763) Burgoyne was a captain in the 11th Dragoons. Burgoyne participated in several amphibious raids on the French coast, and in 1759 he raised and became the colonel of the 16th Light Dragoons. Burgoyne earned credit for leadership skills demonstrated in Portugal in 1762. Following the Seven Years' War, Burgoyne remained in the army; dabbled at popular playwriting, which gained him some notoriety; enjoyed the social life in London; and most important, became a prominent member of Parliament with strong ties to the Tory Party and King George III. By 1775 Burgoyne was one of the most prominent British general officers, and given his relationship with the king and support of the Tory administration, it was natural that he would be dispatched to Boston in 1775 and to Canada in 1776 and 1777. Burgoyne's career previous to the outbreak of the American rebellion had been distinguished and he showed great promise. However, Burgoyne possessed no previous knowledge of, or military service in, North America prior to his arrival at Boston, having earned his reputation as a cavalry commander in Europe. Whether

[1]Burgoyne, a colorful historical figure, has been the subject of numerous biographies. Those consulted by the author include Howson, *Burgoyne of Saratoga*; Hargrove, "General John Burgoyne"; Lewis, *Man Who Lost America*; Lunt, *John Burgoyne of Saratoga*; Glover, *Burgoyne in Canada and America*; Mintz, *Generals of Saratoga*; and Hudleston, *Gentleman Johnny Burgoyne*.

or not Burgoyne could successfully apply his cavalry skills and European experience to the peculiar circumstances of warfare along the waterways and deep woods of Canada and New York remained to be seen. Another professional military officer highly regarded throughout decades of service with a number of armies in Europe, and respected for several insightful publications on military art and science, General Henry Lloyd commented wryly on Burgoyne's departure for Canada: "I am sure this fine flourishing fellow will come home with his arms tied behind his back."[2]

Governor Guy Carleton was fifty-two years old in 1776, having been born of Scotch-Irish stock in Ireland in 1724.[3] His military service had begun in 1742, when he was commissioned an ensign at seventeen years of age. Carleton was a close personal friend of James Wolfe, and they served together in Holland. During the Seven Years' War Carleton had gained considerable military experience. He served with his friend Wolfe at the Siege of Quebec in 1759 and was wounded commanding the 2nd Battalion of the 60th Foot on the left flank of the British battle line at the Plains of Abraham. One indication of the esteem that Wolfe had for Carleton is that Wolfe left his professional library to Carleton in his will.[4] Carleton was again seriously wounded in an amphibious assault on the shores of France in 1761, and at the Siege of Havana, Cuba, in 1762. Carleton was appointed "Lieutenant Governor and Administrator of Quebec" in 1766, and he spent almost ten years administering the Colony of Canada before the Revolutionary War broke out. A skilled and experienced military and civil officer, he was fanatically loyal to the British Crown, and he knew Canada—its weather, geography, and commerce—intimately.

Lord George Germain was King George III's secretary of state for North America from 1755, a position that gave him responsibility for the

[2]Speelman, *Lloyd and the Military Enlightenment*, 92.

[3]There are a large number of excellent biographies of Carleton. Those utilized for this study include Browne, "Guy Carleton, 1st Baron of Dorchester," in *Dictionary of Canadian Biography*, 5:141–155; Smith, "Sir Guy Carleton: Soldier Statesman," in Billias, ed., *George Washington's Opponents*, 103–141; Bradley, *Sir Guy Carleton*; Leroy, "Carleton as a Military Leader"; Nelson, *General Sir Guy Carleton*; and Reynolds, *Guy Carleton*. Carleton's greatest detractor is Canadian historian A. L. Burt, whose critical biography, *Guy Carleton, Lord Dorchester, 1724–1804*, was published in 1955.

[4]Brisebois, "Books from General Wolfe's Library."

war with the thirteen colonies. Germain had been born Lord George Sackville in 1716. He entered military service in 1740, and his noble birth and prominent political and social connections rapidly elevated him to the rank of major general by 1759. At the Battle of Minden, Sackville did not obey an order to launch an attack at a critical moment in the engagement, a lapse for which he was subsequently court-martialed and dismissed from the service, being judged "unfit to serve his Majesty in any military capacity whatsoever." Sackville remained in the House of Lords, and in 1769 a family friend, Lady Elizabeth Germain, died without heirs. Sackville subsequently assumed her title and her estate, becoming Lord George Germain for the remainder of his life. Germain became a strong political supporter of Lord North and King George and was appointed secretary of state for North America. Having never set foot there, Germain lacked any familiarity with the geographical, topographical, economic, and political circumstances in America and Canada. Germain's conduct of the war would subsequently come under considerable criticism. It is generally acknowledged by historians that his handling of the British war effort was vacillating, indecisive, and lacked insight into the actual conditions to be found in the North American theater. When Lord North lost power after Yorktown, Germain also retired from public life. He died at his estate in 1785 following a life marked by general failures and missed opportunities.

These papers present the relationship and communications between these three key British military and political leaders. To place these papers into proper historical context, and to provide an overview of Burgoyne's participation and leadership in the Saratoga Campaign, an essay and conclusions have been prepared.

This previously unpublished caricature of
Lieutenant General John Burgoyne, done by James Sayers and published by Charles Bretherton in London on June 17, 1782, depicts Burgoyne as he appeared during the 1777 Saratoga Campaign and when he subsequently gathered these papers in England. The Burgoyne portraits by Allan Ramsay and Joshua Reynolds were done in 1755–56 and 1766, respectively, and show a considerably younger Burgoyne.
Courtesy National Portrait Gallery, London.

Lieutenant General John Burgoyne and His Leadership in the Saratoga Campaign

At the onset of hostilities between the thirteen American colonies and the home country of Great Britain in 1775, the United Colonies turned their attention to seizing Canada as a potential fourteenth colony. By the fall of 1775 two American columns had descended upon the St. Lawrence River valley, seized British garrisons at Fort Chambly and Fort St. John's, captured Montreal, and blockaded Quebec.[1] When word of this latest American outrage reached London, the British leadership was seriously alarmed. The decision was reached to dispatch a powerful military force either to reinforce the defense of Canada or to regain control of the colony if the Americans had succeeded in wresting control of Quebec from Governor-General Sir Guy Carleton. In the spring of 1776, predominantly because of his political connections, Lieutenant General John Burgoyne was dispatched to lead the detachment of the British army sent to relieve Canada.

With the outbreak of the Revolutionary War, Burgoyne had been promoted to major general and had been ordered to assist the British army in Boston from May to November 1775. He had spent a summer in idleness in Boston, for in truth there was nothing for no less than three major generals to do in that city. His most instructive moment came when he observed, but not did not participate in, the Battle of Bunker Hill, as he subsequently related in a widely reprinted letter to Lord Stanley in London in late June 1775 (U.S. Military Academy Files). This observation provided Burgoyne with a healthy respect for

[1]This fort is also known in French as Fort Saint-Jean.

the Americans' ability at entrenchment, and the capacity of untrained, undisciplined American militia to fight resolutely behind such fortifications. Presumably, his service in Boston must also have afforded Burgoyne some knowledge of American affairs.

Burgoyne had proven that he possessed a talent for independent command, and had demonstrated initiative and innovation in his Seven Years' War service in Portugal. Though possessing nearly four decades of experience, he was still physically robust and energetic enough to command effectively in the demanding Canadian climate. Given the available British generals, his staunch Tory propensities doubtless recommended him to King George III and Lord George Germain as the best choice possible to command the army in Canada. Burgoyne departed Portsmouth, England, in early April 1776 onboard the frigate HMS *Blonde*.

Sharing the voyage to Canada with Burgoyne were two men with whom he would shortly forge deep personal and professional relationships, Major General William Phillips of the Royal Artillery and Major General Friedrich Adolf von Riedesel. Phillips was destined to command the Royal Artillery, Engineers, and Board of Ordnance interests in Canada, as the Ordnance was legally a separate entity in 1777 from the regular British army. General Riedesel took charge of the large German contingent from Brunswick and Hesse-Hanau destined for service in Canada.

Phillips had been born in 1731 and entered the Royal Military Academy in 1746. Upon graduation from Woolwich, Phillips became quartermaster of the 1st Battalion of Royal Artillery on April 1, 1750. He commanded the three companies of the Royal Artillery that were present at the Battle of Minden in 1759, where he won great distinction. He also gained credit for gallantry at the Battle of Warburg in 1760, for the rapidity with which he brought the artillery into action and the efficiency with which he handled it. Phillips actually galloped his horses to maneuver the cannon aggressively on the battlefield, an unheard-of proposition that contributed much to the victory for British arms that day. Phillips's gallantry and experience in combat earned him the attention of the British royal family, and he was regularly promoted, demonstrating great proficiency in every rank in the Royal Artillery from lieutenant fireworker to colonel.[2] His political connections are apparent, for he had become a member of Parliament by 1774. He was beyond question the single most prominent artilleryman in the British army in 1776, and he was a natural selection to serve as the commander of the Artillery Detachment when it was dispatched to Canada in the spring of 1776.[3] Burgoyne and Phillips, in particular, would become intimate friends during the tedious North Atlantic voyage.[4] Because of the division during the Revolutionary War between the British army and the Board of Ordnance, artillery and engineer officers were not permitted to command regular regiments of the British army. During the 1776 and 1777 campaigns, Phillips received special dispensation to serve as Burgoyne's deputy commander.

General Friedrich Adolf von Riedesel of Brunswick, born in 1738, was by 1776 a highly experienced officer who had seen frequent field service and acquired considerable command experience in Europe. He would command the Brunswick and Hessian hired soldiers that served with the British during the 1776 and 1777 campaigns from Canada. Major General Riedesel was a well-seasoned officer, highly regarded by Burgoyne personally and throughout the British army. Under his leadership, the German brigade performed superbly throughout the campaign, and their timely appearance on the battlefields at both Hubbardton and Freeman's Farm won those engagements for the British.

The lead elements of this force had landed at Quebec on May 6, and within hours of their arrival the American blockade of the city precipitously collapsed. Burgoyne arrived at Quebec with still more regiments of British regulars on May 29, 1776. Governor-General Carleton welcomed Burgoyne's nearly forty years of military service, and immediately employed him in leading the pursuit of the fleeing Americans, who were in short order driven out of Canada and back to Forts Crown Point and Ticonderoga on southern Lake Champlain. Burgoyne participated in the entirety of the 1776 campaign, though he saw no actual fighting. Burgoyne commanded the army's advance down Lake Champlain in October

[2]Lieutenant fireworker was the lowest commissioned rank in the British Royal Artillery in the eighteenth century, the equivalent of a 2nd lieutenant in the modern U.S. Army.

[3]Phillips died of a fever while leading a British army in Petersburg, Virginia, in 1781. Phillips has been the subject of only a single biography: Davis, *"Where a Man Can Go."*

[4]Ibid., 41.

1776, but only the Royal Artillery gunboats were engaged, so Burgoyne had little opportunity to exercise any actual leadership.[5] Still, Burgoyne gained considerable familiarity with the geography of Canada and Lake Champlain. He spent the majority of the campaign year focused on logistical and transportation issues and took the opportunity to observe the predominantly French Canadian inhabitants of Canada. He spent much time cooperating with the Royal Navy and nautical transportation, which was absolutely integral to any operations along the rivers and lakes. He also worked together with the individual British and German regiments, forging a strong relationship with the subordinate officers of the army. In short, although the 1776 campaign offered little in the way of personal glory and honor, Burgoyne acquired much knowledge of military affairs as they were conducted in Canada and northern New York Colony. Two memorandums that Burgoyne authored on the 1777 campaign in London (Files 6.16/5 and 6.16/8) clearly document that he had absorbed considerable practical knowledge on military operations in Canada.

In mid-1776 Burgoyne suffered a devastating personal loss, as his wife, Lady Charlotte Stanley Burgoyne, died in his absence on June 7 at Kensington Palace, England. With nothing to do, with no real opportunity of seeing any military action, and once it became apparent that Carleton was not going to assault Fort Ticonderoga in October, Burgoyne took an early departure for England (in part to make arrangements for his wife's estate). While he was waiting at Quebec for transportation across the North Atlantic, Burgoyne carried on a brief correspondence with his friend General Phillips, who remained at Crown Point. On October 23 Phillips wrote (no file #): "I promise you to do my utmost to preserve the army for an early opening of the campaign, and I do most sincerely hope you will come out to us. The next year must divide this army, and we will go together, if it be possible. Take care of our cause in England, I rely on your goodness and regard for me to represent me favorably to the King if you think I deserve it, and keep me third in this army unless a second lieutenant-general is sent." Phillips's appeal suggests that Burgoyne had already discussed with Phillips the campaign for the subsequent year and possessed expectations for both his role and that of Phillips as leaders of the army in the 1777 campaign from Canada.

[5]Clement and Cubbison, "British and German Artillery Gunboats," 247–256.

Burgoyne arrived back in Portsmouth, England, on December 9, and the intrigues for the campaign against Albany in 1777, commonly referred to as "the year of the hangman" because the figure "7" so closely resembled a gallows in eighteenth-century illustrations, began.[6] Carleton had entrusted Burgoyne with a lengthy memorandum describing his proposed operations for the next year, along with an accompanying letter from General Phillips elaborating on the artillery establishment, both of which Burgoyne accordingly provided to Lord George Germain upon reaching London (Files 6.16/6 and 6.16/7). But Burgoyne had other things to discuss with Germain, such as his assumption of the leadership of the army that would move south from Canada that spring. However, as the documents herein testify (File 6.16/2), Lord George Germain and King George III had already made that decision months before.

As early as August 1776, Germain had instructed Carleton to return to Quebec to reorganize the badly shattered Canadian province, while Burgoyne was detached to move to the south and eventually report to Lieutenant General William Howe, the British army commander in chief in North America, who was then heading for New York City.

General William Howe, 5th Viscount Howe (1729–1814), was the youngest brother of the popular brigadier general Lord George Howe, 3rd Viscount Howe, who was killed at Ticonderoga in July 1758. Upon Lord George Howe's death, his younger brother, Admiral Richard Howe of the Royal Navy, became Viscount Howe. As a lieutenant colonel, William Howe had led Wolfe's advance up the slopes of Quebec in 1759, and he completely revised the light infantry tactics of the British army in 1774. An accomplished soldier with considerable experience and an enviable record in North America during the Seven Years' War, Howe was promoted to lieutenant general and assumed command of the British forces in North America on October 10, 1775. His vacillating conduct of the war would earn him considerable criticism in Great Britain.[7]

[6]Glover, *Burgoyne in Canada and America*, 109.

[7]Although Howe would win major victories at New York City in 1776 and Philadelphia in 1777, he failed to persuade the American colonies to accede to British interests. Howe resigned and returned to England in the spring of 1778. General William Howe was knighted as Sir William Howe following his victories in 1776, and he inherited the viscountcy upon the death of his brother Lord Admiral Richard Howe, in 1799.

Governor-General Sir Guy Carleton.
Courtesy National Archives of Canada.

Germain's letter to Carleton (File 6/16.2) had been delivered too late in the 1776 campaign to influence the latter's personal leadership of the October movement upon Fort Ticonderoga, but it indicated that the secretary of state envisioned Carleton remaining in a civil role in Quebec while Burgoyne commanded the army moving out of that province. Germain and Carleton were antagonists, and Germain had no intention of permitting Carleton to garner any victories or honors outside of the province that he governed.[8] The news that Burgoyne carried back to London, amplified by the letter that Phillips had written from Crown Point on November 9, 1776 (File 6.16/7), stating that Carleton had cleared Lake Champlain only to retreat from before Fort Ticonderoga, having barely knocked on its door, certainly did nothing to disabuse Germain of his concept of operations for 1777. Burgoyne's greatest influence on the campaign plans for 1777 was his endorsement of a supporting column that would operate down the Mohawk River corridor from the direction of Lake Ontario, to facilitate the movements of the main British army proceeding from Canada down Lake Champlain and the Hudson

[8]For the acrimonious relationship between Carleton and Germain, refer to Burt, "Quarrel between Germain and Carleton," 202–222.

Lord George Germain, British secretary of state for North America. *Courtesy William L. Clements Library, University of Michigan, Ann Arbor.*

River toward Albany. Burgoyne succeeded in convincing Germain and the king to mandate that this column be an integral part of the operations from Canada.[9]

The great question that had to be resolved was who would command the Canadian column. The short list was limited to either Burgoyne or his friend Major General Henry Clinton (who would shortly be knighted for his contributions to victory around New York City in 1776).[10] Clinton

[9]The author's analysis is supported by Lunt, *John Burgoyne of Saratoga*, 132; but contradicts Howson, *Burgoyne of Saratoga*, 138, which claims that "Burgoyne's 'Thoughts' said very little not said before." In fact, Burgoyne introduced what Lunt referred to as a "right hook" by St. Leger down the Mohawk Valley into the campaign plans for the year, a move not previously contemplated.

[10]Sir Henry Clinton (1730–1795), a major general in the British army, had participated (like Burgoyne) in the Siege of Boston without distinction. Appointed second in command under Howe at New York in 1776, Clinton had served admirably and received his peerage but chafed at serving under Howe. During the 1777 campaign Clinton remained in New York City while Howe attacked Philadelphia. Reinforced in the early fall, Clinton led his command in a belated feint up the Hudson River on behalf of Burgoyne. Appointed British commander in chief in 1778, Clinton's subsequent record was entirely undistinguished. Although he achieved some success in the southern theater, his actions and correspondence suggest defeatism, and he would be in command when Cornwallis surrendered Yorktown in 1781. That was effectively ended Clinton's military service in North America. Clinton and Burgoyne had served together in Boston in 1775–76 and formed a friendship at that time. Clinton did everything that he felt was prudent and reasonable to support Burgoyne's march on Albany.

was senior to Burgoyne, but Burgoyne clearly possessed considerably more familiarity with Canada than did Clinton. Clinton arrived at London from New York City on February 28, 1777.[11] Although historians have not considered this factor, Burgoyne's letters to Clinton in July and October 1776 (Files 17:24 and 18:47a, Henry Clinton Papers) are those of a grieving man pouring out his heart in anguish to an intimate friend; they document the very close relationship that existed between the two men. Clinton had also lost his beloved wife in 1772 and been utterly devastated by her death. Clinton had no intention of supplanting his friend, who so clearly had his heart set on commanding the expedition from Canada; hence Clinton's remark upon his failure to push his own claims to the command: "I had a delicacy upon those matters that would not permit me to do anything of the kind."[12] Once Clinton withdrew his name from consideration, Burgoyne was formally given the command on March 1, and within two days Burgoyne was referring to himself as the commander designate for the expedition (File 20:34, Henry Clinton Papers).[13] On March 10 Clinton and Burgoyne had a congenial dinner together in London, at which the two close friends doubtless exhaustively discussed their plans for the conduct of the 1777 campaign along the entirety of the Hudson River.[14] Around March 26 and immediately after receiving his own instructions and a set of dispatches destined for Carleton, Burgoyne embarked upon the frigate HMS *Apollo* for Canada.[15] Burgoyne arrived at Quebec on May 6 after a relatively swift voyage of only thirty-four days.[16]

Shortly after his arrival in England in December, Burgoyne provided Carleton's memorandum, Phillips's supporting letter, and a report from

[11]Glover, *Burgoyne in Canada and America*, 115.

[12]Quoted in Willcox, "Too Many Cooks," 59.

[13]Howson, *Burgoyne of Saratoga*, 138.

[14]Willcox, "Too Many Cooks," 59.

[15]Glover, *Burgoyne in Canada and America*, 123. The frigate HMS *Apollo*, a fifth-rate Royal Navy ship of thirty-two guns, launched in 1763. It saw extensive service in the American War of Independence but is best known as the vessel that transported Lieutenant General John Burgoyne from England to Canada for the ensuing Saratoga Campaign in the spring of 1777. The ship was broken up following heavy service in 1784, but the name was subsequently used by numerous Royal Navy vessels. It was commanded by Captain Philemon Pownell, Royal Navy, who was an acquaintance of General Burgoyne.

[16]Kingsley, ed., "Letters from Sir Francis-Carr Clerke," 413, 417. This collection of Clerke's letters includes transcriptions of those written during the 1776 and 1777 campaigns.

Carleton documenting his arrangements for winter quarters to Germain (Files 6.16/4, 6.16/6, 6.16/7, and 6.16/8). Burgoyne informed Germain on January 1 (File 6.16/4): "should my attendance in Town become necessary relatively to information upon the affairs of Canada, I shall be ready to obey y^{r} [your] summons upon one day's notice." Burgoyne felt this missive was necessary because he had gone to Bath for his health. Although he had told Clinton in November that "during the passage of the Lake my health suffered a little, but occupation, air & exercise have improved both that & my apparent resolution," the confinement and difficulties presented by a month-long winter's voyage across the North Atlantic must have exacerbated his illnesses.

Burgoyne, shortly after his return to London from Bath, was directed to prepare two detailed memorandums on his proposed expedition for Albany, one consisting of a review and elaboration of Carleton's memorandum and the other a more detailed memorandum of his own approach to the operation (Files 6.16/5 and 6.16/8). The first memorandum essentially presented Carleton's salient points, amplified somewhat. Burgoyne entirely supported Carleton, validating (though elaborating upon) every one of his points. Of perhaps greatest significance, Burgoyne concluded by lending his unqualified support for Carleton's approach to the 1777 campaign: "Most of the foregoing Articles, if not all, are requisite for a vigorous opening of the Campaign."

Today, the second memorandum would be considered the commander's intent for the operation, and would comprise the basis for the commander's senior staff to develop a detailed operations order. Therefore, this memorandum is critical to comprehending Burgoyne's concept of the operation as he attempted to execute it. Of perhaps greatest significance, Burgoyne noted:

> If it be determined that General Howe's whole force should act upon Hudson's River, and to the Southward of it, and that the only Object of the Canada Army be to effect a Junction with that force, the immediate Possession of Lake George would be of great Consequence as the most expeditious and most commodious Route to Albany; and should the Enemy be in force upon that Lake, which is very probable, every Effort should be tried by throwing Savages and Light Troops round it, to oblige them to quit it without waiting for naval Preparations. Should those Efforts fail the Route by South Bay and Skenesborough may be attempted, but considerable

> Difficulties may be expected, as the narrow Parts of the River may be easily choaked up and rendered impassable, and at best there will be necessity for a great deal of Land Carriage for the Artillery, Provisions, &c. which can only be supplied from Canada. In case of Success also by that Route; and [if] the Enemy [is] not removed from Lake George, it will be necessary to leave a Chain of Posts as the Army proceeds for the Securities of your Communication, which may too much weaken so small an Army. Least all these Attempts should unavoidably fail and it become indispensibly necessary to attack the Enemy by water upon Lake George, the Army at the Outset should be provided with Carriages, Implements and Artificers for conveying armed Vessels from Ticonderoga to the Lake.

This discussion in particular dictated the course of the entire Saratoga Campaign, and Burgoyne's concept of operations for advancing south from Fort Ticonderoga accordingly demands additional examination.

Separating Lake Champlain, which flows north into the St. Lawrence River, and the Hudson River, which flows south into the North Atlantic Ocean at New York City, is a height of land, a topographical divide, that separates the two bodies of water. For any military (or, indeed, any commercial) force to traverse this obstacle, two routes were available. Both followed traditional American Indian trading, hunting, and warpaths that had been in use for centuries. The first and predominant route went from the end of the navigable Hudson River, where Fort Edward had been constructed in 1755 by Colonel William Johnson (modern Glens Falls), generally north-northwest to the southern end of Lake George, where Johnson had established Fort William Henry in 1755 and General Jeffery Amherst had built Fort George in 1759. This sixteen-mile route had supported nearly continuous military use from 1755 through 1760, and it had seen steady civilian traffic since then. From the beginning of armed conflict in 1775, this had been the principal American supply route for the Northern Theater Army. Thus, by 1776 this was a well-established and maintained road, at least by eighteenth-century frontier standards. During the Seven Years' War the British had constructed a series of earthworks along this road, so that convoys utilizing it also had recourse to readily available defensive positions.

The second route, which experienced considerably less use, ran between Fort Edward and the southern end of Lake Champlain at Skenesboro, generally north-northeast by way of Wood Creek and Fort

Anne. During periods of high water, Wood Creek was navigable by bateaux from Lake Champlain to Fort Anne. However, during times of low water, the entire route had to be traversed by land. This route had only existed as a road beginning in 1763 when retired British lieutenant colonel Philip Skene had established a community at the southern end of Lake Champlain. The majority of Skene's business and trading interests were performed north along Lake Champlain, using a small two-masted schooner that would eventually become the *Liberty* of the American Continental Army flotilla in 1775. The land passage south was a distinctly minor route, and it had seen relatively little use until Major General Phillip Schuyler, commander of the American Northern Theater, constructed the American Lake Champlain fleet at Skenesboro in 1776. This road was longer than the Lake George road, twenty-four miles between Skenesboro and Fort Edward, and thirteen miles between Fort Anne and Fort Edward, and the terrain was considerably worse, with numerous hills, stream and creek crossings, marshes, and swamps. Burgoyne correctly noted that this route was not the militarily preferred course for an army moving south from Canada.

Although Burgoyne spent considerable time contemplating the movement south from Fort Ticonderoga to the Hudson River, his plans beyond that point were much less tightly formulated, as this discussion indicates: "the sole Purposes of the Canada Army [are] to effect a Junction with General Howe, or after cooperating so far as to get Possession of Albany, and open the Communications to New York, to remain upon the Hudson's River, and thereby enable that General to act with his whole Force to the Southward." Both of Burgoyne's two memorandums contained no real discussion of any movement past Fort Edward; how the army was to maneuver to reach Albany; once arrived there how the army was to be supported in Albany; how a connection was to be established between Burgoyne's army in Albany and the British army in New York City with a strong American blocking force in place at Forts Montgomery, Clinton, and Constitution located in the imposing and constricting terrain of the Hudson Highlands; or what actions the army actually would perform once it reached Albany. Burgoyne's intent was focused on seizing Fort Ticonderoga and continuing the movement south, and thus exclusively on reaching the Hudson

River. Burgoyne's memorandum almost entirely ignored the army's operations south of Fort Edward. Apparently neither King George III nor Lord George Germain noted this deficiency. Burgoyne clearly believed that once the obstacle of the height of land between Lake Champlain and the Hudson River was traversed, there would be no further inhibitions to his ability to reach Albany. The absence of such planning would prove catastrophic to Burgoyne's operations in the late summer and fall of 1777.

Burgoyne arrived at Quebec on May 6 after a relatively uneventful voyage across the North Atlantic. His aide-de-camp, Sir Francis-Carr Clerke, recalled of the journey:[17]

> We were only thirty four Days on our Passage arrived the 6th day of May, without seeing Ice or Privateers; We had one Week's rough weather and contrary Wind, which drove us from the Edge of the Banks to Latitude 41, and obliged to lay to 33 Hours under a ballanced Mizen; during that time it blew as hard and Seas were as high as was ever remembered by any Sailor on board; we would have compounded with the loss of a Mizen Mast at least; however we were so fortunate not to lose anything.[18]

Burgoyne's first, and most important, order of business was to deliver Germain's instructions to Carleton. Various historians have interpreted these orders in different ways, some more accurately than others. Viewed as the strategic objectives and campaign orders from Britain's political leadership (Lord George Germain and King George III) to the theater commander (Governor Carleton), they are actually quite clearly written. Germain's letters were contained in both the original August 22, 1776, letter (File 6.16/1), now finally delivered, and the more elaborate letter

[17]Sir Francis-Carr Clerke (1748–1777). It should be noted that his name was pronounced "Clark" in the common British fashion. Numerous participants accordingly recorded his name, erroneously, as "Clark." He was the 7th Baronet Sir John Clerke. He entered British military service as an ensign in the Foot Guards on 1770, purchased his lieutenancy in the Foot Guards in 1775, and became adjutant of his regiment and captain on February 3, 1776. As a captain he accompanied Burgoyne to Canada as his aide-de-camp in 1776. Clerke served throughout the 1776 campaign, and during the 1777 campaign he also served as Burgoyne's private secretary. He was quite well regarded within the Army. He was mortally wounded at the Battle of Barber's Wheatfield on October 7, 1777, while carrying urgent orders from Burgoyne for a withdrawal from the battlefield; and died at Bemis Heights at Gates's headquarters on October 15. Rogers, ed., *Hadden's Journal and Orderly Books*, 145–146.

[18]Kingsley, "Letters from Sir Francis-Carr Clerke," 417.

of March 26, 1777 (File 6.16/10). In the orders of August 22, Germain instructed Governor Carleton thus: "You should detach Lieut. General Burgoyne, or such other Officer as you should think most proper, with the Remainder of the Troops, and direct the Officer so detached to proceed with all possible Expedition to join General Howe, and to put himself under his Command." Germain then amplified in his March letter that Carleton was to remain in Canada, reestablishing effective government within the province and helping that province recover economically from the damage inflicted by the American invasion of 1775 and 1776. Germain specified, down to the regimental level, the forces available for Governor Carleton to fulfill these strategic objectives. Then Germain continued: "it is the King's Determination . . . to employ the Remainder of your Army upon two Expeditions— the one under the Command of Lieu$^{t.}$ General Burgoyne, who is to force his Way to Albany; and the other under the Command of Lieu$^{t.}$ Colonel S$^{t.}$ Leger, who is to make a Diversion on the Mohawk River." Furthermore, Germain instructed Carleton to order Burgoyne "to pass Lake Champlain, and from thence by the most vigorous Exertion of the Force under his [Burgoyne's] Command to proceed with all Expedition to Albany, and put himself under the Command of Sir William Howe." And finally Germain told Carleton to "direct Lieutenant General Burgoyne & Lieutenant Colonel S$^{t.}$ Leger to neglect no opportunity of doing the same that they may receive Instructions from Sir William Howe. You will at the same time inform them that until they shall have received orders from Sir William Howe It is His Majesty's Pleasure that they act as Exigencies may require and in such manner as they shall judge most proper for making an Impression on the Rebels and bringing them to obedience. But that, in so doing, they must never lose View of their intended Junctions with Sir William Howe as their principal Objects."

Placed into the context of the modern military planning process as practiced by the U.S. armed forces, the stated mission of the strategic leadership (King George III and Lord George Germain) for the 1777 campaign from Canada was that St. Leger and Burgoyne "must never lose view of their intended junctions with Sir William Howe as their principal objects." To accomplish this, the British strategic leadership's commander's intent and stated concept of the operation, with forces

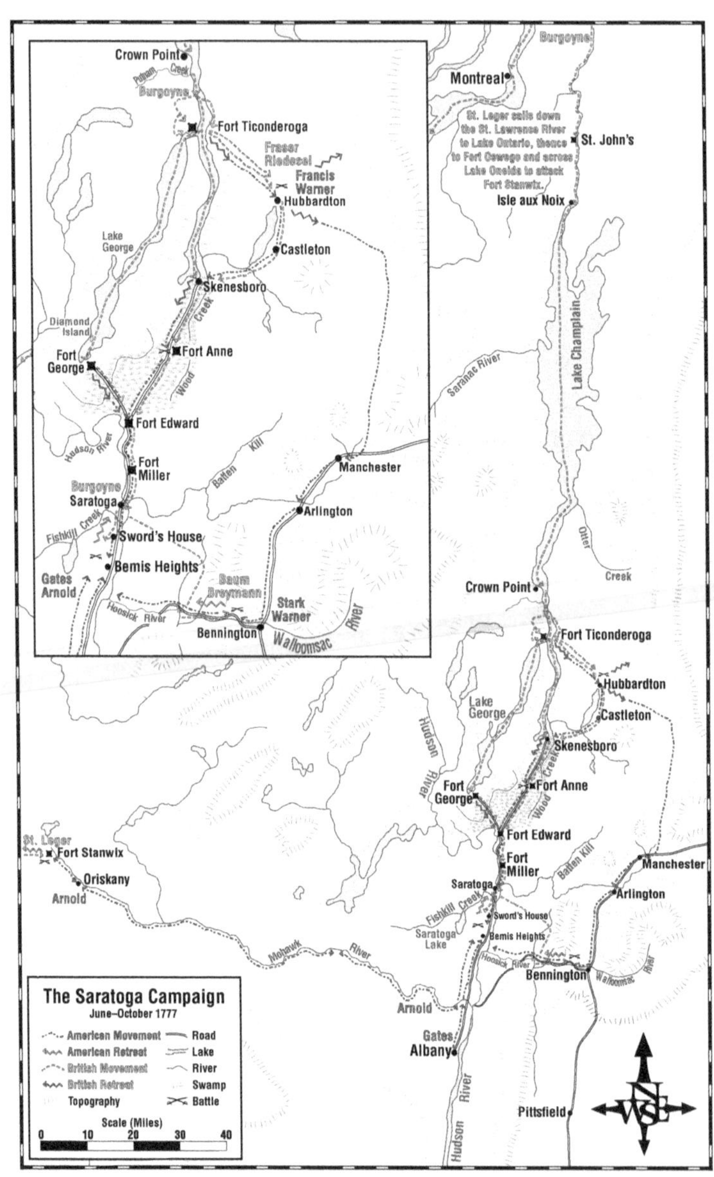

The Saratoga Campaign, June–October 1777.
Map prepared by SunSyne Graphics, http://www.sunsyne.com

available, could be expressed as the following specified tasks. Burgoyne was to command a detachment of 7,173 men to:

1) Pass Lake Champlain;
2) Proceed with all Expedition to Albany; and
3) Put himself under the command of Sir William Howe.

St. Leger was to command a detachment of 675 men to:

1) Make a diversion on the Mohawk River;
2) Proceed forthwith to and down the Mohawk River to Albany; and
3) Put himself under the command of Sir William Howe.

The March 26, 1777, letter also provided, down to the regimental level, the forces available for both of the operations. Burgoyne and Lieutenant Colonel St. Leger were provided instructions that further amplified the commander's intent and specified tasks, and that comprised additional specified tasks:

1) To neglect no opportunity to communicate with Sir William Howe; and
2) To give Sir William Howe intelligence of their movements at the "earliest" opportunity.

Finally, Burgoyne and St. Leger were also informed that, while complying with their assigned primary mission, they had the following flexibility to:

3) Act as exigencies may require; and
4) Act in such manner as they shall judge most proper for making an Impression on the Rebels and bringing them to obedience.

Such instructions would be sufficient, as strategic objectives, for a modern military commander to initiate the planning process for a similar operation.

While consulting together in Quebec, Carleton and Burgoyne attempted to make sense of Sir William Howe's strategic intentions. During the previous year's campaign, Howe's view was that the 1777 campaign would begin by "opening a communication with Canada in the first instance." The implication in Howe's statement (October 9, 1776) is that the Hudson River would be seized. Later in the same letter, he referred to this move as his "primary object."[19] This would be in

---

[19]Nickerson, *Turning Point of the Revolution*, 1:77.

full accordance with the instructions that Burgoyne had received from King George III through Lord George Germain. Howe had followed up this missive with a second letter dated November 30, in which he essentially proposed no fewer than six discrete movements:

1) To hold New York City;
2) To attack Albany from New York City;
3) To hold Rhode Island;
4) To attack Boston from Rhode Island;
5) To protect New Jersey; and
6) To threaten Philadelphia.[20]

Although this strategy was commendable, it was also predicated on Howe's receiving virtually unlimited resources from Britain, a militarily and politically unlikely scenario. Realizing how unrealistic his November plans were, Howe then dispatched another proposal on December 20. Recognizing that he would receive limited forces, Howe proposed defending New York City and Rhode Island and threatening Philadelphia with his main army.[21] Needless to say, Howe's fantastic and delusional assumptions of available troop strength were never realized, and Howe was informed that although he would be reinforced, he would not be augmented to the extent necessary to realize his ambitious November plans. Accordingly, Howe intended to proceed with his plans as he had stated them in late December. He informed Carleton of this intention in a letter written on April 5 (File 6.16/11a). It should be noted that when this letter was written, Burgoyne was in transit across the North Atlantic and Quebec was still inaccessible to shipping because of seasonal winter ice. This letter was received while Burgoyne and Carleton were still working together in Quebec and Montreal. Howe informed Carleton:

> Having but little expectation, that I shall be able, from the want of sufficient strength in this Army, to detach a Corps in the beginning of the Campaign, to act up Hudson's River, consistent with the Operations already determined upon. The Force your Excellency may deem expedient to advance beyond your Frontiers, after taking Ticonderoga will, I fear, have little assistance from hence to facilitate their approach: and as I shall probably be in Pennsylvania when that Corps is ready to advance in to this Province, it

[20]Ibid., 1:78.
[21]Ibid., 1:79.

> will not be in my power to communicate with the Officer Commanding it so soon as I could wish: He must therefore pursue such Measures as may, from circumstances, be judged most conducive to the Advancement of His Majesty's Service, consistently with your Excellency's Orders for his Conduct. The Possession of Ticonderoga will naturally be the first object & without presuming to point out to your Excellency the advantages that must arise by securing Albany [and] the adjacent Country. . . .
>
> . . . still I flatter myself, I have reason to expect, the friends of Government in that part of the Country, will be found so numerous & so ready to give every aid & assistance in their power, that it will prove no difficult task to reduce the more Rebellious parts of the Province. In the mean while I shall endeavour to have a Corps upon the lower part of Hudson's River sufficient to open the Communication for Shipping thro' the highlands, at present obstructed by several Forts erected by the Rebels for that purpose, which Corps may afterwards act in favour of the Northern Army.

Thus, Burgoyne realized even before he entered the Lake Champlain region with his army that Howe would be maneuvering against Philadelphia and that only "a Corps upon the lower part of Hudson's River" would be available to support him. Burgoyne probably drew some confidence from the knowledge that his friend Henry Clinton would likely be commanding this corps.

However, this by no means relieved Burgoyne from the obligation to fulfill the orders given to him by King George through Lord George Germain, which contained peremptory, and not conditional, instructions that Burgoyne was "to pass Lake Champlain, and from thence by the most vigorous Exertion of the Force under his Command to proceed with all Expedition to Albany, and put himself under the Command of Sir William Howe"; and to "never lose View of their intended Junctions with Sir William Howe as their principal Objects." Burgoyne wrote Brigadier General Simon Fraser shortly after Burgoyne returned to Canada, clearly telling him: "The military operations, all directed to make a junction with Howe, are committed to me."[22] Burgoyne later wrote to Lord George Germain in August: "My orders being positive to 'force a junction with Sir Wm. Howe' I apprehend I am not at liberty to remain inactive."[23] Although historians have expended oceans

[22]Atkinson, ed., "Evidence for Burgoyne's Expedition," 139.

[23]Davies, ed., *Documents of the American Revolution*, 14:166.

of ink assessing the effect that Howe's decision had upon the Saratoga Campaign, Burgoyne had no choice but to proceed on his expedition, regardless of where Sir William Howe might or might not be when he arrived at Albany, or what Howe might or might not be doing at that particular time.

Burgoyne would spend the next two months organizing the movement forward from the St. Lawrence River valley, and performing the preliminary movement from the winter garrisons of Canada toward Fort Ticonderoga. The majority of his efforts for these eight weeks were logistical. First, Burgoyne had to roust his soldiers from their winter quarters, organize them into brigades, and maneuver them to Fort Ticonderoga. He had to request Carleton to institute a corvée to move his supplies forward;[24] accumulate mountains of military supplies including provisions—the full panoply of ordnance material, artillery, and medicines; acquire transportation assets such as bateaux, horses, oxen, carts, and wagons with their drivers; and then organize and move en masse up Lake Champlain. American Indian warriors had to be harangued and liaison officers appointed. Once they arrived from their villages, the warriors had to be organized, armed, and equipped. American Loyalist and Canadian units had to have leaders designated and issued beating orders authorizing the enlistment and recruitment of soldiers; then the recruits had to be organized, armed, equipped, trained, and finally moved forward to join the army. One thing that Burgoyne did not have to do was to again wrest control of Lake Champlain from the Americans. Hamstrung because they had expended all available naval supplies in constructing their Lake Champlain fleet the previous season, the Americans did not possess the material means to build a replacement flotilla over the winter. The British navy thus controlled Lake Champlain from Fort St. John's south to Fort Ticonderoga/Mount Independence.

Carleton, with the assistance of Phillips, had fully anticipated a repeat of his southern movement on Lake Champlain in 1777, and he had the

[24]The corvée was a system of required labor in New France, and the requirement was continued by the British after 1760. As militiamen, all habitants were required to work on roads, bridges, fortifications, and transport for the defense and support of the colony; this enforcement of labor was legal and of indeterminate duration. As may well be imagined, it was extremely unpopular with the Canadian residents. A corvée had to be ordered by the Governor, and Governor Carleton instituted one for 1777 to facilitate the movement of Burgoyne's army to the south.

necessary preparations for that offensive well in hand. However, he had not anticipated the detachment of St. Leger down the Mohawk River, and the extensive correspondence regarding that expedition reflects the urgency of the planning that was required to prepare St. Leger's column. More than a dozen of Carleton's and Burgoyne's papers deal with the logistical and administrative organization of that effort (e.g., Files 6.16/17, 17a, 17b, 17c, 6.16/20a–h).

Winter Quarters, 1776–1777

The British army had weathered the harsh Canadian winter in excellent condition, in large part owing to the careful planning and leadership of Governor Carleton and Major General Phillips, who served as army commander in Canada in lieu of Burgoyne. Captain George Pausch, commanding the company of Hesse-Hanau Artillery in Canada, provided his prince with a detailed description of the weekly rations that his soldiers had been issued in Montreal:

> Throughout almost the entire winter the men have received fresh meat and a very good bread. Now however, except for the sick, they receive salted beef or pork, and a very good butter issued one pound per man per week. Almost every time they also receive peas and oatmeal, whenever salted meat is issued. For this uniquely good care the company has General Phillips to thank, who is concerned that portions are as good for them as for his own and the other Royal Artillery companies.[25]

Nutritional food had been plentiful. The troops had occupied relatively comfortable barracks and had been dispersed from Montreal to Quebec and as far south as Isle aux Noix to avoid overcrowding and the resulting spread of diseases. Phillips had ensured that the soldiers were regularly exercised, to include jogging, and drilled on a daily basis. The German soldiers, who had never before conceived of such a thing as running

[25]Burgoyne, trans. and ed., *George Pausch's Journal and Reports*, 46. Two published editions of this journal exist: one prepared by renowned historian William L. Stone in 1886, and a 2003 transcription that includes additional Pausch material prepared by Bruce E. Burgoyne, a historian who has transcribed numerous German documents from the American War of Independence. I have utilized both translations in the preparation of this manuscript but have referenced Burgoyne's edition as more complete and readily available to most readers. Stone, ed., *Journal of Captain Pausch*.

for exercise, were shocked at this practice. Captain Pausch reported in astonishment: "The companies fall out from the barracks and are commanded, by companies, on the parade ground, marched for one-half hour and at times for an hour, and run, which latter is most disagreeable to my company as they have never been drilled in that manner. My poor devils must join the English 'gallop' at both formations daily and at present this requires them to run like hunting dogs."[26] Such exercises were, however, essential for field artillerymen who were frequently called upon to move their heavy, cumbersome artillery pieces by their own strength; and the fact that General Phillips had implemented such a measure indicates that he was in the forefront of military training. The army was in excellent order, and Burgoyne found them not only willing and able but enthusiastic when it came to taking to the field.[27] Burgoyne's young aide-de-camp recalled: "the Army [is] in remarkable high Health and Spirits; and such of the Regiments as we have already seen are amazingly come on in point of Discipline and drill."[28]

Logistical Organization, Spring 1777

The majority of the papers presented in this volume, no fewer than forty-three letters, consists of correspondence between Carleton, Burgoyne, and St. Leger organizing the various logistical issues to support their two columns (Files 6.16/13a through 6.16/15b, 6.16/17a–c, 6.24/1 through 6.24/36, and 6.29/3). Throughout this process, Carleton appears to have done everything within his power to comply with his instructions from Lord George Germain and King George III of March 26, 1777 (File 6.16/10), to render Burgoyne and St. Leger, "proper Artillery, Stores, provisions, and every other necessary Article for his Expedition, and secure to him [Burgoyne] every Assistance in your Power to afford and procure." Many of these papers are routine bureaucratic and

[26]Burgoyne, *George Pausch's Journal and Reports*, 48–50, 52.

[27]The British army's experience in winter quarters in 1776–77 has received almost no attention from academic historians. However, the attention paid to this matter by Carleton and Phillips in particular had a direct impact on Burgoyne's operations, for the army was in excellent condition at the beginning of the Saratoga Campaign. Cubbison, *"Artillery never gained more Honour,"* 66–70.

[28]Kingsley, "Letters from Sir Francis-Carr Clerke," 416.

administrative communications, such as Carleton's letter of November 1776 dealing with obtaining adequate supplies of rum for Canada (File 6.29/3), and organizational correspondence such as beating orders and muster rolls for military units to be raised in Canada. However, all of this correspondence is directly relevant to the conduct of the 1777 Saratoga Campaign, for without the logistical and organizational work being accomplished in Canada, the two expeditions would never have been able to move south against Ticonderoga and the Mohawk River.

Carleton exerted himself to assist Burgoyne and St. Leger. Certainly Burgoyne and Carleton conversed extensively in Quebec for approximately a week from the time of Burgoyne's arrival, until May 14, when both officers proceeded to Montreal to organize further the expedition.[29] Carleton wrote Phillips on May 12, before their departure (File 6.24/3), that "I shall nevertheless go up to Montreal in order to be at hand to give every assistance in my power towards forwarding the King's service in this particular." Burgoyne was at Montreal not later than May 19, as Clerke wrote a letter dated from Montreal on that date. In this letter, Clerke is almost certainly referring to Carleton: "The Behavior of an Officer (about whom we have often conversed) does him the highest honour, he acts with great good Sense and Generosity."[30]

Carleton had already initiated significant efforts to facilitate an advance from Canada in 1777. However, one significant shortfall concerned land-based transportation, specifically horses and wagons. The 1775–76 campaign had seriously depleted the available animals in Canada, and transporting more from Britain was simply impossible. By May 26 Burgoyne had been able to evaluate how many horses he would have available, versus how many would be required, and realized that he faced a significant shortfall (File 6.24/13). On that date Burgoyne notified Carleton: "It also appears to me that seven or eight hundred Horses may become indispensibly necessary for my Progress." Carleton acted swiftly, and by June 6 he and Burgoyne had agreed on contractual terms to obtain the draught animals and wagons (File 6.24/20) and entered into two contracts to obtain them—one contract for 1,000 horses for

[29] Hargrove, "General John Burgoyne," 185–186.

[30] Kingsley, "Letters from Sir Francis-Carr Clerke," 416–418. Burgoyne had the same sentiments; see Davies, *Documents of the American Revolution*, 14:79.

the army (File 6.24/21) and a second contract for horses for the artillery (File 6.24/22), because artillery horses had to be separately arranged and paid for by the Board of Ordnance. By wisely issuing both contracts on the same date, and with the same contractual terms, Burgoyne and Carleton avoided creating artificial competition between the Board of Ordnance and the army. Historian Jane Clark has criticized Burgoyne, claiming that he "delayed a month before asking Carleton for wagons and horses."[31] However, Burgoyne actually made the formal request only twenty days after he arrived in Canada, and this does not appear to be an unrealistic time frame in which to meet with Carleton, organize the campaign, determine appropriate courses of actions for both columns (Carleton had previously only prepared for a single advance down Lake Champlain), estimate needs against available assets, and identify shortfalls. Within less than a month, Burgoyne and Carleton had actually issued contracts to close the identified gaps in logistical capabilities.

The Movement upon Ticonderoga, June 1777

On May 27 Burgoyne reviewed the advance corps of Brigadier General Fraser, and with this step the campaign began moving forward.[32] Burgoyne embarked from Fort St. John's on June 15, 1777 (File 6.24/28). The movement down the lake was not particularly well documented, except through a number of Orderly Books.[33] The army had performed this identical movement the previous October, and there appears to have been minimal need for any correspondence between Carleton and Burgoyne. Phillips and Burgoyne were colocated on board the flotilla so that all of their orders would have been verbal rather than written. By June 30 the army had reached Crown Point, where it stood ready to begin operations against Fort Ticonderoga and Mount Independence.

As a first step in his movement forward, Burgoyne issued two proclamations to the American Indians and local citizens and a set of General

[31]Clark, "Failure of the Burgoyne Campaign," 546.

[32]Bradford, ed., "Lord Francis Napier's Journal," 294.

[33]Clement, ed., *47th Regiment of Foot*; Clement, ed., *Royal Regiment of Artillery*; Clement, ed., *47th Regiment Grenadier Company*; Rogers, *Hadden's Journal and Orderly Books*; O'Callaghan, ed., *Orderly Book of General Burgoyne*; and Phillips, "Brigade Orders of Major General Phillips."

Orders to his army. First, Burgoyne met with the assembled American Indian warriors near the Bouquet River on June 21. He made a lengthy oration to them (File 6.16/15a) in which he set out the conditions under which he expected the Indian warriors to fight. The speech was certainly in a style likely to impress the American Indians, who were used to lengthy narratives and formal discourse in council, and was clearly intended to keep their behavior under control and discipline. However, though doubtless well intentioned, this speech gained Burgoyne no credit, and the American Indians were unlikely to change their way of making war in response to a single lecture, no matter how artfully delivered. The only real result of this piece of oratory was that ridicule was subsequently heaped upon Burgoyne in Britain for it. Edmund Burke mocked it in the House of Commons: "Imagining a riot on Tower Hill, and the Keeper of His Majesty's Lions addressing the animals in his charge: 'My gentle lions, my humane bears, my sentimental wolves, my tender-hearted hyenas, go forth: but I exhort ye as ye are Christians and members of a civilized society, to take care not to hurt man, woman or child.'"[34]

Burgoyne followed this up with a proclamation to the American citizens, in his most grandiose and extravagant language (File 6.16/15b). This "manifesto" was intended to encourage Loyalists and convert Patriots to either neutrality or the cause of the king. As such, it was an early form of propaganda (or Information Operations as it is currently practiced by the modern U.S. Army). It was also a miserable failure. Written in an elaborately formal manner entirely inappropriate for the American frontiersmen and colonists, it became a source of ridicule and propaganda for the American Patriot cause. Most Americans viewed it as bombastic, insulting, demeaning, and pompous—all the British traits that they were fighting against. This manifesto might have been appropriate, popular, and effective in London, but Burgoyne could have benefited from an American editor.

Finally, Burgoyne issued a set of General Orders to his soldiers at Crown Point on June 30, which concluded with the stirring phrase "This Army must not retreat" (no file #). Having expended his literary energies, Burgoyne was now ready to get on with the serious business of the campaign, and to resort to the sword.

[34]Gibbons, "Subtilized into Savages," 88.

Burgoyne set forth, in his *State of the Expedition from Canada*, that the strength of his army on July 1, 1777, at the opening of the campaign and presumably its greatest strength, was as follows:

British	3,576 fit for duty
German	2,919 fit for duty
Artillery	511 fit for duty.[35]

The four strength returns in these papers (Files 6.5/4–7) enable, for the first time, verification of these numbers. On May 1, 1777, the army's strength in Canada was as follows:

British	7,106 present for duty (including Artillery)
German	4,502 present for duty
Total	11,608 present for duty.

On October 1, 1777, the strength of the British army in Canada (including German detachments) was 3,714. Although there were several detachments not with Burgoyne (such as at Fort Ticonderoga and Diamond Island on Lake George), these detachments were still counted against Burgoyne's strength on October 1, and would be until they returned to Canada in late November following Burgoyne's Saratoga Convention. Burgoyne's May 1, 1777, strength was augmented by the arrival of 154 recruits for the Regiments of Foot, which were diverted to the Royal Artillery. Additionally, on March 3, 1777, the *Dublin Journal* reported that "a Draft of seventy Mattrosses, from the Royal Irish Regiment of Artillery, young, able, active fellows, marched off the parade of the Barrack at Chapel-Izod for Cork, there to embark on his Majesty's Service for America. They all went off in high spirits, and expressed the warmest ardour to face the Enemies of their King and Country. So laudable an emulation prevailed through the whole Corps, that many more than the number wanting gallantly offered themselves Volunteers on the occasion."[36] These artillery draftees arrived in time to participate in the Saratoga Campaign.

---

[35]Burgoyne, *Expedition to Canada*, 96–97. It must be noted that these figures are "solely of the army under Lieutenant General Burgoyne." They do not include Carleton's garrisons in Canada or the detachment with St. Leger operating against Fort Stanwix and the Mohawk Valley.

[36]Cubbison, *"Artillery never gained more Honour,"* 69–70. A "matross" was a soldier of the Royal Artillery who ranked lower than a gunner, the equivalent of a private or specialist in today's U.S. Army.

Original copy of Burgoyne's Manifesto to the Americans, issued at the encampment at the Bouquet River, June 24, 1777. *Courtesy Fort Ticonderoga Museum.*

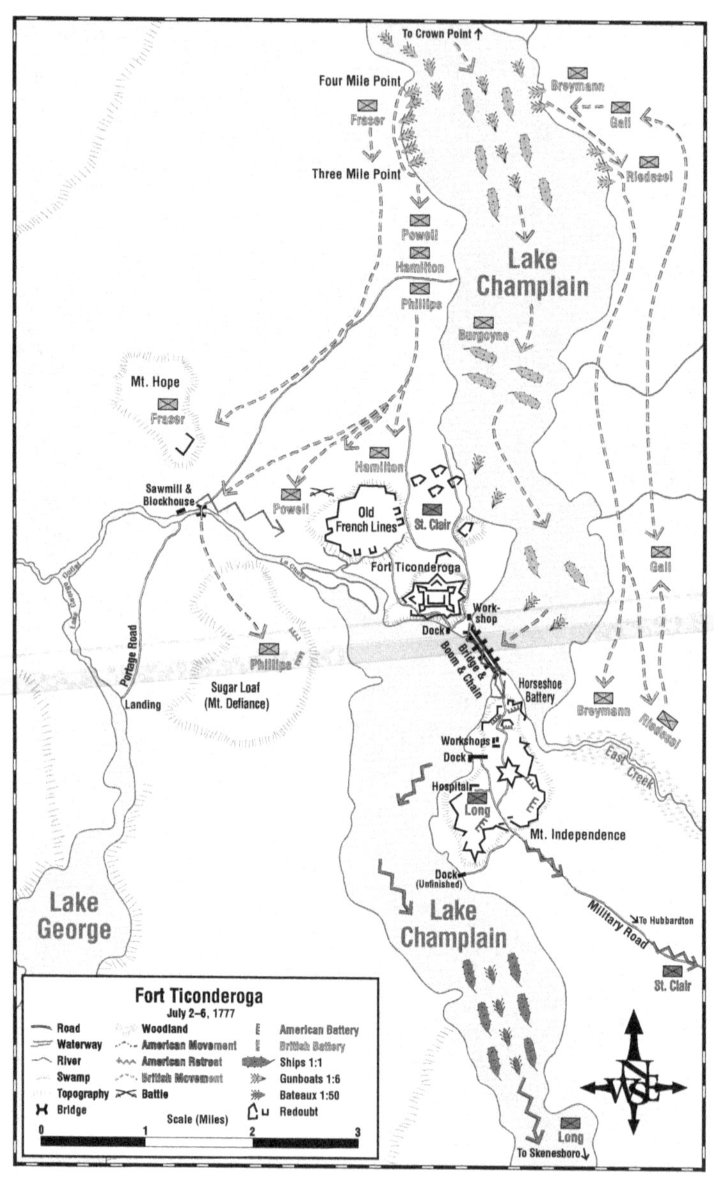

Fort Ticonderoga and vicinity, June–July, 1777.
Map prepared by SunSyne Graphics, http://www.sunsyne.com

These returns document that Burgoyne carried forward 8,118 soldiers from Canada, which is greater than his claimed strength of 7,006 on July 1, 1777. This further suggests either that Burgoyne deliberately understated his strength and had more soldiers initially than his report claims, or that more soldiers were initially detached in Canada that subsequently joined Burgoyne.

Burgoyne described his movements against Fort Ticonderoga in a letter written to Lord George Germain, dated July 11, 1777 (File 6.16/18). His narrative will be presented, and then analyzed, as appropriate:

> On 30th June I ordered the advanced Corps, consisting of the British Light Infantry and Grenadiers, the 24th Regiment, some Canadians and Savages, and ten pieces of Lt. Artillery, under the Command of Brigadier Genl. Frazer [Fraser], to move from Putnam Creek, where they had been encamped some Days, up the west shore of the Lake to four mile Point, so called from being within that distance of the Fort of Ticonderoga.[37] The German reserve consisting of the Brunswick Chasseurs, Lt. Infantry and Grenadiers, under Lt. Colonel Breymann were advanced at the same time upon the East Shore.
>
> July 1st. The whole Army made a movement forward. Brigadier Frazer's Corps occupied the Strong Post called three mile Point on the West shore, the German reserve the East Shore opposite; the right Wing of the Line encamped at four mile point; the left being nearly opposite on the East Shore.

These operations were directed by Brigadier General Simon Fraser (1729–1777), the lieutenant colonel of the 24th Regiment of Foot. He had been appointed a brigadier general for service in Canada in 1776. Fraser, a veteran of the Seven Years' War, was an experienced, professional, and accomplished officer. In command of the British garrison at the Battle of Three Rivers in June 1776, he had handily defeated the American attack with slight loss on the part of his force. Fraser was extremely well regarded within the British army in Canada.[38] Fraser's advance corps was a composite unit intended to precede the main army, while still containing considerable combat power. It consisted of Fraser's own 24th Regiment of Foot; a consolidated battalion of British light

[37]The names of Brigadier General Simon Fraser and his nephew, Captain Alexander Fraser, were consistently misspelled as "Frazer" by Burgoyne. (Burgoyne's original spelling is preserved in all direct quotations from the papers.)

[38]Unfortunately, General Fraser, who played such a key role in the Saratoga Campaign, lacks a dedicated biography.

infantry under the Earl of Balcarres; a consolidated battalion of British grenadiers under Major John Acland; various Loyalists, Canadians, and American Indians; the Company of Select Marksmen under Fraser's nephew Captain Alexander Fraser; a battalion of German light infantry and riflemen under Lieutenant Colonel Breymann; and a light artillery detachment consisting of predominantly 3-pounder cannon.[39]

Burgoyne has received little credit for his operational plans for the advance upon Ticonderoga, as his rapid occupation and emplacement of artillery upon Sugar Loaf Mountain (now Mount Defiance) prevented his full plans from ever being implemented. Burgoyne's intention was to place the German division, under the command of his friend the accomplished major general Baron Riedesel, on the eastern shore of Lake Champlain. Riedesel was to move against Mount Independence, using his infantry and artillery to freeze the American defenders within the natural citadel of the post. He was then to maneuver to the left flank (east) of Mount Independence, and circle to the rear (south) of the post, cutting off the American line of retreat and placing the Hesse-Hanau Artillery in a position to interdict any American maritime retreat south on Lake Champlain. This movement would effectively sever one of the two American lines of communication to Albany. Thus, Burgoyne began his maneuvers by moving the Germans across Lake Champlain, Breymann's Chasseur (Light Infantry) Battalion on June 30, with Riedesel's main contingent following the next day.[40]

Against Fort Ticonderoga proper on the western shore of Lake Champlain, Burgoyne intended to maneuver the British component of

---

[39]Alexander Lindsay, the 6th Earl of Balcarres, was a distinguished Scottish nobleman who spent practically his entire life in the British army (1752–1825). During the Burgoyne campaign he served as a major in the 53rd Foot commanding the British Light Infantry Battalion and was wounded at Hubbardton. Rogers, *Hadden's Journal and Orderly Books*, 333–335, contains a lengthy biography of Balcarres. Major John Dyke Acland (1747–1778) was a member of the House of Commons and an ardent Tory supporter of Lord North. He purchased a captaincy in the 33rd Foot before the American War of Independence broke out, and on December 16, 1775, he purchased the rank of major in the 20th regiment of Foot. He commanded Burgoyne's Grenadier Battalion throughout the Saratoga Campaign and was wounded at both Hubbardton and Barber's Wheatfield. His health suffered severely during the campaign, and in 1778 he returned to England, where he died. His wife's journal is the best source on Major Acland. Thorp, ed., *Acland Journal*.

[40]Historians have paid scant attention to Riedesel's movements on the British left (east) flank, which figured so prominently in Burgoyne's plans. The only scholarly notice is Kingsley, Alexander, and Schnitzer, "German Auxiliaries Project, Part I," 28–41; and "Part II," 53–72.

his force, the two British Regular Brigades under Brigadier Generals James Hamilton and Henry Watson Powell and the large and powerful advance guard under Brigadier General Fraser. The British regulars were intended to move directly against Fort Ticonderoga, again to pin the American defenders within their works surrounding the old French fort. Simultaneously, Fraser was to swing around to the right (west) and secure the American defensive works on Mount Hope and the landing at the La Chute River. Once Fraser had gained the eminence of Mount Hope, he would control the second American line of communications south to Lake George, and thus the Americans would be trapped.

Brigadier General James Hamilton (?–1803), who commanded one of the two British Regular Brigades, was lieutenant colonel of the 21st Regiment. He had been promoted to brigadier general in 1776 for service with the Canadian army. He served with distinction throughout the Saratoga Campaign. In part because of his extremely common name, biographical details are scarce for this officer.[41] Henry Watson Powell (1733–1814), the lieutenant colonel of the 53rd Regiment of Foot, also was promoted to brigadier general for service in Canada in 1776. A subaltern with extensive combat service in the West Indies during the Seven Years' War, Powell was an experienced officer when he was dispatched to Canada with his regiment in the spring of 1776. That Burgoyne would subsequently assign Powell an independent command for much of the Saratoga Campaign suggests he trusted Powell's skills and leadership abilities.[42]

Because his soldiers and American Indian warriors had the farthest distance to traverse, Fraser initiated the movement on June 30, followed by the Regular Brigades on July 1. Burgoyne perceived the American defenses (File 6.16/18) thus:

> A Brigade occupied the old French Lines upon the height northward of the Fort of Ticonderoga. These Lines were in good repair and had several instruments behind them chiefly calculated to guard the North west flank, and they were further sustained by a Block-house. To the left of these works about a mile the Enemy had Saw Mills and a Post sustained by a block-house, and another blockhouse and an hospital at the entrance of

[41]The most comprehensive biography of Brigadier General James Hamilton can be found in Rogers, *Hadden's Journal and Orderly Books*, 468–471.

[42]The only biography of Powell is located in ibid., 464–467. As with many other British officers on the Saratoga Campaign, such as Fraser, Hamilton, and St. Leger, Powell deserves a focused biography.

> Lake George. Upon the right of the French lines, and between them and the old Fort, there were two new block-houses, and a considerable battery close to the water edge. It seemed that the Enemy had employed their chief industry, and were in greatest force, upon Mount Independence, which is high and circular, and upon the Summit, which is table land, was a Star fort, made with pickets and well supplied with Artillery, and a large square of Barracks within it. The foot of the Mount which projects into the Lake was intrenched and covered with a Strong abattis close to the Water. This intrenchment was lined with heavy Artillery pointing down the Lake, flanking the Water battery above described, and sustained by another battery about half way up the Mount.
>
> On the west side the Mount runs the main river and in its passage round is joined by the Water which comes down from Lake George. On the East Side of the Mount [Independence] the Water forms a small Bay into which falls a rivulet, after having encircled in its course part of the Mount to the South East. The side to the South could not be seen but was described as inaccessible. There was a Bridge between the Mount and Ticonderoga which also was unseen.

With this description, Burgoyne revealed his familiarity with the American defenses. The American defensive configuration was astride and blocking Lake Champlain, with Mount Independence on the American right (east), Fort Ticonderoga at the center, and Mount Hope covering the American left (west) and rear.

The main defenses were centered around the old Fort Carillon, built by the French, rechristened Fort Ticonderoga by the British in 1759. The fort had been destroyed by the French during their retreat in 1759, had been only partially repaired during the ensuing British occupation—the northeast bastion and the northern building had never been reconstructed—and by 1777 had been in disrepair for nearly two decades. The "old French fort," as the Americans consistently referred to it, played no role in the Continental Army defensive configuration, merely providing a headquarters and barracks for the American army. To the west, the Heights of Carillon dominated the fort. In 1758 the French general Marquis de Montcalm had constructed a strong breastwork atop the ridgeline, and the British had suffered catastrophic casualties storming it that July. In 1776 the Americans had constructed a major line of earthworks, with embedded redoubts and batteries, on the trace of these French lines. They had constructed four small square redoubts to the rear to protect both flanks from a turning maneuver. To defend the vulnerable flat plain to the north, on the western shore of Lake Champlain, the Americans had constructed an interlocking series of redoubts and batteries that successfully repelled a British probing action in late October 1776. Taken together, these strong defensive fortifications around Fort Ticonderoga constituted a formidable position.[43]

Mount Independence occupied a peninsula that extended from the eastern shore of Lake Champlain to a narrows at Ticonderoga. A tributary of Lake Champlain, East Creek, ran along the northern portion of its defenses. This creek, at its mouth, was deep with steep banks, and the eastern portion of the Mount was covered by swamps and a small stream. Only one entrance to the peninsula was available by land, to the southeast. Here, a road constructed in 1776 led to Rutland, Vermont. Mount Independence was surrounded with infantry parapets and blockhouses/redoubts. A strong star-shaped fort that occupied rocky high ground in the middle of the position was the center of the defenses. A horseshoe-shaped artillery battery located at the northwestern portion of the peninsula controlled a bridge and defensive chain-and-log boom that obstructed the lake. Because the mount was surrounded by water or swampy ground, effective formal siege operations were precluded. Mount Independence was, for all practical purposes, impregnable.[44] Burgoyne recognized that it would have to be outflanked in some manner.

Finally, to secure their line of communications with Lake George, the Americans in 1776 had constructed a large, strong redoubt on Mount Hope. This commanding hill, situated nearly due north of the La Chute River landing, safeguarded the portage to Lake George. They also constructed a blockhouse at the bateaux landing and sawmill of the La Chute River, which drains from Lake George into Lake Champlain. So long as Mount Hope was occupied, a British flanking maneuver around the American left (west) flank was impossible due to distances

[43]For comprehensive information on the Ticonderoga fortifications constructed by the Continental Army in the summer and fall of 1776, refer to Cubbison, *American Northern Theater Army*, 180–199.

[44]The best study of Mount Independence remains Wickman, "Built with Spirit, Deserted in Darkness." Mount Independence is today interpreted and protected as a Vermont State Historical Site in Orwell.

and terrain and the utter absence of roads. The fortifications at Mount Hope commanded any approach from the north, preventing a British flanking maneuver to the west of Fort Ticonderoga.[45]

A promontory that overlooked the entirety of the American positions, as well as the alternate American retreat route south on Lake Champlain, was known as Sugar Hill, or alternately as Sugar Loaf. It entirely commanded Fort Ticonderoga and Mount Independence, and their routes of supply and retreat down both Lakes George and Champlain. From the summit of Sugar Loaf to the Fort Ticonderoga parade ground, the actual range is 2,065 yards; from Sugar Loaf to the main American battery on Mount Independence the true range is 2,350 yards. These were well within the 3,665-yard maximum range of the 12-pounder cannon that the British would eventually place on top of the mountain. Experiments by American officers in 1776 had validated that Fort Ticonderoga and Mount Independence were both within easy cannon range from the heights of Sugar Loaf.[46] The Continental Army's Northern Theater Army commander Major General Horatio Gates chose not to defend Sugar Loaf, because the British had no conceivable way of taking advantage of its commanding location and elevation so long as Mount Hope was controlled by American defenders.[47]

However, the American position had one overwhelming weakness.

---

[45]Remnants of these earthworks are owned and interpreted today by the Fort Ticonderoga Museum, and the outlines of some of the fortifications also survive in the Ticonderoga community cemetery.

[46]Cubbison, *"Artillery never gained more Honour,"* 77–78.

[47]Continental Army Major General Horatio Gates, then commander of the American Northern Theater Army opposed to Burgoyne at Bemis Heights. Gates (1727–1806) is one of the most intriguing, and controversial, characters of the American War of Independence. He had been born in England in 1727, to lower-class parents. His father was a boater and servant by profession but a smuggler at heart, and his mother was a household servant. However, through a fortuitous set of circumstances, his godfather was the powerful Horace Walpole. Intimations abounded throughout his entire life that Gates was somebody's illegitimate son, but precisely whose was never specified, and the rumors were never proven. Gates had purchased a commission in the British army, and by 1755 he was a captain commanding an independent company in New York City. He participated in Braddock's campaign against Fort Duquesne, and during the desperate fight in the wilderness along the banks of the Monongahela River, Gates was severely wounded. He served as a captain throughout the Seven Years' War, in both North America and the West Indies, without again seeing combat or gaining any particular distinction. He did serve as brigade major for two separate generals over two campaigns, earning considerable experience in army administration and bureaucracy. He ended the war as a major but lacked sufficient patronage to avoid being placed on half pay when force reductions occurred at war's end. Gates spent approximately a decade on the half-pay rolls without accomplishment

It was designed to be defended by 13,000 soldiers, which was the size of the army that General Gates had available to him the previous year. But in late June 1777 American force strength was considerably less. Because of difficulties of raising new forces over the winter, the Americans had established Fort Ticonderoga as an "economy of force" mission, occupying it with a minimum garrison, relying on the natural strength of the position and the formidable earthworks constructed in 1776 to secure it. But the new American Commander, Major General Arthur St. Clair, arrived in June to discover that the garrison consisted of approximately 2,000 Continentals and slightly over another thousand militia. St. Clair quickly realized that he could not defend the entirety of the lines. Fundamentally misreading the terrain, St. Clair decided to abandon the position that was farthest away from the British and thus evacuated Mount Hope. By doing so, he entirely exposed his strategic left flank, rendered his primary line of communications to Lake George extremely vulnerable, and left Sugar Loaf undefended.

---

in England, and in 1773 he returned to North America. He purchased a modest western Virginia plantation, which he named "Traveler's Rest." Gates immediately settled comfortably into his new life as a gentleman planter and began to participate in American colonial politics. A fervent Whig, he had been a strong advocate for American liberties and rights even when he lived in England. His experience as a planter in Virginia only strengthened his political convictions. His portraits suggest a shrewdly calculating personality, with a sense of humor, self-confident and sly. He was apparently a good drinking companion and was genial, and outgoing. At the outset of the American War of Independence, Gates quickly offered his services to the fledgling Continental Army, and Washington eagerly employed him as his adjutant general during the Siege of Boston. Gates made his reputation at Boston in 1775–76. He was a highly skilled, extremely efficient administrator. He was meticulously well organized and rapidly made sense and order of the scattered correspondence of the young army working in cooperation with a wide range of officers from different colonies. His radical Whig politics earned him strong friendships with the equally strident New Englanders. Gates prepared for Washington the first set of U.S. Army Regulations, and he played a critical role in establishing procedures for recruitment and training. He had a reputation as a strict disciplinarian, a trait that was desperately needed in the American army, and one that Washington greatly respected. Washington sincerely admired Gates's skills as an administrator and organizer and greatly valued his contributions as adjutant general. Although he had served in the British army from 1749 to 1763, and throughout the Seven Years' War, Gates possessed almost no tactical or strategic experience, had never operated independently, and had no command experience above the company level. Tactically and strategically, Gates preferred a cautious, safe approach to maneuvering and fighting an army. Following his defeat of Burgoyne, Gates engaged in various political intrigues to gain command of the Continental Army that did him little credit, and his reputation was destroyed at the Battle of Camden, South Carolina, in 1780. He never recovered from this, living out the remainder of his years in quiet retirement at "Traveler's Rest." Billias, "Horatio Gates: Professional Soldier," 79–108; Mintz, *Generals of Saratoga*; Patterson, *Horatio Gates*; Nelson, *General Horatio Gates*; and Stitt, "Horatio Gates," 93–115

St. Clair's was a mistake of catastrophic consequences, as Burgoyne rapidly discovered, and exploited to the fullest. Burgoyne reported his subsequent maneuvers (File 6.16/18):

> July 2d. About nine in the morning a smoke was observed towards Lake George, and the Indians brought in a report that the Enemy had set fire to their further blockhouse and had abandoned the Saw Mills, and that a Considerable body were advancing from the Lines towards a Bridge upon the Road which led to the Right of the British Camp. A detachment of the advanced Corps was immediately put in march under Brigadier Frazer supported by a Brigade of the Line, and some Artillery under the Command of Major General Phillips with orders to Proceed towards Mount Hope, which is to the North of the Lines, to reconnoiter the Enemy's position and to take advantage of any Post they might abandon or be driven from.
>
> The Indians under Capt. Frazer,[48] supported by his Company of Marksmen[,][49] were directed to make a Circuit to the Left of Brigadier Frazer's line of March and endeavour to cut off the retreat of the Enemy to their Lines; but this design miscarried through the impetuosity of the Indians who attacked too soon, and in front and the Enemy were thereby able to retire with the loss of one Officer and a few men killed and one Officer wounded. Major General Phillips took possession of the very advantageous

[48]Captain Alexander Fraser (1735–1798) of the Clan Fraser, Scotland. Nephew of Lieutenant Colonel Simon Fraser of the 24th Foot, Fraser served as a subaltern in the Seven Years' War and was wounded at the Battle of Saint Foy (near Quebec) in April 1760. He apparently remained in Canada at the end of the war, providing additional service there as an officer to the British army. As the commanding officer of the Grenadier Company of the 34th Foot, Fraser also served as an assistant superintendent with the Indian Department. In 1776 and 1777 he commanded the Company of Select Marksmen, an elite group of rangers specifically formed to operate with the American Indian warriors as scouts and light infantry. Fraser saw extensive and distinguished service in the Saratoga Campaign. After Burgoyne surrendered, Captain Fraser was selected by Burgoyne to carry his dispatches announcing and explaining the Convention of Saratoga to Canada, for transmittal to England. Thus exempted from the Saratoga Convention, throughout the remainder of the war Fraser served with the Indian Department in Canada. Fraser would conclude the war in command of the Light Infantry Company of the 34th Foot and Fort Oswegatchie on the St. Lawrence River. He remained in the British army and is believed to have died in the West Indies still on campaign in 1798. The only biographical information on Fraser is on a Web site devoted to the Company of Select Marksmen, www.csmid.com. Fraser was known to display considerable tactical skill, daring, and initiative.

[49]The Company of Select Marksmen was formed in the 1776 campaign to serve as marksmen, rangers, scouts, and light infantry that could operate with the American Indians. They served with considerable skill and talent throughout the 1776 Valcour Island and 1777 Saratoga campaigns. They were heavily engaged in nearly every battle of the Saratoga Campaign and suffered severe casualties. They were maintained at double company strength throughout both campaigns. The Company was disbanded immediately before the surrender at Saratoga, and its members returned to their parent regiments. Strach, "Exploits of Captain Alexander Fraser," 91–98.

Post of Mount Hope this night, and the Enemy was thereby entirely cut off from communication with Lake George.

July 3$^{d.}$ Mount Hope was occupied in Force by Brigadier Frazer's whole brigade, the first Brigade British, and two entire brigades of Artillery. The second brigade British encamped upon the left of the first, and the Brigade of Gall[50] having been drove from the East shore to occupy the ground where Frazer's Corps had been on three mile Point, the line became compleat extending from the shore to the westernmost part of Mount Hope, on the same day Major Genl Reidesel encamped on the East Shore in a parallel Line with three mile point, having pushed the reserve forward near the rivilet which is on the East of Mount Independence. The Enemy cannonaded the Camps of Mount Hope and of the German reserve most part of the Day but without effect.

July 4th The Army worked hard at their Communications, and got up the Artillery, tents, baggage, and Provisions. The Enemy at intervals continued the cannonade upon the Camps, which was not in any instance returned. The Thunderer Radeau[51] carrying the battering train and Stores, having been warped up from Crown Point, arrived this day and immediately began to land the Artillery.

July 5th Lt. Twiss[52] the commanding Engineer was ordered to reconnoiter Sugar Hill on the South west side of the Communication from Lake George into Lake Champlain. It had appear'd from the first to be a very advantageous post. And it is now known that the Enemy had a council some time ago upon the expediency of possessing it; but the Idea was rejected upon

[50]Colonel W. R. Van Gall, colonel of the Hesse-Hanau Regiment, served as a brigade commander under Riedesel in both the 1776 and the 1777 campaigns, during which he was recognized as a brigadier general. Colonel Von Gall returned early to Germany following the surrender at Saratoga, thereby incurring the wrath of his sovereign. Little else is known of Von Gall's military or personal career. Doblin, trans., *Officer in the Prinz Friedrich Regiment*, 95.

[51]A radeau was essentially a gigantic floating raft, flat-bottomed, that could be rowed or sailed. Its distinctive design permitted a large number of cannon to be employed, it was musket-proof, and it could be easily built by carpenters rather than skilled shipwrights. A radeau was a distinctive North American vessel, and several of these had been built by the British army on both Lake George and Lake Champlain during the Seven Years' War. The *Thunderer* contained numerous heavy cannon, and during both the 1776 and the 1777 campaigns it had served as the floating British artillery headquarters and chief supply ship. The *Thunderer* had proven itself to be a very poor sailor, though, and generally hindered the operations of the Royal Artillery during both campaigns.

[52]Lieutenant William Twiss (c. 1745–1827) was the senior engineer on both the 1776 Valcour Island and 1777 Saratoga campaigns. He had entered military service in 1760 at fifteen years of age, and was commissioned into the Royal Engineers in 1764. He had served as an engineer at Gibraltar and at Plymouth Harbor in England. A skilled and accomplished engineer, he served on active duty until 1810, leaving the service as a full general. Rogers, *Hadden's Journal and Orderly Books*, 169–171.

the Supposition that it was impossible for a Corps to be established there in force.[53] Lt. Twiss reported this hill to have the entire command of the Works and Buildings both of Ticonderoga and Mount Independence; that the ground might be levelled so as to receive cannon; and that a road to convey them, tho' difficult, might be made practicable in twenty four hours. This Hill also entirely commanded in reverse the Bridge of communication, saw the exact situation of the Vessels, nor could the enemy during the day make any material movement or preparation without being discovered, and even having their numbers counted.[54] It was immediately determined that a battery should be raised upon Sugar Hill for light twenty four Pounders, medium twelves, and eight inch Howitzers. This very arduous work was carried on so rapidly that the battery would have been ready the next day. It is a duty in this Place to do some justice to the zeal and activity of Major General Phillips who had the direction of the Operation. And having mentioned that most valuable Officer, I trust it cannot be thought a Digression to add, that it is to his judicious arrangements and indefatigable pains, during the general superintendency of preparations which Sir Guy Carleton entrusted to him in the Winter and Spring, that the service is indebted for its present forwardness, the prevalence of contrary Winds and other accidents having rendered it impossible for any necessaries prepared in England for the opening of the campaign yet to reach the Army.

As Burgoyne recounted, the Germans had experienced little success in their movements against Mount Independence. They discovered that traversing the terrain was a convoluted exercise, with large areas of marsh, swamp, quicksand, and inundated ground to be negotiated. They found East Creek to be deeper than anticipated, with precipitous banks that more closely resembled cliffs. The Regimental Journal of the Brunswick Regiment commanded by Colonel Johann Friedrich Specht recorded: "Thus, from the very beginning we discovered important impediments we would have to face if we wanted to overcome the enemy in the way we wished."[55] Riedesel, despite his great efforts, would be unable to

[53]This was, in fact, true so long as the Americans remained in possession of Mount Hope.

[54]In Burgoyne, *State of the Expedition from Canada*, xxix, a sentence was inserted in this paragraph providing the artillery ranges from Sugar Loaf to Fort Ticonderoga and Mount Independence.

[55]Doblin, trans., *Specht Journal*, 51. Colonel Johann Friedrich Specht (?–1787), colonel of the regiment of the same name, served as one of Riedesel's brigade commanders throughout the Saratoga Campaign. He would surrender at the Convention on October 17 and eventually return to Brunswick. He allegedly suffered from ill health throughout the campaign. Doblin, *Officer in the Prinz Friedrich Regiment*, 62.

interdict either the American military road leading east into the hills of Vermont or the American main line of communications on the southern bay of Lake Champlain.

Because of Riedesel's inability to work his way around Mount Independence, Gall's Brigade was transferred back to the western shore of Lake Champlain on July 3 to help strengthen the overextended British lines, since Fraser's advance guard was now operating well to the south and west at Mount Hope, the Ticonderoga portage, and Sugar Loaf. Sir Francis-Carr Clerke echoed the observation from Burgoyne's headquarters: "Fraser gained some very material Heights with the Loss of two or three Men only this Evening [July 2], since then the Rebels have been entirely cut off from Lake George."[56]

The transfer of Gall's Brigade seriously depleted Riedesel's strength, making an already challenging job of maneuvering around Mount Independence even more difficult. To provide some compensation for this loss, Captain Fraser's Company of Select Marksmen, at least some if not all of the Loyalists and Canadians, and the majority of the Native warriors were transferred across Lake Champlain on July 3 and 4, and were moved north on the lake to launch a series of raids against American settlements on Otter Creek, well east-northeast of Crown Point. These raids would have a negligible effect on the American populace, no influence whatsoever on the military situation at Fort Ticonderoga and Mount Independence, and precluded Fraser's skilled rangers from supporting the British regulars at a critical juncture in the campaign.[57]

July 4 was occupied in moving up the artillery, which required considerable time and effort. On July 5 Lieutenant William Twiss, the campaign's engineer, moved to the top of Sugar Loaf and examined the terrain. Although when viewed from the lake and Fort Ticonderoga the mountain appears precipitous and the climb impossible, when ascended from the north along the topographical crest leading up to it, the climb is not particularly arduous. It is long with a continuous grade, and a number of rock outcroppings have to be traversed with circumspection. However, in May 2005 the living history Company of Select Marksmen

---

[56]Kingsley, "Letters from Sir Francis-Carr Clerke," 418.

[57]Strach, "Exploits of Captain Alexander Fraser"; and Underwood, "Indian and Tory Raids," 198–199.

pulled, entirely by hand, a full-scale, full-weight reproduction 3-pounder cannon from the base of Mount Defiance to its crest using an informal, unmaintained dirt snowmobile trail, in only a few hours' effort, without any particular difficulty.[58] This experimental archaeology confirmed what Engineer Twiss had discovered in early July 1777, for two 12-pounder cannon were moved up the hill by a large working party under the direct supervision of Major General William Phillips and Engineer Twiss by the afternoon of July 5. Twiss observed, as Lord Francis Napier reported: "A battery begun to be raised on Sugar Hill, a very advantageous situation and entirely commanding the Forts of Ticonderoga & Mount Independence."[59] Sometime on the afternoon of July 5, this large British working party was observed, with great consternation, from Fort Ticonderoga.

During this entire time, Burgoyne provided overall supervision of the main operation from the small frigate *Royal George*, which had been outfitted over the winter. He entrusted his senior commanders, such as Riedesel, Phillips, and Fraser, to command the individual tactical maneuvers.[60] Although at first glance it may appear that this was not a particularly aggressive command post, Lake Champlain was at the geographical center of Burgoyne's army, and Burgoyne could move much faster by water than by land to any point of danger or decision. This actually afforded him the advantage of a headquarters that could communicate effectively with both wings of his army, on either side of the lake. The *Royal George* served as Burgoyne's headquarters afloat from his departure from Fort St. John's in late June until his landing at Skenesboro on July 8.

American Evacuation of Fort Ticonderoga, July 5–6, 1777

With the British already interdicting his line of communications down Lake George, St. Clair wasted little time in evacuating Fort Ticonderoga, and ordered a retreat to be executed under cover of darkness on the night of July 5–6. St. Clair necessarily had to withdraw along two routes. He

[58] See www.hoplologia.org/projects/mtdefiance.html (accessed August 3, 2010).
[59] Bradford, "Lord Francis Napier's Journal," 299.
[60] Kingsley, "Letters from Sir Francis-Carr Clerke," 420.

had six naval vessels available and approximately two hundred bateaux. These included five survivors of the Valcour Island fleet that had fought the previous October: the row galley *Trumbull*, the gondola *New York*, and the smaller sailing ships *Liberty*, *Revenge*, and *Enterprise*. The row galley *Gates* had not been completed in time to fight at Valcour Island. The gondola *New York* quite likely had her three cannon removed to increase its cargo capacity, for no British accounts mention its presence as a fighting vessel. Most likely, absent its armament, the British simply considered the *New York* to be a large bateaux (which, technically, it was).[61]

This provided St. Clair with only enough transportation to move his wounded and sick, and the most valuable of the stores and artillery, from the Ticonderoga fortress complex by water. The majority of his fighting regiments crossed over the Lake Champlain bridge to Mount Independence, and marched east on the 1776 military road in the direction of Hubbardton, Castleton, and then Skenesboro. Burgoyne recounted the British pursuit of the Americans (File 6.16/18):

> July 6th Soon after day light an Officer arrived express onboard the Royal George, where in the night I took my Quarters as the most centrical Situation, with information from Brigadier Frazer that the Enemy were retiring and that he was advancing with his piquets, leaving orders for the brigade to follow as soon as they could accoutre, with intentions to pursue by land.[62] This movement was very soon discernable, as were the British Colours which the Brigadier had fixed upon their Fort at Ticonderoga. Knowing the safety I cou'd trust to that Officer's conduct, I turned my chief attention to the pursuit by Water, by which route I had Intelligence one Column were retiring in two hundred and twenty Bateaux covered by five armed Gallies. The great Bridge of communications through which a way was to be opened was supported by twenty two sunken pieces of large timber at nearly equal Distances: the spaces between were filled by separate floats each about fifty feet long and twelve feet wide, strongly fastened together by Chains and Rivets, and also fastened to the sunken piers. Before this bridge was a Boom made of very large pieces of round timber fastened together by rivetted bolts and double Chains made of Iron an inch and half square. The gun boats were immediately moved forward, and the Boom and one of the intermediate floats were cut with great dexterity and dispatch. And

61 Cubbison, *"Artillery never gained more Honour,"* 81–86.

62 "Accoutre" means that the infantry would put on their accoutrements and other military equipment, such that they were prepared to march and engage in combat.

Commodore Lutwidge[63] with the Officers and Seamen in his department partaking the general animation, a passage was found in half an hour for the Frigates also, through impediments which the Enemy had been labouring for months together to make impenetrable [the log-and-chain barricade across Lake Champlain]. During the operations Major Gen[l] Reidesel had passed to Mount Independence with the Corps of Breyman and part of the left wing. He was directed to proceed by Land to sustain Brigadier Frazer or to act more to the Left if he saw it expedient to do so. . . .

About three in the afternoon I arrived with the Royal George and Inflexible, and the best sailing Gun Boats and Bateaux at South Bay within three miles of Skenesborough at which latter place I learned the Enemy were posted in a stockaded fort, and their armed gallies at the falls below. The foremost regiments viz the 9th 20th and 21st were instantly disembarked and ascended the Mountain with intention of turning the fort and cutting off the Retreat of the Enemy but their precipitate flight rendered this maneuver ineffectual.

The gunBoats and Frigates continued their Course to Skenesborough falls, Capt. Carter[64] with part of his Brigade, and Gun Boats immediately attacked the Gallies, and with so much spirit that two of them very soon struck; the other three were blown up, and the Enemy having previously prepared Combustible materials, set fire to the Fort, Mills, Storehouses, bateaux &c. and retired with the detachment left for that purpose, the main body having gone off when the Troops were ascending the Mountains. A great quantity of Provisions and some Arms were here consumed, and most part of their Officers baggage was burned, sunk, or taken. Their loss in the Attack is not known, about thirty prisoners were made, among which were two wounded Officers.

As Burgoyne described, the British pursuit was performed in three columns, which essentially launched what in nautical terms would be described as a "stern chase" to catch up to the retreating Americans. Brigadier General Fraser and his advance corps were the first to move. They rapidly crossed the bridge over Lake Champlain, continued through the Mount Independence entrenchment, and pursued the Continental Army's land force on the road to Castleton. Following behind him,

[63]Captain Skeffington Lutwidge, Royal Navy, commander of the British fleet.

[64]Captain John Carter, Royal Artillery. He was an seasoned officer with twenty-two years' service by 1777, including combat experience in the Seven Years' War. Carter commanded No. 7 Company, 1st Battalion; and was the second-oldest artillery captain serving under Burgoyne. He subsequently commanded the Park of Artillery during the campaign. Rogers, *Hadden's Journal and Orderly Books*, 91–92.

Riedesel flanked to the east, gained the military road, and marched in Fraser's rear. He would eventually join with Fraser later that day. The British gunboats led the pursuit up Lake Champlain, blasting through the American obstacles across the lake in short order. What is significant in Burgoyne's account is what is omitted, rather than what is included. Specifically, Burgoyne made no note of any instructions for logistical or transportation actions. Instead, his three columns simply galloped off into the American countryside, two by land and one by sea, in pursuit of the enemy. Fraser, for example, took no doctors or medical assets with him, no spare rations, and no additional ammunition. Burgoyne seems to have expended little planning or consideration on the pursuit.

Still, the British gunboats achieved a spectacular victory that afternoon. As Burgoyne recalled, for he viewed the action from the deck of the *Royal George*, the British Royal Artillery gunboats caught the American fleet, which had been confident that the chain-and-log boom that was integral to the Lake Champlain bridge would delay the British for an extended period of time, and were remarkably dilatory in their retreat. St. Clair even failed to designate a commander of the American naval flotilla, and in the absence of positive leadership, the American fighting vessels failed to obstruct the British. The Americans were roused out of their hubris when the British gunboats bore down upon them at Skenesboro, engaged and rapidly sank their fighting vessels, and forced them to destroy their bateaux. Lost onboard the American sailing vessels and bateaux were the most important and irreplaceable of the military and medical stores including ordnance and munitions of the American Northern Theater Army. In the process, the British sustained almost no casualties, losing one lieutenant and one gunner from the Royal Artillery killed, and one volunteer and one other artilleryman wounded. It was a devastating blow to the Continental Army, a loss severe enough that it endangered the very survival of the force.[65]

While Burgoyne crushed the Americans on Lake Champlain, Fraser's advance guard continued its pursuit, following the American retreating columns across dusty roads, through blazing hot temperatures (File 6.16/18):

---

[65]Historians have paid scant attention to the extremely important naval action fought at Skenesboro on July 6, 1777. For further details on this contest, refer to Cubbison, *"Artillery never gained more Honour,"* 81–86.

During these Operations upon the right Brigadier Frazer had continued his pursuit on the road to Castleton 'till one O'clock having marched in a very hot day from four in the morning. Some stragglers of the Enemy had been picked up, from whom the Brigadier learned that their rear guard was composed of chosen men and commanded by Col. Francis[66] one of their best Officers. While the men were refreshing Major Gen[l] Reidesel [*sic*] came up; and arrangements having been concerted for continuing the pursuit, Brigadier Frazer moved forward again and during the Night lay upon his Arms in an advantageous situation.

July 7th. At three in the morning he renewed his march, and about five his advanced scouts discovered the Enemy's Centries [sentries], who fired their pieces and joined their main body. The Brigadier observing a commanding ground on the Left of his light Infantry immediately ordered it to be possessed by that Corps, and a considerable body of the enemy attempting the same they met. The enemy were driven back to their original Post. The advanced guard under Major [Robert] Grant[67] were by this time engaged,[68] and the Grenadiers were advanced to sustain them, and to prevent the right flank from being turned. The Brigadier remained on the Left, where the Enemy aided by Logs and Trees, defended themselves long. After being dislodged and prevented getting to the Castleton road by the Grenadiers they rallied, and renewed the action. They were again driven, and attempted a retreat by Pittsford Mountain, but the Grenadiers scrambled up what had appeared an inaccessible part of the ascent and gained the Summit before them.[69] This threw them into confusion. They were still never the less greatly superior in number and consequently in extent, and the Brigadier in

---

[66]Colonel Ebenezer Francis (1743–1777) commanded the 11th Massachusetts Regiment of the Continental Line, and was the rear guard commander during the American withdrawal from Fort Ticonderoga and Mount Independence. He is generally regarded to have fought with courage, resolution, and considerable skill at Hubbardton. He is buried beneath the battlefield monument at Hubbardton.

[67]Major Robert Grant (?–1777). Following Fraser's promotion to brigadier general in Canada in 1776, Major Grant was the senior officer of the 24th Foot, and commanded that battalion in the 1776 and 1777 campaigns, until his death. His name is so common within the legions of Major Grants of the British army that nothing further can be determined with certainty regarding his life. He was called "a gallant and brave officer." His actions at Hubbardton suggest that he tended to behave somewhat precipitously by nature. The "advance guard" listed here was actually the 24th Regiment of Foot.

[68]The guard had not only been "engaged" but had in fact been quite roughly handled.

[69]This is a rather garbled account of the Battle of Hubbardton. The British light infantry were driven on the left, while the grenadiers successfully advanced on the right. Thus, the battle line rotated counterclockwise as the Americans succeeded on one flank, while the British gained on the other. The grenadiers ascended the steep slopes of Mount Zion, located to the extreme British right or American left flank—that is, the southern flank of the engagement.

Momentary expectation of the arrival of the Germans had latterly weakened his left to support his right. At this critical moment Major Gen$^{l.}$ Reidesel arrived with the foremost of his Column viz. the Chasseur Company and eighty Grenadiers & L$^{t.}$ Infantry. His judgment instantly pointed to him the course to take. He extended upon Brigadier Frazer's left Flank. Major Bernes led the Chasseurs into action with great gallantry and they were equally well sustain'd.[70] The enemy fled on all sides leaving dead upon the field Col. Frances and many other Officers and upwards of two hundred private men[.] [A]bove six hundred were wounded—many of whom perished in the Woods attempting to get off; and one Colonel, seven Captains, ten Subalterns, and two hundred and ten men were made Prisoners.[71] The number of the enemy before the Action amounted by report of Prisoners, to two thousand men, and they were strongly posted.[72] The British detachment under Brigadier Frazer (the parties left at Ticonderoga the day before not having been able to rejoin) consisted only of eight hundred and fifty fighting men. The bare relation of so signal an action is sufficient for its praise. [S]hould the attack against such inequality of numbers before the Germans came up, seem to require explanation—it is to be considered that the Enemy might have escaped by delay;[73] that the advanced guard found themselves on a sudden too near the enemy to avoid action without retreating; and that the Brigadier had supposed the German troops to be very near. The difference of time in their arrival was merely accidental; Major General Riedesel and those he commanded pressed for a share of the glory and they arrived in time to obtain it.[74]

I have only to add upon this event, that the exertions of Brigadier Frazer were but a continuance of that uniform intelligence, activity, and bravery which distinguish his character upon all occasions, and entitle him to be recommended in the most particular manner to his Majesty's notice.

The other Officers and Soldiers of this Corps have prevented any distinctions of Individuals by a general and equal display of Spirit.

---

[70]Major Ferdinand Albrecht von Bärner commanded the Brunswick Chasseur (light infantry) Battalion throughout the Saratoga Campaign.

[71]Colonel Nathan Hale of New Hampshire was the American Colonel captured. The number of prisoners claimed by Burgoyne appears to be accurate.

[72]In fact, the Americans were not posted in battle lines whatsoever at the commencement of the fight. Their forces at Sucker Brook were disorganized and surprised, and the other two regiments were in column of march preparing to move along the road to continue their retreat.

[73]Burgoyne's assessments are most certainly true, as the Americans were actively preparing to depart when the British attacked.

[74]Again, this is absolutely accurate: the arrival of the Brunswick soldiers commanded by Riedesel saved the light infantry that were being badly pressed and having their flank turned; Britain's German allies won the day and gained the field for the British.

The action fought by Fraser and Riedesel on July 7 occurred as much by accident as by design. Fraser had the majority of his advance guard, less the Company of Select Marksmen and American Indians who were detached on their raid on Otter Creek, about 850 men. Because of the haste with which Fraser had initiated his pursuit, and his urgency in pushing it, his advance guard had marched without artillery, surgeons, reserve ammunition, or spare provisions. Burgoyne did little to assist Fraser, as he had raced after the American flotilla on Lake Champlain without issuing any orders for logistical support to follow up the advance guard. Riedesel joined Fraser on the evening of June 6 approximately six miles west of Hubbardton. He only had a portion of his division with him, about 1,100 soldiers.

The American withdrawal from Ticonderoga had been a shambles. It was hastily planned, and most of the soldiers were only told that they were abandoning their fortifications and running from the British. Many of the Americans had been sick to various degrees, and all had been cooped up for the winter in the Ticonderoga encampments with little opportunity to exercise, on preserved rations that lacked adequate nutrition. They were certainly in no condition to perform a forced march in the July heat, with little warning and no preparation. Colonel Ebenezer Francis, 11th Massachusetts Regiment of the Continental Line, initially commanded the rear guard. The American retreat was considerably slowed by two regiments of Massachusetts militia that clogged up the road several miles east of Hubbardton, and troops had been forced to halt for the night at Sucker Brook, a small rivulet in a sheltered glade that afforded good access to drinking water approximately a quarter mile west of Hubbardton. The small crossroads community of Hubbardton consisted of only a few log cabins perched atop a ridgeline. Francis joined forces with the Vermont Green Mountain Boys Regiment commanded by Colonel Seth Warner and Colonel Nathan Hale's 2nd New Hampshire Regiment of the Continental Line at Hubbardton. Colonel Warner assumed command of the rear guard as the senior American officer. Advanced pickets were placed on Sargent Hill, approximately one-half mile west of Sucker Brook. Numerous stragglers and sick had collapsed at Sucker Brook, and Colonel Hale spent most of the night attempting to organize these men and get them back on their feet. The strength of the American force was approximately 1,000 to 1,200; the large number of unaccounted-for stragglers renders it unfeasible to derive any more accurate figure. The Americans almost certainly did outnumber the British, but not by much, particularly considering that many of the Americans at Sucker Brook contributed little or nothing to the defense.

Fraser marched until evening, six miles short of Hubbardton, where he was joined after dark by Riedesel, and they agreed that Fraser would continue the advance before daybreak (about 3:00 A.M.) and that Riedesel would follow in his wake a few hours later. Fraser's advance scouts made contact with the American pickets on Sargent Hill near daybreak (about 5:00 A.M.). The Americans at this moment were preparing to march, and Warner and Francis had their regiments formed in a column on the road atop the ridge, while Hale and his regiment continued trying to assimilate the late arrivals from Sucker Brook.

Fraser halted and called for assistance from Riedesel, but he became impatient and, probably at the urging of his friend Major Grant, determined to attack by himself about 6:30 A.M. The British assault, spearheaded by Grant and the 24th Foot, surprised the American camp at Sucker Brook. Grant was killed instantly at the first fire, when he climbed up on a stump to improve his observation, making himself a marked man at the same time. The British drove the American stragglers in panicked retreat across a quarter mile of open fields and then up a steep ridge now known as "Monument Hill."

By 7:20 A.M. the British began to ascend Monument Hill, and an even steeper promontory to the east, Mount Zion Hill. From this moment on, the fighting became extremely confused amid the thick woods, steep ridges, and small farm fields divided by sturdy fences. During the dry season of mid-July, any marching troop column generated considerable dust, and when combined with the thick blue smoke of the musketry contributed greatly to the confusion.[75] Lieutenant Thomas Anburey with the 24th Foot remembered: "In this action I found all manual exercise is but an ornament, and the only object of importance it can boast of was that of loading, firing, and charging with bayonets." Fraser

[75]The author, a living historian who performed extensive living history events at the Hubbardton battlefield numerous times in early July between 2002 and 2008, including a forced march over the British advance route, can personally attest to these aspects of the battle.

launched a two-pronged attack with the Light Infantry Battalion on his left, the 24th Foot constituting the center, and the Grenadier Battalion on the right. As Anburey recalled: "The grenadiers scrambled up the ascent which appeared almost inaccessible, and gained the summit of the mountain before them; this threw them into great confusion, and that you may form some idea how steep the ascent must have been, the men were obliged to sling their firelocks and climb up the side, sometimes resting their feet upon the branch of a tree, and sometimes on a piece of rock; had any been so unfortunate as to have missed his hold, he must [have] inevitabl[y] been dashed to pieces."[76]

Determined American counterattacks, at least two of them, greatly delayed the British advance. Finally, the British Grenadier Battalion under Major Acland on the right flank achieved success, reaching the pinnacle of Mount Zion, and thus immediately endangering the American left flank and line of retreat to Castleton. Commanding the Light Infantry Battalion on the British left, Balcarres was extremely impressed by the fighting acumen revealed by the Americans, as he later recalled: "Circumstanced as the enemy was, as an army very hard pressed in their retreat, they certainly behaved with great gallantry . . . at all times when I was opposed to the rebels, they fought with great courage and obstinancy."[77] In fact, Balcarres's Light Infantry Battalion was driven back, primarily by Francis's regiment. The fight raged back and forth across Castleton Road and the plateau beyond Monument Hill. As a result, the battle lines actually rotated, from an east–west alignment to a north–south alignment. At about 8:30 A.M., with the British left flank disintegrating, Riedesel arrived, and the rifles of his jaegers proved particularly effective. In the confusion, Colonel Francis saw the Brunswick blue uniforms indistinctly through the smoke and dust, and called for his men to hold their fire. One of his soldiers recalled: "At this time smoke was so thick on the hill, we did not see the enemy until they fired. There being some scattering [scattered] firing, Francis told the soldiers not to fire, they were firing on their own men. Then came a British volley and Francis fell dead." The Brunswick soldiers had arrived at the precise

[76]Jackman, ed., *With Burgoyne from Quebec*, 140, 142. The author has climbed this precise route, in formation, in the uniform and equipage of the 24th Foot, and is in full accordance with the young British lieutenant.

[77]Burgoyne, *State of the Expedition from Canada*, 39, 46.

moment when the Americans, having fought for two hours, were running low on water and ammunition. Riedesel's advance upon the vulnerable American right flank, and the death of Colonel Francis at the critical moment, sealed the fate of the American rear guard.

Defeated, the Americans broke up into small parties, and retreated to the north into the woods on Pittsford Ridge. The British owned the battlefield by about 8:45 A.M., but they had suffered catastrophic casualties. British and German recorded losses were fifteen officers and 183 other ranks killed and wounded. American casualties are unknown, but probably numbered about one hundred Americans killed or wounded. Another 234 American prisoners were taken by the British during the American retreat. Of the forces engaged, British losses were about 22 percent, American about 12 percent, and German about 13 percent. The Americans had clearly outfought the British. Although Fraser had driven the Americans from the field, his advance corps had lost nearly a quarter of its strength, and he ended his pursuit immediately at the top of Monument Hill. Fraser had marched with three days' rations, but he had no spare ammunition or capability of caring for his many wounded, and any further advance was stymied. The Battle of Hubbardton was unquestionably a tactical defeat for the Americans; but the rear guard had successfully accomplished its strategic mission of protecting the withdrawal of the overwhelming majority of the American army, and had simultaneously inflicted severe casualties on the enemy. Burgoyne's account of the battle (File 6.16/18), doubtless received directly from Fraser, Riedesel, and Balcarres, is generally accurate, but it was unquestionably embellished to place his and his army's achievements in the best possible light.[78]

A highly experienced and accomplished cavalryman, Burgoyne well understood the importance of pressing a pursuit of any defeated or retreating force. Historically, any military organization is vulnerable to losing far more men and matériel during a retrograde movement than during the initial action that forced its withdrawal. Burgoyne demonstrated this twice on July 6, when he launched Fraser and Riedesel aggressively from Mount Independence and by pursuing the American

[78]Information on the Battle of Hubbardton is primarily drawn from Williams, "Battle of Hubbardton"; and Ward, *War of the Revolution*, 1:412–414.

flotilla up Lake Champlain with the Royal Navy fleet and Royal Artillery gunboats. He continued his efforts at pursuit on July 7, when he directed the 9th Regiment of Foot, commanded by Lieutenant Colonel John Hill, to move from Skenesboro to Fort Anne, acting on intelligence regarding the route that the badly scattered Americans had taken following their nautical drubbing the previous day.[79]

Colonel Hill proceeded with approximately 160 to 190 rank and file to Fort Anne, where he was aggressively engaged by a strong American rear guard covering the withdrawal of the remnants of the Skenesboro garrison on July 8. The American force consisted of nearly 150 men under the command of Colonel Pierce Long of New Hampshire, augmented by Colonel Henry Van Rensselaer with four hundred New York militia rushed up from Albany. The American attacking force had barely a 3:1 superiority in numbers, the minimum deemed necessary for a successful assault, and given the limited training and experience of the militia, Colonel Long's actual superiority was considerably less. Still, the Americans launched a devastating attack upon Colonel Hill's regulars. Major Forbes of the 9th Regiment recalled: "At half past ten in the morning, the enemy attacked us in front with a heavy and well directed fire; a large body of them passed the creek on the left, fired from a thick wood across the creek on the left flank of the regiment; they then began to re-cross the creek, and attack us in the rear: we then found it necessary to change our ground, to prevent the regiment being surrounded;

[79]Because the name "John Hill" is so common, a biography of Lieutenant Colonel John Hill cannot be compiled with certainty. It is believed that this Colonel Hill was initially commissioned in the 24th Regiment of Foot sometime in 1747 or 1748. He had subsequently transferred to the 13th Foot. During the Seven Years' War he had seen garrison duty at Gibraltar, and following the cessation of hostilities he had served with the garrison at Minorca. He became lieutenant colonel of the 9th Regiment of Foot on September 11, 1775, and accompanied his regiment to Canada, arriving there in May 1776. He was present, but his regiment had not seen any action, in the 1776 campaign. Thus, although Lieutenant Colonel Hill was an officer with nearly thirty years of active service, he had never seen combat. After the surrender at Saratoga he saw no further active service, was promoted to colonel in 1783, and vanished from the rolls of the army in 1784. Rogers, *Hadden's Journal and Orderly Book*, 89–90. The 9th Regiment of Foot sustained heavy casualties at Fort Anne and were nearly broken. Serving as the advance guard for the British Regular Brigade at Freeman's Farm on September 19, 1777, they also suffered severe casualties and were badly broken, taking no further active role (except as reserves) in the engagement. The regiment's less than stellar performance in these two engagements may reflect poor leadership on the part of Hill, but this cannot be confirmed. Only a single primary source is known to exist from this regiment for the Saratoga Campaign: Lamb, *Journal of Occurrences*.

we took post on the top of a high hill to our right. As soon as we had taken post, the enemy made a very vigorous attack, which continued for upward of two hours; and they certainly would have forced us, had it not been for some Indians that arrived and gave the Indian whoop, which we answered with three cheers; the rebels soon after that gave way."[80]

Forbes's account barely acknowledges the intensity of the fighting that afternoon. Hill's men situated on a hill near Fort Anne were heavily assailed. Suffering severe casualties and running low on ammunition, the regiment was on the verge of being shattered when Captain John Money, a British army deputy quartermaster general who had apparently been practicing an Indian war whoop in his spare time for his amusement, unleashed his newly learned skills. However, Forbes's account fails to note that Money was accompanied by a party of real Native warriors, whose arrival doubtless hastened the American withdrawal. The Americans, exhausted and running low on ammunition, had accomplished their mission of stopping the British pursuit in its tracks; and believing that reinforcements were now arriving from the main British army, they accordingly withdrew. American casualties are unknown. British casualties were serious: Lieutenant Haggard was killed, along with one sergeant and eleven rank and file; one captain, two lieutenants, one adjutant, two sergeants, and nineteen rank and file were wounded; and one captain and one surgeon were captured. Out of a force of not more than two hundred, total casualties were near 20 percent. Burgoyne reported (File 6.16/18):

> On the same day (July 7) the Country people about Skenesborough having reported that part of the Enemy were still retreating upon Wood Creek, the 9th regiment was detach'd to take post near Fort Anne to observe their motions. This was effected tho' with much difficulty, the roads being extremely bad and the Bridges broken. The other Troops were employed all that day and night in dragging fifty Bateaux over the falls to facilitate the movement of the rest of the first brigade to Fort Anne to dislodge the Enemy there.
>
> July 8th A report was received from Lt. Colonel Hill commanding the 9th regiment, that the Enemy had been reinforced in the night by a considerable body of fresh Troops, that he could not retire before them with his regiment, but would maintain his ground. The two remaining regiments of the

[80] Burgoyne, *State of the Expedition from Canada*, 81.

first Brigade under Brigadier Powell were ordered to quicken their march, and upon second intelligence of the Force of the Enemy, and firing being heard, the 20th Regt. was ordered forward, and Major General Phillips with some pieces of artillery was sent to take the Command. A violent storm of rain which lasted the whole day prevented these troops from getting to Fort Anne so soon as was intended; but the delay gave the 9th regiment an opportunity of distinguishing themselves by standing and repulsing an attack of six times their numbers.[81] The enemy finding the position not to be forced in Front endeavoured to surround it, and from the superiority of their numbers that inconvenience was to be apprehended and Lt. Col. Hill therefore found it necessary to change his ground in the heat of Action. So critical an order was executed by the regiment with the greatest steadiness and Bravery. The enemy after an attack of three hours were totally repulsed with great loss. They fled towards Fort Edward setting fire to Fort Anne, but leaving a Saw-mill and block-house in good repair which latter was afterwards possessed by the Kings troops. The 9th regiment acquired during their expedition about thirty Prisoners, some stores and Baggage and the Colours of the second Hampshire Regiment.

The accidents to counterballance these several successes are few. The service has lost an Officer of great Gallantry & experience in Major Grant. The other Officers killed are also to be much regretted. Captain Montgomery of the 9th regiment an Officer of much merit was wounded in the Leg early in the action, and was in the act of being dressed by the Surgeon when the regiment changed ground. Being unable to help himself, he and the Surgeon were taken prisoners. I hear he has been well treated and is in a fair way of recovering at Albany. The wounded Officers and men, in general here are also likely to do well.

Although Burgoyne reported the action at Fort Anne to be a victory since Hill's 9th Foot held the field, the regiment had been heavily pressed and had sustained crippling casualties that could scarcely be replaced. Additionally, although the nautical pursuit on Lake Champlain had proved to be a great success, both of Burgoyne's land pursuits had been halted by heavy fighting, coming out considerably worse for wear in the bargain. This was not a good omen either for future engagements or for the continued progress of Burgoyne's campaign.

---

[81] The ardor of the American attack can be gauged from the fact that Hill apparently thought he was heavily outnumbered. As noted, the American force did possess a numerical superiority of 3:1, but since many of the Americans were poorly trained, inexperienced militia, their actual combat superiority was certainly less than this.

Logistics and Transportation at the Southern End of Lake Champlain, July–September 1777

And now Burgoyne had to face the most difficult obstacle that stood between Canada and Albany: the "height of land" between the southern ends of Lakes George and Champlain and the northern end of navigation of the Hudson River at Fort Edward. So long as Burgoyne could move by water, either on the lakes or the river, he could maneuver relatively expeditiously. However, the British had to move the entirety of their baggage trains, sufficient provisions both for the march to Albany and to remain there until a line of communications could be established down the Hudson River to New York City, plus a train of artillery to offer necessary protection against opposition on the way. Traversing this lengthy portage would prove to be the most challenging part of the campaign.

Although his memorandums regarding the proposed campaign had briefly addressed this issue, it appears that Burgoyne laid out no meaningful plans for resolving this logistical and transportation dilemma, and thus underestimated the challenge that it posed to his advance. Sir Francis-Carr Clerke wrote to friends in England on July 17 from Skenesboro in a letter that reflected Burgoyne's perspective: "We are obliged to remain here and at Ticonderoga some little time to get Bateaux over the Rapids at both places; as also to repair the roads from hence to Fort Ann[e]."[82] In the event, this "little time" would consume no less than two full months. Burgoyne reported the beginning of his efforts along the logistical lines (File 6.16/18):

> July 9th & 10th The remains of the Ticonderoga army are at Fort Edward where they have been joined by considerable corps of fresh troops.[83] Roads are Opening to march to them by fort Anne, and the wood Creek is clearing of fallen trees, sunken Stones, and other obstacles, to give passage to bateaux carrying Artillery, Stores, Provision, and camp equipage &c. These are laborious works but the spirit and zeal of the troops are sufficient to surmount them. In the mean time all possible diligence is using at Ticonderoga to get gun boats, bateaux, and Provision vessels into Lake George.

[82]Kingsley, "Letters from Sir Francis-Carr Clerke," 420.

[83]At this point in the campaign, this assertion concerning American reinforcements is almost certainly not true. Except for the Albany militia, none had yet reached Fort Edward.

> A corps of the Army, will be ordered to penetrate by that route which will afterwards be the route of the Magazines, and a junction of the whole is intended at Fort Edward.

With this paragraph, frequently overlooked by historians, Burgoyne articulated his logistical approach. He initially intended to utilize the Fort Ticonderoga–Ticonderoga portage–Lake George–Fort George–Hudson River route. He said as much in a letter written March 2, 1777, to Captain Philemon Pownell of the Royal Navy (File 20:34, Henry Clinton Papers): "to introduce the courses with which I feel for your connection in the naval command provided we have any thing to do on Lake George for I hardly expect we shall be found upon Lake Champlain. At all events I am sanguine enough to believe all lake business will be over early enough in the year to enable whoever commands there to return down the St. Lawrence."

However, since his infantry on July 6 had been disembarked at Skenesboro at the southern end of Lake Champlain, and since his large Royal Naval flotilla could operate from St. John's in Canada all the way to Skenesboro, he decided to continue using the Skenesboro–Fort Anne–Hudson River corridor as his primary route of advance for his infantry. The action fought at Fort Anne by the 9th Regiment of Foot on July 7 also established British possession of the southern Lake Champlain corridor as far as that fort, and if the level of water permitted, bateaux could thus proceed up Wood Creek to this point.

At the same time, Burgoyne conceived the Ticonderoga portage–Lake George–Fort George–Hudson River corridor as the best way to move his heavy baggage and artillery south. This was in accordance with his initial approach formulated in London the previous winter (File 6.16/9): "the immediate Possession of Lake George would be of great Consequence as the most expeditious and most commodious Route to Albany; and should the Enemy be in force upon that Lake, which is very probable, every Effort should be tried by throwing Savages and Light Troops round it, to oblige them to quit it without waiting for naval Preparations. Should those Efforts fail the Route by South Bay and Skenesborough may be attempted, but considerable Difficulties may be expected, as the narrow Parts of the River may be easily choaked up and rendered impassable, and at best there will be necessity for a great deal of Land Carriage for the Artillery, Provisions, &c. which can only be supplied from Canada."

This modified approach of employing both routes, which Burgoyne adapted in mid-July, was actually an improved logistical solution, as it provided dual supply routes that should have significantly improved his ability to pass matériel from Canada to Fort Edward on the Hudson. However, three factors—terrain, American efforts, and weather—intervened to inhibit Burgoyne's ability to move his attendant supplies forward.

First, shipment by boat was relatively rapid, and the large numbers of bateaux, whaleboats, and sailing vessels on Lake Champlain meant that supplies could be readily transported to Ticonderoga, or Skenesboro. From there, however, three land portages would have to be crossed. The first was the relatively short, and well established, portage from the Ticonderoga Landing at the La Chute River, up a relatively steep hill to the landing on the northeastern shore of Lake George. Although only one and one-half miles long and in good repair, the portage rose 250 feet over its entirety. Because of soil conditions around Ticonderoga, when wet the road would become both thick and slippery, and thus any rainfall greatly impeded operations at the Ticonderoga portage. Additionally, all bateaux to be used on Lake George would also have to be hauled up this portage, and the flat-bottomed boats were hardly designed to be easily transported across land. Captain Borthwick of the Royal Artillery had designed a system to move the bateaux more expeditiously, but there is no evidence that this "machine" was ever actually constructed or employed.

The Fort George to Fort Edward portage had seen extensive military use between 1755 and 1758, had been in continuous service since the 1759 campaign of General Jeffery Amherst, and had been the primary Continental Army supply route since 1775. This portage also was relatively well drained, and had only one major creek (Halfway Brook) and two minor brooks (Hampshire or Rocky Brook and Meadow or Five Mile Run) to be crossed.[84] Accordingly, Burgoyne used this route for the majority of his provisions and artillery. The longer portage from Skenesboro to Fort Anne and then to Fort Edward had seen relatively

[84]Bentley, *Old Military Road*, 6–13.

scarce use prior to 1776, and it traversed ground that was poorly drained, ran through numerous low spots and morasses, and had to ford a relatively large number of watercourses. Burgoyne used this route for his four infantry brigades.

The second complication that Burgoyne faced was that American soldiers acting under the orders of American Northern Theater commander Major General Philip Schuyler took measures to damage and obstruct the portage road between Skenesboro and Fort Edward. They wrought considerable mischief along the road, but the delay that these actions caused Burgoyne has been seriously overestimated by most historians. The earliest published histories of the Saratoga Campaign overemphasized the significance of these obstructions. William L. Stone, in his landmark 1877 history, claimed that "this wilderness, in itself so horrible, was rendered almost impenetrable."[85] Nearly every subsequent historian has accepted this assessment; Christopher Ward claimed that "until all Schuyler's work had been undone, progress was impossible."[86] The most recent book-length history of the campaign adheres to this mantra, calling the efforts by Schuyler's men "decisive."[87]

However, Burgoyne's deputy quartermaster general, Captain Money of Fort Anne renown, stated when asked how long Burgoyne's army had been employed in making the roads practicable:

> About six or seven days in making the road between Skenesborough and Fort Anne, and between Fort Anne and Fort Edward. I do not believe the army was delayed an hour on that account: there was a very good road made by the rebels the year before, between Fort Anne and Fort Edward, in which road the rebels had cut down some few trees which took the provincials in our army some few hours to clear.[88]

Certainly, if any of Burgoyne's officers had been aware that Schuyler's work had constituted a significant or campaign-influencing obstacle, it would have been Captain Money as quartermaster. However, the analysis by previous historians notwithstanding, given the fact that the route from Fort George was apparently unobstructed, Burgoyne always had at

[85]Stone, *The Campaign of Lieutenant General John Burgoyne and the Expedition of Lieutenant Colonel Barry St. Leger* (Albany, N.Y.: Joel Munsell, 1877), 29.
[86]Ward, *War of the Revolution*, 1:419–420.
[87]Luzader, *Saratoga*, 81.
[88]Burgoyne, *State of the Expedition from Canada*, 53–54.

least one good road south from Lake Champlain to the Hudson River available to him. Burgoyne's papers contain no acknowledgment that the American delaying tactics of early July had caused him anything more than a passing hindrance. Schuyler's actions were not Burgoyne's bugbear; rather, it was transportation and the realities imposed by the mathematics of logistics.

Between July 8 and the middle of August when he moved south to Fort Edward, Burgoyne made his headquarters at the prominent stone mansion of Lieutenant Colonel Philip Skene, as a guest of that officer, at Skenesboro.[89] This small frontier community was located at the southern end of the South Bay of Lake Champlain, at the farthest southern portion of Lake Champlain that is navigable year-round. Here, the falls of Wood Creek facilitated the construction of water-powered industries such as mills and ironworks. Seasonably, Wood Creek running to the south is navigable to Fort Anne for small boats such as bateaux. The village was located at the bottom of a topographical bowl, consisting of low-lying wet grounds with considerable marshes, surrounded by extremely steep hills. It was established by Skene as a land grant following the Seven Years' War. In 1777 it was a small village with a wharf and some minor industry, all owned and controlled by Skene. During the 1776 campaign it had served as a major American supply depot and shipyard for the Lake Champlain fleet.

Philip Skene (1725–1810) was a British army officer who gained considerable experience in North America and the West Indies during the Seven Years' War. A veteran of the War of the Austrian Succession and Jacobite Rebellion, Skene was already a well-seasoned officer when he came to the Hudson Valley in 1757 with the 27th (Inniskilling) Regiment. In 1764 he left the British army as a lieutenant colonel to establish his small but prosperous settlement at the southern end of Lake Champlain called Skenesboro (now Whitehall). Skene controlled large land grants, was independently wealthy, and was the most prominent settler in the Lake Champlain region. Arrested as a Loyalist at the start of the American War of Independence, he reached Canada and attached himself to Burgoyne's army as an informal political adviser. Numerous contemporaries and historians have intimated that Skene influenced

[89]Morton, *Philip Skene of Skenesborough*, 55.

Burgoyne to his own personal and financial advantage. During the Bennington expedition he purportedly was overeager in accepting "Loyalists" into the army who were most likely American Patriots serving as intelligence agents, and throughout the campaign Skene was accused of overpromoting Loyalist sentiment to Burgoyne.[90]

The third major challenge that Burgoyne faced was not one of his own making, and was one that he could not possibly influence. Specifically, the weather in July and August 1777 was unusually hot and extremely wet. Rain showers fell nearly every day. This factor alone caused Burgoyne considerable difficulties (File 6.16/21).[91]

Burgoyne anticipated that he required a thirty-day stockpile of provisions to permit him to move upon Albany, and then to garrison the town until a line of communications to the main British supply depot at New York City, down the Hudson River, could be established.[92] This seems to be a reasonable assumption, and if anything was the absolute minimal quantity of supplies that Burgoyne could prudently require. It must also be noted that to transport these provisions on the Hudson, Burgoyne had to move sufficient numbers of bateaux across the portage from Lake George.

The largest quantities of stores that Burgoyne had to transport consisted of artillery and provisions. Of these the Royal Artillery and accompanying ordnance supplies (in particular ammunition) was the easiest. The Royal Artillery train, although heavy, was tactically indispensable. Burgoyne was later criticized for the size of his train of artillery, but Carleton and Burgoyne agreed that a substantial amount of artillery was critical to achieve success in any campaign out of Canada. Having both viewed the citadel of Fort Ticonderoga and Mount Independence in October 1776, they were sufficiently impressed by the strength of the American position such that they knew considerable artillery would be required to reduce it. Burgoyne subsequently noted: "I understood this proportion of field artillery to be the same as that proposed by Sir Guy Carleton had he commanded it; it was the proportion recommended by General Phillips, and I formed my opinion

[90]Only one reliable biography of Skene exists, Morton's (ibid.). He was often referred to as "Colonel Skene" during the campaign by Burgoyne's officers.

[91]Barker, ed., "Saratoga and the Kinderhook Tea Party," 31–33.

[92]Burgoyne, *State of the Expedition from Canada*, 21.

conformably to the sentiments of those respectable officers."[93] From his experiences observing the Battle of Bunker Hill, Burgoyne was well aware that the Americans were formidable fighters from behind earthworks; and that the Americans could construct strong fortifications quite well positioned on key terrain in very short order. Burgoyne had observed after Bunker Hill (West Point Burgoyne Letter): "We found the enemy had pushed intrenchments with great diligence, during the night, on the heights of Charles-Town, and we evidently saw that every hour gave them fresh strength" and "Howe's left were staggered . . . the loss was uncommon in officers for the numbers engaged." Burgoyne never forgot the lesson of Bunker Hill. Furthermore, he realized that although the Americans could replace their losses, he could not replace his. Thus, Burgoyne fully intended to use the firepower of his artillery to displace the Americans, rather than depending upon casualty-intensive infantry assaults. Burgoyne also realized that once he occupied Albany he would have to garrison the city, and for that he required adequate numbers of cannon. Accordingly, he intended from the first to bring along with him a strong train of artillery. As Burgoyne had stated in London when planning the campaign (File 6.16/5): "The Artillery after the Light Troops, is the important arm in this American War." And fortunately for the British, the train of artillery had to be moved only once, and except in the rare event of a general engagement, there was no consumption of artillery or munitions.[94]

British Army Rations and Logistics

Provisions were being continuously consumed by the army, requiring daily replenishment. In addition, a surplus of provisions had to be moved forward to enable Burgoyne to stockpile a magazine. The single heaviest and most demanding logistical assets that Burgoyne had to move, provisions entirely dictated his campaign; accordingly, they demand an evaluation both comprehensive and exhaustive.

---

[93] Ibid., 15.

[94] For an exhaustive discussion of Burgoyne's dependence on the Royal Artillery, and the integral role it played in both the 1776 Valcour Island and 1777 Saratoga campaigns, refer to Cubbison, *"Artillery never gained more Honour."*

There are a number of period military manuals that clearly articulate the standard British army ration of the mid-eighteenth century. First, a ration was defined at the time as one day's provisions for one soldier. In the British army of the time, women authorized to accompany the army were afforded half rations, and children were provided one-quarter rations. Williamson's 1782 *Treatise on Military Finance* defined what this daily ration was intended to be:

> The complete ration in every specie is, of flour or bread 1½ lb.[;] beef 1 lb.[;] or pork ½ lb.[;] pease [peas] ¼ pint[;] butter or cheese 1 oz.[;] rice 1 oz. But when the small species are not issued, 1½ lb. of bread or flour, and 1½ lb. of beef, or 10 oz. of pork make a complete ration: when nothing but flour or bread can be distributed, 1 lb. of flour or bread is a ration, as are also 3 lb. of beef, 2 lb. of cheese, or 1½ lb. of rice. Only one ration is issued for each effective officer and soldier, for which they pay 2½ d. [pence]. On board of transports, the ration is two-thirds of a seaman's allowance, for which, each officer and soldier pays 3d. per diem. Exclusive of the ration, the officers and soldiers are commonly supplied, in North America, with three pints of spruce beer each per diem, gratis.[95]

Thomas Sullivan, a private with the 49th Foot, confirmed the following rations as the standard in garrison. Stationed in Boston early in the war, Sullivan reported:

> Of the Provision the Troops Received in Boston. The Provisions were Issued out of the King's Stores, as follows. The Bakers always received 7 Pounds of Flour, for every man in the Regiment or Company, for whom they baked: Out of the 7 lb. of Flour the Baker gave two loaves, weighing 4½ lb. each, which were served twice a week to the troops. Once a week we received 4 lb. of Pork or 7 lb. of Beef; 6 ounces of Butter; 3 pints of Pease or Oatmeal; and ½ lb. of Rice per man. Every Woman had ½ a man's share, and every Child ¼ Rations.[96]

An additional ration item, not always issued but sometimes provided to the soldiers as an antiscorbutic supplement, was sauerkraut (sliced cabbage preserved with fermentation and salt brine). During the occupation of Boston in 1775 and 1776, each soldier in the British army was issued half a pound of sauerkraut per week. Later on in the war soldiers

[95]Williamson, *Treatise on Military Finance*, 57–59.

[96]Boyle, ed., *From Redcoat to Rebel*, 23.

assigned to Rhode Island were issued two pounds per week. Several tons of sauerkraut was documented to have been shipped to the army in Boston from Cork, Ireland, in the fall of 1775.[97]

As regards bread, the British army regularly constructed ovens as it proceeded, and bread was routinely baked from the flour ration. During the Forbes campaign in 1758 in western Pennsylvania, eighteen bake ovens were constructed at Fort Bedford.[98] On the night of August 10, 1758, "through the negligence of the bakers, who were baking biscuit, twelve of our ovens were burned last night." The ovens were promptly rebuilt, with specifications this time that "all the Hatchet men, Masons and those who Understand building Ovens; are to rebuild the Ovens directly of green wood."[99] Ovens were also constructed at several points along the route of advance, and at the Loyalhanna Encampment (later Fort Ligonier). The French army constructed bake ovens at Forts Niagara, St. Frederick (Crown Point), and Carillon (Ticonderoga). When these forts were occupied by the British army during the Seven Years' War, the British promptly began using the same ovens.[100] When the British constructed Fort Stanwix on the Mohawk River in 1758, they included a large baking oven within the fortification's interior.[101]

A British Orderly Book from the Saratoga Campaign specified: "September 27, 1777. Camp at Freemans Farm. Each British Regt. to send a Baker to Mr. Commissary Clark to assist Baking for the Army."[102] The British army issued each soldier a six-pound loaf of bread every four days, for which he paid a fivepence (5d). The army compensated the baker (normally a contractor) the difference between this 5d. and the true cost of the bread. By 1765 the actual price of a six-pound loaf of bread was 7d., so this was a good bargain for the soldier.[103]

An important consideration in British army logistical planning during the American Revolutionary War is that, unlike the circumstances

[97]Bart Reynolds, "Sauerkraut," *The Brigade Dispatch* 32, no. 3 (Autumn 2002): 14; and Tokar, "Logistics and the British Defeat."

[98]Stevens, Kent, Leonard, eds., *Papers of Henry Bouquet*, 2:217.

[99]Ibid., 2:356, 675.

[100]Feister, *Oven Ruins at Crown Point*, 4–6, 27, 28.

[101]Hanson and Hsu, *Casemates and Cannonballs*, 17–20.

[102]Clement, *47th Regiment of Foot*, 80.

[103]Cuthbertson, *Management and Economy of a Battalion*, 22; Williamson, *Treatise on Military Finance*, 53; and Steppler, "Common Soldier," 48.

during the French and Indian War, the British did not maintain control of the countryside; therefore, they could not rely on the North American colonies to provide rations.[104] General Howe's commissary general noted in March 1776: "There is no dependence for supplies for the Army from this Continent."[105] Accordingly, all rations for the army, with the exception of the occasional foraged supplies, had to be brought from England. This had a significant, and detrimental, effect on the quality of rations.

These rations had been purchased by the Department of the Treasury from contractors throughout Great Britain, who in turn had bought the food directly from the farmers.[106] The rations were then consolidated in the port of Cork, Ireland, from which they were shipped to North America. The rations frequently had to wait for transports, obtained initially by the Treasury, but later by the Navy Department. Delays in loading, then weeks in transatlantic shipment, and further delays in being unloaded and transported to the soldiers meant that the rations were often spoiled in whole or in part upon arrival in camp. In its contracts, the Treasury specified that the flour be "of the first Quality, made from wholly Kiln dried Wheat." However, the rations rarely met such standards, and moldy or rotten flour was frequently delivered to the soldiers. This was certainly the case for Burgoyne's army.

During the 1776 Northern Theater campaign, specific orders were issued validating the rations that Burgoyne's army would enjoy during this and the subsequent year's campaign:

> The Stoppages [deductions from a British soldier's pay for rations] from the Army exceeding 2½ pence per day to cease from the 24th of May and that usual Stoppages of 2½ pence per day to remain in force from that time. . . . The Provisions for the Army are to be delivered as follows. A Compleat Ration for one Man for one day, in every Species Flour or Bread one pound & a half, Beef one pound or Pork half a pound[,] Pease one Quarter of a Pint, Butter one Ounce[,] Rice one Ounce Wherever such provisions can be procured for the Army.[107]

This sounds relatively straightforward, but the ration as issued to soldiers on campaign varied greatly. Rations were adjusted regularly in

---

[104]Curtis, "Provisioning of the British Army," 232–241.

[105]Ibid., 232.

[106]Ibid., 233.

[107]Clement, *Royal Regiment of Artillery*, 8.

response to a continuously changing supply situation. Throughout the Forbes campaign of 1758 in western Pennsylvania, General John Forbes established the following ration as his army's standard:

- Eight Pounds of Beef or Five Pounds of Pork per week;
- Seven Pounds of Flour [or previously cooked biscuit] per week;
- One Pint Rice in lieu of one pound more flour per week.[108]

Forbes altered this quantity on July 14: "As the troops are now mostly supplyed with fresh Beef, they are to receive it at the rate of seven pounds per week. And if they gett pork, they are only to have four pounds of pork."[109] Forbes augmented these rations with a supply of bacon and prebaked biscuits. Forbes ordered that "Six or Seven Waggon Loads of Bacon" be purchased, presumably about 12,000 pounds worth.[110] Although this appears to be a large quantity, since bacon was considered to be pork for ration purposes this was only enough meat for the full army of 6,000 men for four days at half a pound per man per day. Forbes probably ordered this bacon as a reserve ration for a forced march or emergency, as it could be consumed without having to be cooked. Draper Woods, deputy commissary, had discussed the matter with Forbes as early as May:

> As Biscuit will be wanted on the march for the use of ranging or scouting partys it would be necessary that the Contractors Agents shou'd order Biscuit to be baked for the above purpose at Lancaster York Town Carlisle &c and by so doing great expence will be saved to the Crown in regard to Carriage of the same, all of which I leave to your Excellency's wise consideration.[111]

Surviving Orderly Books from the 1776 and 1777 Valcour Island and Saratoga Campaigns were specifically perused for mentions of rations. In addition to discussing the quantity of provisions, these Orderly Books also made note of what type of rations were being issued (e.g., fresh beef or salt meat) and offered a few hints regarding the preparation of food once it had been issued:

---

[108]Stevens, Kent, and Leonard, *Papers of Henry Bouquet*, 2:96, 683.

[109]Ibid., 2:208.

[110]Ibid., 2:227–228.

[111]"Letter from Draper Wood to Forbes, Dated Philadelphia May 6th, 1758," Department of Special Collections, the Tracy W. McGregor Library, Headquarters Papers of Brigadier General John Forbes, University of Virginia, Charlottesville.

- June 16, 1776. Isle Aux Noix. "The 20th Regiment, in Garrison at this place were compensated for a scarcity of Fresh Provisions by the immense quantities of all kinds of Fish taken every where round the Island. . . . The Spruce Beer was also served to them & with success."[112]
- June 20, 1776. La Prairie [Canada]. "Bread for four Days will be delivered to the Troops this Evening and to-morrow morning to the 24th Inclusive—they will apply to Mr. Wier Commissary near the Church at La Prairie: Every Regiment may receive at the same time six Oxen from Biscerne, Captain of the Militia, which they will kill, and distribute to the Troops agreeable to the regulation of the Ration; exact Accounts to be kept of the fresh Meat received and delivered."[113]
- June 24, 1776. Montreal. "I desire that it may be ordered that the Messes of the Different Regiments may be obliged to make broth in which Bread, some fat & a Great Quantity of Wild herbs may be mixed among it."[114]
- August 7, 1776. Chamblee. "By Lieutenant General Burgoyne. General Orders. The Physicians to the Army having represented that the following change in the Ration will be very essential towards the Healths of the Men, that half a Pound be taken off the Beef Ration, and a Quarter of a Pound of Rice be added in its place, the Commissaries will begin to deliver it out accordingly."[115]
- November 28, 1776. [Montreal.] "General Orders. During this Winter Provisions are to be issued according to a Complete Ration of every Species as settled and ordered by the Commander in Chief at the opening of the Campaign, but as Rice is now Scarce, that article must be reserved for the Sick and the Hospitals, and instead of one Ounce of Rice must be delivered Two Ounces of Oatmeal, and the delivering must be also twice of Pork to One of Beef. The time of delivery every Four days."[116]
- June 11, 1777. Camp at River Bouquet. "Brigade Orders. Brigadier General Fraser has been pleased to Order a Gill of Rum per Man for the Corps."[117]
- June 15, 1777. Camp at River Bouquet. "Serjt Carral of the 20th Grenadiers and such Butchers of the Corp as he may want, to go up the River to Gallalands Farm in a Bateaux from the Grenadier Battalion this Afternoon to Slaughter in the coal [cool] of the Evening Bullocks sufficient to supply the Corps with two days provisions."[118]

---

[112]Rogers, *Hadden's Journal and Orderly Books*, 54.
[113]Ibid.,' 191.
[114]Clement, *Royal Regiment of Artillery*, 15.
[115]Rogers, *Hadden's Journal and Orderly Books*, 243; and Clement, *Royal Regiment of Artillery*, 38.
[116]Clement, *Royal Regiment of Artillery*, 77.
[117]Clement, *47th Regiment Grenadier Company*, 22.
[118]Ibid., 40.

- June 16, 1777. Camp at River Bouquet. "The Sutlers are not on any pretence to sell Rum or any other Spirits to the Men without a Written Order from a Commission'd Officer and never in less Quantity than a Quart [presumably such a quantity, being relatively expensive, would prevent a soldier from buying enough to get drunk at one time]."[119] "The Quarter Masters to be particularly attentive that provision is regularly sent to the Cartridge makers, of each Battalion, and when Spruce Beer is delivered out to the Men if possible to send them there share."[120]
- June 24, 1777. Camp at River Bouquet. "The Lieut. Genl. Has observed with Satisfaction, that some Corps have got the Art of making flour Cakes without Ovens which are equally wholesome and rellishing with the best bread— He recommends it strongly to the Commanding Officers to bring their Corps into this useful practice as it may frequently happen that the movements of the Army will be too quick to admit a possibility of constructing Ovens."[121]
- July 1, 1777. Camp at Three Mile Point [Lake Champlain near Ticonderoga]. "Evening Brigade Orders. Provisions to be delivered for two Days tomorrow morning to the whole Corps so as to be absolutely distributed among the Men by Eight O'clock at which time they will begin to Cook it as fast as possible."[122]
- September 26, 1777. Camp at Freemans Farm. "The Lieutenant General Desires to Contribute Everything in his Power to the Comfort of the Wounded has Directed, half a Pound of Meat per Day to be added to their Present allowance of Meat."[123]
- September 27, 1777. Camp at Freemans Farm. "As there appears not to be Spruce Beer sufficient for the 4 Regts they will [go] about [getting] it in the morning in the same Order as mentioned yesterday & as the 21st got none this day they & the 20th will begin this rule tomorrow."[124]
- October 3, 1777. [Camp at Freeman's Farm.] "By Lieutenant General Burgoyne. General Orders. . . . the ration of Bread or Flour is for the present fixed at one Pound."[125]
- October 6, 1777. Camp at Freemans Farm. "In the Next Delivery of Provisions— two days Fresh meat will be Issued at the Rate of one Pound of Beef per Ration to Each man, the other two Days will be Salt Provision

[119]Ibid., 45.
[120]Ibid., 46–47.
[121]Ibid., 98–99.
[122]Ibid., 96.
[123]Clement, *47th Regiment of Foot,* 79–80.
[124]Ibid., 81.
[125]Rogers, *Hadden's Journal and Orderly Books,* 325–326.

as usual. His Excellency the Lieu. Genl. is Pleased to make a Present of twelve Barrels of Rum to the troops to be Distributed as follows . . ."[126]

As noted, British army rations also included foraged items, either obtained from the countryside or acquired from the American Indians who accompanied Burgoyne's army. Although foraged rations were a strong lure, their collection was also attendant with great risks. Trade with the American Indians was expressly forbidden. Accordingly, foraged rations would only rarely have been obtained.

A third source of supply for rations that, unlike trade with the Natives or foraging, was officially sanctioned was the purchase of supplies from sutlers, or private businessmen who had been given permission to accompany the army and sell supplies to officers and soldiers. During the Saratoga Campaign the Advance Brigade sutler was a Mr. White. A board of officers from the brigade established prices for his articles early in the campaign:

ARTICLE	POUNDS STERLING	SHILLINGS	PENCE
Madeira per Gallon	0	16	0
Claret [wine] per Dozen	2	8	0
Spirits per Gallon	2	8	0
West Indian Rum per Gallon	0	10	0
[New England?] Rum per Gallon	0	8	0
Porter per Gallon	0	4	0
Hams per Pound	0	1	8
Cheese per Pound	0	1	8
Brown Sugar per Pound	0	1	8
Bohea Tea per Pound	0	1	6
Soape [Soap] per Pound	0	1	4.[127]

During the earlier Forbes campaign of 1758, documented sutler prices had been as follows:

Madeira Wine – 18 shillings per gallon;
West Indies Rum – 10 shillings per gallon;
American (Rye) Whiskey – 5 shillings per gallon;
American Rum – 5 shillings per gallon;
Chocolate – 2 shillings, 6 pence per pound;
Refined (white) Sugar – 2 shillings per pound;
Brown Sugar – 1 shilling, 3 pence per pound;

[126]Clement, *47th Regiment of Foot*, 88.

[127]Clement, *47th Regiment Grenadier Company*, 39, 44.

Leaf Tobacco – 9 shillings per pound;
Roll Tobacco – 1 shilling, 10 pence per pound;
Snuff – 3 shillings per bottle; and
Smoking Pipe – 1 pence each.[128]

Soldiers could have purchased a range of objects from a sutler, but such purchases would have been decidedly limited, as private soldiers were relatively poorly paid and had limited funds available. Most commonly a mess of soldiers would have joined together to purchase a specific article together, such as rum or tobacco. A typical soldier, without earning any additional wages, would have only had available a modest twopence and halfpence and farthing (2¾ d.) as spending money at the end of a week's labor.[129]

Accordingly, a typical soldier's rations in Burgoyne's army at either Skenesboro or Fort Edward between July and September 1777 would have consisted of the following:

- Meat, one pound per man per day of fresh beef or salt beef; or one half pound per man per day of salt pork;
- Bread, 1½ pounds per man per day [alternately, hard bread if performing field service or ranger duties];
- Approximately half a pound per man per day of various incidentals, alternately Oatmeal; Rice; Dried Peas; Sauerkraut; Butter; and/or Cheese;
- One quart per day of Spruce Beer and Rum.

Thus, a daily ration for each soldier included a minimum of four pounds weight (meat, bread, the "various incidentals," and spruce beer/rum). Burgoyne carried forward 8,118 soldiers from Canada (Files 6.5/6, 6.5/7 and 6.5/4). Assuming a loss of some strength due to combat casualties, but adding in supplemental rations authorized for officers, the authorized rations for women and children that accompanied the army, and necessary rations for those civilians that accompanied the army, such as teamsters, a daily throughput of no less than 36,000 pounds per day must have been necessary simply to maintain the army at full rations. However, even this estimate is almost certainly understated, for Burgoyne also contracted that the army would provide forage for the draft animals from the "King's Magazines" (File 6.24/22), and this added significantly to the army's logistical requirements.

[128]Redmon and MacDougall, "Culinary Habits of the Redcoat."
[129]Cubbison, "Eight Pence a Day."

Eighty-five years later, during the American Civil War, the United States Army based its logistical calculations on each horse requiring fourteen pounds of hay and twelve pounds of grain (oats, corn, or barley) daily.[130] A working oxen would require about thirty pounds of forage per day. The British deputy quartermaster general, Captain Money, reported that he had only 180 horse carts (two-wheeled) with five hundred horses, and twenty to thirty oxcarts (two-wheeled) with fifty teams of oxen, operating from Skenesboro.[131] According to Captain Thomas Blomefield of the Royal Artillery: "The whole number of horses detached with the British artillery, previous to the passing the Hudson's river, was about four hundred."[132] Thus, Quartermaster Money was daily feeding nine hundred horses and one hundred working oxen. Considering officers' horses and bat horses, the actual number was probably closer to one thousand horses daily.[133] Thus, Burgoyne's daily forage requirements were approximately 29,000 pounds.

Providing this quantity of forage was a significant effort. Burgoyne had planned to transport feed and forage for the animals from Canada, but as Captain Blomefield recounted, "A quantity of oats was brought forward from Canada, but with respect to other forage they were under the necessity of collecting it in the neighborhood of the encampment."[134] The territory between Ticonderoga and Fort Edward was sparsely populated in 1777, and the quantities of locally grown forage would have been distinctly limited. Compounding this situation, as Burgoyne had anticipated, when the Americans withdrew they had either carried away all the forage with them or destroyed what they could not move. Thus, Burgoyne had to transport all of his animals' feed from Canada, and forage is both bulky and heavy. His draft animals almost certainly were underfed once they left Fort George and Skenesboro.

No primary source documents have been located that positively provide the weight that one of Burgoyne's two-wheeled carts could carry. Most likely, they were at least equivalent to the British army Board of

[130] Risch, *Quartermaster Support of the Army*, 379. Horses and oxen did not materially change between 1777 and 1861.

[131] Burgoyne, *State of the Expedition from Canada*, 56.

[132] Ibid., 92.

[133] "Bat horses" were private horses owned by officers to carry their personal baggage, for which they were paid by the British government.

[134] Ibid., 92.

Ordnance two-wheeled powder carts, which were capable of carrying four barrels of gunpowder.[135] Since a barrel of gunpowder weighed approximately one hundred pounds, these carts could carry, at the absolute minimum, four hundred pounds.[136] However, Burgoyne specifically noted (File 6.24/20): "Five hundred Carts will barely carry fourteen days Provision at a time." This suggests that a 1,000-pound peak capacity for a two-wheeled, two-horse cart on this campaign was likely, although whether or not the carts could carry their maximum load given the conditions of the portage roads and weakened strength of the animals is questionable. Under a best-case scenario of good roads and healthy draft animals, no fewer than thirty-six carts alone had to deliver food to the army every day, with a minimum of another twenty-nine cartloads of forage for the animals, for a total of sixty-five carts arriving at Fort Edward daily just to sustain the army's requirements.

From the formulation of the campaign in London the previous winter, Burgoyne had recognized that to move these provisions and bateaux by land, carriages and animals would have to be contracted for. Burgoyne and Carleton had made such arrangements in late May when they issued two contracts (Files 6.24/21 and 6.24/22) for the general supply train of the army and the Board of Ordnance. The first contract called for one thousand horses with harness and five hundred carts with one driver per cart. However, it appears that the anticipated numbers of carriages and animals were never realized. Although Captain Blomefield suggested that more than sufficient horses were available, the journals of both Major Williams and Lieutenant Hadden clearly articulated that movement of the artillery and stores forward was hindered by lack of animals.[137] Riedesel wrote Lord George Germain (File 6.16/22) that "the want of Carriage greatly retarded the Transport of our Provisions." This problem was doubtless exacerbated by the reduced forage and overwork of the animals, which continuously exhausted and weakened them.

This analysis documents the problems that Burgoyne faced in attempting to build up a month's stockpiles of supplies. Since sixty-five carts, or one-third of his available number, had to arrive every day just to meet

[135]Muller, *Treatise of Artillery*, 128.

[136]Buchanan, ed., *Gunpowder, Explosives and the State*, 175; confirmed through e-mail exchange with Dr. Brenda J. Buchanan, May 10, 2010.

[137]Cubbison, *"Artillery never gained more Honour,"* 93.

the daily requirements, this meant that two-thirds of Burgoyne's carts had to travel the entire distance from either Fort George or Skenesboro to Fort Edward, or no less than between sixteen or twenty-four miles in a single day, to enable Burgoyne to gain a single day's additional rations over any twenty-four-hour period. That it required Burgoyne nearly two months to accumulate an additional month's supply suggests that his carts and draft animals could not maintain such a demanding regimen.

In order for Burgoyne to stockpile thirty days' rations, assuming that his carts could traverse the necessary distances in a single day, and carry a full one thousand pounds of cargo, would thus require a minimum of thirty days under optimum circumstances. In actuality, a full sixty days were needed to stockpile this reserve, from mid-July through mid-September. Either Burgoyne's carts could carry only 500 pounds or they could only traverse half the distance between Lake George or Lake Champlain and Fort Edward in a single day (or some similar combination).

Burgoyne's lengthy delay between Skenesboro and Fort Edward was not occasioned by his selection of a route. In fact, Burgoyne used both routes available to him, specifically to avoid the congestion and delays that employing a single supply corridor could have caused (File 6.16/19). Rather, the delay in his movement forward was a direct result of the distances involved, poor road conditions, shortage of transportation assets (specifically carts and draft animals), and inadequate forage for his horses and oxen. These factors significantly hindered Burgoyne as he struggled to stockpile adequate supplies to support a movement forward.

By July 9 Burgoyne had concentrated his infantry brigades at Skenesboro. Fraser and Riedesel had returned from the battlefield at Hubbardton, and Colonel Hill's rather battered 9th Regiment of Foot had withdrawn from its advance post at Fort Anne. Burgoyne's infantry finally started his movement forward from Skenesboro on July 25, and he reached Fort Edward on July 29, having advanced twenty-three miles in four days. Here Burgoyne again was delayed, struggling with his logistical and transportation difficulties. He would later be quoted: "For every hour that he could devote to planning how he shall fight his army, he must allot twenty to contrive how to feed it." Burgoyne continued his advance seven miles to Fort Miller, where a shallow series of falls on the Hudson River required another short portage, on August 11. By this point in the campaign, Burgoyne was focused nearly entirely on logistical and transportation issues. A letter that Burgoyne wrote to General Fraser from Fort Anne on July 26 dealt exclusively with such issues; it included discussion of assigning a detachment of two hundred men to help repair the roads.[138]

The Battle of Bennington

To alleviate his logistical problems, Burgoyne determined to launch a raid into the countryside to obtain additional stores. He stated that he had done so at the urging of General Riedesel, who presumably hoped to garner more honor for his German division, although it is equally as likely that Riedesel hoped that a rapid raid into the countryside would garner Burgoyne Loyalist recruits, supplies, wagons, and livestock that would permit him immediately to resume the forward momentum of the campaign. The urgings of Lieutenant Colonel Philip Skene may also have played a role. According to Burgoyne's instructions (File 6.16/22): "The Intention of this Expedition is to dive into the Sentiments of the Inhabitants, to remount the Regiment of Dragoons & to attempt furnishing the Army with Horses, Cattle & Waggons."

Burgoyne settled on a strange composition for the expedition. The command was entrusted to German lieutenant colonel Friedrich S. Baum, commander of the Hesse-Hanau Dragoons. Baum had been born in Haste, Hesse, in 1727. He was a highly experienced soldier in the Brunswick service, having begun his military career in 1753 at the age of sixteen. He had apparently seen combat service as a subaltern in the Seven Years' War. Although he possessed twenty-four years of service, he could not utter a single syllable of English and had never led an independent command; besides, his experience in North America was practically nonexistent.[139]

Lieutenant Colonel Baum was assigned his own battalion of German dragoons, approximately half of Captain Alexander Fraser's Company of Select Marksmen, two small corps of Loyalists, and two small

[138]Atkinson, "Evidence for Burgoyne's Expedition," 142.

[139]Baum's woeful performance at Bennington indicates how unprepared professionally and intellectually he was for an independent command in North America against an experienced fighter such as American commander Brigadier General John Stark. Little definite is known of his life; the only extant biography is Gadue, "Lieutenant Colonel Friedrich S. Baum," 37–54.

companies of Canadians, accompanied by a contingent of American Indians and two 3-pounder cannon manned by the Hesse-Hanau Artillery Company. These cannon were English-manufactured bronze 3-pounders, a light and easily maneuverable cannon well suited for this type of expedition.[140] Riedesel recorded the strength of this column as follows (File 6.16/22a):

NUMBER OF THE TROOPS EMPLOYED UPON THAT EXPEDITION

Regiment of [Hesse-Hanau] Dragoons	160
Indians	100
Peter's Corps [American Loyalists]	150
Provincials & Canadian Volunteers	56
Fraser's Company [of Marksmen]	50
Total	516.

> The Provincials & Canadians not being strong enough General Reidesel added to them 25 Chasseurs [Brunswick Light Infantry] & 75 other Soldiers of the Germans.

Thus, this force was composed of soldiers who spoke German, French (Canadian militia), English (Fraser's Company of Marksmen), Provincial English (American Loyalists), and presumably several different American Indian languages. These various military organizations had never previously operated together and were commanded by a German speaker who could not communicate directly with over half of his command except through a translator.

The target was originally Manchester, Vermont, where the Americans were rumored to have a supply depot, but was altered at the last moment to Bennington, Vermont, upon intelligence that considerable supplies were available there. As is documented for the first time in these papers, through a letter from Riedesel to Lord George Germain (File 6.16/22a): "The Changes in his Route were made upon the Report of Colonel Skene, who informed General Burgoyne that there was a very considerable Magazine at Bennington & that it would be very easy to surprise & make himself Master of it."

The Bennington expedition was a rather desperate risk on Burgoyne's

[140]For discussions of these guns, refer to Cubbison, *"Artillery never gained more Honour,"* 27–29.

part. The general had a reputation as a gambler, and this appears to have been a relative long shot indeed. However, like all experienced gamblers, Burgoyne did not hazard anything on this expedition that he could not afford to lose. Although he could easily be criticized for the composition of this force, for it hardly promised mission accomplishment, it employed those elements (the American Indians that had already caused him trouble in management and control, the ineffective Hesse-Hanau Dragoons, and the relatively weak detachments of Canadians) that he could afford to lose without appreciably harming his primary army, or endangering the principal objective of his campaign.[141] Only the selection of the American Loyalists, who could be expected to be extremely effective at interacting with the countryside, seems to have been well suited to the job at hand. Additionally, why Philip Skene, who was serving as Burgoyne's informal political adviser, did not accompany an expedition specifically intended to penetrate into the interior of the country and to recruit Loyalists, and whose personal intelligence had resulted in the selection of the expedition's target, is unknown.

Baum departed Burgoyne's camp on August 11, and by August 14 he had reached the Walloomscoick River, west of Bennington (Baum's initial report, File 6.16/22c). The American Indians contributed little to the expedition, slaughtering valuable cows, horses, and oxen for the bells around their necks and their meat, thus inhibiting Baum from fulfilling one of the important objectives assigned him.[142]

Baum established an extremely poor defensive perimeter above a crossing of the Walloomscoick River. His units were dispersed and were not in position to mass their firepower. The two 3-pounders were separated. Baum failed to establish interlocking fields of fire, the positions were out of communication with each other, and they were incapable of providing mutual support. There had been some brief and inconclusive skirmishes on August 14, and Baum was well aware that he was outnumbered and in trouble. Heavy rains on the night of August 14 and throughout August 15 prevented any American attack from being launched but doubtless only increased the misery of Baum and his soldiers.

---

[141]As confirmed by Burgoyne to Lord George Germain. Davies, *Documents of the American Revolution*, 14:165.

[142]Arndt, "New Hampshire and the Battle of Bennington," 207.

Neither Burgoyne, Riedesel, Skene, or Baum had any intimation of this, but Bennington turned out to be the worst possible destination for an expedition. New Hampshire, in response to Burgoyne's invasion against Ticonderoga, had raised a state regiment at its own volition, and placed it under the command of John Stark, who had just left the Continental Army service in disgust because junior officers had been promoted over his head. Stark was a highly experienced veteran, having served throughout the Seven Years' War as a member and then an officer in the renowned Rogers Rangers. He commanded a regiment in the Continental Army from 1775 to March 1777. New Hampshire enlisted no less than 10 percent of the eligible men in the state, approximately one thousand soldiers. On August 8 Stark had marched to Bennington to safeguard the supplies there. Local New York and Vermont militia poured into Stark's camp, and by the morning of the sixteenth he had roughly two thousand musketmen available. John Stark was a tough, hardened veteran, and with him at the head of his New Hampshire volunteers (at least some of whom were veterans of Stark's own regiment of the Continental Army) and local militia literally fighting in defense of their very homes, Baum faced a formidable adversary.

Alarmed, Baum called for help to Burgoyne, and a second German column under Lieutenant Colonel Breymann with his German advanced guard contingent, about 650 muskets, and two 6-pounder cannon marched on August 15.[143] Belatedly, Philip Skene accompanied Breymann to join Baum. Because of heavy rains and bad roads, Breymann's relief column made only eight miles on their first day (Breymann's report, File 6.16/22b).

On the morning of August 16 the rain ended, and Stark launched a well-coordinated double envelopment attack. Although such a maneuver

[143]Lieutenant Colonel Heinrich von Breymann (?–1777) was the commander of the Brunswick Light Infantry under Riedesel. He was the third-ranking officer among the Brunswickers after Riedesel and Colonel Specht. He was recognized as a competent and aggressive officer, and a strict disciplinarian in the Prussian model. Little that is known about Breymann's military career, personal background, and personality can be confirmed. He was killed at the Battle of Breymann's Redoubt on October 7, 1777. Although historians have claimed that Breymann was a severe disciplinarian and was not popular among his soldiers or other officers in the army, that he had a long-standing quarrel with Lieutenant Colonel Baum, and that he was killed by his own men in an incident of "fragging," primary source evidence for these accusations is generally weak, if not entirely absent.

would be difficult for poorly trained soldiers such as Stark commanded, he apparently determined that even a crudely executed double envelopment could succeed against the faulty defensive configuration that Baum had established. Stark is alleged to have addressed his men before sending them into combat, "See there, men! There the Redcoats are! We'll beat them before nightfall, or Molly Stark sleeps a widow tonight." The fact that Stark's wife was actually named Elizabeth, and that with the exception of the fifty British rangers under Fraser there were no redcoats at Bennington, scarcely detracts from the highly charged (and likely profane) emotional leadership that Stark provided.

Stark's attack succeeded admirably, and although Baum's badly outnumbered soldiers put up a determined defense, they had to fight piecemeal and were simply overwhelmed. The American Indians that had accompanied Baum's expedition departed at the first whiff of gunsmoke (they are not mentioned in any accounts of the battle), and the remainder of Baum's command was killed, wounded, or captured. Baum himself, courageously leading an attempt at swordpoint to break out of the American encirclement, was mortally wounded. The two 3-pounder bronze cannon were captured.[144]

Stark's force, victorious, began to disperse. Most of the men were temporary soldiers, they had scattered during the fighting and started looting, and in any event were either running low on or had expended their ammunition. Colonel Seth Warner at this moment propitiously arrived at the battlefield with the three hundred men of his Vermont regiment, strengthened by other members of the local militia who had arrived too late to take part in the morning's fighting, precisely at the right time to relieve Stark.

When Breymann's troops belatedly approached where they expected Baum's encampment to be, they observed "armed men" beginning to gather. Skene assured Breymann that these men were Loyalists and rode to the front to enlist them. Skene was promptly disabused of his misconception when his horse was immediately shot out from underneath him (File 6.16/22b).

Warner, and whatever men Stark could gather, then launched another double envelopment against both flanks of Breymann's column on the

[144]Cubbison, *"Artillery never gained more Honour,"* 96–101.

road. Breymann's men recoiled under intensive fire, and his column had to perform one of the most difficult military maneuvers: successfully withdrawing from the field while being heavily engaged. Breymann and his German soldiers have scarcely received any credit for their performance that day. Warner's Vermont men, together with what remained of Stark's militia, raked Breymann's column with horrific fire from both flanks and from behind cover, while also attempting to place blocking forces before the Germans to interdict their retreat. The fighting was continuous, at close range and deadly, and it lasted for hours. Eventually, Breymann was able to break contact after sunset, under cover of darkness. He had five bullet holes in his coat and one in his leg, he had lost his two bronze 6-pounder cannon, and nearly a third of his force was captured, killed, or wounded.

The British lost at least one thousand men in total. American casualties are variously estimated; one source gives about thirty killed and forty wounded. Since a considerable portion of the American force were militiamen who fought on their own volition, it is impossible to be any more accurate. Probably American casualties were about one hundred in total, most suffered in the stiff fight between Baum and Stark at the Walloomscoick River. The great significance of the engagement was not in the casualties, for Burgoyne himself stated that he had only risked troops whose loss he could easily afford. But Burgoyne gained no supplies, no reinforcements from the countryside, no wagons, and no draft animals. The expedition was a complete disappointment, as not a single one of Baum's objectives had been realized. Burgoyne's attempts to swell his magazines with a single coup de main had been an abject failure. Before he could resume his southern progress, he would have to continue stockpiling supplies through the painstakingly slow arrival of supply carts. Burgoyne had not really suffered a serious tactical defeat, but it was of considerably greater importance that he had also not gained any advantage, and the slow, tedious work would have to be continued. Sir Francis-Carr Clerke provided the view from Burgoyne's headquarters: "Had the intention of the Expedition succeeded the army would have been at liberty to march without waiting so long for magazines."[145] Even worse from Burgoyne's perspective, Bennington was the first undisputed

[145]Kingsley, "Letters from Sir Francis-Carr Clerke," 422.

American victory in the northern theater since Brigadier General Richard Montgomery had seized Forts Chambly and St. John's two years earlier. The boost to the Americans' morale from defeating the British in an open field battle, could hardly be overestimated.

St. Leger's Column Operates on the Mohawk River

In the meantime, the other prong of Burgoyne's campaign from Canada was playing itself out on the Mohawk River. Burgoyne and Sir John Johnson had recommended such a movement against the Mohawk Valley in 1776, but Carleton lacked sufficient resources to implement this proposal. Carleton continued to support this movement in his plans for the 1777 campaign that Burgoyne had carried back to London (File 6.16/6), but he predicated that such a column could not be dispatched unless "a Reinforcement of four thousand Troops, exclusive of compleating the present Army," was guaranteed "for Canada. . . . With a reinforcement to the above amount, and well composed, a large Corps may be spared to pass Lake Ontario, and to operate upon the Mohawk River." There is no evidence that Carleton actually implemented any preliminary measures to support such an expedition during the winter of 1776–77.

When Burgoyne landed in early May with Germain's instructions (File 6.16/10), they contained peremptory orders:

> It is the King's further pleasure that you put under the Command of Lieut. Colonel St. Leger:

Detachment from the 8th Regiment	100
Detachment from the 34th Regiment	100
Sir John Johnson's Regiment of New York	133
Hanau Chasseurs	342
[Total]	675.

> Together with a sufficient Number of Canadians & Indians, and after having furnished him with proper Artillery, Stores, provisions, and every other necessary Article for his Expedition, and secured to him every Assistance in your Power to afford and procure, you are to give him Orders to proceed forthwith to and down the Mohawk River to Albany, and put himself under the Command of Sir William Howe.

This expedition would be designated the "St. Leger expedition" in honor of its commanding officer, Lieutenant Colonel Barry St. Leger of the 34th Regiment of Foot.[146]

St. Leger (1737–1789) joined the British army in 1756 and fought during the Seven Years' War in Canada, participating in the Louisburg Campaign of 1758, the Quebec Campaign of 1759, and the campaign that captured Montreal and defeated New France in 1760. In 1776 he was lieutenant colonel of the 34th Foot, with a reputation as a solid soldier. However, rumors of heavy alcohol abuse by St. Leger have surfaced.[147] St. Leger's performance during the Fort Stanwix Campaign lacked vigor, careful planning, or resolution, and the remainder of his career was entirely undistinguished. He died in 1789 at a relatively young age, quite possibly of alcoholism. Although Burgoyne clearly thought highly of St. Leger and considered him to be an "able field officer" (File 6.16/9), the latter's lack of accomplishments in command of this campaign raised strong doubts about Burgoyne's character assessment.

As could be expected, the actual numbers that Colonel St. Leger employed with his column varied from the original assignment. British regulars with St. Leger included 42 Royal Artillerymen; 99 soldiers of the 8th Regiment of Foot; 132 regulars of the 34th Regiment of Foot; and 90 Hanau jaegers, for a total of 363 of all ranks. These numbers were augmented by 246 Loyalists of the King's Royal Regiment of New York, 49 Canadians in a Quebec militia company; 105 Indian Department rangers (who would later become Butler's Rangers); and three other Loyalists. Thus, St. Leger marched with 766 soldiers, approximately 100 more than had initially been assigned to him. His column was supported by a small and ineffectual artillery train of two 6-pounder cannon, two 3-pounder cannon, and four 4⅖" cohorn mortars. This allocation of artillery would be capable of supporting his small contingent of regulars in an open field battle or impressing the Natives with salutes, but it was far too feeble to compel anything but a log cabin to surrender through bombardment.

Although this expedition's orders were to proceed down the Mohawk River to Albany, it was also noted that "the Command of Lieut. Colonel

[146]Rogers, *Hadden's Journal and Orderly Books*, 45–47.

[147]For St. Leger's alcohol problems, see Watt, *Rebellion in the Mohawk Valley*, 88.

St. Leger . . . is to make a Diversion on the Mohawk River." Thus, St. Leger's column was intended to make a diversion in support of Burgoyne's major effort, and if St. Leger achieved success, he was to continue to Albany to join Burgoyne.

Carleton, Burgoyne, and St. Leger had to scramble to organize this expedition on short notice, with no meaningful preparations. Carleton immediately began "Assembling the Indians of that Neighborhood to be put under the conduct of Lieutenant Colonel St. Leger." At the same time, a prominent Mohawk Valley Loyalist, John Butler, offered to raise a battalion of Loyalist rangers to serve with the Indians. Carleton documented these initial efforts through a packet of correspondence contained in a letter to Germain dispatched in early July from Quebec (Files 6.16/17, 6.16/17a, 6.16/17b and 6.16.17c). Later in September he forwarded the beating orders issued to Butler to raise his Ranger Regiment (File 6/16/20g), as well as the instructions under which Butler would operate during the campaign (File 6/16/20h).

John Butler (1728–1796) was a distinguished veteran of considerable service with the Provincial Troops during the Seven Years' War and a pioneer settler of the Mohawk Valley. He was a leading citizen of the valley and a close personal friend of Sir William Johnson and his son, Sir John Johnson. When Sir John Johnson departed for Canada in 1776, Butler (who had previously fled the valley in 1775) joined him, and much of their correspondence is included herein. These papers describe the raising of the famous Butler's Rangers, a regiment of Loyalist rangers that caused the American Patriots in the Mohawk Valley considerable problems. Colonel Butler was an experienced and skilled commander; his regiment fought superbly on numerous raids, patrols, and ambushes in northern New York from 1777 to 1783; and many of the veterans of Butler's Rangers would become the earliest settlers of Ontario. His oldest son, Walter Butler, also became a dynamic leader in Butler's Rangers, and would be killed late in the war.

Because of the absence of prior planning and the distance that St. Leger had to travel—from Montreal up the St. Lawrence River, then along the eastern shore of Lake Ontario, via the Oswego River and Lake Oneida, and finally down Wood Creek to the Great Carrying Place, where the 1758 Fort Stanwix (now christened Fort Schuyler) was located—his army did not reach Fort Stanwix until August 2. The American garrison at the fort contained nearly 750 Continentals under the command of a solid officer, Colonel Peter Gansevoort of the 3rd New York Regiment of the Continental Line. Furthermore, as St. Leger subsequently reported (File 6.16/20e), he was surprised to discover the fort to be in good repair, with heavy artillery mounted and a deep ditch containing pickets. The American post was far too strong to be captured in a swift infantry assault, and St. Leger had not brought sufficient artillery with him to lay a proper siege to the fort. Although St. Leger could not have known it, no less than six weeks' provisions were stockpiled within the fort, but St. Leger was at the end of a lengthy and precarious supply line, and he would expend his own provisions well before Fort Stanwix would run low.

Why the situation at Fort Stanwix surprised St. Leger is not documented. Clearly, the lack of advance planning for the operation precluded any scouting being performed during the winter of 1776–77, as there was no apparent need for such patrols. However, the three months between early May, when Burgoyne arrived with orders for the expedition, and early August, when St. Leger actually arrived at Fort Stanwix, should have afforded more than sufficient time to have performed at least some reconnaissance of the post. It is documented that the Oneida and Tuscarora Indians, who strongly favored the American Patriot cause, and whose home villages were just a few miles to the south, alerted the American garrison to the British and Indian approach. It is known that at least one British scouting party was foiled because its attached Indians refused to advance beyond Wood Creek (or into Oneida and Tuscarora country). Quite likely, the Oneida warriors afforded Fort Stanwix protection from British scouting efforts.[148] St. Leger apparently discounted the few fragmentary scouting reports that were received. Regardless of the cause, this was a gross failure of British intelligence.

St. Leger established a strong blockade around the fort, a role for which his Native warriors were particularly well suited. He constructed some defensive breastworks and a battery for his minuscule train of artillery, although he was an experienced enough soldier to recognize that his guns were not adequate to batter through the ramparts of the

[148]Ibid., 120–121, 126.

fort. His men initiated harassment fire against the fort's defenders, which probably served to enhance their alertness and morale rather than degrade the post's defenses.

Receiving notice that Fort Stanwix was under siege, American brigadier general Nicholas Herkimer called on the Tryon County Militia to march to the fort's relief.[149] On August 6, to the east of the fort near a small Indian town named "Oriska," Herkimer's column was ambushed by Natives and Butler's Rangers in a daylong pitched battle that became known as the Battle of Oriskany. The initial attack, while devastating, was initiated too early (File 6.16/20b); as a result, although the vanguard of Herkimer's column sustained horrific casualties, the rear was able to flee the field, and the main portion of Herkimer's column gained a prominent knoll near the road and established a solid defensive laager. For the remainder of the day brutal, close-range fighting raged, with neither side able to sustain an advantage. The Americans held the field at the end of the day but soon retreated, and the Tryon Militia suffered casualties in excess of 250 dead and wounded. Some estimates have placed these casualties as high as four hundred. British casualties were nowhere near as severe. Herkimer's militia was shattered in this fight, and it never regained its pre-Oriskany vigor during the war.

Tragically for the Iroquois Confederation, a band of Oneida warriors fought on the side of the Tryon County Militia while a powerful contingent of Seneca warriors comprised the greater part of the British ambushing party. For the first time in centuries, Iroquois fought Iroquois, and the Confederation disintegrated not merely politically, but in bloodshed and strife. The Senecas, in particular, sustained heavy casualties (for American Indians), from which their nation never fully recovered.

When the exhausted, bloodied British attackers returned to their camp outside of Fort Stanwix, they were greeted with even worse news. While they had been fighting at Oriskany, Lieutenant Colonel Marinus Willet,

[149]Brigadier General Nicholas Herkimer (c. 1728–1777) was the Patriot commander of the Tryon (New York) Militia from the Mohawk Valley. An early settler of the valley and a veteran of the Seven Years' War with the New York Provincial Militia, he provided superb leadership at the Battle of Oriskany. His subsequent death due to a botched leg amputation was a great loss for the Patriot cause in the Mohawk Valley. His home there still survives and has been operated by the State of New York as an important heritage tourism site for decades.

also of the 3rd New York, led a strong sortie against the British camp. With the majority of the British combat power committed against Herkimer's militia, the encampment was virtually undefended, and Willet's men rampaged through it at will, causing considerable destruction, and looting and vandalizing the possessions of the British and their Indian allies.

As St. Leger remained squatted in front of Fort Stanwix, he continued to construct a few rudimentary ditches and went through the motions of besieging the fort, spending nearly three weeks in the effort. On August 20 American major general Benedict Arnold marched a small Continental Army column again toward Oriskany, enlisting the unwilling or unwitting assistance of a Loyalist named Han Yost Schuyler, who carried tales to the Indians that panicked them.[150] Given the Indians' comparatively heavy casualties at Oriskany, the loss of the entirety of their valuable and irreplaceable baggage, and their utter lack of success outside the fort, the Indians were doubtless searching for any real excuse to abandon St. Leger.

By August 22 St. Leger was in full retreat back to Montreal, his campaign largely a failure. He had certainly conducted a more than effective

[150]Major General Benedict Arnold (1740–1801) was an American division commander in the Continental Northern Theater Army. As a teenager Arnold had briefly served with the American Provincials in the Lake Champlain corridor. A self-made businessman, by the outbreak of the Revolution Arnold was quite wealthy, although British revenue laws and taxation had cut into his profits. A fervent Patriot, Arnold had been involved in the American War of Independence since its beginning in April 1775. He had played a prominent role in the capture of Fort Ticonderoga, had been involved in early operations on Lake Champlain in 1775, had participated in the Siege of Boston in 1775, and had then commanded the flanking expedition against Quebec in the fall of 1775 up the Kennebec River. Arnold sustained a serious wound in the leg during the assault on Quebec on January 1, 1776, and although the wound had healed by the 1777 campaign, it left him with a permanent limp. Arnold served in various command positions in Canada throughout the winter of 1775–76, and commanded the American Naval Advance Guard at various actions including the Battle of Valcour Island on Lake Champlain in October 1776. He was among the Continental Army's most formidable and experienced generals and was an exceptional battlefield commander. The British had fought against Arnold on numerous occasions and were highly respectful of his combat prowess. Arnold would serve brilliantly in the 1777 campaign, but his subsequent attempt to turn over West Point to the British, and his treason to the British, destroyed his reputation in both North America and Great Britain. Wallace, *Traitorous Hero*, remains the best of the older biographies. The two finest recent biographies of Arnold are Randall, *Benedict Arnold, Patriot and Traitor*, and Martin, *Benedict Arnold, Revolutionary Hero*. An excellent succinct biography is Wallace, "Benedict Arnold," in Billias, ed., *George Washington's Generals*, 163–192. An interesting Canadian perspective is provided by Wilson, *Benedict Arnold*.

diversion against the Mohawk River, and his virtual destruction of the Tryon County Militia at Oriskany would be of long-term benefit to the British cause in upstate New York, but he had failed to reach the Mohawk River valley, and St. Leger had been entirely unable to reach Albany. He would subsequently return to Lake Champlain and attempt to reinforce Burgoyne, but he would never proceed beyond Fort Ticonderoga, and after August 22 his column was for all practical purposes out of the campaign.

The papers in this volume contain extremely valuable primary sources for St. Leger's campaign, including a record of the campaign by St. Leger (File 6.16/20c); a narrative of the Battle of Oriskany by Colonel John Butler, who played a prominent role in that engagement (File 6/16/20b); and a description of Fort Stanwix as St. Leger viewed it upon his approach (File 6/16/20e). Finally, a letter from St. Leger to Burgoyne "carried through the woods by an Indian" (File 6.16/21a) demonstrates the difficulties that Burgoyne and St. Leger faced in communicating with each other, not to mention the utter impracticability of effective coordination of their mutual efforts.

Burgoyne's Movement on the Hudson River, September 1777

Between August 14 and September 10, Burgoyne made his headquarters at the large home of William Duer, located south of Fort Edward. Duer, a close friend of General Schuyler, was a prominent and wealthy resident of the upper Hudson Valley. He had constructed his magnificent house in 1770. The Brunswick surgeon Julius Friedrich Wasmus called it a "small castle." A local history of Fort Edward described it thus:

> It stood in front of the bluff rising from the Hudson river, and was fifty-two feet square, two stories high; the lower story being eleven feet and the upper one ten feet in height, with a high basement, in which was the kitchen and other rooms. There was a wide hall through the centre of the house upon each floor, with two large square rooms on either side and the staircase on one side of the lower hall, which is said to have been elegantly finished. The windows on the upper story were all bow windows. The roof was nearly flat, built in four triangles, running each way. The house faced

> toward the west and on the rear, or east side, was a wide, two-story veranda, the entire length of the house. On each end was a wing, twenty-two feet square and one and one-half stories high. The frame of the house was of heavy oak timber, the walls being lined with two-inch plank and filled in with brick, over which was lathing and plastering. The windows were all hung with chains and leaden weights. The main part had a cornice carved all around.[151]

Unfortunately, this magnificent house was demolished in 1810, and no contemporary drawings of it are known to exist.

Burgoyne would not resume his march south on the Hudson River until September 13, when his army crossed the river, from the eastern shore to the western shore at Fort Miller. It was only now, two months after he had advanced from Ticonderoga, and a month after the Bennington debacle, that Burgoyne had finally been able to accumulate a full thirty days' worth of provisions.

As the Hudson River flows to the south, it becomes increasingly broader. At its farthest northern reaches, the Hudson can still be crossed by a pontoon bridge. Once the Mohawk River flows into the Hudson at Peebles Island north of Albany, the river becomes extremely wide and cannot readily be crossed without the use of a ferry. In addition, the eastern bank of the river is generally marshy, swampy, and relatively poorly drained. Furthermore, the only road along the Hudson River, known as the "River Road," paralleled the western shore of the river, generally from Fort Miller to Albany. Thus, Burgoyne was compelled to follow the western bank of the Hudson the remainder of the way south.

Although Burgoyne elected not to maintain a continuous line of communications back to Ticonderoga and Canada, he still retained posts at Fort Ticonderoga, Mount Independence, the Ticonderoga landing and portage (including Sugar Loaf), Diamond Island on the southern portion of Lake George, and Fort George. Since these posts were properly outside of Canada, Carleton determined that he was not authorized to garrison them using his Canadian army. Thus, Burgoyne had to detach garrisons for these posts from his own army. Two companies of the 47th Foot were stationed at Diamond Island; and all of the 53rd Foot was detached to Forts Ticonderoga and George. The Prince Frederick

[151]Bascom, *Fort Edward Book*, 130.

Regiment was assigned to the Mount Independence garrison. Burgoyne's logistical rear was commanded by Brigadier General Powell, based out of Fort Ticonderoga. The Lake George and Fort Ticonderoga garrisons consisted of 910 musketmen.

Because of these detachments, before he initiated his movement forward Burgoyne reorganized his army. Riedesel's German division became a single brigade, under the command of Brigadier General Johann van Specht, consisting of the Rheitz regiment, Specht regiment, and Riedesel regiment. The Hesse-Hanau Artillery Company supported this brigade, with two British bronze 6-pounder cannon and two British bronze 3-pounder cannon commanded by the skilled, determined Captain Pausch.

The British Regular Division similarly became a single brigade, under the command of Brigadier General Hamilton, consisting of the 9th, 20th, 21st, and 62nd Regiments of Foot. It was supported by four light 6-pounder cannon, commanded by Captain Thomas Jones of the Royal Artillery.

Brigadier General Fraser's advance corps remained unchanged in composition. Following the casualties sustained at Bennington, Captain Fraser's Company of Select Marksmen contained fifty-six rangers. Of the small loyalist and Canadian contingents, approximately one to two hundred American Loyalists, and about seventy to eighty Canadians remained in the ranks after Bennington. Because of the lateness of the season, and the limited prisoners, scalps, and plunder that the American Indians had garnered throughout the campaign, the majority of Burgoyne's Native allies had gradually departed him, slipping away north to their homes throughout August and September. A remaining fifty American Indian warriors continued to serve with this corps of the army. Artillery assigned to Fraser's corps was four 6-pounder cannon, four light 3-pounder cannon, and two 5½" (Royal) howitzers.

The artillery park consisted of four medium 12-pounder cannon, two light 24-pounder cannon, four light 6-pounder cannon, two 8" howitzers, and two 5½" (Royal) howitzers. A number of bateaux had been transferred with exhaustive effort to operate on the Hudson River, and several of these bateaux were armed. The bateaux fleet and supply trains, carrying the critical munitions and thirty days' worth of provisions stockpiled at such great effort, were further safeguarded by one light 12-pounder cannon, two 8" howitzers, four 5½" (Royal) mortars, and four 4⅖" (cohorn) mortars. The Hesse-Hanau Regiment and the remaining six companies of the 47th Foot were detached to guard Burgoyne's supply trains. Rounding out the army, the few battered survivors of the ill-fated Lieutenant Colonel Baum's Brunswick Dragoons served as Burgoyne's headquarters guards.

The effective combat strength of the army consisted of 2,935 British rank and file, and 1,711 German musketmen. On September 10, 1777, Burgoyne's aide-de-camp Clerke would write friends home in England: "I believe now we shall soon have something to do."[152]

Burgoyne's movement south was not as rapid as one would expect, considering that he was consuming valuable and limited provisions every day. On September 13 he marched nine miles down the west bank of the Hudson River, reaching the Heights of Saratoga, where he constructed light field entrenchments. The next day he remained at Saratoga, improving his field fortifications. During his brief stay at Saratoga, Burgoyne occupied the home of Philip Schuyler. On September 15 he resumed his march but only proceeded as far as Dovegot House, three miles from Saratoga. The next day, he remained at Dovegot, a delay caused by the Americans' destruction of numerous bridges on the River Road. For these two nights Burgoyne made his headquarters at Dovegot House. On the seventeenth Burgoyne performed another short march to Sword's House, only three and one-half miles away. He remained encamped around Sword's House, where he made his headquarters for the next two nights. In six days Burgoyne had progressed only fifteen and one-half miles, not exactly a sweeping rate of advance. It could more properly be described as a crawl.

The morning of September 18, the Americans dispatched heavy reconnaissance parties consisting of the highly experienced and capable Virginia and Pennsylvania riflemen and an accompanying light infantry battalion under the respective commands of Colonel Daniel Morgan and recently promoted Lieutenant Colonel Henry Dearborn, two officers who were veterans of Arnold's expedition to Quebec and the New Year's Eve assault on that city. This force surprised an informal British

[152] Kingsley, "Letters from Sir Francis-Carr Clerke," 424.

foraging party that was scrounging for food four to five hundred yards to the south of the main British camp, killed several British soldiers, and captured twenty men, thus garnering critical intelligence of the British positions, movements, and intentions.[153]

The Battle of Freeman's Farm, September 19

On September 19 Burgoyne resumed his movement forward. The regiments departed between nine and ten o'clock in the morning. Burgoyne's army marched in three columns, with the large supply train and artillery park remaining behind anchored on the Hudson River. On the River Road immediately to the west of the Hudson, Riedesel's German brigade marched due south, as the British left (east) flank. Riedesel's mission was to screen the supply train and to keep the Americans' attention diverted by feinting that his column was the primary British attack. The most important British column was that of Brigadier General Simon Fraser, on the extreme British right (west) flank. Fraser's was the principal British maneuver force, charged with the task of ascertaining the American flank, maneuvering around it, and locating key terrain for Phillips to emplace his artillery upon, from which he could command the Continentals' position and drive them south. Brigadier General Fraser's force consisted of the lightest and most capable soldiers of Burgoyne's army, including Captain Fraser's Select Marksmen, and was well suited for this assignment. Burgoyne personally accompanied the central column, consisting of Hamilton's British Regular Brigade, which was responsible for maintaining contact between Riedesel on the River Road and General Fraser flanking to the west.

Approximately one mile south of Sword's House, the British encountered the obstacle that would become known as the "Great Ravine." Burgoyne and Hamilton's Regular Brigade crossed on a small bridge that the Americans had missed destroying the day before, and then proceeded on a farm track that led to the west. By about noon, General Fraser's advance corps had gained high ground to the west, from which he could readily maneuver around the American flank. The British Regular Brigade was located just north of the several-hundred-acre clearing of

[153]Stanley, ed., *For Want of a Horse*, 145–146.

Freeman's Farm. Freeman's residence, a small log cabin, occupied the top of a knoll overlooking his farm fields to the south and east. By mid-September, the corn crop was nearly ready for harvest. Hamilton's regulars had marched about two and one-half miles that morning, and they were excited to see cleared fields to their front for the first time in many weeks. Riedesel was running late on the River Road, as the Americans had destroyed numerous small bridges that had to be reconstructed. By 1:00 P.M. Burgoyne had been able to communicate with his columns on both flanks and ascertained that they were roughly aligned. He then had Captain Jones's two 6-pounder cannon fire a single shot apiece, to serve as an audible symbol for the general advance to resume.

Major Gordon Forbes of the 9th Foot commanded the strong advance guard for Hamilton's brigade, consisting of approximately one hundred men from his regiment that preceded the advance. As they descended Freeman's knoll and crossed his open fields to the south, they were ambushed by Morgan's riflemen and Dearborn's light infantry, firing from the heavy woods to the south. Forbes's advance guard sustained crippling casualties, with every officer killed or wounded, and the British pickets were broken and driven back in disarray. Morgan's riflemen launched an aggressive pursuit that carried them to the northwest and into the left flank of General Fraser's advance guard, where they were in turn broken and scattered by sustained musketry from Fraser's ranks. Ensign Samuel Armstrong, with the 8th Massachusetts Regiment of the Continental Line, noted: "a reinforcement soon came up to their assistance and obliged us to Retreat to get from their flank Guard which were coming down upon us."[154] In the initial shock, Captain Monin, commanding one of the two Canadian companies, was killed, which greatly demoralized the couple dozen remaining Canadians. While repulsing Morgan's determined attack, Captain Fraser's Select Marksmen absorbed heavy casualties. Lieutenant Anburey recalled: "The very first fire . . . Lieutenant Don of the 21st Regiment received a ball through his heart. I am sure it will never be erased from my memory, for when he was wounded, he sprang from the ground nearly as high as a man."[155] Lieutenant John Don had actually been detached as one of the officers

[154]Boyle, ed., "From Saratoga to Valley Forge," 245.

[155]Jackman, *With Burgoyne from Quebec*, 174.

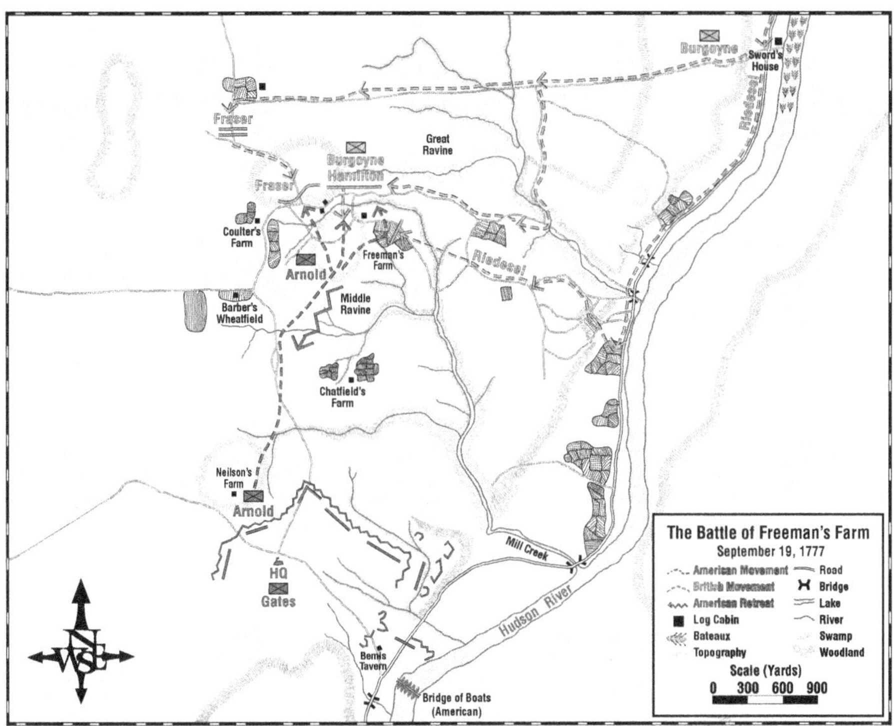

Freeman's Farm and vicinity, September–October, 1777.
Map prepared by SunSyne Graphics, http://www.sunsyne.com

serving with Captain Fraser's Marksmen. Morgan used a turkey call to reorganize his scattered men in the woods south of where they had launched their initial assault. There was a brief lull in the fighting while both sides caught their breath in the woods, and while the Americans summoned additional forces to the battlefield.

About 2:00 to 3:00 P.M. the three British regiments resumed a general advance into the clearing to the south. The 20th Foot was on the left, the 21st Foot held the right flank, while the 62nd Foot fought in the center. The rather battered 9th Foot was placed by Burgoyne in reserve to the right rear (northwest). Jones moved his two 6-pounder cannon onto the knoll at the center of the British position, just south of Freeman's cabin. In turn, the Americans launched a vigorous response from the woods.

Meanwhile, General Fraser's advance guard remained stationary in its position to the west. Burgoyne's tactical scheme depended entirely on Fraser's corps being the primary maneuver element, and if Fraser was recalled from his position on the British flank, Burgoyne's whole concept of operations would be negated. Accordingly, Fraser stayed in position to resume his advance upon the American flank, once the British Regular Brigade under Burgoyne's direct supervision defeated the American attack. Had Burgoyne chosen to divert Fraser's advance corps to join in the fighting with the British Regular Brigade, he would have yielded the initiative, which he was unwilling to do.

The Americans launched a swarm of attacks against the three British regiments exposed in Freeman's fields. The Americans' relentless assaults drove the British to the north into the protection of the woods. During their precipitous advance under heavy fire, the American ranks inevitably became broken, and they would in turn be driven back to the south across the open fields, trampling the ripe crops into the ground. As the British advanced, they encountered deadly accurate rifle fire from Morgan's corps fighting from the shelter of the woods to the south, and in their turn they too would be driven north in disarray. As Ensign Armstrong later wrote recalling the maelstrom: "when we gave them ground, then on turn they gave us ground & so on Alternately, till after Sun-Sit."[156] For the next four hours, Freeman's Farm was the scene of absolutely furious, frenzied fighting.

In the center of the fighting, the two British 6-pounder cannon under Royal Artillery Captain Thomas Jones constituted a highly visible target that the Americans could scarcely miss, and the British gunners were slaughtered almost to the last man. Captain Jones was killed, his subordinate Lieutenant James Hadden had his artillery cap shot through, and out of twenty-two men, nineteen were killed or wounded. Hadden recalled that the guns were silenced at a critical juncture of the fighting, and that he and his few surviving gunners "were forced to abandon the hill and on it my guns."[157] The Americans succeeded in capturing the guns on several occasions, but the British musketry was too heavy for the guns to be dragged away as trophies. The experienced British gunners

[156]Boyle, "From Saratoga to Valley Forge," 245.

[157]Rogers, *Hadden's Journal and Orderly Book*, 165.

had carried off their implements to prevent the Americans from turning the guns around, and in succeeding rushes the British reclaimed their artillery. Captain Benjamin Warren, a company commander with the 7th Massachusetts Regiment of the Continental Line, recorded in his journal: "We beat them back three times and they reinforced and recovered their ground again, till after sunset without any intermissions . . . we took a field piece twice and they retook it again and caried [carried] it off with them."[158]

Although other historians have claimed to identify specific regimental assaults, the available primary sources do not support such a meticulous, detailed account.[159] Given the heavy gunfire, and the choking gray gunpowder smoke that entirely obscured the field, controlled tactical maneuvers were impossible. Even had such tactical control been feasible, all the participants were too heavily engaged to document precise maneuvers. A journal from the Specht's German regiment says it best: "Because this whole affair happened in the woods and among bushes and without even a map, no exact and understandable detailed description of the nature of the region nor of this action itself can be given. Fraser's Corps and that of Lt. Colonel Breymann have taken part in this affair. The various circumstances in it, however, have remained obscure."[160]

Upon hearing the crescendo of firing erupt to his right rear, Riedesel halted his advance down the River Road and detached his own regiment, several additional companies of infantry, and two 6-pounders under Captain Pausch, upon his own initiative. At nearly the same time, departing the death and devastation of the clearing of Freeman's Farm, Major General Phillips hastily returned to the artillery park, then brought Hamilton four additional pieces of artillery, most likely six-pounder cannon, the lightest and most maneuverable pieces available in the artillery train.[161] They arrived just at darkness, in time to support the shattered British battle line at a critical juncture. Riedesel's small column also arrived at sunset upon the exposed American right (east) flank and placed effective enfilading fire against the Americans. Given the onset of night, the heavy casualties suffered, and the expenditure

158 Alexander, ed., "Diary of Captain Benjamin Warren," 211–212.
159 For an example of this, refer to Morrissey, *Saratoga 1777*, 56–72.
160 Doblin, *Specht Journal*, 81.
161 Cubbison, *"Artillery never gained more Honour,"* 110.

of most of their ammunition, the Americans chose to withdraw from the field, carrying their wounded with them.

The three British regiments that faced the worst of the fighting were absolutely devastated. The fate of the 62nd Regiment of Foot was typical. Out of a beginning strength variously estimated at between three and four hundred, the regiment had sustained casualties of 187 killed and wounded, with twenty-five prisoners lost. According to one British officer: "The 62nd had scarce 10 men a company left." From Brigadier General Fraser's brigade, Captain Fraser's Company of Marksmen was the only detachment heavily engaged, and they had lost one lieutenant, one sergeant, and four rank and file killed, with an additional fourteen rank and file wounded, for a total of twenty casualties out of a maximum strength of sixty—a terrible 33 percent loss rate.

Throughout the long afternoon's contest, both Burgoyne and Phillips had remained with Hamilton's brigade at the scene of the heaviest fighting. In the midst of this combat Phillips's aide, Captain Charles Green of the Royal Artillery, was wounded. Captain Green possessed a particularly ostentatious saddlecloth and was accordingly mistaken for the British commanding officer by American sharpshooters. Burgoyne himself would recall:

> Captain Green, aid-de-camp to Major General Phillips, was shot through the arm by one of these marksmen as he was delivering me a message. I learned, after the convention, from the commanding officer of the riflemen [probably Colonel Daniel Morgan] that the shot was meant for me; and as the captain was seen to fall from his horse, it was for some hours believed in the enemy's army that I was killed. My escape was owing to the captain happening to have a laced furniture to his saddle, which made him mistaken for the general.[162]

That General Phillips's aide was seriously wounded while delivering a message to Burgoyne attests to Burgoyne's involvement throughout the day's fight.[163] Unfortunately, no primary source accounts document

[162]Burgoyne, *State of the Expedition from Canada*, 163.

[163]Howson, *Burgoyne of Saratoga*, 209. Anburey recounted a similar story regarding Green's wound, but he was with Fraser's Advanced Corps and not the British Regular Brigade, so his rendition was secondhand. Jackman, *With Burgoyne from Quebec*, 1:180. An anonymous 47th Foot officer also recorded Green's wound, but incorrectly noted him as an officer with the 31st Foot. Stanley, *For Want of a Horse*, 155.

his specific activities during the afternoon's fighting. Sergeant Roger Lamb, present on the field, remembered: "General Burgoyne during this conflict behaved with great personal bravery, he shunned no danger; his presence and conduct animated the troops, for they greatly loved the general; he delivered his orders with precision and coolness; and in the heat, fury, and, danger of the fight maintained those true characteristics of the soldier—serenity, fortitude and undaunted intrepidity."[164]

Petite Guerre in the Middle Ravine, September 20–October 6

Although Burgoyne contemplated an advance the next day, it was obvious that this was impractical. The four regiments and artillery detachment of the British Regular Brigade had been shattered at Freeman's Farm, the German division had been disorganized as it responded to the crisis, and some elements of Fraser's advance guard had also been roughly handled (particularly the Canadian contingent and the Company of Select Marksmen). Burgoyne had to accept that his army was simply incapable of continuing the advance south for the time being. Accordingly, he determined to construct fortifications to safeguard his army, while he interred the dead, treated the wounded, brought up his baggage trains on the Hudson River, and reorganized his army (specifically the badly battered Regular Brigade). Burgoyne instructed his engineers to lay out four sections of strong earthworks. Thus, Burgoyne could claim that he had held the field and gained a victory, even though his advance to the south was entirely halted.

The first section of field fortifications was located on key terrain north of the "Great Ravine," on a prominent bluff overlooking the Hudson River. Here Burgoyne constructed a series of redoubts and batteries to protect his supply trains, and he established his hospital at the base of the escarpment closer to a source of good water. He also brought up his bateaux and constructed a pontoon bridge to the east bank of the Hudson River, where he established a fortified *tete-de-pont* to safeguard gathering of forage that was available there.

---

[164] Lamb, *Journal of Occurrences*, 161.

Riedesel was instructed to withdraw his German brigade from their exposed position on the River Road and to take post on a prominent ridge to the north, and the Regular Brigade also shifted to the east to construct strong breastworks that would comprise the main British defensive position. Burgoyne established his large headquarters marquee just behind these works, in the center of the British lines.

General Fraser's advance corps withdrew from the hill that it had occupied during the Battle of Freeman's Farm and shifted east to the battlefield itself. The large British component of his command, under the supervision of Lieutenant Colonel Balcarres, who commanded the Light Infantry Battalion, constructed a strong entrenched camp around the high ground atop which Freeman's small farm complex had been built. This position subsequently became known as the "Balcarres Redoubt," though in accordance with military engineering dictates of the mid-eighteenth century it was not technically a redoubt. Rather, it was simply a large entrenched camp, with true redoubts on key terrain to its front. The German contingent of the advance guard, under the supervision of Lieutenant Colonel Breymann, constructed another large entrenchment on a higher hillside to the northwest that had not figured in the fighting of September 19 but that commanded the Balcarres Redoubt and was within easy artillery range. As with the other position, this entrenchment was awarded the moniker "Breymann Redoubt," though it too was more a fortified camp or large entrenchment than a legitimate redoubt. The two weak and demoralized Canadian companies occupied two log cabins, which were strengthened to some extent, in a draw between the two major entrenchments. Another pair of true redoubts was constructed on key terrain to the west of the Breymann Redoubt.

It was noted by Captain Pausch of the Hesse-Hanau Artillery that "the dead were buried on the field of battle, instead of on the hill, because breast-works were thrown up there."[165] The numerous British killed were thus buried somewhere in the large cornfield to the east of Freeman's cabin. The graves were not dug to a particularly demanding standard. Lieutenant Digby recorded in his journal: "During the night [Sept. 23–24] it rained heavy, and on the 26th many bodies not buried

[165]Burgoyne, *George Pausch's Journal and Reports*, 78.

deep enough in the ground appeared as the soil was a light sand, and caused a most dreadful smell."[166]

From this moment forth, the British and Americans were engaged in a nearly continuous *petite guerre*, or small skirmish war—a conflict of patrols, scouts, ambushes, and raids conducted between the front of the main British lines and the primary American positions. These conflicts occurred primarily under cover of darkness. The British were attempting simultaneously to cover the front of their works and to perform reconnaissance of the American defensive positions, which remained a mystery to them. The Americans, for their part, were focused on harassing the encamped British and Germans and disrupting the efforts of the British scouts. The battle space contested nightly consisted of the draws and tangles around the Middle Ravine and Mill Creek. The American scouts occupied Chatfield's Farm just to the south of the Middle Ravine, from which every evening they swarmed forth into the no-man's-land between the two armies. The nightly battles were almost always small affairs, squad- or platoon-sized detachments, as larger forces could not effectively operate in the tangled terrain after dark. In this contest, the Americans gained absolute ascendency.

On September 20, 1777, some 150 Oneida and Tuscarora warriors joined the American army. From this date forward, as Dearborn noted, "the Oneidas who joined us the next day after the battle, have brought in more or less prisoners every day."[167] Although most historians have paid this time frame scant attention, and Burgoyne's papers unfortunately fail to document these events, this period was critical to the eventual deterioration of Burgoyne's campaign, and thus deserves comprehensive study.

A daily itinerary documents the slow but steady crumbling of the British situation.

- Sept. 21, 1777 – A German fatigue party of several hundred men clearing roads to their front was attacked by an aggressive American force, which was repulsed, but only after the entire British army was called to arms "in which position it remained two hours."[168]
- Sept. 21, 1777 – The American Indians captured two British soldiers on a raid, as reported (rather gleefully) by a youthful American soldier: "The

[166]Baxter, ed., *British Invasion from the North*, 281.
[167]Brown and Peckham, eds., *Journals of Henry Dearborn*, 107.
[168]Stone, ed., *Memoirs of Major General Riedesel*, 1:153–154.

indians brought in two tworeys [Tories] and the Gennoral [General] delivered them into their hands and I should think it punishment enough for anna [any] human creture [creature]."[169] Another young American soldier had the opportunity to watch the American Loyalists being taunted at the hands of the Native warriors: "This Afternoon a scout of our Indians took a Tory, the Genrl gave him to them for a while they took him & Buried him up to his Neck & had their Pow wow around him, after that, they had him up and Laid him a side of a great fire & turn'd his head & feet a while to the fire, hooting & hollowing round him then he was hand Cuff'd & sent to Albany Goal [jail]."[170] A casual observer suspects that rarely must anybody have been so pleased to be placed into jail.

- Sept. 22, 1777 – The Indians supporting the Americans brought in as prisoners two British Regulars, captured overnight.[171] A young Connecticut soldier, Oliver Boardman, also documented: "A Scout of our Indians took two Regulars Centries . . . after taking their hats from them they Painted their Faces & Brought Them in."[172]
- Sept. 23, 1777 – Large American patrols attacked both flanks of the British lines, and an American Indian contingent assailed the north side of the British camp and captured several Loyalists from the rear of Burgoyne's camp, demonstrating their capability of entirely surrounding the British position. One American officer reported more accurately that "eight tories" were taken prisoner. Musketman Boardman similarly noted: "Our Indians Brought eight . . . Prisners in."[173]
- Sept. 24, 1777 – "Our (German) pickets have frequently been alarmed today by enemy patrols that know how to push through the plain."[174]
- Sept. 24, 1777 – "The indians took savan [seven] tores and broght them to head Quarters and the Genrl delevered them up to the indians to do what they want with them."[175] Another American reported, probably somewhat more accurately: "This morning the Indians brought in three Tories Prisoners, in the Afternoon we sent out severall Scouting Parties but cou'd make no disoveries." Boardman confirmed this, elaborating somewhat: "Our Indians went out & Brought in three Prisoners with a Rope round the Neck of each of them."[176]

[169]Treat, "Journal of Robert Treat," 984–996; and Boyle, "From Saratoga to Valley Forge," 246.
[170]Boardman, "Journal of Oliver Boardman'," 225–226.
[171]Boyle, "From Saratoga to Valley Forge," 246.
[172]Boardman, "Journal of Oliver Boardman," 226.
[173]Stone, *Memoirs of Major General Riedesel*, 155; Boyle, "From Saratoga to Valley Forge," 247; and Boardman, "Journal of Oliver Boardman," 226.
[174]Doblin, *Specht Journal*, 83.
[175]Treat, "Journal of Robert Treat."
[176]Boyle, "From Saratoga to Valley Forge," 247; and Boardman, "Journal of Oliver Boardman," 226.

- Sept. 24, 1777 – The few remaining Indians with the British army that had been dispatched on a scouting party to Saratoga Lake "returned that same night, having seen nothing." One British officer noted that having gained a healthy respect for Morgan's riflemen: "Our few remaining indians appeared very shy at going out on any scouting parties."[177]

Saratoga Lake was located well to the west of the American position, so distant that Burgoyne could not possibly have flanked that far away from the Hudson River, and a scout to Saratoga Lake would almost certainly have avoided any contact with the tough, determined American patrols saturating the ground to the south of Burgoyne's camp. Thus, the Indians were launching a raid in a direction that would avoid any contact, while at the same time affording the illusion that they were actively engaged in supporting the British.

- Sept. 24, 1777 – "This evening, the enemy's retreat shot drove the ball beyond the Regt. Von Riedesel up to the fire watch."[178]
- Sept. 25, 1777 – "At dawn, the enemy again tried something against the Hesse-Hanau pickets . . . to compel one noncomissioned officer with ten men to retreat; 2 of these men were slightly wounded and one sentry [was] cut off."[179] Ensign Armstrong with the 8th Massachusetts Continentals thought that several British soldiers had been killed, but accurately reported that they "took one Prisoner." Private Boardman confirmed these numbers.[180]
- Sept. 25, 1777 – A German scouting party dispatched on the east flank failed to gain any intelligence: "they returned without having seen or learned anything."[181]
- Sept. 26, 1777 – British foragers were captured by the Americans near Saratoga, as Henry Dearborn reported: "We took 18 Prisoners this Day."[182] About thirty Caughnawaga (Montreal Mohawk) Indians arrived in the British camp.[183]
- Sept. 26, 1777 – The advanced British pickets were in action all day, openly besieged by the Americans, who repeatedly assailed the British posts. An Indian raiding party, probably comprised of the Caughnawaga Indians

[177]Stanley, *For Want of a Horse*, 151.
[178]Doblin, *Specht Journal*, 83.
[179]Ibid., 83.
[180]Boyle, "From Saratoga to Valley Forge," 247; and Boardman, "Journal of Oliver Boardman," 226.
[181]Burgoyne, *George Pausch's Journal and Reports*, 83.
[182]Brown and Peckham, *Journals of Henry Dearborn*, 107.
[183]Doblin, *Specht Journal*, 84.

that had just arrived, was dispatched by the British in response; it took one American prisoner and killed two soldiers.[184] Generally, the Americans had the better of this fighting, as reported by Ensign Armstrong: "This Morning the Indians brought in three Hesian prisoners and two of our Men that were taken Prisoners at Ticonderoga, and in the Afternoon they brought in one Tory & an Indian Scalp." Boardman also noted: "This morning our Indians & Rifle Men Brought in three Hessians & two Sailors. About noon they Brought in one Tory & one Sculp. About Twenty taken & Deserted to Day."[185]

- Sept. 27, 1777 – On this date the Americans attempted a new tactic, maneuvering north on the Hudson River in boats, as a German soldier observed: "the enemy made his appearance on the Hudson in bateaux toward evening."[186] However, the fighting was not always one-sided, for on this date the young Connecticut soldier lamented: "A Few of our Men were beyond the out Centries digging potatoes, were captivated by the Enemy."[187]
- Sept. 27, 1777 – Having spent a full week terrorizing the British and Germans, the Oneidas and Tuscaroras departed the American camp. Their duties were assumed by a Company of Stockbridge Mohicans. The *Specht Journal* for October 3 documented with palpable fear and trepidation: "The enemy had a type of Savages in their army, called the Stockbridge Savages, who practiced all possible cruelties on the prisoners."[188]
- Sept. 28, 1777 – "At 9 o'clock at night, the enemy attacked the most remote advanced post of the Hesse-Hanau pickets . . . with overwhelming force compelled the noncomissioned officer with 15 men positioned there to withdraw to the main post."[189] Boardman noted for this day: "Our Indians took two British soldiers Prisners they inform us that their Army is very short on for Provision."[190]
- Sept. 29, 1777 – "About daybreak our (British) picket was fired on from the wood in front."[191] Ensign Armstrong reported: "This day there was Eleven prisoners brought in, six of which were Hessians."[192] Again, the Americans suffered a minor reverse in fighting at another picket post, as

---

184. Burgoyne, *George Pausch's Journal and Reports*, 83.
185. Boyle, "From Saratoga to Valley Forge," 247; and Boardman, "Journal of Oliver Boardman," 226.
186. Doblin, *Specht Journal*, 84.
187. Boardman, "Journal of Oliver Boardman," 227.
188. Doblin, *Specht Journal*, 87.
189. Ibid., 85; and Stone, *Memoirs of Major General Riedesel*, 157.
190. Boardman, "Journal of Oliver Boardman," 227.
191. Digby, *British Invasion from the North*, 284.
192. Boyle, "From Saratoga to Valley Forge," 247.

Boardman noted: "one of our men was killed & three or four wounded. Our Rifle men took six Prisners to Day five of them Hessians & one Tory besides this, one sergeant, one Corporal & one Drummer of the Hessian Troops Deserted."[193]

- Sept. 29, 1777 – Captain Alexander Fraser and his Rangers were engaged in scouting "some distance in the rear of the enemy's camp [probably Saratoga Lake again], saw nothing extraordinary."
- Sept. 30, 1777 – "7 Prisoners were brought in this morning," as reported by Lieutenant Colonel Dearborn.[194] Boardman had a nearly identical narrative: "Our Scout took five Canadians & two Hessians. Four deserters have come in today."[195] Ensign Armstrong rendered a slightly different report: "This Day there was six Canadians brought in as Prisoners."[196]
- Oct. 1, 1777 – A number of American riflemen and Indians that had crept through the British lines to within five hundred feet of Burgoyne's headquarters, "suddenly issued from the woods, snatched a few British soldiers digging potatoes, and carried off the men in the very faces of their comrades."[197] Captain Fraser's Select Marksmen attempted to contest the ground with the Americans and were again out on a patrol. When they saw the rebels burning the mill of a Mr. Jones, who happened to be a local Loyalist serving as their guide, Jones himself went to investigate and was promptly captured by the Americans.[198] Boardman noted: "Two deserters came this morning we learn from them, that the Enemy are very scant for Provision, Bread in particular."[199]
- Oct. 2–3, 1777 – A large British scouting party crossed over onto the east side of the Hudson River. It is likely that this movement was performed to cover the dispatch of messengers from Burgoyne to inform Clinton that Burgoyne intended to resume the offensive again within a few days. Nineteen sailors from the bateaux flotilla on the Hudson River that were engaged in foraging were captured by the Americans, and more of the nearly continuous attacks upon the British pickets occurred. Lieutenant Colonel Dearborn noted: "We took about 40 prisoners."[200] Ensign Armstrong provided a more accurate rendition: "In the Evening our Scout brought in twenty-four Prisoners at one time and six at another."

---

[193]Boardman, "Journal of Oliver Boardman," 227.
[194]Brown and Peckham, *Journals of Henry Dearborn*, 107.
[195]Boardman, "Journal of Oliver Boardman," 227.
[196]Boyle, "From Saratoga to Valley Forge," 247.
[197]Stone, *Campaign of Lieutenant General Burgoyne*, 55.
[198]Bradford, "Lord Francis Napier's Journal," 319.
[199]Boardman, "Journal of Oliver Boardman," 227.
[200]Brown and Peckham, *Journals of Henry Dearborn*, 108.

Boardman recalled: "A Major a Captain & A Lieutenant with an Number of Privates were taken to day. Also a large Number of Cattle Sheep & Horses were brought in with them, Two Hessian Rifle Men have deserted to Day, the whole taken prisners last night & to Day are Thirty Six."[201] As Boardman documented, desertions from the British army were beginning to increase by this time, and both Boardman and Ensign Armstrong confirmed on October 3 that "two Hessians deserted to our Camp."[202]

- Oct. 4, 1777 – "Our (British) picket was fired upon near day break, but as our own posts were strong, and we all slept with our clothes on, it was but little minded."[203]
- Oct. 5, 1777 – The British army by this date finally admitted that they had lost the war of the outposts, and Burgoyne issued General Orders: "All out guards and posts, not intended to be concealed are to light fires 100 yards in their front, that they may the better distinguish any thing advancing within that distance of their station."[204] Yet the harassment still continued, "During the night, the enemy twice alarmed the picket of the Reg. Von Rhetz."[205] And, similarly: "A small party of our sailors was taken by the enemy, also about 20 horses, that strayed near their lines."[206] Boardman wrote on this date: "One Hessian deserted this Morning he informs that several of his fellows were waiting the first opportunity to come off. Also that they are very scant for Provisions. This Afternoon two of the British soldiers deserted, they bring the same news about provision. Taken and Deserted seventeen to Day."[207]
- Oct. 6, 1777 – "Toward noon, the enemy rather intensely alarmed the pickets of the Regt. Von Rhetz." "Toward evening, the enemy again alarmed the pickets Von Rhetz as well as the advance posts of the Hesse-Hanau Regiment down by the water [Hudson River]."[208] The desertions from Burgoyne's army, when combined with the nightly losses caused by the Americans, were becoming a serious drain on the British by this time, as the young soldier from Connecticut recalled: "Four Hessians Deserted this Morning, One Tory was taken, Twenty two have Deserted to Day."[209]
- Oct. 6, 1777 – A large American scouting party, consisting of several hundred men, was out and engaged in heavy skirmishing, but the Americans

[201]Boardman, "Journal of Oliver Boardman," 227.
[202]Boyle, "From Saratoga to Valley Forge," 247; and Boardman, "Journal of Oliver Boardman," 228.
[203]Digby, *British Invasion from the North*, 285.
[204]O'Callaghan, *Orderly Book of General Burgoyne*, 127.
[205]Doblin, *Specht Journal*, 87.
[206]Digby, *British Invasion from the North*, 285–286.
[207]Boardman, "Journal of Oliver Boardman," 228.
[208]Doblin, *Specht Journal*, 87.
[209]Boardman, "Journal of Oliver Boardman," 228.

> became disoriented and were obliged to spend the night in the woods.[210] Sergeant Ephraim Squier, with a Connecticut militia regiment, recorded: "[Oct.] 6th— This morning ordered to march for a covering party . . . no provisions with us, got lost, staid out all night. Rain and cold. No sleep to day and night. Obliged to be still, being just by the enemy."[211] Even with the failure of this large American party, some minor tactical successes were still achieved by the American skirmishers: "Five Prisoners were taken this Morning with a Number of Cattle Sheep &c."[212] Lieutenant Digby recalled: "During the night there were small alarms and frequent popping shots, fired by sentrys from our different outposts."[213]

Throughout this time frame, the Americans entirely precluded the British from gaining any viable intelligence regarding their positions, although some members of Fraser's advance guard perceived, but were unable to penetrate the American picket cordon to confirm, the possible presence of high ground to the west of the left flank of the American fortifications. The Americans clearly gained predominance of the Middle Ravine and Mill Creek. On one notable occasion: "The Americans had the assurance to bring down a small piece of cannon to fire as their morning gun, so near to our quarter-guard that the wadding rebounded against the works."[214]

The Americans, who rarely numbered more than a few score men every night, succeeded in regularly alarming the entire British camp. Every dawn and sunset the British army performed "stand-to" with each man at his defensive post, the artillery ready to fire. Though a prudent and necessary precaution, three continuous weeks of this absolutely exhausted Burgoyne's army. Riedesel described the situation, demonstrating his mastery of the military profession: "The outposts were more and more molested, the army was weakened by sick, wounded and the sending off of detachments, the enemy swarmed in its rear, threatening the strongest positions, the army was as good as cut off from its outposts, while in addition to all this . . . the soldiers had but little rest."[215] Lieutenant Anburey similarly recalled: "Beyond the ground where we defeated our

[210]Brown and Peckham, *Journals of Henry Dearborn*, 108; Boyle, "From Saratoga to Valley Forge," 247–248; and Digby, *British Invasion from the North*, 286.

[211]Squier, ed., "Diary of Ephraim Squier," 693.

[212]Boardman, "Journal of Oliver Boardman," 228.

[213]Digby, *British Invasion from the North*, 286.

[214]Jackman, *With Burgoyne from Quebec*, 181.

[215]Stone, *Memoirs of Major General Riedesel*, 157.

enemy, all is hostile and dangerous in an alarming degree. . . . It seems to be the plan of the enemy to harass us by constant attacks, which they are enabled to do without fatiguing their army." He continued: "We have within these few evenings . . . been under arms most of the night."[216] Major Acland, the commanding officer of the Grenadier Battalion with Fraser's advance corps, remembered: "our camp being within a mile & half of the enemies our advanced pickets & patrols were perpetually engaged with the enemies so that neither night or day were we free from skirmishes near some part of the camp or other."[217] The wife of General Riedesel recorded: "The army were engaged daily in small skirmishes, but all of them of little consequence. My poor husband, however, during the whole time could not get a chance either to go to bed or undress."[218]

The contributions of the Oneida, Tuscarora, and Stockbridge Mohican warriors who fought for the Continental Army during the three weeks of late September and early October 1777 have received scant recognition by historians. Clearly they played a major role in the American success in the war of the outposts, and their services were welcomed and appreciated at the time by such men as Daniel Morgan and Henry Dearborn as they contested ground with the British army. Together, the riflemen and soldiers of the Continental Army and their Native allies decisively won this little-heralded phase of the campaign.

Further complicating the British situation, while Burgoyne hesitated for three weeks, his army continuously consumed the thirty days' rations that had been accumulated with such great efforts. Burgoyne was forced to place the army on half rations on October 3, 1777.[219] Even worse, the draft animals of the army were starving, as nearly all of the forage in the vicinity had been used up. The Americans, and particularly their American Indian allies, crowded in on all sides around the British encampment. Individual British foragers, and even small parties, were regularly scooped up by the Americans. Desertion was becoming rampant. Burgoyne's army was in desperate circumstances, hungry, exhausted, demoralized—and much worse, Burgoyne had lost the initiative, with his freedom of action severely constrained.

---

[216]Jackman, *With Burgoyne from Quebec*, 177, 181.

[217]Thorp, *Acland Journal*, 31.

[218]Baroness Von Riedesel, "Her Revolutionary Journal," in Rankin, ed., *Narratives of the American Revolution*, 322.

[219]Rogers, *Hadden's Orderly Books and Journal*, 325–326.

Of Burgoyne's personal and leadership activities during the three weeks between September 20 and October 6, little is known. Once he had advanced from Fort Miller, his correspondence for all practical purposes ceased, as he simply could not get messengers through to his garrisons on Lake George and at Fort Ticonderoga. Only a few intrepid, and one suspects incredibly lucky, messengers managed to thread their way south to Clinton. The papers herein do document Burgoyne's efforts to establish communications with Sir Henry Clinton in New York City. Burgoyne had managed to get at least one earlier message through Clinton to Lord Howe, which had been dispatched while the American Northern Theater Army was still disorganized and reeling from defeat and retreat at Ticonderoga (File 6.16/23a). This letter was written by Burgoyne on August 6. What date it reached New York City and who carried it are not known.[220] Clinton sent this letter on to Howe as requested by Burgoyne, and it reached him in Philadelphia on October 7. Clinton certainly sent a dispatch (which has not been documented) in response to Burgoyne.

The great obstacle that had to be overcome, of course, was that two large contingents of the Continental Army controlled the ground between Burgoyne and Clinton. Direct communications were impossible. A dispatch sent down Lake Champlain, then down the Richelieu and St. Lawrence rivers, and finally around New England via the North Atlantic to New York City would typically require six weeks to be delivered, and the excessive time involved precluded use of this line of communications. This meant that Burgoyne had to solicit volunteers to wear civilian clothes and carry concealed dispatches through the two American armies to Clinton. Needless to say, this was an extremely hazardous venture. If caught, such messengers were legally spies and would almost certainly be unceremoniously hanged in accordance with contemporary military laws. It says much for Burgoyne's charisma, and the morale of his army, that he apparently never lacked for volunteers for what practically amounted to a suicide mission.

The messages had to be either concealed or verbal. Sometime before Burgoyne departed Boston in late 1775, he and Clinton had established

[220]One successful courier was Joseph Bettys of Ballstown, New York, who was later one of the Canadian Department's most successful Secret Service operatives. He is believed to have carried messages for Burgoyne in 1777.

what they referred to a as a "cipher" so that they could write with candor between each other, without fear of their true intentions being revealed (File 18:47a, Henry Clinton Papers). The fact that Burgoyne and Clinton established such a cipher so early on is compelling evidence of the considerable friendship that had been forged between them in 1775. Roughly shaped like an hourglass, this cipher outline cut from a piece of paper would be used to write a legitimate military dispatch within its boundaries, and then the remainder of the sheet of paper would be filled in with a seemingly trivial, personal letter. One might reasonably assume that such a cipher would have been carefully safeguarded, but Burgoyne managed somehow to lose his, as he explained in a letter to Clinton dated September 23, 1776 (File 6.16/23b): "I have lost the old Cipher, but being sure from the Tenor of your Letter, you meant it to be so read, I have made it out." Apparently Burgoyne made a new cipher from memory, and Clinton and Burgoyne used this cipher to write to each other at least as early as November 1776, and they employed this cipher throughout 1777.

Although their routes are not documented, most likely Burgoyne's carefully disguised messengers crossed the pontoon bridge over the Hudson River under cover of darkness and proceeded south on the eastern shore of the Hudson River. The greatest portion of Gates's army was on Bemis Heights, opposing Burgoyne on the western bank of the river. The American army in the Hudson Highlands similarly had its strongest garrisons at Forts Montgomery and Clinton on the western bank of the river. Finally, to the south the Mohawk River flowed from the west into the Hudson River, and by traversing the Hudson's eastern bank a perilous crossing over this tributary could be avoided. By employing an eastern route, a messenger would marginally improve his chances of successfully reaching New York City.

The papers in the volume document that at least three of Burgoyne's messengers reached Clinton, although only one of Clinton's messengers similarly made it through the American lines to Burgoyne. Burgoyne related (File 6.16/24): "[September] 21st. A Messenger Arrived from Sir Henry Clinton with a Letter in Cyphers informing me of his intention to attack Fort Montgomery in about 10 Days from the date of his Letter, which was the Tenth Sept^{r}[.] [T]his was the only Messenger of many that I apprehend were dispatched by Sir William Howe and him that had reached my Camp." This establishes a rough time frame of eleven days for a messenger from Clinton to reach Burgoyne.

Based on a brief comment in one of Burgoyne's notes, he dispatched his messages in triplicate to increase the probability that they would get through. Burgoyne sent Clinton a brief written message on September 23, then dispatched two officers with detailed verbal messages on September 27 and 28 that were duplicates of the same primary dispatch.

The first communication, written on September 23, contained a letter in cipher, and presumably provided a longer verbal message (File 6.16/23b). This message was carried by Lieutenant Daniel Taylor of the 9th Regiment of Foot, a Loyalist originally from Kinderhook, New York, whose knowledge of the local topography and community contacts were invaluable for this purpose. Lieutenant Taylor reached Clinton on October 5. The second dispatch was a verbal message that Burgoyne transmitted on September 27. Carried by a "Captain Scott," it was received by Clinton at Fort Montgomery on October 9 (File 6.16/23e). Actually this was Lieutenant Thomas Scott of the 24th Foot, who had been detached to Fraser's Company of Select Marksmen in 1776 and 1777, had earned a reputation as a hardy and strong officer capable of independent action, and must have garnered some knowledge of woodcraft and stealth from service with the American Indian warriors that often accompanied Fraser's Rangers.

A third copy of this dispatch was sent by Burgoyne on September 28. A "Captain Campbell" carried this brief written message, doubtless also in cipher, with a considerably longer and more detailed verbal message. Campbell also reached Clinton on October 5 (File 6.16/23c). Burgoyne wrote: "The bearer, Capt. Campbell, an officer of Great Merit, and full Confidence, is Charged with an Exact duplicate of my Message to your Excy, dispatched Yesterday by another Officer, I request the most Speedy Answer by Triplicates." There were numerous Captain Campbells in Burgoyne's army. This is believed to be Captain Colin Campbell of the Royal Highland Emigrants, who was on detached service during this campaign with the Indian Department, of which his brother, Major John Campbell, was superintendent. As with Lieutenant Scott, it appears that service with the Indians was deemed to increase the likelihood that a covert messenger could successfully negotiate the challenges of a comparatively long and extremely dangerous passage—while avoiding innumerable American patrols in the process.

A message written by Clinton in response to Captain Campbell's arrival was sent on October 8, with a courtesy copy sent to Lord Howe; but there is no record that this message ever actually passed through the American cordon to Burgoyne, for the copy that Burgoyne had within his papers (File 6.16/23d] was actually the copy of record provided by Clinton to Howe. Captain Campbell attempted to carry this message to Burgoyne but was forced to turn back. Returning to the City of New York, as a reward for his courage and the hazards that he had faced Captain Campbell was given a commission as a captain in the 1st Battalion, 71st Regiment, on October 14, 1778.[221] Captain Campbell was fortunate, in that he escaped apprehension.

At least one other messenger was considerably less fortunate. Lieutenant Taylor, attempting to pass behind the Continental Army garrison at New Windsor on the western shore of the Hudson, was captured on October 10. He had the misfortune to encounter American soldiers wearing British army uniforms and had "discovered himself to them." Lieutenant Taylor could not possibly have known it, but this was not an uncommon event, for a number of shiploads of British army uniforms had been captured by American privateers, and the clothing was confiscated and routinely issued to the worst clad among the Continental Army. Facing interrogation by General George Clinton, governor of New York and commander of the state militia, Lieutenant Taylor swallowed "a small silver ball of an oval form, about the size of a fusee bullet, and shut with a screw in the middle." Unfortunately for Taylor, in 1777 common medical techniques included the liberal use of purgatives of various types, and a Continental Army surgeon was swiftly summoned who prescribed the appropriate treatment ("a strong dose of tartar emittic"), which soon brought the incriminating evidence to the light. Desperate, Taylor grabbed it and successfully concealed it again. General Clinton, losing patience with the game, calmly "demanded the ball on pain of being hung up instantly and cut open to search it. This brought

[221]This information is provided by Mr. Erick Schnitzer, interpretive ranger at Saratoga National Historical Park, in a living history unit's Web site: www.62ndregiment.org.

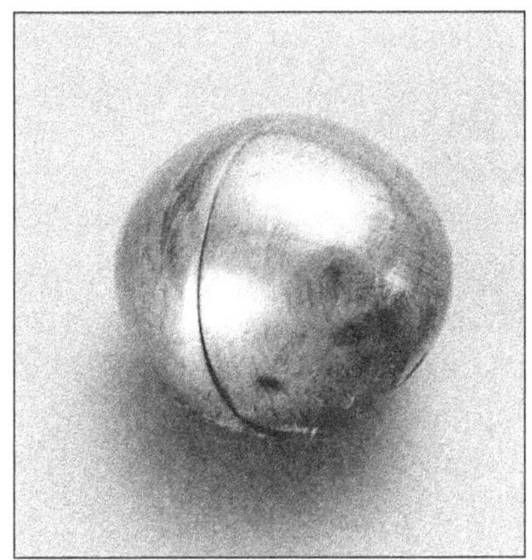

This is the silver musket ball swallowed by Lieutenant Daniel Taylor, 9th Regiment of Foot, in the presence of Brigadier General George Clinton of the New York State Militia at New Windsor, New York, on October 8, 1777. It contained a message from Sir Henry Clinton to Burgoyne that would never be delivered. *Courtesy Fort Ticonderoga Museum.*

it forth." Contained within this silver musket ball was the message from Clinton to Burgoyne that he had written on October 8 from Fort Montgomery (identical to File 6.16/23d sent by Clinton to Howe).[222] Trapped, Taylor "confessed his being an Express from General Clinton to General Burgoyne when taken. And that he had been employed as an Express also from General Burgoyne to General Clinton." His message intercepted, Taylor was given a general court-martial on October 14, but the outcome of the trial was scarcely in doubt, and he was hanged on the morning of October 17.[223] It was also noted that Isaac Van Vleck was "taken up as a spy" with Taylor at New Windsor, but his fate is unknown. If he was a civilian, as his name indicates, he would not have received the courtesy of a court-martial that a commissioned British officer was afforded, and doubtless was summarily hanged.[224]

Before Burgoyne resumed his advance in early October, he attempted to send another set of messengers to Clinton, presumably under the cover of the movement of a force across the Hudson River on October 2 and 3, but there is no evidence that any of them ever got through. Surgeon James Thacher with the Continental Army recorded that one "Nathan

[222]Clinton, *Public Papers of George Clinton*, 1:404, 413–414.

[223]Ibid., 1:443–444.

[224]Ibid., 1:415.

Palmer" was seized near Peekskill "under suspicious circumstances" and shortly thereafter hanged as a British spy by General Israel Putnam during this time frame. Thacher noted: "Messengers or persons in the character of spies are frequently suspected of passing from one British commander to the other."[225] With the Americans fully on the alert, it appears that no messengers successfully negotiated the passage between Burgoyne and Clinton in early October.

Regarding Burgoyne's other activities during this period, besides his efforts to communicate with Clinton, almost nothing is documented. One glimpse, however, is afforded to us through the efforts of the renowned American historian William L. Stone in 1886:

> On one of my visits to the [Saratoga] battleground I pointed out to Mr. Wilbur, on whose land we were then standing, the place designated by the Brunswick Journal as Burgoyne's Headquarters. "That" exclaimed Mr. Wilbur "explains what I have often wondered at." He then stated that when he first plowed up that particular spot, he was accustomed to find great quantities of old gin and wine bottles, and that, until now, he had often been puzzled to know "how on earth those bottles came here!"[226]

Burgoyne made his headquarters in his marquee tent, pitched in the center of the British main lines. The Baroness Von Riedesel, who had accompanied her husband on the campaign, was extremely critical of Burgoyne, noting of him during this critical juncture: "General Burgoyne was very fond of indulging, he spent half the night in singing and drinking . . . he was very fond of champagne."[227]

Certainly at this time Burgoyne was under considerable stress. When John McAlpine, a Scottish emigrant who lived near Crown Point and had proven himself to be a devoted Loyalist, as he had served as a volunteer throughout the 1776 and 1777 campaigns, asked to be permitted to return to his home in early October 1777, he was summoned to meet with Burgoyne personally.[228] McAlpine recorded: "how great was my disappointment when, in place of any reward or even bare mention of it, I found a very cold, indifferent reception from General Burgoyne, who

[225]James Thacher, *A Military Journal*, 99.

[226]Stone, *Saratoga Battle-Grounds*', 92.

[227]Von Riedesel, "Her Revolutionary Journal," 331.

[228]Alternately spelled "M'Alpine." I have used the modern spelling and pronunciation of the name "McAlpine."

asked me if I was seriously going to leave him at this critical time of danger" and "he passionately then turned upon me, saying vehemently that I might depend on it I had for ever forfeited his recommendations, liberality and friendship & he had rather that I had joined the rebels than have deserted him in the present critical juncture."[229]

Burgoyne delayed in his fortifications for nearly three weeks, consuming his rations; losing the war of outposts to his front, flanks, and rear; and hoping for either Sir Henry Clinton or Colonel St. Leger to move to his relief. Finally, by early in October, Burgoyne realized that he could no longer remain in place. He would have to either resume his advance or retreat back to Ticonderoga while he still could.

Burgoyne's Reconnaissance in Force, Barber's Wheatfield, October 7

During the various failed attempts at British reconnaissance, all of which had been turned away by the alert American patrols, an intimation of "high ground" to the west of the American primary fortifications had been discerned, but could not be confirmed. Burgoyne determined to assemble a reconnaissance in force of picked men, approximately 1,500 soldiers consisting of the battalions of British Light Infantry and Grenadiers and the 24th Regiment of Foot from Fraser's advance corps, and a composite force of Hessian infantry with the core being the Riedesel Regiment under Colonel Von Specht, acting directly under Riedesel. This reconnaissance in force included a strong contingent of artillery: two 12-pounder cannon and four 6-pounder cannon manned by the Royal Artillery, and two 6-pounder cannon of the Hesse-Hanau Artillery. Burgoyne personally accompanied the column, joined by Major General Phillips, Brigadier General Fraser, and Major General Riedesel. Brigadier General Hamilton remained behind commanding the British lines. Burgoyne's intent was to gather forage for his starving draft animals, move forward to confirm the location of the high ground, and then occupy it. If successful, he intended to have Phillips bring up the artillery train the next day, supported by the entirety of his army, to drive

[229]M'Alpine, *Genuine Narratives and Concise Memoirs*, 32–35.

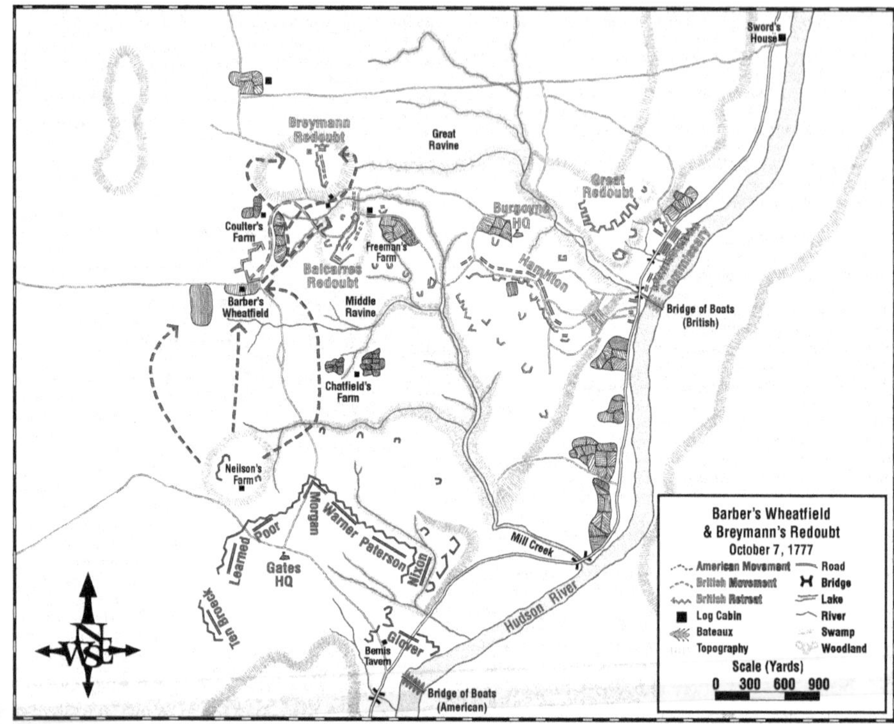

Barber's Wheatfield and vicinity, October 7, 1777.
Map prepared by SunSyne Graphics, http://www.sunsyne.com

the Americans out of their strong defensive position. Burgoyne's entire scheme of maneuver was rather desperate. It was entirely predicated on this detachment of 1,500 soldiers being able to absorb and repulse any American counterattack, and then being able to locate, occupy, and hold the high ground around the American left (west) flank, thus setting the conditions for the continued advance of the remainder of his army and his train of heavy artillery the next day. In the gambling vernacular so familiar to Burgoyne, the effort was a long shot indeed.

Burgoyne's column departed the Balcarres Redoubt at 11:00 A.M. on October 7, marched past the abandoned Coulter's Farm on rutted farm lanes, and occupied a large wheatfield located immediately south of Barber's Farm at about 1:00 P.M. (the times are approximate, not precise). Here Burgoyne deployed his infantry and artillery to his front, with the Light Infantry Battalion on the right (west) occupying another open farm field separated from the wheatfield by a thin stretch of wood; the Grenadier Battalion with the two 12-pounders anchoring his left (east) flank astride the farm road continuing to the south; and the Germans and remainder of the artillery, a line of British and Hessian six 6-pounders, occupying the center. The 24th Regiment of Foot was stationed astride the road that they had marched up, slightly to the left rear (northeast) in reserve. While members of the Quartermaster Department gathered desperately needed forage from the wheatfield for the use of his animals, Burgoyne and his senior officers ascended to the roof of the cabin, endeavoring with their field glasses to perceive the valuable rise to their south. They were not successful, as this promontory, although it was within artillery range of the Neilson House on the Continental Army's western flank, was not visible from the wheatfield.[230] At some point in the early afternoon, Burgoyne issued orders to post a small detachment of the 20th Foot to the north of Barber's Wheatfield to maintain communications with the Balcarres Redoubt.[231]

This was a brief calm before the storm, for Burgoyne's advance had been discovered nearly as soon as his column departed their works, and Gates had immediately ordered out an overwhelming response to turn aside Burgoyne's thrust. About 3:00 P.M. the blow fell in a classic double envelopment, launched from the cover of the woods upon both of Burgoyne's flanks. The grenadiers, astride the road and thus closest to the Americans, were the first to fold. Shortly thereafter the light infantry, assailed in front and flank, collapsed. With the grenadiers fragmenting, the British withdrawal route was immediately endangered. Brigadier General Fraser perceived the deteriorating tactical situation at a glance. He immediately summoned his own regiment, the 24th Foot, forward from reserve and began to deploy it to cover a British retrograde movement, which he realized was now inevitable. In the process,

[230] This has been confirmed by extensive "boots on the ground" terrain research performed by the author at Saratoga National Historical Park. Historians commonly refer to this engagement as the Battle of Bemis Heights, although the fight was nowhere near this ridge. I have chosen to use the more accurate "Battle of Barber's Wheatfield."

[231] Burgoyne, *State of the Expedition from Canada*, 71.

Fraser was mortally wounded. With his fall, the British disintegration was complete.

Burgoyne remained on the battlefield until it was apparent that the fight was lost. He then issued orders to General Phillips for the detachment to conduct a general retreat, and simultaneously dispatched his aide-de-camp with an order to the artillery to withdraw from the field, never delivered as Sir Francis Clerke was mortally wounded and captured.[232] All eight artillery pieces were seized, and the British reconnaissance in force fled in disarray to the north beyond Coulter's Farm, past which they had confidently marched only a few short hours before. Burgoyne's gambit had been crushed.

Burgoyne then returned to the Balcarres Redoubt to frantically organize a desperate defense there, for most of its garrison had been stripped to participate in the morning's reconnaissance. The shattered British and German soldiers streaked in panic and confusion back to the redoubt. Lieutenant Digby, who had accompanied the ill-fated reconnaissance, recalled:

> On our retreating, which was pretty regular, considering how hard we were pressed by the enemy, General Burgoyne appeared greatly agitated as the danger to which the lines were exposed was of the most serious nature at that particular period. I should be sorry from my expression of *agitated,* that the reader should imagine the fears of personal danger was the smallest cause of it. He must be more than man, who could undisturbed look on and preserve his natural calmness, when the fate of so many were at stake, and entirely depended on the orders he was to issue. He said but little, well knowing we could defend the lines or fall in the attempt.[233]

Lieutenant Thomas Anburey of the 24th Foot had remained in the entrenched camp, being assigned to guard duty that morning, and was thus present as Burgoyne reached the camp:

> The troops came pouring into camp as fast as they could, and shortly after Generals Burgoyne, Phillips and Riedesel. It is impossible to describe the anxiousness depicted in the countenance of General Burgoyne, who immediately rode up to the quarter guards, and when he came to that of our regiment, I was across the ravine, posting a sergeant's guard. Upon

[232]Ibid., 71–72.

[233]Digby, *British Invasion from the North*, 288–289.

> enquiring eagerly for the officer, I came to him. "Sir," said the General, "you must defend this post to the very last man." You may easily conceive, upon receiving those orders, I judged everything to be in a dangerous situation. There was not a moment for thought, for the Americans stormed with great fury the post of the light infantry, under the command of Lord Balcarres, rushing close to the lines, under a severe fire of grape-shot and small arms. This post was defended with great spirit, and the enemy, led on by General Arnold, as gallantly assaulted the works.[234]

Fortunately for the British, Burgoyne took active charge of the defenses of the Balcarres Redoubt, for the aggressive Arnold had arrived on the battlefield determined to immediately launch an attack against the British earthwork, the first that the American pursuit encountered. Under Arnold's direct leadership, the American Continentals and militia launched a furious assault on the British entrenched camp. The British defenders were hard-pressed, but the American assaults were finally repulsed, owing predominantly to deadly artillery fire.[235] Burgoyne urgently dispatched one of his aides, Captain the Earl of Harrington, with a note to Brigadier General Hamilton "for all the works in the rear of the camp . . . to be manned."[236]

Arnold backed off while yet another assault pressed in, attempting to discern a weakness in the British arrangements. He astutely observed that the draw between the main Balcarres Camp and the Breymann Redoubt to the northwest was guarded only by a pair of log cabins. Arnold directed Morgan, Dearborn, and other American forces to sweep up that defilade, while Burgoyne and the British defenders were fully occupied in repulsing yet another furious wave of American frontal attacks against both the British and German entrenched camps. The few Canadians put up a token resistance, but were tumbled out of their position in short order. In moments Arnold and his men were in the rear of the Breymann breastwork, and it was entirely exposed to their assault. Turning swiftly to their left (north) Arnold's troops overwhelmed the comparatively few German defenders, now fighting in two directions, and killed Lieutenant Colonel Breymann. With his death, the German resistance crumbled, and the two 6-pounder cannon in the works

[234]Jackman, *With Burgoyne from Quebec*, 184–185.

[235]Cubbison, *"Artillery never gained more Honour,"* 123–124.

[236]Burgoyne, *State of the Expedition from Canada*, 72.

were seized. Fortunately for the British, it was now sunset, and Arnold had been critically wounded by a gunshot wound to the leg. With his wounding, the American attacks ceased for the night.

The Breymann Redoubt occupied a hill thirty feet higher in elevation than the Balcarres Redoubt and was only 1,500 feet to the north, well within the "point-blank" range of the 6-pounder cannon captured by the Americans. Once the Breymann Redoubt had been seized, given its higher elevation and close artillery range, the Balcarres Redoubt would no longer be tenable.[237] In turn, if the Balcarres Redoubt fell, the main British lines across the Mill Creek ravine would be similarly enfiladed. Accordingly, on the evening of October 7 Burgoyne ordered a general retreat across the Great Ravine to the main British fortified camp, approximately half a mile to the rear (north) of the breastworks of the British Regular Brigade and Riedesel's German division. The day ended with the British having sustained not one but two crushing defeats. Burgoyne's reconnaissance in force had been smashed—and with it his delusion of capturing Albany that year.

British Retreat to Saratoga and the Convention of Saratoga, October 7–17, 1777

Having crossed the Great Ravine to his Great Redoubt, Burgoyne began organizing his army for the now inevitable retreat to Canada. On October 8 Brigadier General Simon Fraser died of his wounds. That afternoon he was buried inside one of the British redoubts, in a somber funeral service attended by all of the senior officers of the British army, Burgoyne included, conducted despite the accompaniment of heavy American artillery fire. Although General Gates had not yet bestirred himself, the Continental Army was beginning to tighten the noose around Burgoyne.

The mass of American cannonballs raining down around his positions convinced Burgoyne of the necessity of a rapid departure, and the British withdrawal commenced at 8:00 P.M. with the march of the advance guard, followed by the artillery park and supply train an hour later. Burgoyne lacked sufficient carriage to evacuate his seriously wounded

[237]Cubbison, *"Artillery never gained more Honour,"* 125.

soldiers from his army field hospital, and he had to leave them behind. Accordingly, he "sent in a flagg, desiring Genl Gates to take care of the Sick and wounded he left behind, as he lay under a Necessity of moving his Army, which consented to be taken as Prisoners of War, being in number about four hundred."[238] This was a common practice in the eighteenth century, and Gates responded honorably and appropriately.

By three o'clock in the morning of October 9, the rear of Burgoyne's column closed at Dovegot House. In six hours of marching, they had traversed five and one-half miles. This was certainly not the spirited pace that would be required if Burgoyne held out any hope of returning safely to Ticonderoga. Desertion remained a serious concern in the British ranks, intimating that discipline and morale was disintegrating. One American officer reported that "40 or 50 Deserters come to our Camp this morning."[239] Worsening the rapidly deteriorating British situation, torrential rains began to descend at about ten o'clock on the morning of October 9.[240] Burgoyne instructed that the retreat resume at about 4:00 P.M., and by 9:00 P.M. the British column had reoccupied the earthworks located on the Heights of Saratoga that they had constructed approximately one month previously (September 13–15). Again, Burgoyne's march was dilatory, he gained only two and one-half miles in five hours of effort, and inexplicably the retreat ground to a halt at Saratoga, with nearly the entire night remaining.

By this point in the campaign, Burgoyne had displayed an utter lack of determination and resolution. Following the Battle of Freeman's Farm it must have been apparent to him that he lacked the combat power to shove the Continental Northern Theater Army out of the way and to reach Albany. However, rather than returning to Canada while he still could, he instead remained in place, clearly trusting that his friend Sir Henry Clinton would launch an effective attack in his support. Clinton eventually did so, but too late to help Burgoyne. Taken within this context, Burgoyne's General Orders of June 30 (no file #) that stated "This Army must not retreat" were not mere hyperbole. Rather, it is obvious that Burgoyne absolutely believed that this statement constituted his mission. Burgoyne himself had informed the Baroness Von Riedesel,

[238]Boyle, "From Saratoga to Valley Forge," 249.

[239]Ibid.; and Boardman, "Journal of Oliver Boardman," 229.

[240]Riedesel, "Her Revolutionary Journal," 329–330.

the wife of General Riedesel, that "the English never lose ground."[241] Certainly, Burgoyne delayed the resumption of his movement forward as long as possible, hoping that his advance would coincide with Clinton's. But following the debacle of October 7, Burgoyne knew that he had no option except to retreat. Yet, for some reason, his movements were slow and confused. The baroness would later note of this period, recording a tactical opportunity to take an isolated American detachment that Burgoyne had not exploited, with the comment: "They might easily have been prisoners by our own troops, had not General Burgoyne lost his head."[242] It appears that Burgoyne suffered some type of breakdown in early October, whether physical through exhaustion from the constant skirmish warfare that continuously kept the British camp alarmed, mental from the stress imposed by a dangerous situation, or self-induced through the liberal consumption of alcohol. His papers, however, fail to reveal any insight into such a possibility.[243] But the aggressive, self-confident, hard-hitting, and swiftly moving cavalry commander was entirely absent in early October 1777.

Lieutenant Colonel Sutherland with the 47th Regiment of Foot actually marched to the Batten Kill Creek on October 10 to scout the retreat route north and found it still open, though Americans were entrenched north of Fort Edward and whether or not Burgoyne could have continued his withdrawal beyond that point is questionable. An abortive American attack was launched across Fishkill Creek on the morning of October 11, but it scarcely mattered, as by that date Burgoyne was not only stalled in place, but trapped. Possibly hastened by this aggressive American probe, Burgoyne ordered his army to continue the retreat on the evening of October 12 based on Sutherland's successful reconnaissance. It was only two miles to Batten Kill Creek, seven miles to Fort Miller, and another seven to Fort Edward. A long night's march could have readily carried Burgoyne from Saratoga to Fort Edward, but it was not to be, as he inexplicably canceled his orders just as the march was beginning. Only his few remaining Indian allies, in the van of the column, managed to get away.

[241]Ibid., 319.

[242]Ibid., 329.

[243]Burgoyne candidly wrote Lord George Germain at the end of the campaign: "I am sunk in mind and body." Davies, *Documents of the American Revolution*, 14:237.

The only thing more dilatory than Burgoyne's retreat was Gates's pursuit, although what supervision the American commander failed personally to provide was substituted for by aggressive subordinate leadership that was acting to tighten the loop around Burgoyne, generously assisted by Burgoyne's stinted marches.

By the morning of October 13, Burgoyne's situation was desperate. The Continental Army entirely surrounded his army. Most of Burgoyne's provisions were now expended, and his troops had been on half rations for more than a week. The draft animals were dying in place from starvation, as all forage had long since been used up. American riflemen crept along the south bank of Fishkill Creek and east bank of the Hudson River, and prevented the British from even obtaining water except under cover of darkness. Numerous American artillery batteries were similarly emplaced, and they ranged the entire British camp, sweeping the ground with deadly accurate artillery fire. Corporal George Fox of the 47th Regiment distinctly remembered: "They had three batteries playing upon us . . . here a six pound ball took the bottom of my knapsack off."[244]

Two councils of war held at Burgoyne's headquarters on October 12 and 13 determined that the situation was indeed hopeless (File 6.16/24i). On the evening of October 13, at precisely 9:00 P.M., Burgoyne sent a note to Gates (File 6.16/24a) "upon a Matter of high moment to both Armies." The "matter of high moment" was, of course, the capitulation of the British army.

Burgoyne's and Gates's officers met at 10:00 A.M. the next morning. Burgoyne was represented by Major Robert Kingston, his adjutant general and military secretary, and Captain James Craig of the 47th Regiment of Foot, who had been badly wounded at Hubbardton and had served as one of Burgoyne's aides-de-camp during his convalescence.[245] Gates was represented by Lieutenant Colonel James Wilkinson, his extremely young aide-de-camp. For the first time, the papers published

[244]Houlding and Yates, "Corporal Fox's Memoir of Service," 160.

[245]Major Robert Kingston (c. 1736–c. 1793) entered the British army as an ensign in 1756. He had served with Burgoyne in Portugal with the 16th Dragoons in 1761. He remained with that corps through 1768. He accompanied Burgoyne to Canada as his adjutant general in 1777 and was promoted to lieutenant colonel in August 1777. Upon the death of Sir Francis Clerke at the Battle of Barber's Wheatfield on October 7, he became Burgoyne's secretary. Kingston became a major general in 1793 and he is believed to have died shortly thereafter. Rogers, *Hadden's Journal and Orderly Books*, 62–65.

herein permit a complete picture from Burgoyne's perspective of the surrender negotiations, as they provide all correspondence between the two commanders, including four previously unpublished communications.

At this meeting, to the consternation of the British officers, Gates's chief representative, Wilkinson, introduced terms previously prepared by Gates (File 6.16/24c). This was in direct contravention of the established eighteenth-century military custom that dictated that the commander who had been forced to yield would propose the conditions under which he would capitulate.[246] For the victor to propose such terms was unprecedented, and a breach of tradition. Furthermore, Gates's first statement was: "Genl. Burgoyne's Army being exceedingly reduced by repeated Defeats by desertion Sickness &c. their Provisions exhausted their military Horses, Tents and Baggage taken or destroyed their retreat cut off and their Camp invested they can only be allowed to surrender Prisoners of War." This was a most impertinent opening proposal, not to mention a violation of the tenets of eighteenth-century honors and protocol.

Still, Burgoyne had little choice but to respond, accepting some of the terms, discarding or modifying others (File 6.16/24c). However, Burgoyne found Gates's sixth article to be particularly egregious: "These terms being agreed to and signed The troops under his Excellency Genl. Burgoyne's Command may be drawn up in their Encampments where they will be ordered to Ground their Arms and may thereupon be marched to the River side to be passed over in their way towards Bennington." An army that had been forced to surrender after an honorable resistance would expect to march out of its fortifications to yield, thus indicating that it still held its own works, and remained capable of a defense. Thus, by permitting Gates to occupy his entrenchments, Burgoyne would admit that he was no longer capable of maintaining an effective defense, and had been defeated. Such an admission would have obviously proven false Burgoyne's delusion that he was entering into a "convention" instead of being forced to surrender, so he adamantly rejected this article thus: "This Article inadmissible in any extremity sooner than this Army will consent to ground their Arms in their Encampments they will rush on the Enemy determined to take no Quarter." Burgoyne must have become absolutely livid over this article,

[246]Wright, "Sieges and Customs of War," 639.

and with the backing of a second council of war on October 14 (File 6.16/24i), he sent Major Kingston back to Lieutenant Colonel Wilkinson with a curt demand (File 6.16/24d): "If General Gates does not mean to recede from the sixth Article the Treaty ends at once. The Army will to a Man proceed to any Act of Desperation rather than submit to that Article. The Cessation of Arms ends this Evening."

Gates ceded to Burgoyne, for the truce continued through the next morning, when Burgoyne returned the negotiations to a more traditional format by submitting his own proposals to Gates (File 6.16/24e). This proposal by Burgoyne, dated October 15, would essentially set the Convention that would be signed. The critical terms were the initial two: "1st The Troops to march out of their Camp with the Honours of War and the Artillery of the Intrenchments which will be left as hereafter may be regulated" and "2nd A free Passage to be granted to this Army to Great Britain upon Condition of not serving again in North America during the present Contest and a proper Port to be assigned for the Entry of Transports to receive the troops wherever Genl Howe shall so order." The first essentially abrogated Gates's original, and demeaning (to the British), proposals of October 14. The second removed Burgoyne's army from North America, but was craftily framed such that Burgoyne's army would not be considered to be prisoners of war, and thus the British government could simply use Burgoyne's army to replace other soldiers in Britain or other garrisons worldwide, and then dispatch the relieved soldiers to North America. Burgoyne must have been gratified, if not surprised, when Gates accepted this term. In short order, another council of war (File 6.16/24i) met on October 15 and found the negotiations to be acceptable. They were, to the British, much more than acceptable, and Burgoyne hastily agreed to the unexpectedly generous terms shortly after he had obtained the concurrence of his subordinate generals.

Why Gates was so conciliatory cannot positively be ascertained. By this date, he had certainly received news that Clinton had attacked and seized Forts Montgomery and Clinton on October 6 and captured Fort Constitution across the Hudson River from West Point on the next day. As the negotiations were proceeding, Sir Henry Clinton was moving unobstructed north up the Hudson, and he would reach the New York State capital at Kingston on October 16. Gates must have been panicked that he would have to defend against Clinton's army before it could seize his logistical base at Albany, and he was clearly in haste to finish with Burgoyne, preferably through negotiations, but if not through force of arms.

Burgoyne must have suspected that Clinton was pressuring Gates, though there is no evidence that any letter from Clinton had made its way through the tight American cordon to reach him. In any event, Burgoyne's messengers to Clinton had taken between eleven and twelve days to reach their destination. Clinton's letter (File 6.16/23d) written from Fort Montgomery on October 8 could not possibly have reached Burgoyne by the time that he initiated a ceasefire with Gates (Lieutenant Taylor, carrying one copy of the message, had only reached New Windsor by October 10). Accordingly, Burgoyne wrote two additional notes to Gates, one on October 15 (File 6.16/24f) and the other dated October 16 (File 6.16/24g), attempting to delay the negotiations. These thinly veiled efforts proved not to be successful, and Gates sent a terse verbal message to Burgoyne to either sign or fight. Not wishing to lose the generous terms, and with the condition of his army deteriorating nearly by the hour, Burgoyne agreed to the famous Convention of Saratoga on October 16 (File 6.16/24h).

The next morning it was all over, and Burgoyne's army laid down and marched away from their arms and artillery, and became prisoners of the Continental Army. The ceremony was conducted with decorum and honor, and the American army demonstrated considerable discipline during the exercise. Colonel Dudley Colman, who commanded a regiment of Massachusetts militia at the surrender, wrote home shortly afterward:

> It may I think be reckoned among the extraordinary events history furnishes us with, to have 5,000 and upwards of veteran, disciplined troops . . . surrounded, and their resources and retreat so cut off in the field, as to oblige them to surrender prisoners of war, without daring to come to further action, is an event I do not recollect to have met with in history, much less did I ever expect to see it in this war, I confess I could hardly believe it to be a reality when I saw it, the prospect was truly extremely pleasing to see our troops paraded in the best order, and to see march by as prisoners, after they had laid down their arms, those who but a few days before had pretended to despise us. I can but mention the good order observed by our troops on seeing them march by, no laughing or mark of exultation were to be seen among them, nothing more than a manly joy appeared on the countenances of our troops, which showed that they had fortitude of mind to bear prosperity without being too much elated, as well to encounter

Harry A. Ogden (1856–1936), *Burgoyne's Surrender.*
A late-nineteenth-century depiction by the renowned military artist, carefully researched and relatively accurate, of Burgoyne offering his sword to Major General Horatio Gates on the battlefield of Saratoga, October 17, 1777, who courteously returned it to Burgoyne.
Courtesy Fort Ticonderoga Museum.

> the greatest hardships and dangers it has likewise been observed to me by several of the British officers that they did not expect to be received in so polite a manner, and they never saw troops behave with more decency, or a better spirit on such an occasion.[247]

The Convention Army

Under the provisions of the Convention, Burgoyne's army was to march to Boston, and from there be returned to England. Burgoyne himself became a guest at the Albany mansion of General Philip Schuyler on

[247]Tulloch, ed., "Eye-Witness of Burgoyne's Surrender," 279–280.

Jacques Milbert, *Spot Where Burgoyne Surrendered* (Paris, 1825). This painting depicts the surrender of Burgoyne's army at the site of Fort Hardy on the Hudson River, as viewed from the east bank across the river. *Courtesy Fort Ticonderoga Museum.*

October 18, where Burgoyne, Phillips, and Riedesel, with their large staffs and considerable contingents of personal servants, proceeded to eat the Schuylers out of house and home for the next two weeks, only departing Albany for Boston on October 27.[248] Burgoyne had indeed reached Albany in 1777, but not in the manner he had envisioned in London that spring.

The army, however, marched immediately, and within weeks was installed around Boston. What was intended to be a relatively brief sojourn while the Crown provided transportation became a lengthy stay as Congress reviewed Gates's Convention, and ultimately rejected it. Thus, Burgoyne's soldiers unexpectedly found themselves stranded for an extended duration in Boston. The army had embarked in June upon what was meant to be a summer campaign. The replacement uniforms intended for the 1777 campaign had been captured by American

[248]Strach, *History of the Schuyler Mansion.*

Scott's *March of British Prisoners* (1877) depicts the progression of the British and German "Convention Army" from Saratoga to Boston, following its capitulation on October 17, 1777. *Courtesy Fort Ticonderoga Museum.*

privateers, so that Burgoyne's army had been forced to retain their worn coats, which had already survived one rigorous Canadian campaign, and patch them for a second year's service. By mid-October, the clothing of Burgoyne's army was badly worn, and the papers document one effort by Burgoyne to address this situation, which was being exacerbated by the onset of a New England winter (Haldimand Papers, File 21834). Also included is one additional letter from Burgoyne documenting that, even under parole, the exigencies of army administration and bureaucracy never really ended (Haldimand Papers, File 21834).

Within seven months, Lieutenant General John Burgoyne would be back in Britain, seeking a court-martial before Parliament (which he was denied by Germain) to salvage his reputation.[249] As General Henry Lloyd had accurately predicted, Burgoyne had returned "with his arms tied behind his back."

[249] Lewis, *Man Who Lost America*, 223.

Papers of Lieutenant General John Burgoyne Relating to the Saratoga Campaign, 1777

Special Collections and Archives, U.S. Military Academy[1]

Letter from Major General John Burgoyne to Lord Stanley,[2] Boston, June 25, 1775

Boston, June 25, 1775

Boston is a peninsula, joined to the main land only by a narrow neck, which on the first troubles Gen. Gage fortified; arms of the sea, and the harbour, surround the rest: on the other side one of these arms, to the North, is Charlestown (or rather was, for it is now rubbish), and over it a large hill, which is also, like Boston, a peninsula: to the South of the town is a still larger scope of ground, containing three hills, joining also to the main by a tongue of land, and called Dorchester Neck: the heights as above described, both North and South, (in the soldier's phrase) command the town, that is, given an opportunity of erecting batteries above any that you can make against them, and consequently are much more advantageous. It was absolutely necessary we should make ourselves masters of these heights, and we proposed to begin with Dorchester, because from particular situation of batteries and shipping (too long to describe, and unintelligible to you if I did) it would evidently be effected without any considerable loss: every thing was accordingly

[1]A printed version of this letter may be found at the Massachusetts Historical Society, Boston, www.masshist.org/bh/burgoyne.html (accessed August 12, 2010).

[2]Lord Edward Stanley (1752–1834), 12th Earl of Derby, Burgoyne's brother-in-law, and younger brother to Burgoyne's wife.

disposed; my two colleagues[3] and myself (who, by the bye, have never differed in one jot of military sentiment) had, in concert with Gen. Gage,[4] formed the plan: Howe was to land the transports on one point, Clinton in the center, and I was to cannonade from the Causeway, or the Neck; each to take advantage of circumstances: the operations must have been very easy; this was to have been executed on the 18th. On the 17th, at dawn of day, we found the enemy had pushed intrenchments with great diligence, during the night, on the heights of Charles-Town, and we evidently saw that every hour gave them fresh strength; it therefore became necessary to alter our plan, and attack on that side.

Howe, as second in command, was detached with about Two Thousand men, and landed on the outward side of the peninsula, covered with shipping, without opposition; he was to advance from thence up the hill which was over Charles-Town, where the strength of the enemy lay; he had under him Brigadier-General Pigot;[5] Clinton and myself took our stand (for we had not any fixed post) in a large battery directly opposite to Charles-Town, and commanding it,[6] and also reaching to the heights above it, and thereby facilitating Howe's attack. Howe's disposition was exceeding soldier-like; in my opinion it was perfect. As his first arm advanced up the hill, they met with a thousand impediments from strong fences, and were much exposed. They were also exceedingly hurt by musquetry from Charles-Town, though Clinton and I did not

[3]Major General William Howe and Major General Henry Clinton, whom Burgoyne had accompanied to Boston in April 1775.

[4]General Thomas Gage, British commander in chief of North America, and governor of Massachusetts. Gage had served without particular distinction in the Seven Years' War; as a lieutenant colonel of the 44th Foot, he fought with Braddock at the Battle of the Monongahela, raised the 80th Regiment of Foot (Gage's Light Infantry), and was promoted to colonel. He served as a brigadier general in North America throughout the 1756–60 campaigns. Upon the return of General Jeffery Amherst, Gage became commander in chief of North America, a position that offered him considerable challenges but little reward. He was recalled to England shortly after Bunker Hill.

[5]Brigadier General Robert Pigot (1720–1796), lieutenant colonel of the 10th Regiment of Foot, local brigadier general in North America. He commanded the left wing with great valor at Bunker Hill and was rewarded with a colonelcy of the 55th Foot. He served throughout the Revolutionary War without any particular distinction, his most prominent moment coming in 1778 when he successfully defended Rhode Island against a combined French-American attack led by Continental Army major general John Sullivan.

[6]The Copp's Hill Battery, at Boston. This battery had been established on April 23, 1775, and contained six 24-pounder cannon. It was located northeast of the North Burying Ground (now known as Copp's Hill Burial Ground), located atop the prominent Copp's Hill in the North End of Boston. Since the eighteenth century, the Burial Ground has expanded and it now covers the site of the battery. The National Park Service maintains interpretation at this site.

perceive it, till Howe sent us word by a boat, and desired us to set fire to the town, which was immediately done. We threw a parcel of shells, and the whole was instantly in flames. Our battery afterwards kept up an incessant fire on the heights; it was seconded by a number of frigates, floating batteries, and one ship of the line.

And now ensued one of the greatest scenes of war that can be conceived: if we look to the height, Howe's corps ascending the hill in the face of entrenchments, and in a very disadvantageous ground, was much engaged; and to the left the enemy pouring in fresh troops by thousands, over the land; and in the arm of the sea our ships and floating batteries cannonading them; strait before us a large and a noble town in one great blaze; the church steeples, being of timber, were great pyramids of fire above the rest; behind us the church steeples and heights of our own camp covered with spectators of the rest of our army which was not engaged; the hills round the country covered with spectators; the enemy all anxious suspense; the roar of cannon, mortars, and musquetry; the crush of churches, ships upon the stocks, and whole streets falling together in ruin, to fill the ear; the storm of the redoubts, with the objects above described, to fill the eye; and the reflection that perhaps a defeat was a final loss to the British empire in America, to fill the mind; made the whole a picture and a complication of horror and importance beyond any thing that ever came to my lot to be witness to. I much lament Tom's absence[7]—it was a sight for a young soldier that the longest service may not furnish again; and had he been with me would likewise have been out of danger; for, except two cannon balls that went an hundred yards over our heads, we were not on any part of the direction of the enemy's shot. A moment of the day was critical: Howe's left were staggered; two battalions had been sent to reinforce them, but we perceived them on the beach seeming in embarrassment what way to march; Clinton, then next for business, took the part, without waiting for orders, to throw himself into a boat to head them; he arrived in time to be of service, the day ended with glory, and the success was most important, considering the ascendancy it gave the regular troops; but the loss was uncommon in officers for the numbers engaged.

[7]Burgoyne's nephew, Thomas Stanley (1753–1779), and younger brother to Lord Stanley and Burgoyne's wife. He had departed London to serve as a volunteer with the British army in Boston but had apparently not arrived as of late June 1775. Eventually commissioned as a major, he died in service with the British army in Jamaica in the West Indies in 1779.

Howe was untouched, but his aide-de-camp Sherwin was killed;[8] Jordan, a friend of Howe's, who came, *engage du cœur,*[9] to see the campaign, (a ship-mate of ours on board the Cerberus, and who acted as aid-de-camp) is badly wounded.[10] Pigot was unhurt, but he behaved like a hero. You will see the list of the loss. Poor Col. Abercrombie,[11] who commanded the grenadiers, died yesterday of his wounds. Capt. Addison, our poor old friend, who arrived but the day before, and was to have dined with me on the day of the action, was also killed;[12] his son was upon the field at the time. Major Mitchell is but very slightly hurt; he is out already;[13] young Chetwynd's wound is also slight[.][14] Lord Percy's regiment[15] has suffered the most, and behaved the best; his Lordship himself was not in the action: — Lord Roden[16] behaved to a charm; his name is established for life.

Sir Henry Clinton Papers, File 17:24

Letter from Major General John Burgoyne to Major General Henry Clinton, [Fort] Chambly, [Canada], July 7, 1776

My dear Clinton:
Though without a guess by what means or in what place this letter will reach you, I cannot let pass the chance of a safe conveyance without

[8]Captain Sherwin of the 67th Regiment of Foot, Howe's aide-de-camp, was killed at Bunker Hill.
[9]Literally, "engaged of the heart."
[10]Most likely Lieutenant Jorden of the Royal Navy, reported wounded at Bunker Hill.
[11]Lieutenant Colonel James Abercrombie of the 22nd Regiment of Foot, killed at Bunker Hill.
[12]Captain Addison of the 52nd Regiment of Foot, killed at Bunker Hill.
[13]No Major Mitchell of the British army was reported to be wounded at Bunker Hill. Quartermaster Mitchell of the 38th Regiment of Foot was reported wounded.
[14]Ensign Chetwynd of the 52nd Regiment of Foot was wounded.
[15]Brigadier General Hugh Percy, colonel commanding the 5th Regiment of Foot.
[16]Lord Francis Rawdon-Hastings (17541826). Commissioned an ensign in the 15th Foot in 1771, then a lieutenant in the Grenadier Company of the 5th Regiment of Foot, joined his new regiment in Boston in 1774, participated in all three assaults at Bunker Hill, assumed command of his company after his company commander was wounded, and commanded the Grenadier Company for the remainder of the engagement. He would shortly be promoted to captain in the 63rd Regiment of Foot and given a company, in recognition for his valor. Burgoyne's assessment proved correct: Lord Rawdon served with considerable skill and accomplishment throughout the Revolutionary War.

assuring you of the sense my mind constantly bears of your friendship, of the interest it takes in your glory, and consequently of the impatience it feels to hear of your proceedings.

I wrote at [underline indicates emphasis in original] you twice before I left England, once in cipher when I expressed my sentiments at full. I also informed you of my destination, unsought for, to Canada. I had the good fortune to arrive early, and from the moment of my landing have been in chase of the rebels. Their attempt upon Three Rivers was founded in rashness and executed with timidity, two principles which compounded make a consummation of preposterous conduct.[17] Their flight up the Sorrell before the part of the army I had the honour to command was most unsoldierlike and disgraceful.

We are now exerting every faculty of army and Provincials to prepare for passing the Lake. The quantity of vessels necessary for force and provision and transport of the troops makes the work tedious and laborious; I will not, however, relinquish the sanguine hopes, the favourite idea upon which I lay my head every night to my pillow, of joining you and my friend Howe before winter. If you are with him I have desired him to communicate a plan I have formed for a secret and separate expedition; whether it will take place I cannot say; it is under contemplation and preparation. Not knowing, through how many hands this letter may pass, I do not think it discreet to insert it here.[18]

Your friendship, my dear General, claims some account of myself as well as of public transactions, but I will not lay so cruel a tax upon your sensitivity as to enlarge upon my personal situation. Suffice it to know that, after enduring a conflict of two months in England to disguise from Lady Charlotte what I suffered on her account, I left that truest

[17]A British advance post at the town of Three Rivers on the St. Lawrence River was attacked on the morning of June 8, 1776, by elements of the American Northern Theater Army. The attack was poorly planned, ill-conceived, and clumsily executed by the Americans, in large part due to faulty command decisions by Brigadier General William Thompson. The attack was easily repulsed by the British garrison with the assistance of the Royal Navy on the St. Lawrence. The American assaulting forces sustained extremely heavy casualties and were essentially destroyed in the debacle. For more detailed information on the Battle of Three Rivers, refer to Cubbison, *"Artillery never gained more Honour,"* 41–42; and Cubbison, *American Northern Theater Army*, 100–119. Although Burgoyne played no role in this engagement, his assessment of American leadership is entirely accurate.

[18]This paragraph strongly intimates that Burgoyne was considering an expedition down Lake Champlain and the Hudson River under his command to join General William Howe in New York City as early as July 1776.

friend, amiable companion, tenderest, best of women and of wives, to whose qualities and virtues I have been habituated through a long course of years without a single error on her part, in a state of health that affords me little chance of seeing her more.[19] The suspense is scarcely tolerable. She is hourly before my eyes. Her excellencies increase upon every reflection, as do every fault I ever committed towards here [her]. They are not, indeed, many, and those are unknown to her. I have ever aimed at fortitude; I hope I am not wholly devoid of it. But I never was put to so severe a trial as this separation. I would have sacrificed fortune or ambition, and all that in the flight of imagination can depend upon them to avoid this campaign. A sense of duty to the King, to my profession, and to the country in so important a cause enable me, and barely enabled me, to overcome my private emotions. I, however, embarked very ill. I am now perfectly well in health and throw myself, a volunteer, into every occupation that can divert thought. I find this practice of use and shall continue it while doubt remains. The decision once past and, should it so please God, against my hopes, I close all interesting and valuable prospects of life.

Observing how much I have said upon a subject I meant only to touch, I am in doubt whether I ought not to tear the paper. I know too well your mind to think you can read it without pain. Glance it over, send me a sign, and think no more on it.

Phillips, who was my shipmate on the voyage from England, I believe writes to you by this conveyance.[20] He is perfectly well and indefatigable in his department. We often talk of you. Gardener is most respectfully yours. We join in love and compliments to Drummond[21] and Lord Rawdon.[22] The latter has a young brother here, who promises to fullow his Lordship's steps in military and manly pursuits. Major Carleton,[23] who is now with me, desires to be remembered by you.

---

[19]Burgoyne's wife, the Lady Charlotte Stanley, was the daughter of Edward Stanley, 11th Earl of Derby and Elizabeth Hesketh. She married Burgoyne, against her family's wishes, in 1749, eloping to France. She died in 1776, while Burgoyne was in Canada. By every evidence, they were deeply in love with each other and enjoyed an extremely happy marriage.

[20]Major General William Phillips, Royal Artillery, previously introduced.

[21]Captain Duncan Drummond, Clinton's aide-de-camp.

[22]In January 1776 Lord Rawdon was appointed an aide-de-camp to Clinton. He served as Clinton's aide for much of the war but later demonstrated considerable acumen for command in the southern theater.

[23]Major Thomas Carleton (c. 1735–1817), the younger brother of Sir Guy Carleton. A lifelong soldier, he joined the 20th Regiment of Foot in 1753. He had experience as an ensign and lieutenant

Adieu, my dear Clinton. Believe me in every wish for your glory and happiness, and in every sentiment of respect and affection,

The faithfulest of your friends,
J: Burgoyne.
Compliments to Lord Cornwallis.
[To] Lt. Gen Clinton

6.16/1

Extract of a Letter from Lord George Germain to Sir William Howe, Whitehall, August 22, 1776

I herewith transmit to you a Copy of a Dispatch sent to General Sir Guy Carleton, which I think makes it unnecessary, for me to enter into a Discussion of that part of your Letter which relates to the difficulties that might arise upon a junction of your respective Armies. A Duplicate of this Dispatch is sent herewith which, for fear any accident should happen to the Original, you will transmit to Sir Guy Carleton by the first opportunity.

6.16/2

Extract of a Letter from Lord George Germain to Sir Guy Carleton, Whitehall, August 22, 1776[24]

The rapid success of His Majesty's Arms in driving the Rebels out of Canada, does great honor to your conduct; & I hope soon to hear that

on the European continent during the Seven Years' War. He was assigned as the major of the 29th Regiment of Foot at the relief of Quebec in May 1776, was promoted to lieutenant colonel of the regiment upon the death of Lieutenant Colonel Patrick Gordon in 1776, and held that position throughout the American War of Independence in Canada. He served throughout the war without particular distinction, accompanying the Burgoyne campaign as a quartermaster general and secretary to his older brother in Canada. During the postwar years he served as the lieutenant governor of New Brunswick, a post in which he prospered and rendered great service. His career appears to have been overshadowed by his older brother and retarded by an argumentative disposition. His best biography is a lengthy entry in the *Dictionary of Canadian Biography*.

24 This letter was printed as Appendix No. 2 in Burgoyne, *State of the Expedition from Canada*, ii–iii. There is no difference in content between this version and the printed copy, there are only minor differences in punctuation and capitalization.

you have been able to pursue them cross the Lakes, & to possess those Posts upon the Frontiers, which may effectually secure your Province from any future Insult.

His Majesty in appointing you Commander in Chief of His Forces in Canada was pleased to extend your Commission to the Frontiers of His Provinces bordering thereupon, wisely foreseeing that it might be necessary, for the compleating your Plan of operations, that you should march your Army beyond the limits of your own Government. I trust, before this letter reaches you, that you will, by your Spirit and Activity, have cleared the Frontiers of Canada of all the Rebel Forces; and will have taken the proper Measures for keeping possession of the Lakes. That Service being performed, His Majesty Commands me to acquaint you, that there still remains another part of your Duty to be undertaken which will require all your abilities & the strictest application—the restoring Peace & the establishing good order & Legal Government in Canada[.] It is an object of the greatest Importance to this Country— The Difficulties attending it are immense— but his Majesty depends upon your zeal and upon your experience for carrying it into Execution. His Majesty, ever anxious for the Happiness of His Subjects, Commands me to inform you, that no time should be lost in beginning so important a Work, and that you do therefore Return to Quebec; detaching Lieut. General Burgoyne, or such other officer as you shall think most proper, with that part of your Forces which can be spared from the immediate defence of your Province, to carry on such Operations as shall be most conducive to the success of the Army, acting on the side of New York—And that you direct the Officer so detached to communicate with & put himself as soon as possible, under the Command of General Howe. You will order such Artillery as you shall judge necessary to proceed with this Detachment— And as a great quantity of heavy Cannon & Military Stores were sent upon the supposition that Quebec might have been in the hands of the Rebels you will, upon Requisition from General Howe, supply him with such Cannon & Stores, as may not be wanted for the protection of Canada.[25]

[25]Although written in August 1776, this letter was delayed by unseasonably early ice in the St. Lawrence River in the fall of that year, and it could not be delivered to Governor Carleton in Quebec until May 1777.

[*No file #*]

Major General William Phillips to Lieutenant General John Burgoyne, Fort Crown Point, October 23, 1776

My Dear Sir—
I have passed a very unpleasant time since here and lament your absence most sincerely. I stand alone unable to bear up against the sloth and changes of this atmosphere. You will scarcely suppose that there is neither reconnoitering post nor scout sent forward, but as the whim of a drunken Indian prevails. I have endeavored in vain to form a small detachment to feel the pulse of the enemy; the answer is that it is wrong to teach these rebels war. There are deserters who are daily accounts of the panic of these people. Two men came in from Albany who report that there are ships of war and other vessels, amounting to thirteen, in the Hudson River beyond the highlands on the way to Albany; that the Royalists are all waiting with eager impatience for assistance. I do really believe that Howe's Army will take the post of Crown Point, when we leave it, which is this day determined after bringing away all the artificers from Isle Aux Noix and St. John. I will, before you leave this country, send you the report of the engineers concerning this place. I must be of opinion that, notwithstanding the success upon the lake, we terminate the campaign ill. It was upon the positive declaration that a post was to be established here, at all events, that I proposed sending the troops back into Winter Quarters for the power of more easily supplying the corps here, and to be left for the winter with provisions; for I do protest that otherwise I think the army should have moved forward and a trial made at Ticonderoga. Had we failed in a strong feint we could but have retired, and I must think there were good chances of success from the very strong panic which has taken the rebels. But it is the humor here to suppose that it is no disgrace to retire if it is not done in the face of the enemy. I have been uniform in my ideas of the manner this army was to have proceeded upon the lake. One brigade to attend the fleet, the rest to move at the moment of success. Had it been so, the army

might have been at Crown Point the 15th, and the fleet and armed vessels going up the lake towards Ticonderoga with a show of attacking with the army and strong parties towards Lake George and Skenesborough we should have destroyed their communications if we had not frightened them out of Ticonderoga. I never was of opinion to attack the entrenchments seriously, but I am and shall ever be of opinion that every art of war should be practiced upon these people, whose ignorance renders stratagem and surprise so easy to succeed. I am tardy in saying all this as it has been our joint opinion, and it is a flattering, most flattering, most satisfactory reflection to me that we have agreed, I think, almost in every proposal and plan for this campaign. I shall be very happy, as a citizen, that Howe succeeds, even to Crown Point, but, as an officer, I wish this Army might have been allowed the share in the war which it should, in my opinion, have had. I write my mind freely to you and repose my griefs in the bosom of a friend, such I believe you, such I respect and regard you for at my heart. I do not talk to the folks here thus, my pride of soldiership forbids it. The army seems distressed and hurt at the langor which governs every movement. I still fear a dreadful winter, but still I shall be myself, nor let chagrin prey upon me, nor will I grow languid in the public service. I promise you to do my utmost to preserve the army for an early opening of the campaign, and I do most sincerely hope you will come out to us. The next year must divide this army, and we will go together, if it be possible. Take care of our cause in England, I rely on your goodness and regard for me to represent me favorably to the King if you think I deserve it, and keep me third in this army unless a second lieutenant-general is sent. I will leave you some of my letters open; read them, as it is possible they may contain something worthy your remembrance concerning the detail. Seal them with a common impression, when I take the liberty of consigning them to your care. Yours Sincerely, W. Phillips.

Sir Henry Clinton Papers, File 18:47a

Letter from Major General John Burgoyne to Major General Henry Clinton, Quebec, November 7, 1776

My Dear Clinton
I wrote to you at the opening of the Campaign under cover to Genl Howe.[26] My mind, at that time agitated by the most anxious suspense, I am afraid paid too little regard to my friend's sensibility. That suspense soon after ended in the confirmation of a calamity to which I had never dared to look forward, & I would not fain be more cautious of mentioning it in a manner to excite you pain; but there is a luxury of sorrow, ungenerous perhaps but irresistible, in attracting the sure participation of a fellow sufferer; in drawing a tear from me who has felt like ourselves; who has known what it is to be united to that rare character of female excellence which God occasionally bestows on earth to teach us happiness, & to try us with resignation.

The news of this event reached me in the most critical period of our operations, when the labour of preparation was within a few days of being completed, & an attack upon the enemy, in which I then expected to have a considerable share, was projected & promising for execution. I passed the regular stages through imperfection at first, & emotion afterwards, to perfect misery. I made however an effort on my mind & I succeeded so far as to return to my duty in the field in such a composure as should not injure the King's Service, effect my honour, or be troublesome to those about me. During the passage of the Lake my health suffered a little, but occupation, air & exercise have improved both that & my apparent resolution. The latter will continue its progress. Till it settles first into a calm melancholy & next into a private devotion of memory—should it go further & approach to forgetfullness, may I stand as despicable in the eyes of those I most value as shall do in my own!

Such is [two words illegible] & upon such exertions I shall perhaps receive from the particularity of my friend's compliments upon my fortune— I hesitate upon the propriety of the term, & much doubt

[26] Burgoyne's letter to Clinton from Chambly, July 7, 1776 (File 17:24, Clinton Papers).

whether it would not be more for the honor of the heart to sink under [two words illegible] as mine than to sustain it.

In this situation, callous as I am to every personal pursuit or interest, think me not indifferent to the lot of the few who upon the solid estimation of worth I have learned to value— Judge of my [single word illegible] at hearing no authoritative account of you or your proceedings—flying, imperfect, improbable rumors have reached me—I shall not be satisfied till I know your own sentiments upon the situation you have been in, for as to your conduct in every circumstance wherein you can possibly engage in arms. I shall rest easy in the conviction that you must do everything a soldier ought; & this conviction I shall be proud to maintain should it ever be necessary in the face of ignorance or impertinence.

As to our affairs here, I have no person to complain of, that I confess all my plans have been disappointed. I acquainted you from England with the order & the circumstances, not the inclination that destined my services to Canada. You will have heard long since of the precipitous retreat of the enemy after raising the siege of Quebec. Having driven them beyond St Johns on the side of Lake Champlain came necessity all operations became to stand still & naval force could be prepared. Lake Ontario was nevertheless open & as soon as boats could be ready for that route I proposed to put myself at the head of only three British Battalions with a Corps of Artillery some Canadians & a large body of Indians which we had at command, to have taken my route by Oswego & Fort Stanwix, & have established myself upon the Mohawk River. This plan I formed after many conversations with Sir John Johnston[27] who was in person with our army & gave me minute intelligence both of the Country & the disposition of the people. I was convinced of the practicability of the one & the favorable cast of the other, & with proper provision of spare arms, & money, I think he & I together should have

[27]Sir John Johnson (1741–1830) was the eldest son of Sir William Johnson and assumed the office of baronet upon his father's death in 1774. Driven from his home in the Mohawk Valley because of his Loyalist leanings in 1776, Johnson raised the King's Royal Regiment of New York, and served throughout the American War of Independence. Although his career was by no means as distinguished as that of his father, and he lacked his father's leadership and vibrant, energetic personality, Sir John Johnson was an important early leader in the development of the Province of Ontario and Canada; he died in Montreal in 1830.

raised a combination in that country of great effect—a powerful diversion in regard to our army & a yet more positive assistance to that of Genl Carleton when ready to cross Lake Champlain, for I cannot suppose any General would have remained at Ticonderoga Fort Edward or any other post above the junction of the Mohawk & Hudson Rivers.[28] The ideas & reasoning upon my plan was approved—it failed for want of sufficient store of provision. My efforts next turned to estimate & facilitate the proportion of a naval force—our friend Phillips had infinite merit in that Department. Seven hundred batteaux, four vessels of great force & six & twenty artillery row boats were built & equipt & they sailed & destroyed the enemys fleet in less than three months.[29]

But here again my plan for sustaining the fleet with a corps of the army in order to take sudden advantage of a defeat, was at first adopted & afterwards over rated & the commander in chief embarked alone to command the fleet leaving the whole of the army, artillery excepted & with what to the great displeasure of Phillips he would not suffer that General to proceed, to be brought forward by degrees after the naval operation should have had effect. I still adhere in opinion to my first disposition as to the army, but I should be unjust to Genl Carleton, if I [one word illegible] that odd & misplaced as his post may appear he had of the naval department only, he had reasons to justify that proceeding— They would carry me no farther in the occasion proper to open them to you now.

---

[28]This is the earliest evidence that Sir John Johnson and Burgoyne formulated the plan for a diversion expedition, which it was hoped would be successful and could be exploited to become a flanking column, down the Mohawk River from Oswego. In 1777 this expedition would be commanded by Lieutenant Colonel St. Leger.

[29]There were actually twenty-two Royal Artillery gunboats that participated in the 1776 campaign on Lake Champlain and five major vessels. The first, the gondola *Loyal Convert*, had been captured by the British Royal Navy from the Americans on the St. Lawrence River in early May. It had been outfitted with seven 9-pounders and a number of swivels. The largest British vessel was the *Inflexible*, a formidably large ship that mounted no fewer than eighteen 12-pounder cannon. The British fleet counted two schooners, the *Carleton* and the *Maria*. The *Maria*, named for Carleton's wife, served as the flagship of the fleet, and Carleton sailed aboard this vessel. Both ships were heavily armed, the *Carleton* mounting twelve 6-pounders and the *Maria* carrying an impressive fourteen 6-pounders. The fifth British ship was a distinctive class of vessel, specifically designed for military use on interior waters in North America: the radeau *Thunderer*. The *Thunderer* carried at least fourteen cannon: six 24-pounder cannon, six 12-pounder cannon, and two 8" howitzers. Cubbison, *American Northern Theater Army*, 230–232.

You will have heard of the compleat victory obtained over the enemy's fleet— I joined the General with two brigades of the army at Crown Point; He held the attack of Ticonderoga at so advanced a season of the year, inexpedient— It was too strong for a coup de main. The blow could not be followed. The lake was secured & without it, & the place must necessarily fall with small loss & in short time by a regular attack next spring. In these reasons Philips & I acquiesced upon the idea that Crown Point was to be maintained; but I could have wished to throw a corps of Indians & light troops round the enemy's post, to have felt their pulse & attempted their convoys from Lake George & Fort Edward— Finding nothing of that sort or any other operation was in contemplation, I thought myself at liberty to withdraw on my way to England & left the General consulting the speediest & properest means to make Crown Point (all the buildings of which were burnt) tenable for one brigade for the winter. The greatest difficulty therein appeared to be the supply of provisions. This task I undertook & in my passage down established a conveyance & arrangement of posts that ensured success before the Lake should become impracticable. I cannot express my surprise nor concern at hearing since the post has been judged untenable for want of season to cover the troops & fortify them, & that the whole is coming back. I think this step puts us in danger, besides conveying a bad impression to the publick, of losing the fruits of our summer's labour & certain victory— It may perhaps be a race which shall build fastest for a new navel dispute next spring, the Lake which was positively & effectually secured by possessing Crown Point being again entirely open. I must honour Carleton's abilities & judgement, I have lived with him upon the best terms & bear him real friendship— I am therefore doubly hurt that he has taken a step in which I can be no otherwise serviceable to him than by silence; for I cannot bring myself to think that he might not have held the post if he had ordered the troops to cover themselves, to construct huts instead of barracks & called in his own good sense to direct the fortification without being guided by the drawings & technical reasonings of dull, formal, methodical, fat, engineers.

You will not wonder, my dear friend, at my return to England—a secondary station in a secondary army is at no time agreeable; but many circumstances combine to render it in the present instance uncommonly dissatisfactory. My private [single word illegible] are yet more forcible—a mind sunk at time in distress, a constitution unfitted to severity of cold, a few duties yet remaining to the memory of Lady Charlotte, compel me to break through the bars of ice & snow which are forming to seclude this country from the rest of the globe for the next six months. I mean not however to withdraw myself from the American War unless french one breaks out— An uncommited cipher in the world— The portion lost which made prosperity an object of solicitude—my prospects are closed— Interest, ambition, the animation of life is over. Profession & honour is all that remains, & I would rather that finished in a professional grave, than to the slow wasting, decrepitude & infirmness Of the age.

Accept the confidence with which I write as our testimony of my friendship; could I express my impatience to see you you would find it astonishing. I remember a sort of one you made not a sacrifice in America; I will therefore hope a few months to see you in person for [end of sentence illegible].

I am yours;
J. Burgoyne

P.S.
My love to Drummonds, respects & best wishes to Lord Rawdon. I presume the cipher but as this goes by an officer have thought not necessary to use it. Keep in your own breast my opinion of what has passed here.[30]
J.B.

6.16/3

Extract of a Letter from Genl. Sir William Howe to Lord George Germain, New York, November 28, 1776. Rec'd December 30 [1776]

I have the honor to acknowledge the receipt of your Lordship's Dispatches of the 11th. 12th & 21st of June— Four different Letters of the 22d August, inclosing one to Sir Guy Carleton of the same Date.

[30] This is the earliest mention of a cipher having been established between Burgoyne and Clinton.

6.16/4

Copy of a Letter from Genl. Burgoyne to Lord George Germain, Hartford Street [London,] January 1, 1777[31]

My Lord,
My Physician has pressed me to go to Bath[32] for a short time & I find it requisite to my health & spirits to follow his advice— But I think it a previous duty to assure your Lordship, that should my attendance in Town become necessary relatively to information upon the affairs of Canada, I shall be ready to obey y^r [your] summons upon one day's notice.

Your Lordship being out of Town, I submitted the above intentions a few days ago—personally to His Majesty in His Closet—and I added—"that as the arrangements for the next Campaign might possibly come under His Royal Contemplation before my return, I humbly laid myself at His Majesty's feet for such active employment as he might think me worthy of."

This was the substance of my audience on my part. I undertook it & I now report it to your Lordship, in the hope of your patronage in this pursuit; a hope my Lord founded, not only upon a just sense of the honour your Lordship's friendship must reflect upon me, but also upon a feeling, that I deserve it, in as much as a solid aspect, and sincere personal attachment can constitute such a claim.

I leave in the hands of M^r. Doiley[33] such of the Memorandums confided to me by Genl Carleton as require dispatch—should your Lord think proper to carry them into execution.

I also leave in that gentleman's hands the copy of an application relative to Boats for the Artillery & which I take the liberty to submit to your Lordship, as well worthy of Consideration, upon the supposition that the Enemy should arm upon Lake George & that any Operation should be advisable by that Route.[34]

---

[31]This letter was printed as Appendix No. 1 in Burgoyne, *State of the Expedition from Canada*, i–ii. There is no difference in content between this version and the printed copy; and there are only minor differences in punctuation and capitalization.

[32]Bath, in southwest England, was a spa town whose waters were considered to be therapeutic for a range of ailments. The English gentry regularly visited Bath to "take the treatment."

[33]Mr. Christopher D'Oyly, an undersecretary of state to Lord George Germain.

[34]This is the letter from Phillips to Carleton dated November 9, 1776 (File 6.16/7). This constitutes early evidence that Burgoyne intended to follow the Lake George route south, rather than continuing on Lake Champlain from Fort Ticonderoga.

I likewise leave the Disposition of Winter Quarters which I received by the last ship from Canada. I find no Dispatch is come to your Lordship by that occasion & I conceived those Papers might be of use.

I have the honour to be &c.
J. Burgoyne

6.16/6

Memorandum of General Carleton relative to the next Campaign communicated to Lieut. General Burgoyne to be laid before Government

A Reinforcement of four thousand Troops, exclusive of compleating the present Army, is necessary for Canada.

It would be desirable to increase the present Establishment of British Regiments to an hundred per Company, as part of the desired reinforcement.

With a reinforcement to the above amount, and well composed, a large Corps may be spared to pass Lake Ontario, and to operate upon the Mohawk River.[35]

Another Corps might possibly be employed to penetrate to Connecticut River.[36]

Six Months Provisions for at least twenty thousand men at full rations, ought to be sent out early in the Spring. The Number of Mouths to feed including Savages, Canadians, Artificers & Seamen &c. upon the Lakes may be reckoned a full third more than the Troops.

Canada will furnish flour sufficiently, but the drain of live Cattle has been so great the last Campaign that very little can be expected.

A Corps of Boatmen is absolutely necessary for all Operations in a Country so much intersected with Lakes and Rivers as that wherein the Canadian Army must act.

35 This expedition would become the Mohawk River diversion commanded by Lieutenant Colonel Barry St. Leger.

36 This expedition was never implemented.

6.16/7

Copy of a Letter from Major General Phillips to Genl. Carleton, St. John's, November 9, 1776[37]

Sir,

The late expedition upon the Lake has fully made to appear the great utility of Gun Boats when they are served by the Royal Artillery. That it is an armament peculiarly adapted to the service of the lakes in almost every case that can happen, and possessing singular advantages in light wind & calms, by covering our own vessels, or attacking those of the Enemy, of which the instance in the action of the 11th October strongly evinces the truth.[38]

It appears to me an object very worthy your Excellency's consideration for the next Campaign & I take the liberty of submitting to you Sir, whether it would not be proper to make a Demand from England for a certain number of these Boats, calculated to mount Guns upon, to be sent from thence framed, so as to be put together in Canada.

Their being sent from England becomes necessary because they can be constructed there with seasoned Timber, so as to render the Boats, Platforms, Carriages for guns &c. &c. sufficiently strong for the Service they are intended.

The gun boats which was built here were of a very good construction, but being new Timber cut from the woods were not buoyant on the Water, consequently not so useful as could be wished, nor strong enough to resist the force of heavy Guns & Howitzers.

The building a number of boats of this sort here would also interfere with & retard the refitting & fitting out the armament as it now stands for the ensuing Campaign. I therefore repeat that I think Gun Boats should be constructed in England, I am positively of opinion that a certain number should be ordered for this Service.

The Boats upon this principle which came from England this year, must have been constructed by different persons. They were allmost

---

37 The original of this letter is located in the George Germain Papers, William L. Clements Library, University of Michigan, Ann Arbor. It was previously published for the first time in Cubbison, *"Artillery never gained more Honour,"* 62–63. This copy of the letter is identical to the original except in minor variations of capitalization and punctuation. This letter accompanied Carleton's Memorandum (File 6.16/6).

38 Phillips is referring here to the Battle of Valcour Island.

all different one from the other some were indeed very good, others but indifferent, & two so very bad that they could not with the utmost endeavor be put together here.

From the experience we have had of these Boats, and from the reports of the Officers of Artillery & the gentlemen of the Navy, they are not so perfect at any rate as they might and ought to be; — I have therefore directed a drawing of a Gun Boat upon larger dimensions having increased the length 5 feet, & so on according to that Proportion.

These Boats so constructed are calculated to carry heavy 12 Pounders, light 24 Pounders, 8 Inch Howitzers, in the bow, upon sliding carriages or moveable Platforms such as have been made here this year & used with much success. There may be also mounted upon the stern of these Boats two light 3 or 6 Pounders, to secure a defensive fire against an attack during the time the gun in front is in action against an Enemy.

The conveniency & security of carrying Ammunition is particularly attended to. The boats sent from England this year were remarkably insufficient in this particular.

I beg further to suggest that it be recommended that if the Navy construct these Boats it may be done at one Dock Yard or if by Contract, by one Person. As by this means the Timbers will be all conformable to the plan, & there will be no difficulty in putting the Boats together when they arrive in Canada.

I submit to your Excellency's consideration whether there should not be Boats demanded as follows.

For 12 P^{dr} [Pounder] heavy Brass – 4
For 24 P^{dr} Light do – 8
For 12 P^{dr} Medium do – 8
8 Inch Howitzers – 4
[Total] – 24

I am not certain whether there are not 24 P^{drs} cast upon a medium construction weighing about 36 Cwt.[39] Should it be so, I would offer to your Excellency to have 4 such guns in place of the four heavy 12 P^{drs}—

The Gun Carriages, Platforms, Iron Works, & every other particular necessary to mount these Guns upon these Boats, to be sent from England.

[39]Referring here to old English units of hundredweight. In the eighteenth century, an English hundredweight was a modern 112 pounds. Thus, a 24-pounder of 36 hundredweight would weigh 4,032 modern pounds.

It will be necessary also that some of the Artillery before mentioned be sent with the Boats & the Ammunition required for the whole[.] I enclose a Return upon that subject.

Capt. Blomefield[40] of the Royal Artillery who has acted during the Campaign as my Major of Brigade,[41] is perfectly acquainted with the

[40]Captain-Lieutenant Thomas Blomefield (1744–1822) had been born in 1744 to the Reverend Thomas Blomefield. Blomefield had apparently considered a career in either the Royal Navy or the army and in fact sailed for one cruise on board the HMS *Cambridge*, an 80-gun ship of the line in 1755. He subsequently entered Woolwich in February 1758. Blomefield proved himself surprisingly adept at his studies at Woolwich, attracting the attention of John Muller, then master instructor of fortification and artillery, and graduating as a lieutenant fireworker in only eleven months. He served throughout the remainder of the Seven Years' War, participating in campaigns in Europe, the West Indies, and North America. Blomefield was present at the formal siege of Havana in 1762, in which the field artillery played a prominent role. In 1771 Blomefield had become aide-de-camp to General Conway, then master general of ordnance; he must have excelled at this position, for when Lord Townshend assumed the post Blomefield was kept on. In 1776 Blomefield joined the Canadian detachment, most likely as a means of seeing further active duty and progressing his career. Blomefield served with distinction during the 1776 and 1777 campaigns and was severely wounded at the Battle of Barber's Wheatfield on October 7, 1777. Following his return from Canada, Blomefield was appointed inspector of artillery and of the brass foundry at Woolwich in 1780. Steadily promoted, Blomefield commanded the artillery employed in the siege and capture of Copenhagen, Denmark, between August 16 and September 5, 1807, when the British government determined to capture the Danish fleet before the French could seize it. This was one of the few cases in British history where the designer and caster of an entire series of cannon would command them in battle. Blomefield went on to design a complete system of artillery that would serve as the standard for British artillery for fifty years. Historian and Royal Artillery Officer Adrian Caruana would state of Blomefield:

> the volume of production of the various pieces, and the extent to which they were used, make Blomefield a major figure in ordnance design. Blomefield's work as Inspector of Artillery, as a result of which the standard of British ordnance was raised to a level equal to that of any other nation, can hardly be over estimated. His influence was considerable, since he effectively controlled the production of all ordnance for some forty years; brass ordnance by his direct command of the foundry, and iron ordnance by his control of the Woolwich proof, to which all ordnance was subjected. In deed, as an influence on ordnance, no other designer was in a position of power for so long a time. While purely as a designer he may not have been as important as others, the control he exercised and the influence he wielded, makes him the equal of any other designer in the history of British ordnance.

Blomefield died as a full general near Woolwich in 1822. He was still on active service. "Major General Sir Thomas Blomefield"; and Caruana, "Sir Thomas Blomefield," 95–100. No definitive biography of Blomefield, one of the most significant officers in the history of the Royal Artillery, has been written.

[41]Brigade major was one of the few established staff positions in an eighteenth-century army. The officer assigned as brigade major was detailed from his usual position with the line and was to receive greater pay and allowances for the significantly increased workload and responsibilities that the position entailed. The brigade major's functions were similar to those of the adjutant general of the modern army. Essentially, he was responsible for all of the administrative duties and functions of the brigade headquarters, including but not limited to the preparation and

intention relative to these Boats, the Artillery for them, & their compleat equipment.

As that Officer is going to England I will request of you Sir, should your Excellency approve of what I have wrote on this Subject to recommend that Capt. Blomefield may have the care of seeing & attending upon the Construction of these Boats & their equipment in England.

I am etc.
W. Phillips

6.16/8

Winter Quarters For the British Troops as ordered by his Excellency, the Commander in Chief [Governor of Canada and General Sir Guy Carleton], November 1, 1776[42]

Head Quarters of the Army
Montreal
Royal Artillery
29th Regiment
General Hospital

Kings R. Regt New York
La Chine
La Point Claire
St Anne

The Royal Regt. Emigrants
La Chenaye
Terre Bonne
Riviere du Chine

Brigr General Fraser's Corps
Upon the South of the River St. Lawrence

---

dissemination of orders, compilation of reports, maintenance of official brigade papers, and organization and preparation of the correspondence of the commanding officer of the brigade. The brigade major was also directed to assist a brigade commander, however it was deemed to be appropriate and necessary.

[42] This letter accompanied Carleton's Memorandum (File 6.16/6).

La Prairie
Longuevil
Boucherville
Varennes et Isle Therese
Verchenes et Isle Toucharet
Grand St Ours

First Brigade
Commanded by Brigadier General [Henry Watson] Powell

Left of the Brigade
31st & 53d Regiments
Chambly
Belloeuvil
S$^{t.}$ Charles
S$^{t.}$ Denys
S$^{t.}$ Antoine
S$^{t.}$ Ours
Sorel
Upon the River Sorrel

Right of the Brigade
47th & 9th Regiments
Isle Jesus
Rivieres des Prairies
Saut du Recolet
S$^{t.}$ Genevieve
S$^{t.}$ Lawrence
Upon the River S$^{t.}$ Lawrence & District of Montreal

Second Brigade
Commanded by Brigadier General [James] Hamilton

Left of the Brigade
34th & 62nd regiments
Quebec
District of Quebec

Right of the Brigade
21st & 20th Regiments

Isle aux Noix
St. John

6.29/3

Copy of Extract of a Letter from His Excellency Genl Carleton, November 25, 1776

Of the rum ordered here by the Lords of the Treasury from the different Islands, only the Grenada & Barbados proportions have been Received and some from Halifax forwarded by the Dep^y Qua^r Mr Genl [deputy quartermaster general] Lieut. Colonel Shirrett, before Genl Howe left that place, the exact amount of which cannot be ascertained at present, but falls greatly short of what their Lordships had designed for this Army; it is now too late to make any Contracts here for a supply of this Article against the next Campaign of which I think it necessary their Lordships should be informed—

6.16/5

Memorandums & Observations related to the Service in Canada, submitted to Lord George Germain [by Lieutenant General John Burgoyne]

General Carleton's Requisitions

"A Battalion of Seamen consisting of 300 at least—that the expensive expedients to which we have been obliged to have recourse this year of detaining Transports on account of their Seamen—might be avoided in future; even if it should be in our power to use it; but as there may not be a number sufficient of those Ships in the River to furnish us as before, should in that case be at a loss to man our vessels again, and it seems most probable, that we shall have the same if not greater occasion for them next spring, at least it must be necessary to be provided against all which may happen, as I find it impossible to remain here."

The above is an extract of a Letter from General Carleton to Genl Burgoyne Dated Crown Point 22^d Octr 1776.

Observations [of General Burgoyne]

The reasons stated by Gen[l] Carleton in favor of the proposed Corps of Seaman may appear to apply—particularly to the Service of Armed Vessels & it may be imagined that he has already, including the Crews of Frigates and Transports wintering in the River S[t.] Lawrence a sufficiency of Men for that purpose, even upon a supposition that the Lakes should be again disputed.

But I beg leave to Suggest the expediency of such a Corps for the Boats appropriated to the Baggage, Ammunition, provisions, intrenching Tools, Artillery Stores & various other indispensible Stores of an Army.

A certain number of good watermen dispersed in the Battalion Boats, particularly in those of the foreign Troops, who cannot learn to row well, would be of great use in point of regularity & expedition.[43]

I am considering the late War, the Battalion Boats were always rowed by their own Soldiers & I believe the Stores and Artillery Boats were also supplied with rowers from the Regiments; but it must be considered that the Regiments at that time were more than double in numbers to the present Establishment.

After deducting upon a moderate calculation the sick, Hospital Guards, General Officers Guards, many small drains of Regimental Service not to be avoided and perhaps attachments assistant to the Artillery, the Battalions exclusive of Grenadiers & light Infantry which are separated from them, will hardly exceed 300 Rank & File. If from that number it is to be also deducted, the Guards for the Boats when the troops land & for the conveyance & Care of Stores that follow the Army, the Battalions will be much weaker than they ought to be for any Operation.

The Canadians supply this Service very ill, their great practice on the water being in Canoes which paddle. They are very awkward with an Oar. They are besides under no discipline, and continually desert or pretend sickness.

The Corps proposed would enable the Commander in chief, to release

[43]By "foreign Troops" Burgoyne is referring to the Brunswick and Hesse-Hanau regiments hired for military service in North America to augment the British army. They had arrived in 1776 and had participated under Burgoyne's command in the October 1776 campaign down Lake Champlain.

great part of his present Sea forces, as soon as the Passage of the Lakes was accomplished.

To facilitate this Measure it is humbly submitted, that men taken from Rivers in England, might Answer the purpose—without interfering with the present call for able Seamen; and with all due deference to Genl. Carleton, I should imagine, that such a Body thrown into independent Companies of 60 each, with proper Naval Officers would answer better than what is called in the Demand a Battalion.

Requisition [of General Carleton]

An Augmentation of artillery consisting of two Companies & the whole number of Companies on the Service in Canada— Completed to an hundred Men each

Observations [of General Burgoyne]

I think it a duty to press upon your LordShip my Opinion upon the expediency of this proposal. The Artillery after the Light Troops, is the important arm in this American War. The assistance obliged to be given from the line to that Service the last Campaign, was a great weakening to the Regiments, at the same time it was a very inadequate substitute for trained Artillery Men.

Requisition [of General Carleton]

Six Months provisions to be sent out as early as possible in the Spring, calculated at the full ration, for one third more than the effective of Soldiers and Seamen.

Observations [of General Burgoyne]

The reason of this demand is to supply Canadians, Savages, Artificers,[44] and some waste which, in spite of every possible precaution and diligence in the Commissaries Department will in some degree happen, from the accidents and inconveniencies (particularly leakage) attending water Carriage.

The Canadian Corvée, without which the force could Not go on must receive provisions. The Savages also expect it for their women and must be indulged.

[44]The artificers accompanying the Royal Artillery comprised valuable skilled craftsmen such as blacksmiths, wheelwrights, and carpenters. Often civilian employees, or soldiers specifically detached for this duty, they provided the British army with skilled labor.

Salt provisions[45] are indispensably necessary for the upper Posts at Niagara &c. where there is great negotiation with the Savages. They must also be solely depended upon, for the movement of every Body of Troops acting beyond St. John's by the Lake Champlain or beyond the Island of Montreal by the lake Ontario.

For an expedition by the latter route, provision should be carried for at least three times the number of the Forces the expedition sets out with, as it may be expected to be joined by large Bodies of both Savages and civilized Inhabitants, before they reach a Country of supply. The obvious measure of the Enemy will be to drive the Country at the first news of a Corps penetrating by Oswego & Fort Stanwix. It is well known that Schuyler had taken precautions for doing it last year.[46]

It is much to be feared that Canada will not afford provisions (corn excepted) for the maintenance of even the Troops which are to remain in the Province next Year.

Upon the whole therefore I am persuaded the demands of Gen[l.] Carleton in this article will be found to be put as low as can be made consistent with the probable exigencies of the Service.

Requisition [of General Carleton]

A Reinforcement of Four Thousand Men

Observations [of General Burgoyne]

In a letter to me since I received Gen[l.] Carletons Memorandum he expresses himself thus— "I have the more reason to expect the Reinforcements which I have requested, will be sent out to me, as Lord Cornwallis and his regiments which were to have composed a part of this army, have been employed otherwise & a very Strong Regiment of German was exchanged for a weak battalion of English." The Idea upon which the General thought this reinforcement necessary has been

---

[45]Salt provisions refer to rations that had been preserved with salt, such as "salt pork," "salt beef," "salt fish," or sauerkraut. These were the principal rations of the British army during the American War of Independence. Although these foodstuffs were moderately well preserved by such methods and could tolerate long storage and rough handling during extended transportation, they lacked nutrition, and a steady diet on such rations would result in sickness and scurvy.

[46]In other words, the American army would remove all food, provisions, crops, cattle, and anything else usable as it retreated. Thus, the British army would have to carry all of its materials, equipment, and provisions as it advanced forward. Previously, Arnold had removed all such material during the withdrawal from Canada in 1776. In the event, this is exactly what Schuyler did during the next year's campaign.

explained In a Memorandum I had the Honor to present to your Lordship soon after my return. I have only to add that the effective rank and File, by the last returns amount only to 10,174 in which number is comprised a good deal of useless stuff vizt. Men recruited in Germany for the British Regiments and sent over last year, not one tenth of whom in the Opinion of the Officers of those Regiments will be fit for the ranks from Infirmities, Malingering habits, Desertion, or profligacy of Disposition. Many of the Irish Recruits & Drafts are equally bad. In the German Regiments, there are also many unserviceable Men.

The Royal Highland Emigrants[47] have among them considerable numbers of Recruits from the Rebel Prisoners[48] & to judge of their future behavior by that of last Summer, great numbers of them may be expected to desert.

The Royal Regiment of New York,[49] are not yet anything like Soldiers, having wanted Commissioned Officers and Serjeants to train them.

Upon the whole therefore when a moderate deduction of sick is added to the useless, the whole of the Canada Army as it now stands, allowing for the Recruits arrived in the Autumn & I believe not all comprised

[47]The Royal Highland Emigrants were raised in 1775 by Lieutenant Colonel Allan Maclean, who was empowered to "enlist for His Majesty's Service, in any of His Provinces of North America, such Highlanders or such other Loyal Subjects." The regiment was raised in Canada, predominantly in the St. Lawrence River valley, and consisted of large numbers of British army veterans who had participated in campaigns against New France in Canada during the Seven Years' War and who determined to remain in Canada following their discharge. The regiment contained numerous veterans of the 42nd, 77th, and 78th Regiments of Foot, which were all raised in the Highlands and were Scottish regiments in dress, traditions, and customs. The Royal Highland Emigrants had given very good service in the Siege of Quebec during the winter of 1775–76.

[48]Following the unsuccessful New Year's Eve attack by the American Patriots under Brigadier General Richard Montgomery and Colonel Benedict Arnold, a number of American prisoners voluntarily enlisted into the Royal Highland Emigrants. Most apparently did this to obtain better living conditions, with the intent of deserting at the first opportunity. They proved extremely unreliable soldiers, many did in fact desert, and most were subsequently returned to captivity.

[49]The King's Royal Regiment of New York, informally referred to as the "Yorkers," were formed by Sir John Johnson in June 1776. It was raised predominantly from Mohawk Valley Loyalists who had fled to Canada with Johnson. The Regiment served in Canada throughout the war, being primarily used as a garrison and labor regiment. Its only active field service on a regular campaign was the Fort Stanwix Campaign of 1777. However, it must be noted that detachments of this regiment regularly and frequently participated in a large number of raids on the Patriot-held Mohawk Valley throughout the war. Following the Treaty of Paris, the regiment was disbanded, and it provided many original settlers for the Province of Ontario. Johnson had complained of a lack of trained officers and NCOs to prepare his regiment for active service. Thus, in late 1776 when this memorandum was prepared, the King's Royal Regiment of New York remained unproven.

in the Returns, will not exceed 8000 Men, of such Troops as I believe your Lordship would wish to risk the fate of an offensive Campaign upon, on the reputation of any General you may think proper to recommend to His Majesty.

I humbly conceive it will be thought expedient to leave at least 3,000 Men in Canada— General Carleton may possibly think 1,000 more necessary

The danger of any attack upon Canada in force may probable appear Chimerical, when we have an Army Advanced beyond the lakes, and I readily acquiesce in that Opinion. Altho' there are some examples that shew the Enemy capable and inclined to that sort of enterprise vizt. The March of Arnold[50] by the Chaudiere[51] before he knew or had cause to expect the rapid success of Montgomery[,] who had drawn the force of Canada to oppose him & thereby Quebec was left exposed.[52]

A second example was the Attack upon Trois Rivieres last year an offensive Operation conceived upon a retreat, and attempted by beaten, disconcerted sickly Men.

A third example is the project well known to have been conceived by Mr. Washington, for penetrating into Boston with a Corps of 5,000 Men & thereby changing ground with General Howe, at the time he

[50]In the fall of 1775 Colonel Benedict Arnold had led an American expedition from Boston up the Kennebec River, with the intent of surprising the British garrison of Quebec and capturing the city. The Kennebec River route, seldom used except by a few small parties, had never served as a route for a major military force. The march was a record of difficulties, challenges, hunger, and privations. Arnold's column arrived across from Quebec on November 9, 1775. This incursion has been documented in various histories, the most renowned treatment being the historical fiction novel by Kenneth Roberts, *Arundel.*

[51]The Chaudière River (French for "cauldron" or "boiling river") is 115 miles in length. It runs from Lac-Mégantic in extreme southeastern Quebec Province generally north until entering the St. Lawrence River opposite Quebec.

[52]Brigadier General Richard Montgomery (1738–1776), who had commanded the American Northern Theater Army in its advance from Fort Ticonderoga and Fort Crown Point, New York, to Quebec. Montgomery had served with the 17th Foot during the Seven Years' War, seeing considerable active service throughout the war, and afterwards in the West Indies and in suppressing Pontiac's Rebellion. He then mustered out of the British army and became a prominent leader in New York Colony. When the rebellion began, Montgomery accepted a commission in the Continental Army. Known as an aggressive, energetic, skilled, and extremely popular officer, he was one of the most experienced officers serving with the American army. He was killed at the head of his soldiers in the assault on the City of Quebec on New Year's Eve, 1775.

meant to Attack the Works at Dorchester a little before the evacuation of Boston.[53]

But not to lay any hope upon the possibility of future rashness in like projects. I conceive that the number of Troops I have mentioned will be found Necessary, first to guard against small incursions, to secure your convoys of supplys which must all pass first up the St. Lawrence to Sorell, and afterwards by that river and Lake Champlain a very long Track. 2nd To keep the Mutinous parts of the Country in due subjection & 3rd To enforce the Duty of Corvee which will be indispensably necessary for the supply of the Army, even among the well affected.

I conceive the disposition of the regular Troops left in Canada would be

a garrison in Quebec— 500
Posts upon the Chaudiere & in the disaffected parishes of Point Levi— 300
Garrison at Montreal & posts between that Town & Oswegatchie— 300[54]
At Trois Rivieres— 100
Chain from Sorell to Chamblee— 100
St. Johns— 200
Isle aux Nois[55]— 300
La Prairie, Vergore & some other Towns upon the South Shore of St.

[53]Burgoyne's "Mr. Washington" is in fact General George Washington, commander of the Continental Army then besieging Boston. The British officers regularly referred to Washington as "Mr. Washington" to deliberately avoid military titles, as they did not recognize officers' ranks in an army in rebellion against the king.

[54]Fort Oswegatchie, known by the French as Fort La Presentation, was constructed by the Frenchman Abbe Piquet at the intersection of the Oswegatchie River and St. Lawrence River in 1749. The French intended for it to serve as an Indian mission, trading post, and stop for transportation traffic using the St. Lawrence River. It was captured by the British in 1760, and renamed Fort Oswegatchie. In 1776 it was garrisoned by a detachment of the 8th Regiment of Foot, and a successful attack on the American strategic rear at the Cedars was launched in May 1776 from the fort.

[55]Isle aux Noix, or the "Isle of Nuts" as translated from the French, is an island located in the middle of the Richelieu River, nine miles north of the modern U.S.–Canada border at Rouse's Point (thirteen miles north of Point au Fer) and eleven miles south of St. John's. The French constructed a fortification on this island in 1759, as cannon mounted here could control both east and west channels of the river, and siege works were obviously obstructed by the intervening river. The British captured it following a determined siege in 1760. It was used as a storehouse and resting point by both the French and British during the Seven Years' War and by the Americans during their advance into Canada in 1775 and 1776. The island is very low and poorly drained, and in the eighteenth century it was known as a particularly unhealthy locale. The British would subsequently construct Fort Lennox on the island, which was garrisoned well into the nineteenth century; today it is maintained as a Parks Canada National Historical Site.

Lawrence opposite the Isle of Montreal with Posts of Communications to St. Johns— 200
For Escorts of Convoys over Lake Champlain— 400
Allowance for sickness— Desertion & other Casualties— 600
[Total] 3,000

It may be thought that Canadian Militia might supply part of these purposes, & I beg leave to observe it is so intended, the above calculation being made much too low without their assistance. It will be necessary to have Chains of Canadian Patroles and posts in the woods behind the Regulars, to intercept the communications between the Enemy and the ill-affected in Canada, to prevent desertion and procure intelligence, and for many other services that will be obvious for keeping the Country quiet.

These Services will be supplied by the several parishes, as their situation be respectively. So the objects & amount in the whole to 500 Men. Another great call upon the Canadians will be for workmen at the Fortifications of Sorell, St. John's, Chamblee & Isle aux Noix to the latter place it may be expedient to send the disobedient and refractory as a punishment, it being a place from which they can not desert. To compleat the necessary works in the course of next Summer will probably require 2000 Men.

A still greater call upon the Canadians will be for the Transport of all provisions, Artillery, Stores and Baggage of the Army from the repositories to the water, and afterwards all the carrying Places. This service may at the Opening of the Campaign require 200 Men, besides a very large proportion of carts and horses & will happen at the time of sowing of the Corn.

It is to be hoped that 1,500 or 2,000 Men Armed may be attached to the Army Destined to follow the Enemy. When these numbers are cast up, Canada will be found to contribute to the full what the Country can afford. I will venture to assert much more than they will afford [underline indicates emphasis in original], if any diminution is made in the numbers of regulars proposed to be left among them. Should there be grounds to suppose that France is taking an under hand in America, or has any future views towards the recovery of Canada, all the reasons for having a respectable Force there will derive double weight— For safe as the Country may be against a second seduction by the Rebels, it is obvious to the Slightest observation that many parts of it are liable to be seduced by the French, and it cannot be doubted that there are emissaries ready for such an employment.

Requisition [of General Carleton]

Twenty four Gun Boats to be constructed in England capable of carrying light 24 Pounders[,] heavy 12 Pounders & 8 Inch Howitzers & those pieces also to be sent from England.[56]

Observations [of General Burgoyne]

Tho this requisition is not comprised in the Memorandums given me by Genl. Carleton, I thought it proper to subjoin it as an object of great importance. For the detail and utility of the Boats Proposed, in justice to Major Gen[l] Phillips, I refer your Lordship to a Copy of that Gentleman's Letters to Gen[l] Carleton upon the subject & I beg leave to add that should it be found necessary to drive the Enemy from Lake George where it is probably if not obvious they will Strengthen themselves during the Winter, these Boats would Be of the utmost consequence, as they would bear the Transport by land from Ticonderoga to Lake George, infinitely better than those built of green Timber, would be from the Improvement made in the Construction of much greater Service when there, than any now built, and would save great time in the Campaign as it will probably be necessary otherwise to wait the building of them at Ticonderoga or Crown Point.

It would also be very proper to have Carriages constructed here of Seasoned Timber, of which Cap[t] Blomefield has a drawing, for conveying Boats, as well those built in America, as those now proposed over Land.[57]

I beg leave to Close these Observations with submitting to your Lordship the expediency of Transporting every Article Destined for the Service, in Canada early in the year and at once.

---

[56] These gunboats were flat-bottomed bateaux with a single mast, approximately twenty-eight feet in length, and mounting a single gun in the bow. They had been used previously by the British army in the Seven Years' War on the St. Lawrence River and had proven effective in inland waters. The British shipped a number of these gunboats in pieces from England and constructed additional gunboats at St. John's in the summer and fall of 1776. They had borne the brunt of the naval engagement at Valcour Island and had proven to be extremely effective on Lake Champlain in 1776. For more on these gunboats, refer to Cubbison, *"Artillery never gained more Honour."*

[57] It should be noted here that Burgoyne is demonstrating an excellent grasp of the difficulties that his army would face advancing south from Fort Ticonderoga.

Most of the foregoing Articles, if not all, are requisite for a vigorous opening of the Campaign[.] And the Provision which is to proceed to Lake Ontario for the whole years supply, ought to leave Montreal early in the Summer.

The Passage up the St. Lawrence both below and above Quebec is precarious, and at best extremely dilatory after the Month June, when the Westerly Winds prevail; and in the Autumn no dependence can be had of a Passage at all.

(Signed)
J. Burgoyne

6.16/9

Thoughts for conducting the War, from the Side of Canada [by Lieutenant General John Burgoyne][58]

When the last Ships came from Quebec, a Report prevailed in Canada, said to have been founded upon positive Evidence, that the Rebels had laid the Keels of several large vessels at Skenesborough, and Ticonderoga, and were resolved to exert their utmost Powers to construct a new, and formidable Fleet during the Winter.[59]

I will not, however, give Credit to their Exertions in such a Degree as to imagine the King's Troops will be prevented passing Lake Champlain early in the Summer; but will suppose the Operations of the Army to begin from Crown Point.

But as the properest means to form effective Plans, it to lay down every probable Difficulty, I will suppose the Enemy in great force at Ticonderoga. The different Works there are capable of admitting twelve thousand Men.

[58]This letter was printed as Appendix No. 3 in Burgoyne, *State of the Expedition from Canada*, iii–xii. The letter's content is not altered, with minor variations in capitalization, spelling and punctuation.

[59]Burgoyne did not anticipate this correctly, for the Americans were incapable of making such an effort.

I will suppose him also to occupy Lake George with a considerable naval Strength in order to secure his Retreat, and afterwards to retard the Campaign, and it is natural likewise to expect that he will take Measures to block up the Road from Ticonderoga to Albany by the Way of Skenesborough, by fortifying the strong Ground at different Places, and thereby oblige the King's Army to carry a weight of Artillery with it, and by falling trees, breaking bridges, and other obvious Impediments to delay, though he should not have Powers or Spirit finally to resist its Progress.[60]

The Enemy thus disposed, upon the side of Canada, it is to be consider'd what Troops will be necessary, and what Dispositions of them will be most proper to prosecute the Campaign with Vigour and Effect.

I humbly conceive the operating Army (I mean exclusively of the Troops left for the Security of Canada) ought not to consist of less than eight thousand Regulars Rank and File; the Artillery required in the Memorandum of General Carleton; a Corps of Watermen; two thousand Canadians including Hatchet Men and other Workmen; and a thousand or more Savages.

It is to be hoped that the Reinforcements, and the victualing Ships may all be ready to Sail from the Channel and from Cork[61] on the last day of March. I am persuaded that to sail with a Fleet of Transports earlier is to subject Government to Loss and Disappointment: it may reasonably be expected that they will reach Quebec before the 20th of May, a period in full time for opening the Campaign; the Roads and the Rivers and Lakes, by the melting and running off of the Snows, are in common Years impracticable sooner.[62]

But as the Weather long before that time will probably have admitted of Labour in the Docks, I will take for granted that the Fleet of last year, as well Batteaux as armed Vessels will be found repaired, augmented

---

60 It is important to note that this is precisely what happened during the summer of 1777, and Burgoyne fully anticipated that American Northern Theater commander Major General Philip Schuyler would employ this tactic against him.

61 The port of Cork, Ireland, was the logistical hub of the British army in North America. Most of the rations, in particular, destined for the British army were gathered at Cork and shipped aboard transport ships contracted by the Treasury Department to North American ports.

62 Burgoyne had not wasted his year in Canada; clearly he had gained full familiarity with the environmental conditions in Canada that directly affected military operations in that theater.

and fit for immediate Service. The Magazine that remain of Provisions, I believe them not to be abundant, will probably be formed at Montreal, Sorell and Chamblee.[63]

I conceive the first Business for those entrusted with the chief Powers, should be, to select and post the Troops destined to remain in Canada; to throw up the Military Stores, and Provisions with all possible Dispatch, in which Service the abovementioned Troops, if properly posted, will greatly assist; and to draw the Army destined for Operation to Cantonments within a few Days March of St. John as conveniently may be. I should prefer Cantonments at that Season of the Year to Encampment, as the Ground is very damp, and consequently pernicious to the Men, and more especially as they will have been for many Months before used to Lodging heated with Stoves, or between Decks in Ships.

All these Operations may be put in Motion together, but they severally require some Observation.

I should wish that the Troops left in Canada supposing the Number mentioned in my former Memorandum to be approved, might be made up as follows

	RANK & FILE
The 31st Regt. British, exclusive of their Light Company & Grenadiers	448
Maclean's Corps	300
The 29th Regiment	448
The ten additional Companies from Great Britain	560
Brunswick & Hesse Hanau to be taken by Detachment, or compleat Corps, as Major Genl. Riedesel shall recommend, leaving the Grenadiers, Light Infantry & Dragoons Compleat	650
Detachments from the other British Brigades, leaving The Grenadiers & Light Infantry compleat, and Squaring the Battalions equally	600
[Total]	3,006[.]

[63]"Magazine" here refers to a supply depot, not a store of ammunition. This was a common eighteenth-century use of the military term: "A place in which stores are kept, of arms, ammunition, provisions, etc. Every fortified town ought to be furnished with a large magazine, which should contain stores of all kinds, sufficient to enable the garrison and inhabitants to hold out a long siege, and in which smiths, carpenters, wheelwrights, etc. may be employed, in making every thing belonging to the artillery, as carriages, wagons, etc." Society of Gentlemen in Scotland, *Dictionary of Arts and Sciences*, 3:2.

My reason for selecting the 31st Regt. for this Duty is, that when I saw it last, it was not equally in Order with the other Regiments for Services of Activity.

I propose the 29th Regiment, as it is not at present brigaded.—

I propose Maclean's Corps because I very much apprehend Desertion, from such Parts of it as are composed of Americans, should they come near the Enemy. In Canada whatever may be their Disposition it is not so easy to effect it.

And I propose making up the Residue of Detachment, because by selecting the Men least calculated for Fatigue, or least accustomed to it, which may be equally good Soldiers in more confin'd Movements, and better provided Situations, the effective Strength for Operation is much greater, and the defensive Strength not impaired.

I must beg leave to state the expeditious Conveyance of Provisions and Stores from Quebec, and the several other Depositories, in order to form ample Magazines at Crown Point, as one of the most important Operations of the Campaign, because it is that upon which most of the rest will depend. If sailing Vessels up the St. Lawrence are alone to be employed, the Accident of contrary Winds may delay them two Months before they pass the Rapids of Richlieu, and afterwards St. Peter's Lake.[64] Delays to that extent are not uncommon, and they are only to be obviated by having a Quantity of small Craft in readiness to work with Oars—From the Mouth of the Sorell to Chamblee rowing and tracking is a sure Conveyance, if sufficient Hands are found. From Chamblee to St. Therese (which is just above the Rapids) land Carriage must be used and great Authority will be requisite to supply the Quantity necessary.

A Business thus complicated in Arrangement; in some parts unusual in practice, and in others perhaps difficult, can only be carried to the desired Effect by the Peremptory Powers, warm Zeal, and consonant Opinion of the Governor and though the former are not to be doubted, a failure in the latter, vindicated or seeming to be vindicated, by the plausible Obstructions that will not fail to be suggested by others, will be sufficient to crush such Exertions, as an Officer of a sanguine temper,

[64] The "Rapids" referred to here traverse several miles of the Richelieu River between Chambly and St. Jean. These rapids are dangerous and severe enough to preclude nautical travel on the Richelieu River between the two towns.

entrusted with the future Conduct of the Campaign, and whose personal Interest and fame therefore consequentially depended upon a timely Outset, would be led to make.

The Assembly of the Savages, and the Canadians will also entirely depend upon the Governor.

Under these Considerations it is presumed that the General Officer employed to proceed with the Army will be held to be out of the reach of any possible Blame 'till he is clear of the Province of Canada, and furnished with the proposed Supplies.

The Navigation of Lake Champlain secured by the superiority of our naval force, and the Arrangements for forming proper Magazines so established as to make the Execution certain, I would not lose a day to take Possession of Crown Point with Brigad^r Fraser's Corps, a large body of savages, a body of Canadians, both for Scouts, and for Work, and the best of our Engineers and Artificers well supplied with intrenching Tools.[65]

The Brigade would be sufficient to prevent Insult during the time necessary for collecting the Stores, forming Magazines, and fortifying this Post: all which should be done to a certain degree previous to proceeding in force to Ticonderoga, to such a Degree, I mean, as may be supposed to be effected in the time of transporting Artillery, preparing Fascines, and other Necessaries for Artillery Operations and by keeping the rest of the Army back during that period, the transport of Provisions would be lessened, and the Soldiers made of Use in forwarding the Convoys.[66]

But though there would be only one Brigade at Crown Point at that time, it does not follow that the Enemy should remain in a state of Tranquility. Corps of Savages supported by Detachments of Light Regulars

[65]This is exactly how Burgoyne would organize Fraser's advance corps throughout the 1777 campaign.

[66]A fascine is a tightly bound bundle of sticks, twigs, and branches. When completed, fascines were to be approximately six inches in diameter. They could be made to any length, although six feet and sixteen feet were typical. They could be used in construction to build roads or embankments, or to fill in marshy or wet ground. Fascines were most typically used in sieges to resist musketry and form batteries and fortifications or to fill in obstacles such as wet or dry ditches. Fascines could resist musketry, and when stacked together they comprised strong entrenchments. They could be manufactured entirely from natural materials, readily obtained from any wooded or brushy area.

should be continually on foot to keep them in Alarm, and within their works, to cover the reconnoitering of General Officers, and Engineers, and to obtain the best Intelligence of their Strength, Position, and Design.

If due Exertion is made in the preparations stated above, it may be hoped that Ticonderoga will be reduced early in the Summer and it will then become a more proper Place of Arms than Crown Point.[67]

The next Measures must depend upon those taken by the Enemy, and upon the general Plan of the Campaign as concerted at home. If it be determined that General Howe's whole force should act upon Hudson's River, and to the Southward of it, and that the only Object of the Canada Army be to effect a Junction with that force, the immediate Possession of Lake George would be of great Consequence as the most expeditious and most commodious Route to Albany; and should the Enemy be in force upon that Lake, which is very probable, every Effort should be tried by throwing Savages and Light Troops round it, to oblige them to quit it without waiting for naval Preparations. Should those Efforts fail the Route by South Bay and Skenesborough may be attempted, but considerable Difficulties may be expected, as the narrow Parts of the River may be easily choaked up and rendered impassable, and at best there will be necessity for a great deal of Land Carriage for the Artillery, Provisions, &c. which can only be supplied from Canada. In case of Success also by that Route; and the Enemy not removed from Lake George, it will be necessary to leave a Chain of Posts as the Army proceeds for the Securities of your Communication, which may too much weaken so small an Army.[68]

Least all these Attempts should unavoidably fail and it become indispensibly necessary to attack the Enemy by water upon Lake George, the Army at the Outset should be provided with Carriages, Implements and Artificers for conveying armed Vessels from Ticonderoga to the Lake.

---

[67]In fact, this is what occurred. Following the evacuation of Fort Ticonderoga and Mount Independence by the Continental Army in early July, Burgoyne established these two posts as his logistical center for operations of his army to the south. The British army maintained large garrisons at Fort Ticonderoga and Mount Independence supporting Burgoyne's army with maritime transportation until his surrender, only evacuating these facilities in early November.

[68]During the campaign, this is precisely how Burgoyne established his line of communications, protected by posts at Fort Ticonderoga/Mount Independence, the landing at the La Chute River at the northern extremity of the Ticonderoga portage, Diamond Island in Lake George, and Fort George at the southern end of Lake George.

These Ideas are formed upon the supposition that it be the sole Purposes of the Canada Army to effect a Junction with General Howe, or after cooperating so far as to get Possession of Albany, and open the Communications to New York, to remain upon the Hudson's River, and thereby enable that General to act with his whole Force to the Southward.

But should the Strength of the main American Army be such as to admit of the Corps of Troops now at Rhode Island remaining there during the Winter, and acting separately in the Spring, it may be highly worthy of Consideration whether the most important Purpose to which the Canada Army could be employed, supposing it in Possession of Ticonderoga, would not be to gain the Connecticut River.[69]

The Extent of Country from Ticonderoga to the inhabited Country upon that River opposite to Charles Town is about sixty Miles and though to convey Artillery and Provisions so far by Land would be attended with Difficulties, perhaps more than those above suggested upon a Progress to Skenesborough, should the Object appear worthy, it is to be hoped Resources might be found. In that Case it would be adviseable to fortify with one or two Strong Redoubts the Heights opposite to Charles Town and establish Posts of Savages upon the Passage from Ticonderoga to those heights to preserve the communication and at the same time prevent any Attempt from the Country above Charles Town, which is very populous, from molesting the Rear, or interrupting the Convoys of Supply while the Army proceeded down the Connecticut, should the Junction between the Canada and Rhode Island Armies be effected upon the Connecticut it is not too sanguine an Expectation that all the New England Provinces will be reduced by their Operations.[70]

[69]As noted previously, the British army did not implement this alternative component of Burgoyne's plan.

[70]Redoubts are a form of fortification, normally constructed of dirt, stone, earth, logs, or sod in North America; more commonly constructed of brick and stone in Europe. A redoubt was a fortification of no fixed size or design, completely enclosed, and was sized and designed based on the terrain feature it was intended to defend. They were usually manned with infantry, although redoubts might also contain a few pieces of light or field artillery. A redoubt could be rapidly constructed with immediately available materials and could enable a relatively small force to defend a fixed position. Redoubts were extensively used in the eighteenth century in both North America and Europe. For a detailed study of redoubts, refer to Cubbison, *Historic Structures Report.*

To avoid breaking in upon other Matters, I omitted in the beginning of these Papers to state the Idea of an Expedition at the Outset of the Campaign by the Lake Ontario and Oswego to the Mohawk River which, as a Diversion to facilitate every proposed Operation, would be highly desirable, provided the Army should be reinforced sufficiently to afford it.[71]

It may at first appear from a view of the present Strength of the Army that it may bear the sort of Detachment proposed by myself last year for this Purpose, but it is to be considered that at that time the utmost Object of the Campaign, from the advanced Season, and unavoidable Delay of Preparation for the Lakes, being the Reduction of Crown Point and Ticonderoga unless the Success of my Expedition had opened the Road to Albany, no greater Numbers were necessary than for those first Operations. The Case in the present year differs, because the Season of the Year affording a Prospect of very extensive Operations, and consequently the Establishment of many Posts, Patroles &c. will become necessary, the Army ought to be in a state of Numbers to bear those Drains, and still remain sufficient to attack any thing that probably can be opposed to it.

Nor, to argue from probability, is so much force necessary for this Diversion this year, as was required for the last, because we then knew that General Schuyler with a thousand Men was fortified upon the Mohawk, when the different Situation of things is considered, Viz. the Progress of Gen$^{l.}$ Howe, the early Invasion from Canada, the threatening of the Connecticut from Rhode Island &c. it is not to be imagined that any Detachment of such force as that of Schuyler can be supplied by the Enemy for the Mohawk.[72] I would not therefore propose it of more (and I have great Diffidence whether so much can be prudently afforded) than Sir John Johnson's Corps, an hundred British from the second Brigade, and an hundred more from the 8th Regt. With four

[71]This obviously became the St. Leger expedition against Fort Stanwix. Refer to Burgoyne's previous letter to Henry Clinton in which he noted that together with Sir John Johnson he had developed the concept for this diversionary column down the Mohawk River during the 1776 campaign.

[72]This was a miscalculation on Burgoyne's part, as the Americans in the spring of 1777 established a strong and capable garrison at Fort Stanwix on the Great Carrying Place between the Mohawk River and Wood Creek.

Pieces of the lightest Artillery and a body of Savages, Sir John Johnson to be with the Detachment in Person, and an able Field Officer to command it. I should wish L$^{t.}$ Col$^{onl.}$ S$^{t.}$ Leger for that Employment.

I particularize the second Brigade because the first is proposed to be diminished by the 31st Regiment remaining in Canada, and the rest of the Regiment drafted for the Expedition being made also part of the Canada Force, the two Brigades will be exactly squared.

Should it appear upon the Examination of the really effective numbers of the Canada Army that the Force is not sufficient for proceeding upon the above Ideas with a fair prospect of success, the alternative remains of embarking the army at Quebec, in order to effect a junction with General Howe by sea, or to be employed separately to co-operate with the main designs, by such means as should be within their strength upon other parts of the continent. And though the army, upon examination of the numbers from the returns here, and the reinforcements designed, should appear adequate, it is humbly submitted, as a security against the possibility of its remaining inactive, whether it might be expedient to entrust the latitude of embarking the army by sea to the commander in chief, provided any accidents during the Winter, and unknown here, should have diminished the Numbers considerably; or that the enemy from any Winter Success to the Southward should have been able to draw such force towards the Frontier of Canada and take up their Ground with such Precaution as to render the intended Measures impracticable or too hazardous. But in that case it must be considered that more Force would be required to be left behind for the Security of Canada than is supposed to be necessary when an Army is beyond the Lakes, and I do not conceive any Expedition from the Sea can be so formidable to the Enemy, or so effectual to close the War, as an Invasion from Canada by Ticonderoga, this last Measure ought not to be thought of; but upon positive Conviction of its Necessity.

Hertford Street
Feb$^{y.}$ 28th 1777
(signed)
J. Burgoyne

Sir Henry Clinton Papers, File 20:34

Letter from Major General John Burgoyne to Captain Philemon Pownell, Royal Navy, March 2, 1777[73]

Hertford Street, March 2d 1777

My dear Sir
I should have acknowledged the friendly Letter you honoured me with sooner, had I not waited the decision of my destination for the ensuing Campaign, & also to inform myself whether there was a probability of my being able to accept your kind invitation on board the Apollo.

It is now fixed that I return to Canada, & the command of the army is to be mine whenever we reach the bounderies of the province; but this last is intelligence you will keep to yourself. I only mention it to introduce the courses with which I feel for your connection in the naval command provided we have any thing to do on Lake George for I hardly expect we shall be found upon Lake Champlain. At all events I am sanguine enough to believe all lake business will be over early enough in the year to enable whoever commands there to return down the St. Lawrence & keep Levrels [?] in the Ocean.

I met Lord Sandwich at a dinner yesterday; & I need not say how happy I was to receive from his mouth, without any previous opening on my part, intimation that I might have my passage on board the Apollo. He spoke of it as a certainty provided I could be ready in time, & gave me the flattery of adding that he dared to say the arrangement would be as agreeable to Capt. Pownell as to myself. He assured I can not have higher gratification than in being thus known to possess your friendship.

Whether it will be possible to avoid a Convoy I [blotted illegible] but request you to give me a line of information as quick as possible of the time you can be ready that I may go in it accordingly.

If there is any encumberance with [blotted illegible] can be useful to you let me know at the same time.

I was sorrowed to find you had quitted Perth before my arrival & thus

---

[73]Captain Philemon Pownell had commanded the frigate HMS *Blonde*, aboard which Generals Burgoyne, Phillips, and Riedesel had traveled on their way to Canada in the spring of 1776. In March 1777 Captain Pownell commanded the frigate HMS *Apollo*.

I was prevented the honour of being presented to your family. I hope they are in health, & I have the honour to be with much respect Dear Sir & I am your most faithful and affec^{t} Honourable Servant

J: Burgoyne

6.16/10

Extract of a Letter from Lord George Germain, to General Sir Guy Carleton, Whitehall, March 26, 1777[74]

My Letter of the 22^{d} August 1776, was intrusted to the Care of Captain LeMaitre, one of your Aid de Camps. After having been three times in the Gulph of S$^{t.}$ Lawrence, he had the Mortification to find it impossible to make his Passage to Quebec, and, therefore, returned to England with my Dispatch, which tho it was prevented by that Accident from reaching your Hands in due time, I nevertheless think proper to transmit to you by this the earliest opportunity.[75]

You will be informed, by the Contents thereof, that as soon as you should have driven the Rebel Forces from the Frontiers of Canada, it was His Majesty's pleasure that you should return to Quebec, and take with you such part of your Army as, in your Judgement & Discretion, appeared sufficient for the Defence of the province, that you should detach Lieut. General Burgoyne, or such other Officer as you should think most proper, with the Remainder of the Troops, and direct the Officer so detached to proceed with all possible Expedition to join General Howe, and to put himself under his Command.

[74]This letter was printed as Appendix No. 4 in Burgoyne, *State of the Expedition from Canada*, xii–xvii. There are no substantive differences; only relatively minor variations in capitalization and punctuation were noted.

[75]The August 22, 1776, letter was finally delivered to Governor Carleton in early May 1777, more than eight months after it had been dispatched. Routine travel times were six weeks following the prevailing winds from New York City to London and eight weeks from London to New York City. However, fall and winter communications by ship to Canada were tenuous at best, and such lengthy transit times, though rare, were not unprecedented. This example validates the challenges of military and government communications in the age of sailing ships. Willcox, "Too Many Cooks," 57.

With a View of quelling the Rebellion as soon as possible, it is become highly necessary that the most speedy Junction of the two Armies should be effected, and therefore, as the Security + good Government of Canada absolutely requires your Presence there; it is the King's Determination to leave about 3000 Men under your Command for the Defense + Duties of that Province, and to employ the Remainder of your Army upon two Expeditions—the one under the Command of Lieut. General Burgoyne, who is to force his Way to Albany; and the other under the Command of Lieut. Colonel St. Leger, who is to make a Diversion on the Mohawk River.

As this plan cannot be advantageously executed without the Assistance of Canadians + Indians, His Majesty strongly recommends it to your Care, to furnish both Expeditions with good and sufficient Bodies of those Men: and I am happy in knowing that your Influence among them is so great, that there can be no room to apprehend you will find it difficult to fulfill His Majesty's Expectations.[76]

In order that no time may be lost in entering upon these important Undertakings, General Burgoyne has received Orders to sail forthwith for Quebec & that the intended Operation may be maturely considered, and afterwards carried on in such manner as is most likely to be followed by Success, he is directed to consult with you upon the Subject, and to form and adjust the Plan as you both shall think most conducive to His Majesty's Service.

I am also to acquaint you that as soon as you shall have fully regulated every thing relative to these Expeditions (and the thing relies upon your zeal that you will be as expeditious as the nature of the Business will admit) it is His Majesty's Pleasure that you detain for the Canada Service

The 8th Regt., deducting 100 for the Expedition to the Mohawk	460
Battalion Companies of the 29th and 31st Regiments	896
Battalion Companies of the 34th, deduct 100 for Exped to the Mohawk	348
Eleven additional Companies from Great Britain	616
Detachments from the two Brigades	300
Detachments from the German Troops	650

[76]Lord George Germain, ensconced in England and never having served or traveled to America, clearly had no conception of the difficulties and expenses involved in recruiting and retaining American Indian warriors.

Royal Highland Emigrants 500
[Total] 3770.

You will naturally conclude that this Allotment for Canada has not been made without properly weighing the several Duties which are likely to be required. His Majesty has not only considered the several Garrisons, and Posts which probably it may be necessary for you to take, Vizt. Quebec, Chaudiere, the disaffected Parishes of Point Levis, Montreal, and Posts between that Town and Oswegatchie, Trois Rivieres, St. John's, Isle aux Noix, La Prairie, Vergere, and some other Towns upon the South Shore of St. Lawrence, opposite the Isle of Montreal, with Posts of Communication to St. John's. But he hath also reflected that the several operations which will be carrying on in the different Parts of America must necessarily confine the Attention of the Rebels to the respective Scenes of Action and secure Canada from external Attacks and that the internal Quiet which at present prevails is not likely to be interrupted, or if interrupted will soon be restored by your Influence over the Inhabitants. He therefore trusts that 3000 Men will be quite sufficient to answer every possible Demand. It is likewise His Majesty's Pleasure that you put under the Command of Lieut. General Burgoyne

The Grenadiers & Light Infantry of the Army (except of the 8th Regt and the 24th Regt) as the advanced Corps under the Command of Brigadier General Fraser — 1,568
First Brigade Battalion Companies of the 9th, 21st & 47th Regts, deducting a Detachment of 50 from each Corps to remain in Canada — 1,194
Second Brigade Battalion Companies of the 20th, 53d & 62d Regts, deducting 50 men from each Corps to remain as above — 1,194
All the German Troops, except the Hanau Chasseurs & a Detachment of 650 — 3,217
The Artillery, except such parts as shall be necessary for the Defence of Canada
[Total] 7,173.

Together with as many Canadians & Indians as may be thought necessary for this Service, and after having furnished him in the fullest & compleatest manner with Artillery, Stores, Provisions, and every other Article necessary for his Expedition, and secured to him every Assistance which it is in your power to afford and procure, you are to give him Orders to pass Lake Champlain, and from thence by the most vigorous

Exertion of the Force under his Command to proceed with all Expedition to Albany, and put himself under the Command of Sir William Howe.

From the King's Knowledge of the great preparations made by you last year to secure the Command of the Lakes and your Attention to this Part of the Service during the Winter, His Majesty is led to expect that every thing will be ready for General Burgoyne's passing the Lakes by the time you and he shall had adjusted the plan of the Expedition.

It is the King's further pleasure that you put under the Command of Lieut. Colonel St. Leger.

Detachment from the 8th Regiment	100
Detachment from the 34th Regiment	100
Sir John Johnson's Regiment of New York	133
Hanau Chasseurs	342
[Total]	675.

Together with a sufficient Number of Canadians & Indians, and after having furnished him with proper Artillery, Stores, provisions, and every other necessary Article for his Expedition, and secured to him every Assistance in your Power to afford and procure, you are to give him Orders to proceed forthwith to and down the Mohawk River to Albany, and put himself under the Command of Sir William Howe.

I shall write to Sir William Howe from hence by the first packet, but you will nevertheless endeavour to give him the earliest Intelligence of this Measure, and also direct Lieutenant General Burgoyne & Lieutenant Colonel St. Leger to neglect no opportunity of doing the same that they may receive Instructions from Sir William Howe. You will at the same time inform them that until they shall have received orders from Sir William Howe It is His Majesty's Pleasure that they act as Exigencies may require and in such manner as they shall judge most proper for making an Impression on the Rebels and bringing them to obedience. But that, in so doing, they must never lose View of their intended Junctions with Sir William Howe as their principal Objects.

In case Lieutenant General Burgoyne, or Lieutenant Colonel St. Leger should happen to die, or be rendered through Illness incapable of executing those great Trusts you are to nominate to the respective Commands such Officer, or Officers, as you shall think best qualified to supply the place of those whom His Majesty has, in his Wisdom, at present appointed to conduct those Expeditions.

6.16.11

Extract of a Letter from Sir William Howe to Lord George Germain, New York, April 2, 1777

Your Lordship will receive inclosed a Copy of my Letter to Sir Guy Carleton, which goes in a few Days by a Frigate convoying Sir John Johnson, Lieut. Col. Maclean and several Officers both British & Canadian, lately returned from their Captivity, together with a few Recruits for the several Corps in Canada.[77]

6.16/11a

Copy of a Letter from Genl Sir William Howe to General Sir Guy Carleton, New York, April 5, 1777 In Sir William Howe's of April 2, 1777

Copy
New York 5th April 1777

Sir,
Having but little expectation, that I shall be able, from the want of sufficient strength in this Army, to detach a Corps in the beginning of the Campaign, to act up Hudson's River, consistent with the Operations already determined upon. The Force your Excellency may deem expedient to advance beyond your Frontiers, after taking Ticonderoga will, I fear, have little assistance from hence to facilitate their approach: and as I shall probably be in Pennsylvania when that Corps is ready

[77]Colonel Allan Maclean (1725–1797) was first commissioned in the renowned Scotch Brigade of the Dutch service, participating in the Siege of Bergen op Zoom in 1747. He entered British service in 1756. He was severely wounded at the assault on Ticonderoga on July 8, 1758. Promoted to captain commanding a New York Independent Company of the British army, he was also wounded at the Siege of Niagara in 1759. In 1775 he raised the Royal Highland Emigrants, and he was instrumental in the defense of Quebec in 1775–76, for which he gained considerable commendation from Governor General Carleton. He served with the British army in Canada throughout the remainder of the American War of Independence, seeing no more active service. He returned to England, where he died in 1797, following a long and distinguished military career. Rogers, *Hadden's Journal and Orderly Books*, 547–555.

to advance in to this Province, it will not be in my power to communicate with the Officer Commanding it so soon as I could wish: He must therefore pursue such Measures as may, from circumstances, be judged most conducive to the Advancement of His Majesty's Service, consistently with your Excellency Orders for his Conduct.

The Possession of Ticonderoga will naturally be the first object & without presuming to point out to your Excellency the advantages that must arise by securing Albany the adjacent Country—I conclude they will engage the next attention; but omitting others, give one leave to suggest, that this situation will open a free intercourse with the Indians, without which we are to expect little assistance from them on this side.

The further Progress of this Corps—depending so much upon the Enemy's Movements, cannot be foreseen at this distance of time—still I flatter myself, I have reason to expect, the friends of Government in that part of the Country, will be found so numerous & so ready to give every aid & assistance in their power, that it will prove no difficult task to reduce the more Rebellious parts of the Province. In the mean while I shall endeavour to have a Corps upon the lower part of Hudson's River sufficient to open the Communication for Shipping thro' the highlands, at present obstructed by several Forts erected by the Rebels for that purpose, which Corps may afterwards act in favour of the Northern Army.[78]

Major Edmestone of the 48th Regt having been long detained a Prisoner at Albany & having procured leave to come here to negotiate his exchange, I have sent him back with directions to inform Mr. Schuyler,[79] that if he permits him to go to Canada, I shall release a Major in exchange. He has information of too delicate a nature to commit to Paper

[78]Howe is referring to the Hudson Highlands, where there were two fortified positions. The strongest position included Forts Montgomery and Clinton at the mouth of Popolopen Creek and Anthony's Nose on the Hudson River, at the present location of the Bear Mountain Bridge. A secondary position, considerably weaker and unfinished, was Fort Constitution at Constitution Island across from West Point farther north on the Hudson.

[79]Major General Philip Schuyler (1733–1804) was the American Northern Theater commander, serving as the theater commander rather than an army commander. A wealthy New York aristocrat who had served the British army as a quartermaster throughout the Seven Years' War, Schuyler was an extremely skilled and accomplished officer who performed superbly in the 1776 and 1777 campaigns. He was a committed Patriot and a close personal friend of George Washington. He took responsibility for the fall of Fort Ticonderoga in July 1777 and, as a result, lost his command, though the eventual American victory at Saratoga would owe much to Schuyler's leadership and efforts. Following Burgoyne's surrender at Saratoga, Schuyler hosted Burgoyne and his staff at his mansion in Albany. Again, note that Howe is referring to him here as "Mr. Schuyler" to avoid providing him with any military rank.

& of the utmost importance in favour of the Northern Army advancing to Albany, which I trust he will find some means of communicating, even tho' he should not obtain leave to go to Canada in person.

I beg your Excellency may be pleased to favour me with the earliest Intelligence of your Movements, and flatter myself some method will be found of conveying it immediately to New York.

With my most earnest wishes for your health & success—I have the honour to be &c.

(signed)
W. Howe

6.16/12

Extract of a Letter from Sir Guy Carleton to Lord George Germain, Quebec, May 9, 1777

I received by Capt. Le Maitre[80] who arrived here with General Burgoyne in the Apollo the 6th Inst.,[81] your Lordship's several Dispatches from No. 3 to 7 inclusive, your separate letter of 26th March last, and the others from No. 9 to 16 inclusive with the annexed Papers.

6.16/13

Extract of a Letter from Sir Guy Carleton to Lord George Germain, Quebec, June 26, 1777 Rec. August 3

I acquainted your Lordship in my Letter No. 19, that the Troops order'd to be detached from the Army in Canada, to serve upon Expeditions

[80]Captain Francis Le Maistre had been commissioned as an ensign in the 98th Foot in 1760 and fought in the West Indies. He had then served as adjutant in the 7th Regiment of Foot in Canada, as brigade major during the blockade of Quebec in 1775–76, and subsequently as Carleton's aide. Carleton dispatched him to London in May 1776 with news of the successful defense of Quebec. He had a prominent military career, generally connected with Carleton, and would become one of the earliest and most preeminent English settlers of Quebec Province in Canada.

[81]HMS *Apollo. Inst.*, for "Instant," was commonly utilized in the eighteenth century to mean "the same month."

under Lieutenant General Burgoyne and Lieutenant Colonel St. Leger, had been immediately put under their respective Commands. Lieutenant General Burgoyne proceeded on the Service allotted to him by your Lordship about the 17th Instant, having sent on part of his Army some time before, and the last of it left St. John's about the 20th. Major General Phillips serves upon this Expedition, and I have the Satisfaction of being able to assure you that all the Troops, as well Foreign and National, are in high Health & good Discipline.

This Army has been joined by the Indians of St. Regis, Sault St. Louis, Lake of the Two Mountains, and St. Francis, and the Hurons are immediately to follow: the whole of which Indians amount above 500 Warriors, but it is necessary to observe, that there is always an uncertainty as to the Force of the Indians, Parties being continually leaving them and returning, as their Humour leads them.

By Accounts from Michellimakinac [Fort Michilimackinac] I learn that all the Western Nations are desirous of coming down, and that the Difficulty is to prevent the Number of them from being so great as to cause Distress to His Majesty's Service. One Body consisting of 120 are just arrived (part of those I ordered last Year) they will follow General Burgoyne as fast as possible.

Having learnt by Intelligence from the Frontiers of this province that considerable Numbers of Loyal Inhabitants were waiting for the Approach of the Army; to furnish them with Opportunities of escaping from among their Rebellious Neighbors, and that they will take Arms. I have made out Blank Commissions, and delivered them to General Burgoyne, to form two Corps, as he shall find occasion, wishing to make up, as far as I am able, for his Want of Powers, and that in some degree he may avail himself of a favorable Disposition in these people, and turn it to public Utility immediately, lest the favorable Moment should be lost in Delay.[82]

Lieut. Colonel St. Leger has likewise begun his Movements, taking with him the Detachment of the 34th & the Royal Regiment of New York, which is increased to about 300 Men, and a Company of Canadians. He will be joined by the Detachment of the 8th, and the Indians

[82] These "two Corps" became Peters's and Cressup's corps of Loyalists. Although these two commands served faithfully throughout the campaign and sustained severe casualties at Bennington, the "considerable numbers" that Sir Guy Carleton anticipated turned out to be only a few score in actuality.

of the Six Nations,[83] with the Missesages, as he proceeds: About a Hundred of the Hanau Chasseurs have since arrived, and they are on their way to join him.[84]

That Your Lordship may be more particularly informed of all these Matters, I transmit the Orders which I have issued on this Occasion, together with Copies of all Letters worth your Notice, which have passed between Lieutenant General Burgoyne, Major General Phillips, and me, on the Subject of the Arrangement they have thought proper to propose, a List of which papers is herewith inclosed.[85]

6.16/13a

Copy of a Letter from Sir Guy Carleton to Lieut. Genl. Burgoyne, Montreal, June 10, 1777 In Sir Guy Carleton's of June 26, 1777

Montreal 10th June 1777

Sir

Although I have communicated to you every thing I was made acquainted with relative to you, and Lieutenant Colonel St. Leger Expeditions I cannot let you depart without giving you all the Orders concerning them in the manner: they are contained in Lord George Germain's Letter of the 26th March 1777 for your further Guidance and Instruction, an Extract from which Letter is herewith inclosed, and I inclose you extracts of two Letters from Lord Barrington, the one respecting the Brigadiers, the other the Recruits of the 33d Regiment going under your Command.[86]

---

[83] The Six Nations of the Iroquois Confederation consisted of the Seneca tribe (to the west), and the Cayuga, Onandaga, Oneida, Tuscarora, and Mohawk tribes (to the east). Sir William Johnson, an adopted Mohawk, had enjoyed particularly strong relationships with the Iroquois, which were continued by the British after Sir William's death in 1774.

[84] This battalion of German "hunters" or "light infantrymen," experienced German woodsmen equipped with German short-barreled hunting rifles, joined St. Leger en route to Fort Stanwix on August 26, 1777. Commanded by Lieutenant Colonel Carl von Kreutzbourg, they served throughout the entirety of the Siege of Fort Stanwix.

[85] These orders and letters are preserved as File 6.24, provided in this volume.

[86] William Wildman Shute Barrington, 2nd Viscount Barrington (1717–1793), British secretary of war in 1776 and 1777, and member of the King's Privy Council. At the time, the position of secretary of war held little real power or authority.

I also inclose for your private Information a Copy of a Letter which I have received from General Sir William Howe, wishing you a happy and successful Campaign

I am &c.
G.C.
[Copy to] Lieutenant General Burgoyne

6.16/14

Extract of a Letter from the Honorable Sir William Howe to Lord George Germain, New York, July 5, 1777

I had the Honor to receive, by the Somerset, transmitted by Mr. D'O'yly Copies of your Lordship's Letters to Sir Guy Carleton, of the 26th of March, and John Stuart Esqr. Of the 2nd of April, together with the several States of the Anspach Corps, Detachment of Artillery, Chasseurs, &c.

6.16/15

Extract of a Letter from Lieutenant General Burgoyne to Lord George Germain, Camp on the River Bouquet, near Lake Champlain, June 22, 1777

Operations of Consequence being so near, I should have postponed this Dispatch, but that I was unwilling to omit the immediate Opportunity that offers of conveying to Your Lordship Intelligence so satisfactory as I imagine will be that of the general Cordiality of the Indians.

Five Hundred of those of the nearest Nations arrived punctually at the Rendezvous I had fixed for them, and a larger Number are daily expected. I met them yesterday in Congress; and I inclose to Your Lordship the Substance of what passed. I gave them the War Feast according to their Custom in the Evening, and this Morning a considerable Detachment are gone forth, supported by regular Light Infantry, to break in upon the Enemy's Convoys & Communications from the Side of Connecticut, and to cover the Reconnoitering of the Country on the other Side Ticonderoga, towards South Bay which is the Route I imagine they mean to retreat by when Ticonderoga shall be forced— A plan that I shall endeavour to disconcert, as well as that of retreating by Lake George.[87] Should they try to pass cross the Green Mountains, to Connecticut River, I should hope they would be much exposed to my pursuit. I have taken the Occasion of the above Detachment to disperse a Manifesto, a Copy of which I herewith inclose.

6.16/15a

Substance of the Speech of Lieut. Genl. Burgoyne to the Indians in Congress at the Camp upon the River Bouquet, June 21, 1777. And of their Answer[88]

Chiefs and Warriors.

The Great King, Our common Father and the Patron of all who seek and deserve his Protection; has considered with Satisfaction the general Conduct of the Indian Tribes from the beginning of the Troubles of America. Too sagacious and too faithful to be deluded or corrupted, they have observed the violated Rights of the Parental State they love, and burned to vindicate them. A few Individuals alone, the refuse of a small Tribe, at the first was led astray; and the misrepresentations, the specious Allurements, the insidious Promises and diversified plots in which the Rebels are exercised, and all of which they employed for that effect, have served only in the end to enhance the honour of the Tribes in general by demonstrating to the World how few and how contemptible are the Apostates. It is a Truth known to you all that these pitiful examples excepted (and they probably have before this day hid their faces in shame) they collective voices and hands and hearts of the Indian Tribes over this vast continent, are on the side of Justice, of Law, and of the King.

[87] This was the "Otter Creek Raid" of early July 1777, previously mentioned.

[88] This letter was printed as Appendix No. 6 in Burgoyne, *State of the Expedition from Canada*, xxi–xxv. There are no substantive alterations, only minor variations in capitalization and punctuation.

The restraints you have put upon your resentment in waiting the King your Father's call to Arms (the hardest proof, I am persuaded, to which your affection could have been put) is another manifest and affecting mark of your adherence to that principle of connection, to which you were always fond to allude, and which it is mutually the Joy and the duty of the Parent to cherish.

The Clemency of your Father has been abused; the offers of his Mercy have been despised; and his further patience would in his Eyes become culpable in as much as it would with hold redress from the most grievous Oppressions in the Provinces that ever disgraced the history of Mankind.

It therefore remains for me, the General of one of his Majesty's Armies, and in this Council His Representative, to release you from those bonds which your Obedience imposed— Warriors, you are Free— Go forth in might of your valour and your cause—strike at the common enemies of Great Britain and America— Disturbers of public order, peace and Happiness—destroyers of Commerce; Parricides of the State.

The circle round you, the Chiefs of His Majesty's European forces, and of the Princes his Allies, esteem you as Brothers in the War. Emulous in glory and in friendship, we will endeavour reciprocally to give and to receive Examples. We know how to value, and we will strive to imitate, your perseverance in enterprise, and your constancy to resist hunger, weariness and pain. Be it our task, from the dictates of our Religion, the laws of our Warfare, and the principles and interest of our policy, to regulate your passions when they overbear, to point out where it is nobler to spare than to revenge; to discriminate degrees of guilt; to suspend the up-lifted stroke; to chastise and not to destroy.

This War to you my friends is new. Upon all former Occasions in taking the field you held yourselves authorized to destroy wherever you came, because every where you found an Enemy. The Case is now very different.

The King has many faithful Subjects dispersed in the Provinces, consequently you have many brothers there; and these People are the more to be pitied, that they are persecuted or imprisoned wherever they are discovered or suspected; and to dissemble is to a generous mind a yet more grevious punishment.

Persuaded that your Magnanimity of Character, joined to your principles of affection to the King, will give me fuller Control over your minds than the military Rank with which I am invested, I enjoin your most serious Attention to the Rules which I hereby proclaim for your invariable Observation during the campaign.

I positively forbid bloodshed when you are not opposed in Arms.

Aged Men, Women, Children and Prisoners must be held sacred from the Knife or Hatchet, even in the time of actual conflict.

You shall receive Compensation for the Prisoners you take, but you shall be called to account for Scalps.

In Conformity and Indulgence to your Customs, which have affixed an Idea of Honour to such Badges of Victory, you shall be allowed to take the Scalps of the Dead when killed by your fire and in fair Opposition; but, on no account, or pretence, or subtlety, or prevarication, are they to be taken from the wounded, or even dying; and still less pardonable, if possible, will it be held, to kill Men in that condition on purpose, and upon a Supposition that this protection to the wounded would be thereby evaded.

Base lurking assassins, Incendiaries, Ravagers and Plunderers of the Country, to whatever Army they may belong, shall be treated with less Reserve; but the latitude must be given you by order, and I must be the Judge of the Occasion.

Should the enemy, on their part dare to countenance acts of Barbarity towards those who may fall into their hands it shall be yours also to retaliate; But 'till Severity shall be thus compelled, bear immovable in your hearts this solid maxim, it cannot be too deeply impressed, that the great essential Reward, worthy service of your Alliance, the Sincerity of your Zeal to the King, your Father and never-failing Protector, will be examined and judged, upon the Test only of your steady and uniform Adherence to the Orders and Councils of those, to whom His Majesty has entrusted the direction and the honour of his Arms.

Answer from an old Chief of the Iroquois

I stand up in the name of all the Nations present to assure our Father that we have attentively listened to his Discourse. We receive You as our Father because when you speak We hear the Voice of our great Father beyond the Great Lake.

We rejoice in the approbation you have expressed of our Behaviour.

We have been tried and tempted by the Bostonians; but We have loved our Father and our Hatchets have been Sharpened upon our Affections.

In proof of the Sincerity of our professions our whole villages able to go to War are come forth. The Old and Inform, our Infants and Wives alone remain at home.

With one common Assent we promise a constant Obedience to all you have ordered and all you shall order, and may the Father of Days give you many and Success.

6.16/15b

Copy of Manifesto issued by Lieut. Genl. Burgoyne

By John Burgoyne Esquire, Lieutenant General of his Majesty's Armies in America, Colonel of the Queen's Regiment of Light Dragoons, Governor of Fort William in North Britain, one of the Representatives of the Commons of Great Britain in Parliament, and commanding an Army & Fleet employ'd on an Expedition from Canada, &c. &c. &c.

The Forces entrusted to my command are designed to act in concert, and upon a common principle, with the numerous Armies & Fleets which already display in every Quarter of America, the power, the justice, and, when properly sought, the mercy of the King.

The cause in which the British Arms are thus exerted applies to the most-affecting Interests of the human Heart: and the military Servants of the Crown, at first called forth for the sole purpose of ensuring the Rights of the Constitution, now combine with love of their Country & duty to their Sovereign, the other extensive incitements which spring from a due sense of the general privileges of Mankind. To the eyes and ears of the temperate part of the public, and to the breasts of suffering Thousands in the provinces, be the melancholy appeal whether the present unnatural Rebellion has not been made a foundation for the compleatest system of Tyranny that ever God in his displeasure suffered for a time to be exercised over a forward & stubborn Generation.

Arbitrary imprisonment, confiscation of property, persecution & torture, unprecedented in the inquisition of the Romish Church are among the palpable enormities that verify the affirmative. These are inflicted, by Assemblies & Committees who dare to profess themselves friends to Liberty, upon the most quiet Subjects, without distinction of age or sex, for the sole Crime, often for the sole suspicion, of having adhered in principle to the Government under which they were born, & to which by every tye [tie] divine & human they owe allegiance. To consummate these shocking proceedings the profanation of religion is added to the most profligate prostitution of common reason; the consciences of Men are set at nought; & multitudes are compelled not only to bear Arms, but also to swear subjection to an usurpation they abhor.

Animated by these considerations; at the head of Troops in the full powers of Health, discipline & valour; determined to strike where necessary, and anxious to spare where possible, I by these presents invite and exhort all persons, in all places where the progress of this army may point—and by the blessing of God I will extend it far—to maintain such a conduct as may justify me in protecting their Lands, habitations & Families. The intention of this Address is to hold forth security not depradation to the Country.

To those whom Spirit & principle may induce to partake the glorious task of redeeming their Countrymen from Dungeons, and reestablishing the blessings of legal Government I offer encouragement and employment; and upon the first intelligence of their associations I will find means to assist their undertakings. The domestic, the industrious, the infirm & even the timid Inhabitants I am desirous to protect, provided they remain quietly at their Houses, that they do not suffer their Cattle to be removed, nor their Corn or Forage to be secreted or destroyed; that they do not break up their Bridges or Roads; nor by any other acts directly or indirectly endeavor to obstruct the operation of the King's Troops, or supply or assist those of the Enemy.

Every species of Provision brought to my Camp will be paid for at an equitable rate, in solid Coin.[89]

In consciousness of christianity, my royal Master's clemency & the honor of soldiership, I have dwelt upon this Invitation & wished for more persuasive terms to give it impression: And let not people be led to disregard it by considering their distance from the immediate situation of my Camp—I have but to give stretch to the Indian forces under my direction, and they

---

[89]"Hard" currency, known as specie, was universally in short supply in the North American colonies. In fact, the shortage of silver and gold coins had adversely impacted the American invasion of Canada in 1775–76. Thus, Burgoyne's promise to pay in copper, silver, or gold currency was a considerable enticement to many colonists.

amount to thousands, to overtake the hardened Enemies of Great Britain and America, I consider the same, wherever they lurk.

If notwithstanding these endeavors & sincere inclinations to affect them, the phrenzy [frenzy] of hostility should remain, I trust I shall stand acquitted in the eyes of God and Man in denouncing & executing the vengeance of the State against the willful outcasts— The Messengers of justice & of wrath await them in the Field; and devastation, famine & every concomitant horror that a reluctant but indispensible prosecution of military duty must occasion, will bar the way to their return.[90]

Camp at the River Boquet
June 24th 1777
J. Burgoyne

By Order of his Excellency the Lieut. General
Robt Kingston, Secretary.

[*No file #*]

General Orders issued by Lieutenant General John Burgoyne, June 30, 1777[91]

Gen[l] Orders Crown Point June 30th 1777
Parole S[t] David C:S: Wales

G. O. The Army Embarks tomorrow to Approach the Enemy[.] We are to contend for the King and the constitution of Great Britain to vindicate Law and to relieve the Oppressed. A Cause in which His Majestys Troops and those of the Princes His Allies will feel equal exactment. The Services required of this particular Expedition are critical and conspicuous[.]

[90]Threatening the American colonists with attack or "devastation, famine &. . . horror" by American Indians was an extremely poorly considered idea. Indian raids on the American frontiers had slaughtered thousands of colonists, destroyed hundreds of families, and caused hundreds of farms and scores of communities to be burned. North American colonists well remembered the French and Indian raids of the recent Seven Years' War and generally distrusted and hated the Native Americans. This threat served to recruit scores of hundreds of volunteers for the Patriot militia and Continental Army against Burgoyne in this campaign. By late September, the American Northern Theater Army had been so expanded by recruits obtained in this manner that Burgoyne was significantly outnumbered at Bemis Heights.

[91]Clement, *47th Regiment of Foot*; and Rogers, *Hadden's Journal and Orderly Book*, 81–82.

During our progress occasions may Occur, in which, not difficulty nor labour nor life are to be regarded. This Army must not retreat.

When Orders are given and no particular time Named they are to be executed not only with punctuallity but with the utmost dispatch. No Officers to go to the Advanced Corp of the Army without leave & having permission one never to go beyond the Outposts of those Corps—without previous leave from the Officers Command^{g} them.

The General to beat tomorrow in place of the Revalley [reveille] at the dawn of Day, the Assembly to beat an hour afterwards at which time the whole will embark. A Field Officer with 100 British, and 100 Germans to remain at Chimney Point to take charge of the provisions & Stores at that place. The Wings are to take up their new encampment in Two Lines. So soon as the Regiments are encamp'd a working party of 20 Men and a Subaltern from each will parade in front of their respective Regiments.

His Excellency Sir Guy Carleton has been pleased to make the following promotion in the Army. 53^{d} Regimt. M$^{r.}$ Hamilton to be Ens^{n} in room of Ens^{n} Davies deceased[.] Quarter Master Price of the 53d Regt. is Appointed Lieu$^{t.}$ in the [Royal Highland] Emigrants[.] Serj$^{t.}$ Major John Chambers of the 53^{d} Regt. Is Appointed Quarter Master in the Room of Lieu$^{t.}$ Price. M$^{r.}$ May is Appointed Ensign in the Emigrants. Cap$^{t.}$ Green of the 31st Reg$^{t.}$ is appointed Aide-de-Camp to Maj$^{r.}$ Gen$^{l.}$ Phillips during the Campaign.

6.16/16

Extract of a Letter from Sir William Howe to Lord George Germain, New York, July 15, 1777

Various Accounts have been lately brought from the Northern part of this province, in regard to the Army from Canada, and I have this Day had the Satisfaction to receive a Letter from Lieut. General Burgoyne with a Confirmation of his being before Ticonderoga, a Copy of which your Lordship has inclosed. Intelligence otherwise leaves no Room to doubt his being in possession, but it does not come from Authority so certain as to justify me in a positive Declaration of the Fact.

6.16/16a

Copy of a Letter from Lieut. General Burgoyne to Genl. Sir William Howe, before Ticonderoga, July 2, 1777

Camp before Ticonderoga July 2nd: 1777.

Sir

I wait some necessaries of the heavy Artillery which have been retarded by contrary Winds upon Lake Champlain to open Batteries upon Ticonderoga.[92]

The Army is in the fullest Powers of Health and Spirits. I have a large Body of Savages and shall be joined by a larger in a few days. Ticonderoga reduced I shall leave behind me proper Engineers to put it in an impregnable state, and it will be Garrisoned from Canada where all the destined supplies are safely arrived, my force therefore will be left complete for future operations.[93]

The Enemy do not appear to have the least suspicion of the King's real Instructions relative to the Campaign after the Reduction of Ticonderoga.[94]

I shall implicitly follow the Ideas I communicated to Your Excellency in my Letters from Plymouth and Quebec.

I have the honour to be, Sir
Signed J Burgoyne

[92]Artillery supplies for Burgoyne's army were contained in the radeau *Thunderer*, a notoriously poor sailing vessel. For this, refer to Cubbison, *"Artillery never gained more Honour,"* 72–73.

[93]When faced with the decision, Governor Carleton determined that Ticonderoga properly lay "outside" of the borders of Canada and that he could not, within the confines of his orders, garrison a post beyond the borders of that province. Accordingly, Burgoyne had to withdraw regiments from his army to garrison Ticonderoga.

[94]The surprise, of course, was on Burgoyne, for Howe also had no intentions of following the "King's real Instructions."

6.5/6

Monthly General Returns of the British Troops, Canada, May 1, 1777 (Copy)

Monthly General Returns of the British Army Serving under His Excellency General Sir Guy Carleton, Head Quarters at Quebec 1st May 1777

	OFFICERS PRESENT										
	COMMISSIONS										
	General	Lieut General	Major General	Brigdr General	Colonel	Lieut Colonel	Major	Captain	1st [Lt]	2d [Lt]	Ensigns
Regiments											
Staff	1	1	1	3							
9th						1	1	7	11		5
20th						1	1	8	9		4
21st						1	1	7	11	3	
24th						1	1	8	11		7
29th						1	1	5	7		7
31st						1	1	8	9		8
34th						1	1	6	11		6
47th					1	1	1	6	7		6
53d						1	1	8	11		6
62d						1	1	8	11		5
Artillery							1	5	2	10	
Rl. H. Emigrants							1	6	6		6
Rl. Regt New York							1	3	6		7
Total	1	1	1	3	1	10	13	85	112	13	68

	OFFICERS PRESENT									
	STAFF									
	Qr Mar Genl	Dy Qr Mr Genl & Assistants	Adj General	Dep Adj General	Majors Brigade	Aid de Camps	Adjutants	Quar Masters	Chaplains	Surg & Mates
Regiments										
Staff	1	5		1	3	7			1	
9th							1	1		1
20th							1	1		2
21st							1			2
24th							1	1		2
29th							1			2
31st							1	1	1	2
34th							1	1		2
47th							1	1		2
53d							1	1		2
62d							1	1		2
Artillery							1	1	1	2
Rl. H. Emigrants							1	1		2
Rl. Regt New York							1	1		2
Total	1	5		1	3	7	13	11	3	25

	OFFICERS ABSENT				
	COMMISSIONS				
	Colonels	Lieut Colonels	Majors	Captains	Subalterns
Regiments					
Staff					
9th	1			1	2
20th	1				4
21st	1			1	3
24th	1				1
29th	1			3	5
31st	1				2
34th	1			2	2
47th				2	5
53d	1				2
62d	1				2
Artillery				2	1
Rl. H. Emigrants		1		3	7
Rl. Regt New York		1		1	1
Total	9	2	[0]	15	37

	OFFICERS ABSENT				
	STAFF				
	Ad^{j} General	Chaplains	Adjutants	Qu^{r} Masters	Sur^{gs} & Mates
Regiments					
Staff	1				
9th		1			1
20th		1			
21st		1		1	
24th		1			
29th		1		1	
31st					
34th		1			
47th		1			
53^{d}		1			
62^{d}		1			
Artillery					
R^{l}. H. Emigrants					
R^{l}. Regt New York					
Total	1	9	[0]	2	1

	OFFICERS VACANT		
	Captains	Lieutenants	Ensigns
Regiments			
Staff			
9th			1
20th		1	1
21st		2	
24th			
29th			
31st			
34th			
47th			
53d			
62d			1
Artillery			
Rl. H. Emigrants			
Rl. Regt New York			
Total	[0]	3	3

	EFFECTIVE RANK AND FILE	
	Sergeants Present	Drum[rs] & Fifes Present
Regiments		
Staff		
9th	30	22
20th	30	20
21st	30	20
24th	30	22
29th	22	15
31st	29	22
34th	24	18
47th	29	20
53d	28	20
62d	30	22
Artillery	12	12
Rl. H. Emigrants	30	16
Rl. Regt New York	15	5
Total	339	234

	EFFECTIVE RANK AND FILE							
	Present fit for Duty	Sick in Quarters	Sick in Hospital	On Command	Recruiting	Recruits not joined	Prisoners with the Rebels	Total
Regiments								
Staff								
9th	531	17	1					549
20th	487	20	20					527
21st	478	47	6		1			532
24th	470	54	6					530
29th	346	1	43	121				511
31st	493	14	15	18				540
34th	381	30	4	120		1		536
47th	377	19	14	90	1		2	503
53d	483	28	5	15				531
62d	379	15	18	136				548
Artillery	236	3	11					294
Rl. H. Emigrants	304	3		45			46	398
Rl. Regt New York	148	6	3					157
Total	5113	257	146	545	2	1	48	6156

	WANTING TO COMPLEAT TO THE ALLOWANCE			ALTERATIONS SINCE LAST RETURN			
	Sergeants	Drums & Fifes	Rank & File	Inlisted	Dead	Discharged	Deserted
Regiments							
Staff							
9th			11		2		
20th			33		1		
21st			28		3		
24th			30				
29th		2	49		1	1	
31st			20		1		
34th			24				
47th			57		2	1	
53d			29		5		
62d			12	2		1	
Artillery			24				
Rl. H. Emigrants		4	162	1			
Rl. Regt New York				7		3	
Total	[0]	6	479	10	15	6	[0]

6.5/7

Monthly General Returns of the German Troops, Canada, May 1, 1777

General Monthly Returns of the German Troops serving under His Excellency General Sir Guy Carleton Head Quarters at Quebec May 1st 1777

	OFFICERS PRESENT							
	COMMISSION							
	Major General	Brig^{dr} Generals	Colonels	Lt Colonels	Majors	Captains	Lieutenants	Cornets and Ensigns
Regiments								
Staff	1	2						
Regiment of Dragoons			1	1	1	4	3	4
Batt^{n} of Grenadiers				1		4	7	4
Reg^{t} Prince Frederick				1	1	5	9	4
Reg^{t} of Rhetz				1	1	5	10	5
Reg^{t} of Riedesel			1	1	1	5	7	4
Reg^{t} of Specht			1		1	5	10	5
Reg^{t} of Light Infantry					1	5	9	4
Reg^{t} of Hanau			1	1		6	8	5
Total	1	2	4	6	6	39	63	35

	OFFICERS PRESENT										
	STAFF										
	Dep^y Adj^t General	D^y Q^r Mr Genl	Aid de Camp	Major Brigade	Pay-master	Sec-retary	Ad-jutants	Qua^r Masters	Chap-lains	Judge Ad-vocates	Sur-geons and Mates
Regiments											
Staff	1	1	3	2	1	1					
Regiment of Dragoons							1	1	1	1	5
Batt^n of Grenadiers							1				5
Reg^t Prince Frederick							1	1	1	1	6
Reg^t of Rhetz							1	1	1	1	6
Reg^t of Riedesel							1	1	1	1	6
Reg^t of Specht							1	1	1	1	6
Reg^t of Light Infantry							1	1			6
Reg^t of Hanau							1	1	1	1	4
Total	1	1	3	2	1	1	8	7	6	6	44

OTHER PERSONS ATTACHED TO THE STAFF				
	Clerks	Artificers	Hautboys[95]	Provost & Servants
Regiments				
Staff	2	11		
Regiment of Dragoons	1	3	1	2
Batt^{n} of Grenadiers				2
Reg^{t} Prince Frederick	1		4	2
Reg^{t} of Rhetz	1		4	2
Reg^{t} of Riedesel	1		4	2
Reg^{t} of Specht	1		4	2
Reg^{t} of Light Infantry				
Reg^{t} of Hanau			6	2
Total	7	14	23	14

	Sergeants & other non Commissioned Officers not rank & File	Drummers Fifers & Trumpeters	Officers Servants
Regiments			
Staff			4
Regiment of Dragoons	24	8	27
Batt^{n} of Grenadiers	40	20	26
Reg^{t} Prince Frederick	49	13	37
Reg^{t} of Rhetz	50	16	40
Reg^{t} of Riedesel	50	15	38
Reg^{t} of Specht	50	15	40
Reg^{t} of Light Infantry	49	14	34
Reg^{t} of Hanau	46	20	
Total	358	121	246

[95]Musicians.

EFFECTIVE RANK AND FILE					
	Present fit for Duty	Sick in Quarters	Sick in Hospital	On Command	Total
Regiments					
Staff					
Regiment of Dragoons	213	6			219
Batt^n^ of Grenadiers	425	3			428
Reg^t^ Prince Frederick	490	10			500
Reg^t^ of Rhetz	494	14			508
Reg^t^ of Riedesel	499	14			513
Reg^t^ of Specht	497	19			517
Reg^t^ of Light Infantry	427	18	1		446
Reg^t^ of Hanau	504	3	1		508
Total	3549	87	2		3639

	WANTING TO COMPLEAT				ALTERATIONS SINCE LAST RETURN		
	Sergeants & other Non Comm[d] Officers	Drums Fifers & Trumpeters	Privates Soldiers Chasseurs and Dragoons	Officers Servants	Recruited	Dead	Deserted
Regiments							
Staff							
Regiment of Dragoons			26			2	1
Batt[n] of Grenadiers			24	1			
Reg[t] Prince Frederick	1	3	35	3		2	
Reg[t] of Rhetz			26	1		1	
Reg[t] of Riedesel		1	22	1	1	1	
Reg[t] of Specht		1	18	1			1
Reg[t] of Light Infantry	1		82	3	2	4	
Reg[t] of Hanau	2	1	53				
Total	4	6	286	10	3	10	2

6.5/5

Return of the Additional Companies, Quebec, July 1, 1777

Return of the Additional Companies of the 8th 9th 20th 21st 24th 31st 34th 47th 53rd 62d Regiments, Quebec, 1st July 1777

	Officers Present					
	Captains	1st Lieutenants	2nd Lieutenants	Ensigns	Sergeants Present	Drummers & Fifers Present
Companies of Regiments						
8th		1			1	1
9th				1	2	2
20th	1	1		1	3	2
21st	1	1	1		3	2
24th	1	1		1	2	2
29th	1	1		1	3	2
31st	1	1		1	3	2
34th				1	2	1
47th		1			2	1
53rd	1	1			3	2
62nd	1			1	2	2
Total	7	8	1	7	26	19

	EFFECTIVE RANK & FILE						
	Present fit for duty	Sick in Quarters	Sick in Hospital	On Command	Recruiting	On Furlough	Total
Companies of Regiments							
8th	23		1				24
9th	44		1	3			48
20th	50	3	3				56
21st	48	6	2				56
24th	34	6	2				42
29th	50	4	2				56
31st	56						56
34th	36	4		15			55
47th	21	1	5				27
53rd	50	3					53
62nd	55	1					56
Total	467	28	16	18	[0]	[0]	529

	WANTING TO COMPLEAT TO THE ALLOWANCE			ALTERATIONS SINCE LAST RETURN				
	Sergeants	Drums & Fifes	Rank & File	Inlisted	Dead	Discharged & Recommended	Discharged & not Recommended	Deserted
Companies of Regiments								
8th	1							
9th	1		8					
20th								
21st								
24th	1		14					
29th				1				
31st								
34th			1					
47th			9					5
53rd			3		1			1
62nd				1			1	
Total	3	[0]	35	2	1	[0]	1	6

ABSENT NOT YET ARRIVED						
	Captains	Lieutenants	Ensigns	Serjeants	Drummers	Rank & File
Companies of Regiments						
8th	1		1	1	1	34
9th						
20th						
21st						
24th						
29th						
31st						
34th		1		1	1	
47th			1	1		15
53rd						
62nd		1		1		
Total	1	2	2	4	2	49

6.5/4

Monthly General Return of the Army in Canada, October 1, 1777

Monthly General Return of the Army in Canada Serving under His Excellency General Sir Guy Carleton, Head Quarters at St. Johns 1st October 1777

	OFFICERS PRESENT									
		COMMISSIONS								
Regiments	No of Companies	General	Brigdr General	Colonel	Lieut Colonel	Major	Captain	1st [Lt]	2d [Lt]	Ensigns
Staff		1	1							
8th	10				1	1	4	6		6
29th	11				1	1	5	7		7
31st	11				1	1	6	7		8
34th	11					1	4	6		4
Royal Highland Emigrants	10				1		8	6		7
Detachments from British [Regiments with Burgoyne]	6						6	3	2	7
Detachments from the Germans [Regiments with Burgoyne]	7						6	12		
Total	66	1	1	[0]	4	4	39	47	2	39

	OFFICERS PRESENT										
	STAFF										
	Q^r Ma^r Genl	D^y Q^r Mr Genl	Asst Qr Mr Gen-erals	Ad-jutant Gen-erals	D^y Ad-jutant Gen-erals	Majors of Brig-ade	Aids de Camp	Chap-lains	Ad-jutants	Quarter Masters	Surgeons & Mates
Regiments											
Staff	1	1	2	1		2	4				
8th									1	1	2
29th									1	1	2
31st								1	1	1	2
34th									1		1
Royal Highland Emigrants									1	1	2
Detachments from British [Regiments with Burgoyne]									1		
Detachments from the Germans [Regiments with Burgoyne]											
Total	1	1	2	1	[0]	2	4	1	6	4	9

	EFFECTIVE RANK AND FILE	
	Sergeants Present	Drum[rs] & Fifes Present
Regiments		
Staff		
8th	25	20
29th	23	15
31st	25	16
34th	21	15
Royal Highland Emigrants	30	20
Detachments from British [Regiments with Burgoyne]	18	9
Detachments from the Germans [Regiments with Burgoyne]	53	15
Total	195	110

	EFFECTIVE RANK AND FILE								
	Present fit for Duty	Sick in Quarters	Sick in Hospital	On Command	Recruiting	Recruits not joined	On Furlough	Prisoners with the Rebels	Total in Canada
Regiments									
Staff									
8th	382	24	5	109	1	27			548
29th	389	32	0	57			1		473
31st	415	14	23	35					487
34th	352	17	6	11		2			388
Royal Highland Emigrants	345	0	13	54	5		37		454
Detachments from British [Regiments with Burgoyne]	209	34	24	24					291
Detachments from the Germans [Regiments with Burgoyne]	597	0	3	0					600
Total	2689	121	74	284	6	29	38	[0]	3241

	WANTING TO COMPLEAT TO THE ALLOWANCE			ALTERATIONS SINCE LAST RETURN			
	Sergeants	Drums & Fifes	Rank & File	Inlisted	Dead	Discharged	Deserted
Regiments							
Staff							
8th			12				
29th		2	31			10	
31st	1		21				
34th				19	2		
Royal Highland Emigrants			106	1		1	3
Detachments from British [Regiments with Burgoyne]							
Detachments from the Germans [Regiments with Burgoyne]							
Total	1	2	170	20	2	11	3

6.24

Correspondence of Sir Guy Carleton Relating to Genl. Burgoyne's Expedition

List

1. Extract of a Letter from Sir Guy Carleton to Lord George Germain dated Quebec 20th May 1777. Inclosure in Sir Guy Carleton's of 26th June 1777 received 3rd August.
2. Copy of a Letter from Sir Guy Carleton to Major General Phillips, dated Quebec 8th April 1777.
3. Copy of a Letter from Sir Guy Carleton to Major General Phillips, dated Quebec 12th May 1777.
4. Copy of Orders for the Troops to serve under Lieutenant General Burgoyne.
5. Copy of a Letter from Capt. Foy to Lieut. Colonel St. Leger, dated Quebec 12th May 1777.
6. Copie d'une Lettre Circulaire aux Colonels des Milices & aux Commissairies Canadiens de Transport. [translation: Copy of a Circular Letter to the Militia Colonels and Canadian Commissaries of Transportation]
7. Copy of a Letter from Capt. Foy to Capt. Fraser Assistant Superintendent of Indian Affairs, dated Quebec 13th May 1777.
8. Copy of a Letter from Sir Guy Carleton to Lieutenant General Burgoyne, dated Quebec 19th May 1777.
9. Copy of a Letter from Sir Guy Carleton to Lieut. Colonel Bolton of the 8th Regiment, dated Quebec 18th May 1777.
10. Copy of a Letter from Sir Guy Carleton to the Officer commanding at Oswegatchie, dated Quebec 18 May 1777.
11. Copy of a Letter from Sir Guy Carleton to Colonel Butler dated Quebec 18th May 1777.
12. Copy of a Letter from Capt. Foy to Capt. Mackay, dated Quebec 19th May 1777.
13. Extract of a Letter from Lieut. General Burgoyne to Sir Guy Carleton, dated Montreal 26 May 1777.
14. Proposed Disposition of the Hospital for the Service in Canada.
15. List of the Staff proposed for the Expedition under Lieutenant General Burgoyne.
16. Copy of a Letter from Lieut. Colonel St. Leger to Lieut. General Burgoyne dated 15th May 1777.
17. Extract of a Letter from Sir Guy Carleton to Lieut General Burgoyne, dated Quebec 29th May 1777.

18. Extract of a Letter from Sir Guy Carleton to Lieut. General Burgoyne, dated Quebec 28th May 1777.
19. Extract of a letter from Sir Guy Carleton to Lieut. Govr. Cramahé dated Montreal 9th June 1777.
20. Copy of a Letter from Lieut. General Burgoyne to Sir Guy Carleton, dated Montreal 7th June 1777.
21. Copy of Proposals for furnishing Horses, Carriages and Drivers for the Service of the Army, under the Command of Lieutenant General Burgoyne.
22. Copy of Proposals for furnishing Horses & Drivers for the Service of the Artillery on the Expedition under Lieut. General Burgoyne.
23. Copy of a Letter from Sir Guy Carleton to Lieutenant General Burgoyne dated Montreal 7th June 1777.
24. Extract of a Letter from the Secretary at War to Sir Guy Carleton dated 17th August 1776.
25. Extract of a Letter from the Secretary of War to Sir Guy Carleton dated 25th March 1777.
26. Copy of a Letter from Capt. Foy to Lieut. Colonel St. Leger dated Montreal 10th June 1777.
27. Copy of a letter from Sir Guy Carleton to Lieut. Genl. Burgoyne dated St. John's 13th June 1777.
28. Copy of a Letter from Lieut. General Burgoyne to Sir Guy Carleton dated St. Johns 15th June 1777.
29. Copy of a Letter from Sir Guy Carleton to Lieut. General Burgoyne dated Montreal 17th June 1777.
30. Copy of a Letter from Major General Phillips to Sir Guy Carleton dated St. John's 17th June 1777.
31. Copy of a Letter from Major General Phillips to Sir Guy Carleton dated St. John's 17th June 1777.
32. Copy of a Letter from Sir Guy Carleton to Major General Phillips, dated Montreal 18 June 1777.
33. Copy of Orders—Montreal 18th June 1777.
34. Copy of a Letter from Major General Phillips to Sir Guy Carleton dated St. John's 19th June 1777.
35. Copy of a Letter from Sir Guy Carleton to Major General Phillips, dated Quebec 26th June 1777.
36. Copy of Letter from Sir Guy Carleton to Lieutenant General Burgoyne, dated Quebec 26th June 1777.

6.24/1

No. 1. Extract of a Letter from Sir Guy Carleton to Lord George Germain, Quebec, May 20, 1777 Received July 2

Lieutenant General Burgoyne shall have every Assistance in my power, and my most ardent Wishes for the Prosperity of the King's Arms—The Troops & Armament destined for his Expedition had immediate Orders to receive and follow his Directions, that he may combine their Movements as he thinks proper. The same so far as concerns Lieutenant Colonel St. Leger's Expedition, the Hanau Chasseurs excepted. I have no such Corps in my Army, nor any Information concerning it in your Dispatch, but it is set down as part of the Corps I am to put under his Command. At first I thought it might be a Mistake, and that the Brunswick Chasseurs were meant, Lieutenant General Burgoyne says not; that these are to go with him, and that he thinks the Hanau Chasseurs are on their way hither. All the Indians in the Neighborhood of Niagara and Lake Ontario have orders to join Lt. Coll. St. Leger. Those in the lower part of the Province, and those ordered last year from Michilimackinac, are to attend Lieutenant General Burgoyne; Three Hundred Canadian Militia are also to make the Campaign, to be disposed of by Lieutenant General Burgoyne, which Canadians, with those necessary for scouring the Woods towards the New England Provinces, and a great number which must be employed for the forwarding all things for those two Expeditions, is I think in the first Dawning of good Order and Obedience as much as ought in prudence to be demanded from this unfortunate Province.

The Marine has been greatly improved and augmented which the Impatience of last Year's Service would not permit. Those on Lake Champlain have been put under Lieutenant General Burgoyne's Command, and the greatest part of those on Lake Ontario will attend Lt. Col. St. Leger—

6.24/2

No. 2. Copy of a Letter from Sir Guy Carleton to Major General Phillips, Quebec, April 8, 1777[96]

Head Quarters Quebec the 8th Apr. 1777

Sir

My dispatches from the Secretary of State inform me that it is His Majesty's pleasure I should remain in Canada; and that I should detach Lieutenant General Burgoyne with a certain part of the Army, which is so particularly detailed that nothing is left to me but the seeing these Commands put into execution, and, in the case of the death or illness of General Burgoyne, the naming of his successor. As it is my intention to provide everything for this detachment with the same care and attention to the good of the service as it I were to command it myself, I shall propose that you accompany General Burgoyne, and doubt not he will be happy in the thoughts of having such able assistance, while I can only express my sorrow at not having it in my power to testify to you, by a greater mark, the high sense I entertain of the Zeal and Activity with which you have constantly executed the orders which occasions have required my giving you, as well as of the obligations I am under to you for the great trouble which you have so heartfully taken upon you, in the management of our publick works, which, by your diligence, I have the satisfaction of finding in such forwardness as that the expedition under General Burgoyne will be able to proceed without delay—

An other detachment is in like manner ordered to be made under Lieutenant Colonel St. Leger.

I want as soon as possible, for the Information of General Burgoyne, as exact an Account as can be had of the bateaux—of what are ready, what will be ready, and when.

I have received your dispatches of the 5th Instant.

I am Sir &c &c.
(Signed) G.C.

---

[96]Likely misdated here, this letter was probably written on May 8, 1777.

PS I must likewise beg leave to know how far the orders given some time ago, with respect to transporting provisions to St. John's, and Oswegatchie, have been carried into execution, and I trust you will press the Commissary upon this point as much as possible.

6.24/3

No. 3. Copy of a Letter from Sir Guy Carleton to Major Genl. Phillips, Quebec, May 12, 1777

Head Quarters Quebec 12th May 1777.

Sir
I receive your Letters of the 9th and 10th Instant.

You will have learnt from my last Letter; that General Burgoyne is to take the Command of the Troops that are to go out of the province, and you will see by the enclosed orders that I put them immediately under him; But, tho I have nothing further to do with them, I shall nevertheless go up to Montreal in order to be at hand to give every assistance in my power towards forwarding the King's service in this particular.

I am Sir &c. &c.
(Signed) G. C.

6.24/4

No. 4. Copy of Orders for the Troops to serve under Lieut. Genl. Burgoyne

Head Quarters Quebec 10th May 1777.
Parole St. Benedict

The King having thought proper to order, that a detachment from the Army under my Command, be sent upon an expedition under Lieutenant General Burgoyne, and that this detachment be composed of the Grenadiers, Light Infantry and 24th regiment, together with the

9th, 20th, 21st, 47th, 53rd, and 62nd regiments (except detachments of 50 men from each of the six last mentioned regiments) and all the German Troops, except a detachment of 650, these Corps will accordingly hold themselves in readiness to march at the shortest Notice, orders for which will be given them by Lieutenant General Burgoyne, to whom in the meantime, they will make all reports, as well as to the Commander in Chief.

The detachments of 50 men with a Captain[,] two Subalterns, and noncommissioned officers in proportion, from each of the six regiments as above, will assemble at the present Head quarters of their respective regiments and there, remain till further orders.

The Artillery, and the departments of the Quartermaster General, Hospital, and Commisariate will likewise supply Lieutenant General Burgoyne, with such returns as he may call for to enable him to lay before the Commander in Chief, the portions of the several Articles they are capable of furnishing.

6.24/5

No. 5. Copy of a Letter from Capt. Foy to Lieut. Colonel St. Leger, Quebec, May 12, 1777

Head Quarters Quebec 12th May 1777.
Sir

The King having been pleased to signify his pleasure thro' the Secretary of State, that a detachment from this Army to consist of one hundred men from the 8th regiment[,] one hundred men from the 34th Regiment, Sir John Johnson's Corps,[97] and the Hanau Chasseurs, be sent under your Command upon an expedition, concerning which you will receive further instructions, I am to acquaint you that the commander in chief directs you to order one hundred Men accordingly, and Officers in proportion, of the 34th Regiment to hold themselves in immediate readiness for this service, orders to the same effect are immediately to be dispatched to the 8th Regiment and Sir John Johnson's Corps, as will

[97] The King's Royal Regiment of New York.

be to the Chasseurs when they arrive, and the whole are to obey such further Orders as you shall give them.

I am Sir &c. &c.
(Signed) E. Foy[98]

6.24/6[99]

No. 6. Copie d'une Lettre Circulaire aux Colonels des Milicies aux Commissaries Canadiens de Transport

Copie
Quartier General Quebec 12 Mai 1777

Monsier
Le Roi agent commandé qu'un Detachment dé L'Armée in Canada, sort employé sur une Expedition, sous les Ordres du Lieutenant General Burgoyne, Je suis ordonné a vous signifier le plaisier du Commandant in Chef, que vous obeissiez a toutes les Requisitions qui pouront vous etre faites, de la part du dit Luetenant General Burgoyne, sort en Corvées, on autres chores dependents de votre Department, communiqueant nean moins a son Excellence tout ce qui regarde en particulier la Milice.

Je Suis &c.
(Signé) E. Foy[100]

[98]Captain Edward Foy (c. 1730–1778) first entered the British service as a private in the Royal Regiment of Artillery in 1750, became a cadet at the Royal Military Academy in Woolwich in 1754, and was commissioned a lieutenant fireworker in the Royal Artillery in 1755. He served with distinction at the Battle of Minden in 1759 and was a veteran artillery officer with (*continued*) over twenty years' service by the time of the American War of Independence. He held a variety of positions on Carleton's officer staff in 1776 and 1777, serving most of 1777 as adjutant general. He died in Canada in 1778, having earned a reputation as an able and faithful secretary and having rendered lifelong service in the British Royal Artillery. Rogers, *Hadden's Journal and Orderly Books*, 381–386.

[99]This brief letter was translated from the original French through the generosity of my colleague John Magrath, of the U.S. Army Combat Studies Institute, Fort Leavenworth, Kansas.

[100]This is not particularly good French, and it appears to have been copied by an English clerk or secretary to whom French was a second language.

[TRANSLATION: Copy of a Circular Letter for the Militia Colonels and Commissaries of Canadian Transport]
Copy
General Headquarters in Quebec, 12 May 1777

Sir
The King, having commanded that one detachment of the army in Canada be employed on an expedition under the command of Lieutenant General Burgoyne, I have ordered you at the pleasure of the Commander in Chief, who you will obey for all the requisitions which arise, you make on behalf of the said Lieutenant General Burgoyne whether by corvée or other dependent chores from your department, communicate to his Excellency everything with particular regard for the militia.

I am, &c.
(Signed) E. Foy

6.24/7

No. 7. Copy of a Letter from Capt. Foy to Capt. [Alexander] Fraser, Assistant Superintendent of Indian Affairs, Quebec, May 13, 1777

Head Quarters Quebec 13th May 1777.

Sir
I have it in command to signify the General's Pleasure to you, that you wait upon Genl. Burgoyne, as soon as you are able, after the receipt of this, in order to receive his commands relative to the Assembling the Indians, and such other directions as he shall think proper to give you in regard of that department[.]

I am Sir &c &c
Signed E. Foy

6.24/8

No. 8. Copy of a Letter from Sir Guy Carleton to Lieut. Genl. Burgoyne, Quebec, May 19, 1777

Quebec the 19 of May 1777

Sir
I inclose Letters for the commanding Officer of the 8th Regiment, Colonel Butler Superintendent of Indian Affairs, the Officers at the Posts of Oswegatchie and Michilimackinac, the three first contain full orders and directions for preparing the detachment for Lieutt. Col. St. Leger assembling the Indians which are to join him and for giving him every assistance which these Officers have it in their power to afford. But as I refer Lieut. Col. Bolton & Col. Butler to Lieutt. Col. St. Leger for fixing the rendezvous both of the detachment of the 8th and the savages it will be proper that he should communicate his Sentiments upon that subject to them; I will only offer it as my opinion that Cataraqui is the properest place for that purpose[.]

Captains Tise And John[101] being gone up to Montreal will carry these letters and receive any instructions you shall be pleased to give them[.]

I am Sir &c &c
(Signed) G.C.
[To] Lieutt. Genl. Burgoyne

6.24/9

No. 9. Copy of a Letter from Sir Guy Carleton to Lieut. Col. Bolton of the 8th Regt., Quebec, May 18, 1777

Head Quarters Quebec 18 May 1777

Sir
It being the Kings pleasure that I put under the Command of Lieutt. Col. St. Leger to be employed upon an expedition

[101]Otherwise unidentified.

A Detachment from the 8th Regiment 100 Men
A Detachment from the 34th the Same [100 Men]
Sir John Johnson's Regiment of New York and
a Corps of Hanau Chasseurs[.]

You will accordingly direct that one hundred Men with Officers in proportion to the strength of the Regiment hold themselves in immediate readiness to march and to obey all orders they shall receive from Lieut. Col. St. Leger[.]

The King having further Signified his pleasure that a Sufficient number of Indians be joined to this detachment you will therefore employ every means in your Power to assemble as many Indians as you can communicate with, and prevail upon them to put themselves with proper leaders, who will be appointed by Colonel Butler, under the command of Lieut. Col. St. Leger and to exert their utmost efforts under his direction in the Service of their King and Father.

You will consult with Lieut. Col. St. Leger in regard of the Rendezvous both of the Troops & Savages & give every assistance in your power to promote the Service upon which he is employed.

I am Sir &c &c.
Signed G.C.
[To] Lieutt. Col. Bolton

6.24/10

No. 10. Copy of a Letter from Sir Guy Carleton to the Officer commanding at Oswegatchie, Quebec, May 18, 1777

Head Quarters Quebec 18 May 1777

Sir
Lieut. Col. St. Leger with a detachment under his Command being to pass by your Post I desire you will give him every possible assistance and any Armed Vessels he shall require is to follow his directions.

I am Sir &c &c.
Signed G.C.
The Officer Commanding at Oswegatchie

6.24/11

No. 11. Copy of a Letter from Sir Guy Carleton to Col. Butler, Quebec, May 18, 1777

The King having thought proper that a detachment from this Army together with a Sufficient number of Indians should be employed upon an expedition under the command of Lieut$^{t.}$ Colonel S$^{t.}$ Leger, I am therefore to request that you will exert the zeal which has ever distinguished your Conduct by now using every Means in your Power to collect as large a body as possible of the Indians of the Six Nations & any other you can communicate with & to dispose them to act with all their vigour in concert with his Majesty's Troops and under the direction of Lieut$^{t.}$ Col. S$^{t.}$ Leger. The providing & appointing of proper leaders (who will have the usual allowances) to this body of Indians, is left to your care and judgment, and I hope your health will permit you to accompany this expedition as I know no Person so capable of the conducting & management of the Indians.

I should be glad you would transmit me a list of the officers you think proper to nominate, and acquaint me what pay they should be allowed and whether any of them should have Rank, and what, likewise what Rank & pay you think yourself entitled to.

As for the Provincials that have come in, Sir John Johnson's Regiment being to go upon this expedition, I think they should join that Corps, at least as many as will compleat it; it will be right in you to make these people acquainted that for their Encouragement his Majesty has thought proper to declare that he will give two hundred acres of Land to all Such of them as shall take arms & serve till the War be ended[.]

I am Sir &c &rc
Signed G.C.
Colonel Butler Superintendent of Indian Affairs—Niagara

6.24/12

No. 12. Copy of a Letter from Capt. Foy to Capt. Mackey, Quebec, May 19, 1777

Head Quarters Quebec 19th May 1777

Sir
I am communicated to acquaint you that the Companies of Monin & Boucherville[102] are ordered to march with all possible Expedition to Montreal there to receive further Orders from you who are to follow such directions & Commands respecting the three Canadian Companies as shall be given you by Lieutenant Genl. Burgoyne.

Mr. Honre [Henri] Genier is appointed Adjutant to the three Companies of Canadians.

I am &c &c.
(Signed) E. F.

6.24/13

No. 13. Extract of a Letter from Lieut. Genl. Burgoyne to Sir Guy Carleton, Montreal, May 26, 1777

Sir
I Judge by the Letters your Excellency has honoured me with, that the time of your setting out for Montreal is yet uncertain, I take leave to Submit to your Excellency by express such circumstances of the Publick Service as require decision, and further powers to carry them into execution than those I am invested with. I have to propose to your Excellency a Corvée of a thousand Men to attend the Expedition for a limited time for the Purposes of labour and Transport. The Troops will be saved thereby from the harassing duties which at the Outset of a Campaign your Excellency well knows are productive of disease, and the ranks will be properly full for their Service in Arms.

[102] The two companies of French Canadian militia destined for Burgoyne's expedition.

It also appears to me that seven or eight hundred Horses may become indispensibly necessary for my Progress, and I have good assurances that the transport of them to Crown Point by Land is very practicable.[103] So large a number may not be requisite for Operations against Ticonderoga, but I submit to you, Sir, the expediency of having the arrangement so prepared that they may be ready upon a short call. It is with great deference to your Excellency's knowledge of the Country that I mention my particular modes of furnishing these Supplies, but I conceived there would be no difficulty of obtaining the horses, if your Excellency thought proper to Stipulate a reasonable price for the hire per week with one man to two horses for the Care and driving of them, and the expense to Government would be much more moderate than purchasing them outright[.] I have the same confidence that the Corvée of working men above proposed would be palatable to the Country if you thought proper to issue a Proclamation limiting the time of their Service, and wherever I might be at the expiration of the Term I should hold myself indispensably bound to fulfill your intentions therein.

I inclose to your Excellency Lists of the Staff &c., as proposed by the Officers at the head of the several departments, and upon all those Subjects I request your orders as soon as may be. Colonel Carleton[104] writes to you himself, and it is with great Satisfaction I learn his inclinations to give me his assistance if the Arrangement meets your Approbation.

My great Opinion of the Talents of Captain Foy, confirmed by your Excellency's advice, induced me to mention as an Officer most desirable to me; but I do not mean to press any Appointment that may interfere with your Inclinations, convenience or designs respecting that Gentleman.

In regard to the preparations I have made for proceeding, your Excellency will find that none have been retarded for want of the above points being decided.

A Corvée has been employed to repair the roads, necessary for Land Carriage, and the flour, which was the only short Article of Provision at St. John's, thrown up from Chamblee. The Caulking of Batteaux and other remaining work in the Docks has been pressed by M. G. [Major General William] Phillips with his usual assiduity.[105] The troops are

[103] In 1777 there was no land route between St. Jean and Crown Point, and land transportation of livestock between these points was utterly impracticable.

[104] Lieutenant Colonel Carleton at this time.

[105] "Persistent application or diligence; unflagging effort."

contracted in their Quarters and have received their Camp Equipage. The Indians with Capt. Frazer's Superintendency have received their call and wish only the Nomination of their rendezvous. The State of the Ground for encamping at different Stations upon the Lake has been examined and found Sufficient, tho' there never was so much Water known at this Season. I propose to see General Frazer's brigade assembled tomorrow and to move them forward on Thursday. The rest of the Troops will follow in regular progression. I thought myself justified by the full Powers your Excellency entrusted me with in the Liberty to remove the 31st Regiment from their old Quarters to S[t.] Therese, that the passage to Chambleé might thereby be left free for the German Troops and the 62nd Regiment, and that in the interim the Transport from Chamblee to S[t.] John's might be assisted and enforced by a Corps at S[t.] Therese.

Upon the whole, Sir, I see no impediment to all my Force being very near the Point of their embarkation by the end of this week, and I request your Excellency's final orders for the time when S[t.] John's, and the Isle Aux Noix may be occupied by the Troops you may think proper to Post there[.]

6.24/14

No. 14. Proposed Disposition of the Hospital for the Service in Canada

Montreal 26th May 1777

Proposed Disposition of the Hospital for the Service of Canada with his Excellency Gen[l.] Sir Guy Carleton Commander in Chief—

1 Physician
1 Surgeon
1 Apothecary
8 Mates 2 of whom are Sick

The Hospital for Gen[l.] Burgoyne's Expedition from which a flying Camp is to be taken & the residue to hold ready to move as occasion may require—

1 Physician
2 Surgeons
2 Apothecaries
14 Mates
300 Sets of Bedding with Stores in proportion for the flying Hospital.
300 Sets with Stores ready to follow.
For the Service under Col. St. Leger
Mr. Blaxham First Mate
Mr. Salmon Supernumerary [Mate]

N.B. Lieut. Col. St. Leger much wishes the Surgeon of the 34th Regt. to go with his Detachment & it is submitted to His Excellency that he may be added to the Hospital for that occasion.

(Signed) Robert Knox, Inspector of Hospital in Canada[106]

6.24/15

No. 15. List of the Staff proposed for the Expedition under Lieut. Gen. Burgoyne

Staff proposed for the Expedition under Lt. Genl. Burgoyne & submitted for the decision of his Excellency Sir Guy Carleton.

Lieut. Genl. Burgoyne
Major Genls. Phillips & Reidesel
Brigr. Genls. Fraser, Powell, Hamilton, Specht and
Brigade Majors Freeman, Muir, Kirkman, Cleece
Quarter Master General Lt. Col. Carleton
Deputy [Quarter Master General] Capt. Money
Assistants— Any two of the four now on the List that Lt. Col. Carleton shall appoint[,] Cornet Grant to join his Regt.
Deputy Adjutant Genl Capt. Foy

[106]Doctor Robert Knox was appointed "Physician to the Forces in North America" on January 1, 1776. Knox was a graduate of St. Andrews University in Edinburgh in 1750, and he had served as a military physician with the British army on the continent of Europe during the Seven Years' War and then returned to private practice. He was a physician at Middlesex Hospital, England, when he accepted an appointment to travel to Canada. "Physician to the Forces" was a prestigious post, with not more than ten such doctors serving in North America and the West Indies at any given time during the Revolutionary War. Knox was also the personal physician to Sir Guy Carleton. Knox had served in the 1776 campaign and been present at the Battle of Valcour Island. Maguire, "Knox's Account of Valcour Island," 141–150.

Chaplain to the Staff Mr. Brudenal[107]
Commissary Department as per List already submitted
Hospital as per [List already submitted]
Assistant Paymaster Mr. Gaddis[108]
Provost Martial [blank]
Artillery
Engineers
All the Civil List of the Naval Department under the acting Commsrs [Commissioners] & Comptr [Comptroller]
Lt. Shanks
Lieut. Twiss

6.24/16

No. 16. Copy of a Letter from Lieut. Colonel St. Leger to Lieut. Genl. Burgoyne, May 15, 1777

May 25th 1777.

My Dear General
Your having done me the Honor to intimate to me that it was the Commander in Chief's Pleasure that I should be consulted concerning a proper place of Rendezvous for the Detachment of the 8th Regiment & the Indians destin'd for the Expedition under my Command[,] I take the Liberty to lay before you the difficulty I am under to determine a Point of such Consequence & beg leave to submit to you (the proper Channel to the Commander in Chief) whether the better to enable me to make the necessary Arrangements with Precision & without the least chance of Confusion or misunderstanding, it would not be proper to communicate to me the different Nations, that are to be Employed &

[107]The Reverend Edward Brudenell (?–1805) acted as chaplain to the British army in Canada in 1776–77. Almost nothing is known of his religious career or life outside of his involvement in the Burgoyne campaign. Thorp, *Acland Journal*, xxxiii; and Rogers, *Hadden's Journal and Orderly Books*, 106.

[108]David Geddes (1751–1811) served as paymaster to Burgoyne's army. Born to a modest Scottish merchant family, Geddes had immigrated to Canada in the early 1770s and had begun to establish a solid reputation as a merchant. The post of paymaster to a British army was a lucrative one, and apparently Geddes took advantage of the opportunity. Geddes, "'David Geddes,'" 425–476.

the Magazines they are to be supplied from 'till a junction is effected with them— because from some Questions I have put to the Commissary General, he seems to be at a loss to decide upon this very material Point, having peremptorily affirm'd that Niagara could not supply a proper Quantity, and moreover said, not having it in Command from proper Authority to correspond with me he did not think himself at Liberty to Answer my Questions, or to give into my desires, you will therefore do me the Honor to Communicate this to his Excellency the Commander in Chief that he may be pleased to send me and others concerned in the various Arrangements of this Detachment such Orders that no delay may be given to the fulfilling of his intention[.]

I have the Honor to be Dear General y^{r} most Obedient & most humble Serv$^{t.}$
Barry S$^{t.}$ Leger
[To] General Burgoyne

P.S. The Commander in Chief having been pleased to tell me that I should be assisted by a Proportionate Staff, I request his Permission to Nominate that part of it, that will be most immediately concerned in contributing to the Success of the Expedition— To the Deputy Adjutant General's departments Cap$^{t.}$ Ancrum of the 34th, who goes as a Capt of that Regiment's Detachment, Lieut$^{t.}$ Lundy of McCleans Corps to that of the Q$^{r.}$ Masters, L$^{t.}$ Cross who is likewise one of the officers named for the Detachment of the 34th as Major of Brigade— I wish much for M$^{r.}$ Blake Surgeon of the 34th to go as Hospital Surgeon assisted as his Excellency may think proper, I esteem M$^{r.}$ Farqhuarson on Account of the very great Activity of his mind & Person as the fittest Commissary for a Flying Camp. An inspector of Batteaux will be necessary such a person is at this Moment at Montreal, having fled from the Mohawk River to avoid persecution, he formerly served under General Bradstreet in the same Capacity, his name is Kisick. This Man I beg leave to submit to his Excellency's consideration. The Waggon Master's Departm^{nt} has been already well fitted by the General at Quebec, as for any other assistance that may be thought necessary, I have no Choice.[109]

[109]As Sir Guy Carleton noted (File 6.24/18), this is a ridiculously large staff for the relatively small force that St. Leger commanded. However, regardless of Carleton's concerns, St. Leger went

6.24/17

No. 17. Extract of a Letter from Sir Guy Carleton to Lieut. General Burgoyne, Quebec, May 29, 1777

In the present situation of the Province, having a vast number of Men employed in the Fur Trade &c.[,] Fisheries, and by way of a beginning only, which, I think never can be too Gentle, while I expected to Conduct the Expedition in Person, a Draft of three hundred Militia was ordered.

And this is as much, considering the numbers destin'd to watch the several Inlets into the Province, for the Transporting Provisions, Stores &c. as we can hope to Effect.

Orders are this day given for each Parish to furnish two able Married Men for each Deserter from it, which is the only Expedient I can think of at present, to supply the deficiency. I shall Order the Horses and Corveés you require, if upon mature consideration, you think it advisable.

You may be assured however that as far as in my Power, I shall do every thing that depends on me to Assist you, and the Service you are going upon—

I am &c
(Signed) Guy Carleton

---

ahead with these appointments in mid-June 1777. The officers identified were Captain William Ancrum and Lieutenant William Crofts of St. Leger's own 34th Foot as quartermaster general and assistant quartermaster, along with Lieutenant James Lundy of the Royal Highland Emigrants as an additional assistant quartermaster. Mr. James Kusick served as bateaux master. Mr. John Farquharson served as commissary; Charles Blake of the 34th Foot as surgeon; and Mr. Austin Piety as conductor of artillery. St. Leger's military secretaries (essentially, his military aides who functioned as clerks) were Lieutenant William Osborne Hamilton and Ensign George Clergis of the 34th Foot. Captain Ancrum survived the campaign, being promoted to major, and served as commandant at Detroit from 1784 to 1786. Surgeon Blake doubtless regretted his decision, as he lost his instruments, medicines, and other valuable personal property when his baggage was looted by American Indians during the retreat from Fort Stanwix. Watt, *Rebellion in the Mohawk Valley*, 74–75, 254.

6.24/18

No. 18. Extract of a Letter from Sir Guy Carleton to Lieut. Genl. Burgoyne, Quebec, May 28, 1777

I have your Letter by Express, The Commissary has had Positive Orders to follow your directions in every thing & L$^{t.}$ Col. S$^{t.}$ Leger being destined to Command a Corps Cooperating with you, was instructed by me to consult you upon all Occasions. I therefore take for granted that M$^{r.}$ Day[110] will obey such Commands as you shall give him for forming Magazines for Lieut$^{t.}$ Col. S$^{t.}$ Leger at such places as when the Rendezvous of their different Detachments are determined upon shall be indicated to him, I must Observe that Niagara is entirely out of the Question.

As to his Staff I must refer him to you[.] Only I would Observe that he seems to require a Staff sufficient for a great Army— What you think proper to allow him I shall approve of, but this he must settle and arrange with you[,] and I think he should take such as may be necessary for him from the Staff already established & not make new creations.

I cannot appoint a Surgeon as Mr. S$^{t.}$ Leger requires for his Detachment nor can I allow a Regiment to remain without their Surgeon, but if the Gentleman in question chooses to resign his Commision in the Reg$^{t.}$ he belongs to in Order to accompany Lieut$^{t.}$ Col. S$^{t.}$ Leger I shall not object to it.[111]

I would suggest my Wishes that you make the necessary Arrangements for the Forwarding of the Provisions which are to pass thro' this Province for your Army after you shall be advanced, to which Arrangement I shall give all the Assistance in my Power.

I am Sir with great regard &c.
(Signed) G.C.

---

[110]Nathaniel Day was Carleton's commissary general. In this capacity, he made massive purchases from Canadian citizens to supply the army with local foodstuffs. Gabriel, ed., and Vergereau-Dewey, trans., *Quebec during the American Invasion*, xliv.

[111]It is very unlikely that a surgeon on duty in Canada would willingly choose to resign his commission for a single season's campaign. However, Surgeon Blake of the 34th Foot did accompany St. Leger, apparently without resigning his commission.

6.24/19

No. 19. Extract of a Letter from Sir Guy Carleton to Lieut. Govr. Cramahé,[112] Montreal, June 9, 1777

Extract
Montreal 9th June 1777

General Burgoyne having made a Requisition for a Corvee of Canadians to assist the Troops going upon an Expedition under his Command, I beg you will give orders that the utmost diligence be used by the Commissary for the Corvées & all the Officers of Militia, that a body of five hundred be immediately drawn from the District of Quebec for this Service; & as soon as they can be assembled, that they proceed without delay under proper Leaders to St. John's, giving me & the Commanding Officer there an Account thereof. I desire likewise that Mr. Baby[113] be directed to send me immediately a State of the Number of Militia Men contained in the District of Quebec, and from thence up to three Rivers.

Please likewise to send me Mr. Rowselle's Commission which is to be dated the same as the others, and that of Mr. Southers to be dated the day of his presenting his Mandamus.[114]

Understanding that the Ship with the Naval Stores is arrived, I should be glad that such part as is required for the Vessels upon the Upper Lakes be selected out of them and sent up with all Expedition. The charge of it to be given to Captain Thomson who I intend to send to these Lakes in order to procure from him an exact Report of the State and Condition of the Vessels there. Mr. Robertson will be able to assist him in getting up the Stores from Quebec.[115]

---

[112] Hector Theophilus Cramahé (1720–1788), lieutenant governor of Canada from 1771 to 1782. Cramahé held a wide variety of civil offices during the British administration of Canada, from 1760 until his death. A former British officer, he provided inestimable service preparing Quebec against attack by the Americans in the fall of 1775. Gabriel, *Quebec during the American Invasion*, 126.

[113] Francois Baby (1733–1820), a prominent French merchant and fur trader. Baby had fought as an officer with the French militia against the British during the Seven Years' War. Following the French surrender, he reestablished his commercial concerns and reconciled with the British authorities. Baby became close friends with both Governors Carleton and Haldimand. He served as a captain in the Quebec militia and was promoted to adjutant general of militia and commissary of military transportation in 1776, in reward for his loyal service during the 1775–76 Siege of Quebec. Gabriel, *Quebec during the American Invasion*, xli–xlii.

[114] Latin for "we order," a legal writ (today properly referred to as a "writ of mandate") that orders a public agency or governmental body to perform an act required by law when it has neglected or refused to do so.

[115] The other individuals referred to in this correspondence are otherwise unidentified.

6.24/20

No. 20. Copy of a Letter from Lieut. Genl. Burgoyne to Sir Guy Carleton, Montreal, June 7, 1777

Having had the honor to represent to your Excellency the necessity of being Provided with a certain number of Horses and Carriages for the Artillery, victual & other indispensible Purposes of the Army, when it shall be Obliged to quit the borders of the Lakes & Rivers; and having Understood from your Excellency that such Provision could not be made by the Ordinary methods of Corvée, and that if proposed without compulsion to the Country the effect would be precarious, dilatory and expensive. I have now the honor to lay before your Excellency proposals of Contracts for an Expeditious supply of a Necessary number of Horses for the Artillery, and Two hundred Carts with two Horses each for other Purposes.

I am too ignorant of the Prices of the Country, to offer any Judgment upon the reasonableness of these Proposals; nor have I any long acquaintance with Mr. Jordan[116] or other motive for wishing him the preference if other Persons can be found equally capable, responsible & expeditious, I have only interfered thus far, upon a conviction, after considering the Route the Kings's Orders directs, and lacking all Possible Methods of information upon the Supply to be expected as we proceed, that to depend upon the Country altogether would be to hazard the Expedition.

Your Excellency will Observe that in Order to save the Public expense as much as Possible I have reduced this requisition much below what would be adequate to the Service, meaning to Trust to the resources of the Expedition for the rest. Five hundred Carts will barely carry fourteen days Provision at a time, & Major General Phillips means to demand as few Horses as Possible, Subject to what ever future augmentations future

[116]Jacob Jordan (1741–1796), a prominent English merchant in Montreal, was also the seigneur for a township on the Winooski River in the Vermont Colony. Jordan was certainly a well-placed and important merchant, as he was the Canadian agent for Harley and Drummond of London, who had the lucrative contract to remit specie for army pay and expenses.

Services may require. The present number will be about four hundred. There will then remain unprovided for (for expeditious movements) the Transport of Batteaux from Lake George to Hudson's River, and the Carriage of the Tents and Baggage of the Army, and many other contingencies I need not trouble your Excellency to point out to you.

I have the honor to be with true respect &c. &c. &c.
(Signed) J. Burgoyne

6.24/21

No. 21. Proposal for furnishing Horses, Carriages, and Drivers for the Service of the Army under the Command of Lieut. Genl. Burgoyne

Proposals for Furnishing Horses, Carriages, and Drivers for the Service of the Army on the Expedition under the Command of Lieutenant Gen[l.] Burgoyne

Vizt.

1000 Horses with Harness

500 Carts to carry & Cart drawn by two Horses[,] 1 Driver to each Cart.

One half the number to be rendezvoused at Chatteau gay in 15 days from the date of the Contract, the remainder in 30 days.

The Carts and Harness within the same space at S[t.] Johns.

The Commissary appointed by the Crown to grant a Certificate of the delivery.

All Horses, Carts, Harness &c. are to be kept compleat, and every incidental expence of Conductors to be paid by the Contractor; except provisions for the Drivers, and Forage for the Horses.

When the Kings magazines cannot supply Forage with convenience to the Service the Contractor is to have a liberty of doing it and upon producing proper Certificates to be paid at the rate by which the Kings Magazines are to be supplied[.]

The Contractor to be paid for this Service at the Rate of seven Shillings Halifax Currency per day for each Cart, with two Horses, and Driver to Commence from the day of rendezvous.

All Horses Killed, Dying in the Service or taken by the Enemy, to be paid for, on thou Cases certified by the Kings Commissary, at the rate of Ten Pounds each, Carts taken or destroyed Five pounds, Harness three pounds.

The Contractor to be paid ever two months by warrant granted upon the Commissaries Certificate.

This Contract to be in Force 150 Days[.]

Penalty for performance[.]

Signed J.J.[117]
Montreal 6th June 1777

6.24/22

No. 22. Proposals for furnishing Horses & Drivers for the Service of the Artillery on the Expedition under Lieut. Genl. Burgoyne

Proposals for Furnishing Horses and Drivers for the Service of the Artillery, on the expedition, under the Command of Lieutenant General Burgoyne.

Vizt.

Horses

1 Driver to every two Horses

One half of the Number to rendevous at Chatteau Gay in 15 days from the date of the Contract[,] the remainder in 30 Days.

The Commissary appointed by the Crown to grant a Certificate of the delivery.

All Horses and Drivers to be kept compleat in numbers, and every incidental expence of conductors, to be paid by the Contractor, except Provisions for the Drivers, and Forage for the Horses.

Where the King's Magazines cannot supply Forage, with convenience to the Service[,] the Contractor is to have a Liberty of doing it, and upon producing proper Certificates to be paid at the Rate by which the Kings Magazines are to be supplied.

---

[117]Jacob Jordan.

The Contractor to be paid for this Service, at the rate of Six Shillings per day for every two Horses, and one Driver, to Commence from the day of Rendivous.

All Horses, killed, Dying in the Service or taken by the Enemy, to be paid for on thou Cases Certified, by the King's Commissary, at the rate of Ten Pounds each.

The Contractor is to be paid every two months by Warrant granted upon the Commissary's Certificate[.]

This Contract to be in Force 150 Days[.]

Penalty for Performance[.]

Signed J.J.
Montreal 6th June 1777.

6.24/23

No. 23. Copy of a Letter from Sir Guy Carleton to Lieut. Genl. Burgoyne, Montreal, June 7, 1777

Montreal 7th June 1777.

Sir

I have received your Letter of this days date on the subject of a Contract for Horses for the Artillery and other purposes of the Army and enclosing proposals for the same.

It is sufficient that you see the Necessity of this measure for my approving of it & therefore I wish you wou'd conclude such Agreements as appears to you to be just as reasonable, and with such person as you shall think proper (there seems to me no cause of objection against the terms or person proposed) and I shall be happy if any assistance I can give may forward this business[.]

I am Sir &c. &c.
(Signed) G.C.

6.24/24

No. 24. Extract of a Letter from the Secretary at War to Sir Guy Carleton, August 17, 1776

His Majesty being persuaded that at the time you Appointed Lt. Colonels Nesbitt[,] Fraser, Powell and Gordon, to act as Brigadiers you were satisfied the same would be for the benefit of the Service, has been pleased to approve of their appointment: and they will accordingly receive pay as such during their continuance in Canada.[118]

But I have his Majesty's Orders to observe to you that whenever any of the said Officers shall lead their Brigades out of the Province of Canada, in Order to Join the Troops under General Howe, there will be a necessity for their Command ceasing as Brigadiers; to Prevent the impropriety of their bearing a higher Rank & pay than Several of the Lieutt. Colonels who are their Seniors in that Army— Your Excellency will therefore be pleased to give such directions hereupon as you may Judge most Expedient.

[118]Lieutenant Colonel William Nesbit was commissioned as an ensign in the 36th Regiment of Foot on April 20, 1751. He had subsequently served in the 31st, 70th, and 69th Foot and was promoted to lieutenant colonel of the 4th Foot on April 16, 1763. He saw limited active service during the Seven Years' War. He participated in the actions at Lexington and Concord and Bunker Hill, then transferred to Quebec with the 47th Foot in the spring of 1776. Nesbit was appointed a local brigadier general for service in Canada at that time. He fell seriously ill in September of that year and died in November. Rogers, *Hadden's Journal and Orderly Books*, 175–176. Lieutenant Colonel Patrick Gordon was commissioned as a captain-lieutenant in the 1st Royal Foot Guards on January 22, 1755. He saw limited active service during the Seven Years' War and left the service on half pay at the end of the war. He returned to active service as lieutenant colonel of the 29th Foot at the beginning of the American War of Independence and accompanied that regiment to Canada in the spring of 1776, whereupon he was appointed a local brigadier general. On July 24, 1776, he was riding alone on an inspection tour between Fort St. John's and Chamblee when he was ambushed and mortally wounded by an American partisan named Whitcomb. He died at Fort St. John's shortly thereafter and was buried in Montreal. Gordon was the first British general killed in action during the Revolutionary War. Rogers, *Hadden's Journal and Orderly Books*, 4–5.

6.24/25

No. 25. Extract of a Letter from the Secretary at War to Sir Guy Carleton, March 25, 1777

I agree with your Excellency for the Reasons dated in your Dispatch of the 29th November that it is best not to turn over the English Recruits of the 33rd Regiment; but I should think it advisable to distribute the German Recruits for that Corps among the Regiments serving under your Command, as the Agent informs me that under the idea that this Measure would be adopted, the Officers recruiting for the 33rd have for some time been employed in raising Men to replace them.

6.24/26

No. 26. Copy of a Letter from Capt. Foy to Lieut. Colonel St. Leger, Montreal, June 10, 1777

Montreal 10th June 1777.

Sir
I have it in command to send you the enclosed extract of a Letter from Lord George Germain containing the instructions which is to be your guidance when you shall proceed upon the expedition which you are to command.

I am Sir &c. &c.
(Signed) E. F.

6.24/27

No. 27. Copy of a Letter from Sir Guy Carleton to Lieut. General Burgoyne, St. John's, June 13, 1777

St. Johns 13th June 1777.

Sir
The Canadians which are to serve on the expedition going under your command, having been drafted from the Militia of the several Parishes upon promise of being allowed to return to their families by the first of November, being the time they expect the Winter to set in; and all those ordered, or to be ordered, upon Corvees for different purposes of the Troops which pass the Lakes, consenting to this Service upon the faith of being dismissed by the same time, I am to request that you will allow both the one and the other to return accordingly, unless any of them shall choose to remain with you of their own free will and inclination.

I am sir &c. &c. &c.
Signed G.C.
[To] Genl. Burgoyne

6.24/28

No. 28. Copy of a Letter from Lieut. Genl. Burgoyne to Sir Guy Carleton, St. John's, June 15, 1777

St. John's June 15th 1777.

Sir
I am sorry to inform your Excellency that the four men of the Canadian Companies whose names are enclosed deserted last night with their Arms[,] Provisions, and every other Article they had.

I trouble your Excellency with the report, thinking that if one or more of these men could be apprehended, they would be very proper Subjects for an Example, and I should have no Scruple in trying them by a Court Martial, it is supposed they are gone directly home, and I submit to your Excellency whether a party sent directly to their Parishes might not have good effect.

I have the honour to be with great Respect
Sir
Your most Obedient Humble Servant
J. Burgoyne

P.S. You will excuse my Paper and Pen being just Embarking
[To] Sir Guy Carleton

6.24/29

No. 29. Copy of a Letter from Sir Guy Carleton to Lieut. General Burgoyne, Montreal, June 17, 1777

Copy
Montreal 17th June 1777

Sir
I have received your letter enclosing a List of deserters from the Companies of Canadians, under your command. No time has been lost in giving orders for every Possible means to be used to apprehend them, and at whatever time they are taken they shall be sent to you, to proceed against them as you shall think proper.

I am Sir &c. &c.
Signed G.C.
[To] General Burgoyne

6.24/30

No. 30. Copy of a Letter from Major General Phillips to Sir Guy Carleton, St. John's, June 17, 1777

Copy
St. Johns June 17th 1777.

Sir
I take the Liberty with great respect to report to your Excellency that unless you are so good to Order the 29th Regiment to St. John for two Months, to Assist the Transport of the Expedition it will be impossible the Service can go on. That regiment Incamping here for the Summer Months, will expedite every service here & the 31st Regiment, may do the duty of the Garrison—so much it is necessary that I shall be obliged to keep a Battalion from crossing the Lake until your Excellency is so good as to send the 29th Regiment, which may move even by Companies supposing the Regiment cannot Assemble easily together.

As your Excellency has entrusted to me during the Winter the Care of the Post, it has given me such knowledge that I will venture to offer, for your Excellency's Consideration—that the 31st regiment be Ordered to take up the following Chain, Observing that the Company at Pointe au fer,[119] may or may not be withdrawn hereafter as your Excellency shall see proper, as the Post is strong and Secure, but at present it is of Absolute necessity there should be a Company at Point au Fer as it is an intermediate Depot between St. John & Crown Point.

Posts to be occupied by the 31st Regiment June 1777

	Companies
Pointe au Fer	1
Isle Aux Noix	2
St. John's	4
Chambly	1
	8 Companies

[119]Point au Fer ("point of iron") is located on the west bank of Lake Champlain in modern-day Clinton County, New York. It is located four miles south of the modern town of Rouse's Point, on the current U.S.–Canada border. It was a traditional stopping post on Lake Champlain, as it provided good camping, a sheltered beach, and a well-located resting point before a convoy began the difficult passage of Lake Champlain to the south.

Sorel the
Additional Company
Of the Regt 1

9 Total.

Should your Excellency be pleased to allow of this distribution I will request your Excellency will send me by Express your approbation and I will direct the Route of the 31st Accordingly.

I will venture to offer an opinion relating to the Detachment of the 6 Regiments which are on the Expedition namely the 9th–20th–21st–47th–53rd–62nd. It is that they be Ordered directly to Montreal where the Hospital is, and where there is an Excellent Barracks to receive them, as they Recover, and your Excellency is Sensible that these Detachments are Composed of the Sick Men from each of the Six regiments— I apprehend the German Detachment to be much the same, and unless the Men are together in one Body I greatly fear they never will be serviceable.

I trust to your Excellency's Goodness to pardon this intrusion on your time, it is great respect and sincere attention for your Excellency which dictates every Line I ever write to your Excellency.

I will hope an immediate Answer to this Letter, as I must Arrange the movement of Brigadier Genl. Hamiltons Brigade accordingly.

I have the honor to be Sir with the Greatest respect
Your Excellency's most Obedt & Most Humble Servt.
(Signed) Wm Phillips

6.24/31

No. 31. Copy of a Letter from Major General Phillips to Sir Guy Carleton, St. John's, June 17, 1777

St Johns June 17th 1777.

Sir
It is with great reluctance, I write when I am obliged to give your Excellency so much trouble, but I am under the necessity of reporting

to your Excellency, that I have received reports, from the Quartermaster General Assistants, that the Corvées necessary for the Transport of the Army from Chambly to the Portage, and from the Portage to this place, are most of them run away in such manner that the Transport of Provisions is nearly stopt, and I am apprehensive unless means be found to forward on this Service, that the Army under Lieutenant General Burgoyne may shortly want provisions.

I would offer to your Excellency's consideration, whether part of Brigadier General Macleans Corps, should not be ordered to the South of the River St. Lawrence, and on the Parishes, on both sides of the River Sorel, to enforce such orders, for the necessary Corvées required, as will enable this Service to go on.

I had the Honour to send your Excellency an Express this day, requesting the 29th Regiment to be sent to St. John's, in order that by Detachments to St. Therese, the communication and Corvées may be kept on for the Transport of provisions and Stores— I have been obliged to order the 62nd Regiment to remain behind for some days in hopes the 29th will soon Relieve it[.]

Major St. George Dupré[120] Commissary of the Transport of the Army, by Corvées, can never be of any use Remaining in Montreal; I will hope your Excellency will have the goodness to order him upon the Communication on the Sorel, and the South of the River St. Lawrence, as Vercheres–Varrones–Boucherville–Longueuil–La Prarie [underline indicates emphasis in original] in order by his presence, and by his Activity, he may urge on the different Corvées, without which I must repeat, to be really under Apprehensions for the supply of the Troops at Crown Point.

If Brigadier Genl McLaine was to reside a few days at Chambly, it might perhaps be of use, by giving Countenances and protection to the Officers of Militia in the Execution of their Orders.

---

[120]Major Saint-Georges Dupré was a prominent citizen and major of British militia in Montreal. Dupré was arrested by General David Wooster of the Continental Army in the winter of 1775–76 during the American occupation. Appointed a commissary for transportation in 1776 upon the British resurgence in Canada, he served in this position throughout Burgoyne's 1777 campaign, his primary service being involved with supervising the Canadian labor and forwarding supplies from Canada to Burgoyne to the south. He appears to have been a competent, dedicated supervisor in this service. He is most well known as a son-in-law to the infamous Luc de la Corne. Rogers, *Hadden's Journal and Orderly Books*, 276.

I repeat how extremely sorry I am to be obliged to write thus, which nothing but the real state of Facts, shou'd oblige me to do.

I have the Honour to be Sir &c.
Signed Phillips

6.24/32

No. 32. Copy of a Letter from Sir Guy Carleton to Major General Phillips, Montreal, June 18, 1777

Montreal 18th June 1777.

Sir
I received one letter from you of Yesterdays date late last night and another this morning.

As it is my earnest desire to give every Assistance to the expedition under general Burgoyne. The 29th Regiment shall move immediately, and Encamp at St. Therese about halfway between Chamblee and St. John—being the properest place for that communication.

The 31st Regiment shall be disposed of as you propose, except as to point au Fer which is contrary to my orders,[121] but if you find that a Company can be of use at Riviere La Colle,[122] one shall be sent there. The Emigrants for the greatest part shall cross to the Southside for the purposes you desire and Mr. St. George[123] shall go over there to attend to that Service, as shall also Brigadier Maclean to give every Assistance in his Power.

I should be glad you would order the Detachment of the 20th and 21st to move directly to this place, where the other similar detachments except that of the 62nd, which I shall order to Quebec[,] shall also be assembled agreeable to your proposition.

I am Sir with great respect your most &c.
(Signed) G. C.

---

[121] In other words, Point au Fer was (and is today) out of Canada, and thus beyond Carleton's purview, as he had no authority beyond the boundaries of the province of Canada.

[122] The Lacolle River enters the west bank of the Richelieu River at Ash Island, approximately midway between the Isle aux Noix and Point au Fer. Chambers, *Atlas of Lake Champlain.*

[123] Saint-Georges Dupré, previously introduced.

6.24/33

No. 33. Copy of Orders, Montreal, June 18, 1777

Montreal 18th June 1777.
Parole St. Ann & Boston

The thirty-first Regiment is to take, and to move immediately to the Posts of St. John and the Isle Aux Noix four Companies to each place, one Company of those at Isle Aux Noix, to move to Riviere la Colle, in case Major General Phillips, shall think it necessary, and the signify the same to them. The Companies at all those Posts, to be aiding and assisting in the Transport of Provisions, Stores & all things passing for the Troops, under the Command of Lieut. Genl. Burgoyne.

The 29th Regiment to march and encamp, at or near St. Therese, detaching two Companies to Chambly, this Regiment will likewise be aiding, and Assisting in forwarding everything necessary for General Burgoyne's Troops, the Royal Highland Emigrants will detach a Company to Sorel for the like Service and Brigadier General Maclean will make a tour to the places on that River, and order such further part of his Regiment, to take Post there, as he finds may be necessary for the above purposes or for assisting the Officers of Militia in executing orders sent to them[.] Mr. St. George dupré Commissary for the transport will pass over to the South side of the River St Lawrence and use his utmost diligence to forward these Services, and to see that the different Corvées are supplied, demanding the assistance of the nearest Troops, where it may be necessary, who are to comply with such request as he shall make.

6.24/34

No. 34. Copy of a Letter from Major General Phillips to Sir Guy Carleton, St. John's, June 19, 1777

St. Johns June 19th 1777

Sir

I just now receive your Excellency's letter and orders of the 18th Instant, and I send off an Officer Express, that he may return on the Instant, so that I may be able to leave St. John tomorrow, convinced I hope that every Agreement has met your Excellency's approbation— I have always offer'd my Opinions with the utmost respect, and it has ever been the greatest Satisfaction to me, when they have at all coincided with those of your Excellency.

Two Companies of the 29th Regiment being ordered by your Excellency to Chambly of which I am very glad, will allow the 31st Regiment to be divided equally. Four Companies to St. John, and four Companies to the Isle Aux Noix, which shall take place the instant the 29th Regiment arrives.

I will venture to Trespass upon your Excellency's Goodness, to allow my request, that the remaining six Companies of the 29th Regiment may be divided.

One to the little portage
One to the upper portage
Four to St. John

The reason for this arrangement is that being so posted they will communicate from Chambly to the Isle Aux Noix in the Transport of Provisions and Stores, for Lieut. General Burgoyne's Expedition and I beg to assure your Excellency that as not upon Slight Grounds, I have formed my wishes upon this subject, but upon mature deliberation, and with the advice of every person concerned in the different Transport here, and it is meant to not employ the 29th Regiment other than for this duty; the 31st being the Garrison of this place the Isle Aux Noix will have sufficient duty in that Service, I will therefore still hope your Excellency, will be so good to allow of this distribution of the 29th Regiment.

I have but one more Article to trouble your Excellency upon, which is that of Pointe au Fer, it is at present a Depot for provisions, being lodged there when the Wind will not permit the Vessels to go further, in order not to lose time, as, also for Artillery Stores; there are, also Rafts made there for Transporting the provision Carts—belonging to Mr. Jordan and many other Articles for the publick Service.

Will you therefore, Sir, permit me to most respectfully request of your Excellency to load a Company from the 31st at the Isle Aux Noix to take Charge of the Post, which becomes serious from the reasons I have given— May I presume to offer my Opinion that although Pointe au Fer is beyond the Latitudinal Limits of the province it is certainly within the Frontier which I have ever conceived to extend to Crown Point & Ticonderoga this duty will be required only for a few weeks, the Company may return to its Station at Isle Aux Noix, and at the same time be of essential use to the Service.

I had the honour to write to your Excellency this morning, informing you, Sir, that I had ordered the Detachments of the 20th, 21st and 53rd Regiments, to move to Sorel, to be in readiness there for further orders, which I have now received from your Excellency, that they are to be Quartered at Montreal— I still continue their Route for Sorel by Water, as it is the easiest for the sick, which the Surgeons here have reported upon and requested that mode of conveyance and it will prevent al[l] interference with the Transport of the Army by Land Carriage— I have directed Lieut. Duport[124] Assistant to the Quarter Master General at Sorel to assist in forwarding the Rout of these Detachments to Montreal, and I will still request a Surgeons Mate from the Hospital, may be sent with the Medicines to meet them there in case they shou'd stand in need.

I now am to take leave of your Excellency, which I do with the most sincere feelings of Gratitude for a thousand favors and acts of Friendship you have conferred upon me.

I shall not fail to Report to Lieutenant General Burgoyne, your Excellencys marked Goodness to him in ordering the 29th Regiment, and the Emigrants with Brigadier General Maclean to assist the Transport for the Service of his expedition[.] I am sure he will have every Grateful feeling upon the Occasion.

---

[124]Lieutenant Robert Duport of the 47th Foot. He served in North America during the Seven Years' War, was appointed an assistant quartermaster general on August 22, 1776, in Canada. He never rose higher than captain, and little is known of his activities or talents. Rogers, *Hadden's Journal and Orderly Books*, 260–261.

I hear your Excellency inte[n]ds to stay somedays at Montreal, at which I exceedingly rejoice as the Consequence of your presence in this part of the provi[n]ce at present from the dignity of your Situation cannot fail of being of real use.

I have the Honour to be Sir &c.
(Signed) Wm Phillips

6.24/35

No. 35. Copy of a Letter from Sir Guy Carleton to Major General Phillips, Quebec, June 26, 1777

Quebec 26 June 1777—

Sir
Your Dispatches of the 19th June arrived at Montreal after I was set out which has prevented my answering them sooner; Orders are given for moving the 29th Regiment exactly as you desired & you may dispose of a Company of the 31st Regt at Point au Fer, as I am fully persuaded of the utility of such a Step, but I shall lay the blame if any be imputed to me for exceeding my Order, upon you.

I desire you will remind Genl. Burgoyne to send me a state of the Troops under his Command after the Recruits now on their way have joined him and I intend to compleat his Regiments from the best men of the additional Companies.

I am Sir
With great regard Your Most &c.
(Signed) G. C.
[To] Major Genl. Phillips

6.24/36

No. 36. Copy of a Letter from Sir Guy Carleton to Lieut. General Burgoyne, Quebec, June 26, 1777

Copy
Quebec 26 June 1777

Sir
Mr. Jordan being under apprehensions of not being able to find the number of Men which he shall want for his Horses, has applied to me to order him from the Country as many as will make up his deficiency, but I saw great impropriety in commanding People for supplying a purpose for which you had made a contract, as I do great inconveniences which must arise from ordering Corvées, one part of which is to be paid while other are not[,] mean time, in order to forward the Service which Mr. Jordan has undertaken as much as I could, I have given him permission to employ any part of the Corvée ordered for your Army to which no particularly Duty had been assigned by you, which he shall require to assist in conducting his Horses to you.

Two hundred & forty eight men of five hundred ordered from this District have already set out for St. John's, & two hundred & three are now here to set out today or tomorrow & forty four have been sent to replace Deserters.

I am with great regard Sir &c. &c.
Signed
G.C.
[To] Lt. General Burgoyne

6.16/18

Copy of a Letter from Lieut. Genl. Burgoyne to Lord George Germain, Head Quarters Skensboro House, July 11, 1777[125] Rec. August 23 [1777]

Head Quarters at Skensborough House July 11th 1777

My Lord
I have the honour to acquaint your Lord Ship that the Enemy dislodged from Ticonderoga and Mount Independence on the 6th instant, and were driven on the same Day beyond Skenesborough on the right, and to Huberton on the Left, with the loss of an hundred and twenty eight pieces of Cannon; all their armed vessels and Batteaux, the greatest part of their baggage, and ammunition, Provision and Military Stores, to a very large amount.

This Success has been followed by events equally fortunate and rapid. I subjoin such a detail of Circumstances as the time will permit; and for his Majesty's further information, I beg Leave to refer your Lordship to Captain Gardner my aid de Camp,[126] whom I have thought it necessary to dispatch with news so important to the King's service, and so honourable to the Troops under my Command.

Journal of the late Principal proceedings of the Army.

Having remained at Crown Point three days to bring up the Rear of the Army, to establish the Magazines and the Hospital and to obtain intelligence of the Enemy, on 30th June I ordered the advanced Corps, consisting of the British Light Infantry and Grenadiers, the 24th Regiment, some Canadians and Savages, and ten pieces of Lt. Artillery, under the Command of Brigadier Genl. Frazer, to move from Putnam Creek, where they had been encamped some Days, up the west shore

---

[125]This letter was printed as Appendix No. 7 in Burgoyne, *State of the Expedition from Canada,* xxv–xxxvi. As with his other letters, only minor differences in capitalization and punctuation are noted.

[126]Captain Henry F. Gardner entered the British army as a cornet in the 16th Light Dragoons, the regiment of which Burgoyne was then lieutenant colonel, in 1761. He remained in the army, becoming promoted to captain in 1772. He became aide-de-camp to Burgoyne upon embarkation for Canada in the early spring of 1776, and served as Burgoyne's aide until he returned to England. He remained in the British army, being promoted to lieutenant colonel and serving until at least 1792. Rogers, *Hadden's Journal and Orderly Books*, 242.

of the Lake to four mile Point, so called from being within that distance of the Fort of Ticonderoga. The German reserve consisting of the Brunswick, Chasseurs, Lt. Infantry and Grenadiers, under L$^{t.}$ Colonel Breyman[127] were advanced at the same time upon the East Shore.

July 1st.

The whole Army made a movement forward. Brigadier Frazer's Corps occupied the Strong Post called three mile Point on the West shore, the German reserve the East Shore opposite; the right Wing of the Line encamped at four mile point; the left being nearly opposite on the East Shore. The Royal George & Inflexible Frigates with the Gun boats were anchored just without the reach of the Enemy's Batteries.[128]

The rest of the Fleet had been some time without Guns in order to assist in carrying provisions over Lake Champlain.

The Enemy appeared to be posted as follows a Brigade occupied the old French Lines upon the height northward of the Fort of Ticonderoga. These Lines were in good repair and had several instruments behind them chiefly calculated to guard the North west flank, and they were further sustained by a Block-house.[129]

To the left of these works about a mile the Enemy had Saw Mills and a Post sustained by a block-house, and another blockhouse and an hospital at the entrance of Lake George.[130] Upon the right of the French lines, and between them and the old Fort, there were two new block-houses, and a considerable battery close to the water edge.[131] It seemed that the Enemy had employed their chief industry, and were in greatest force, upon Mount Independence, which is high and circular, and upon the Summit, which is table land, was a Star fort, made with pickets and well supplied with Artillery, and a large square of Barracks within it.[132]

---

[127]Lieutenant Colonel Heinrich von Breymann, previously introduced.

[128]Both the *Royal George* and *Inflexible* were rated as "small" frigates. The *Inflexible* employed eighteen 12-pounder cannon. Both were commanded by Royal Navy officers and manned by Royal Navy sailors. They had been constructed by Sir Guy Carleton in 1776 during the contest for dominance of Lake Champlain, which the British had eventually won at the Battle of Valcour Island and by subsequent engagements on the lake in October 1776.

[129]"Instruments" here refers to military fortifications such as redoubts and batteries.

[130]The fortifications at Mount Hope, mentioned above.

[131]This refers to the string of strong redoubts constructed by the American army in 1776 to control the plateau immediately west of Lake Champlain and the flat ground leading to Fort Ticonderoga from the north (Crown Point).

[132]Mount Independence, previously mentioned.

The foot of the Mount which projects into the Lake was intrenched and covered with a Strong abattis close to the Water. This intrenchment was lined with heavy Artillery pointing down the Lake, flanking the Water battery above described, and sustained by another battery about half way up the Mount.

On the west side the Mount runs the main river and in its passage round is joined by the Water which comes down from Lake George. On the East Side of the Mount [Independence] the Water forms a small Bay into which falls a rivulet, after having encircled in its course part of the Mount to the South East. The side to the South could not be seen but was described as inaccessible. There was a Bridge between the Mount and Ticonderoga which also was unseen.

July 2[d.]

About nine in the morning a smoke was observed towards Lake George, and the Indians brought in a report that the Enemy had set fire to their further blockhouse and had abandoned the Saw Mills, and that a Considerable body were advancing from the Lines towards a Bridge upon the Road which led to the Right of the British Camp. A detachment of the advanced Corps was immediately put in march under Brigadier Frazer supported by a Brigade of the Line, and some Artillery under the Command of Major General Phillips with orders to Proceed towards Mount Hope, which is to the North of the Lines, to reconnoiter the Enemy's position and to take advantage of any Post they might abandon or be driven from.

The Indians under Capt. Frazer, supported by his Company of Marksmen[,] were directed to make a Circuit to the Left of Brigadier Frazer's line of March and endeavour to cut off the retreat of the Enemy to their Lines; but this design miscarried through the impetuosity of the Indians who attacked too soon, and in front and the Enemy were thereby able to retire with the loss of one Officer and a few men killed and one Officer wounded. Major General Phillips took possession of the very advantageous Post of Mount Hope this night, and the Enemy was thereby entirely cut off from communication with Lake George.

July 3[d.]

Mount Hope was occupied in Force by Brigadier Frazer's whole brigade, the first Brigade British, and two entire brigades of Artillery. The second brigade British encamped upon the left of the first, and the

Brigade of Gall having been drove from the East shore to occupy the ground where Frazer's Corps had been on three mile Point, the line became compleat extending from the shore to the westernmost part of Mount Hope, on the same day Major Gen[l] Reidesel [*sic*] encamped on the East Shore in a parallel Line with three mile point, having pushed the reserve forward near the rivilet which is on the East of Mount Independence. The Enemy cannonaded the Camps of Mount Hope and of the German reserve most part of the Day but without effect.

July 4th

The Army worked hard at their Communications, and got up the Artillery, tents, baggage, and Provisions. The Enemy at intervals continued the cannonade upon the Camps, which was not in any instance returned.

The Thunderer Radeau[133] carrying the battering train and Stores, having been warped up from Crown Point, arrived this day and immediately began to land the Artillery.

July 5th

Lt. Twiss the commanding Engineer was ordered to reconnoiter Sugar Hill on the South west side of the Communication from Lake George into Lake Champlain. It had appear'd from the first to be a very advantageous post. And it is now known that the Enemy had a council some time ago upon the expediency of possessing it; but the Idea was rejected upon the Supposition that it was impossible for a Corps to be established there in force.[134] Lt. Twiss reported this hill to have the entire command of the Works and Buildings both of Ticonderoga and Mount Independence; that the ground might be levelled so as to receive cannon; and that a road to convey them, tho' difficult, might be made practicable in twenty four hours. This Hill also entirely commanded in reverse the Bridge of communication, saw the exact situation of the Vessels, nor could the enemy during the day make any material

[133]A radeau was essentially a gigantic floating raft, flat-bottomed, which could be rowed or sailed. Its distinctive design permitted a large number of cannon to be employed on board, it was proof against musketry, and it could be easily built by carpenters rather than skilled shipwrights. A radeau was a distinctive North American vessel, and several of these had been built by the British army on both Lake George and Lake Champlain during the Seven Years' War. It contained numerous heavy cannon, and during the 1776 and 1777 campaigns the *Thunderer* served as the floating British artillery headquarters and chief supply ship. The *Thunderer* proved a very poor sailor and generally hindered the operations of the Royal Artillery on both of these campaigns.

[134]This was, in fact, true so long as the Americans remained in possession of Mount Hope.

movement or preparation without being discovered, and even having their numbers counted.[135]

It was immediately determined that a battery should be raised upon Sugar Hill for light twenty four Pounders, medium twelves, and eight inch Howitzers. This very arduous work was carried on so rapidly that the battery would have been ready the next day. It is a duty in this Place to do some justice to the zeal and activity of Major General Phillips who had the direction of the Operation.

And having mentioned that most valuable Officer, I trust it cannot be thought a Digression to add, that it is to his judicious arrangements and indefatigable pains, during the general superintendency of preparations which Sir Guy Carleton entrusted to him in the Winter and Spring, that the service is indebted for its present forwardness, the prevalence of contrary Winds and other accidents having rendered it impossible for any necessaries prepared in England for the opening of the campaign yet to reach the Army.

July 6th

Soon after day light an Officer arrived express onboard the Royal George, where in the night I took my Quarters as the most centrical Situation, with information from Brigadier Frazer that the Enemy were retiring and that he was advancing with his piquets, leaving orders for the brigade to follow as soon as they could accoutre, with intentions to pursue by land.[136]

This movement was very soon discernable, as were the British Colours which the Brigadier had fixed upon their Fort at Ticonderoga.

Knowing the safety I cou'd trust to that Officer's conduct, I turned my chief attention to the pursuit by Water, by which route I had Intelligence one Column were retiring in two hundred and twenty Batteaux covered by five armed Gallies.[137]

The great Bridge of communications through which a way was to be opened was supported by twenty two sunken pieces of large timber at nearly equal Distances: the spaces between were filled by separate

135In Burgoyne, *State of the Expedition from Canada*, xxix, a sentence was inserted in this paragraph providing the distances from Sugar Loaf to Fort Ticonderoga and Mount Independence.

136"Accoutre" means that the infantry would put on their accoutrements and other military equipment, such that they were prepared to march and engage in combat.

137The "five ships" (actually six) were the survivors of the Valcour Island fleet that had fought the previous October. These were the row galleys *Gates* and *Trumbull*, the gondola *New York*, and the smaller sailing ships *Liberty*, *Revenge*, and *Enterprise*.

floats each about fifty feet long and twelve feet wide, strongly fastened together by Chains and Rivets, and also fastened to the sunken piers. Before this bridge was a Boom made of very large pieces of round timber fastened together by rivetted bolts and double Chains made of Iron an inch and half square.

The gun boats were immediately moved forward, and the Boom and one of the intermediate floats were cut with great dexterity and dispatch. And Commodore Lutwidge[138] with the Officers and Seamen in his department partaking the general animation, a passage was found in half an hour for the Frigates also, th'rough impediments which the Enemy had been labouring for months together to make impenetrable. During the operations Major Genl. Reidesel had passed to Mount Independence with the Corps of Breyman and part of the left wing.

He was directed to proceed by Land to sustain Brigadier Frazer or to act more to the Left if he saw it expedient to do so.

The 62^d Regiment British, and the Brunswic [Brunswick] regiment of Prince Frederic were left at Ticonderoga and Mount Independence in the place of the parties of Frazers Brigade which had remained in possession of the Stores and the rest of the Army were ordered to follow up the River as they could be collected without regard to the place of Corps in the Line.

About three in the afternoon I arrived with the Royal George and Inflexible, and the best sailing Gun Boats and Batteaux at South Bay within three miles of Skenesborough at which latter place I learned the Enemy were posted in a stockaded fort, and their armed gallies at the falls below.

The foremost regiments viz the 9th 20th and 21st were instantly disembarked and ascended the Mountain with intention of turning the fort and cutting off the Retreat of the Enemy but their precipitate flight rendered this maneuver ineffectual.

The gunBoats and Frigates continued their Course to Skenesborough falls, Capt. Carter[139] with part of his Brigade, and Gun Boats immediately attacked the Gallies, and with so much spirit that two of them very soon struck; the other three were blown up, and the Enemy having previously prepared Combustible materials, set fire to the Fort, Mills, Storehouses, batteaux &c. and retired with the detachment left

[138] Captain Skeffington Lutwidge, previously introduced.

[139] Captain John Carter, Royal Artillery, previously introduced.

for that purpose, the main body having gone off when the Troops were ascending the Mountains.

A great quantity of Provisions and some Arms were here consumed, and most part of their Officers baggage was burned, sunk, or taken. Their loss in the Attack is not known, about thirty prisoners were made, among which were two wounded Officers.

During these Operations upon the right Brigadier Frazer had continued his pursuit on the road to Castleton 'till one O'clock having marched in a very hot day from four in the morning. Some stragglers of the Enemy had been picked up, from whom the Brigadier learned that their rear guard was composed of chosen men and commanded by Col. Francis[140] one of their best Officers. While the men were refreshing Major Genl Reidesel came up; and arrangements having been concerted for continuing the pursuit, Brigadier Frazer moved forward again and during the Night lay upon his Arms in an advantageous situation.

July 7th.

At three in the morning he renewed his march, and about five his advanced scouts discovered the Enemy's Centries [sentries], who fired their pieces and joined their main body. The Brigadier observing a commanding ground on the Left of his light Infantry immediately ordered it to be possessed by that Corps, and a considerable body of the enemy attempting the same they met. The enemy were driven back to their original Post. The advanced guard under Major Grant[141] were by this time engaged, and the Grenadiers were advanced to sustain them, and to prevent the right flank from being turned. The Brigadier remained on the Left, where the Enemy aided by Logs and Trees, defended themselves long. After being dislodged and prevented getting to the Castleton road by the Grenadiers they rallied, and renewed the action. They were again driven, and attempted a retreat by Pittsford Mountain, but the Grenadiers scrambled up what had appeared an inaccessible part of the ascent and gained the Summit before them. This threw them into confusion. They were still never the less greatly superior in number and consequently in extent, and the Brigadier in Momentary expectation of the arrival of the Germans had latterly weakened his left to support his

[140] Colonel Ebenezer Francis, 11th Massachusetts Regiment of the Continental Line, previously introduced.

[141] Major Robert Grant, commanding the 24th Regiment of Foot, previously introduced.

right. At this critical moment Major Gen$^{l.}$ Reidesel arrived with the foremost of his Column viz. the Chasseur Company and eighty Grenadiers & L$^{t.}$ Infantry. His judgment instantly pointed to him the course to take. He extended upon Brigadier Frazer's left Flank. Major Bernes led the Chasseurs into action with great gallantry and they were equally well sustain'd.[142] The enemy fled on all sides leaving dead upon the field Col. Frances and many other Officers and upwards of two hundred private men[.] [A]bove six hundred were wounded—many of whom perished in the Woods attempting to get off; and one Colonel, seven Captains, ten Subalterns, and two hundred and ten men were made Prisoners.[143] The number of the enemy before the Action amounted by report of Prisoners, to two thousand men, and they were strongly posted. The British detachment under Brigadier Frazer (the parties left at Ticonderoga the day before not having been able to rejoin) consisted only of eight hundred and fifty fighting men. The bare relation of so signal an action is sufficient for its praise. [S]hould the attack against such inequality of numbers before the Germans came up, seem to require explanation—it is to be considered that the Enemy might have escaped by delay; that the advanced guard found themselves on a sudden too near the enemy to avoid action without retreating; and that the Brigadier had supposed the German troops to be very near. The difference of time in their arrival was merely accidental—Major General Riedesel and those he commanded pressed for a share of the glory and they arrived in time to obtain it.

I have only to add upon this event, that the exertions of Brigadier Frazer were but a continuance of that uniform intelligence, activity, and bravery which distinguish his character upon all occasions, and entitle him to be recommended in the most particular manner to his Majesty's notice.

The other Officers and Soldiers of this Corps have prevented any distinctions of Individuals by a general and equal display of Spirit. On the same day (July 7) the Country people about Skenesborough having reported that part of the Enemy were still retreating upon Wood Creek, the 9th regiment was detach'd to take post near Fort Anne to observe their motions. This was effected tho' with much difficulty, the roads being extremely bad and the Bridges broken. The other Troops

[142]Major Ferdinand Albrecht von Bärner commanded the Brunswick Chasseur (light infantry) Battalion throughout the Saratoga Campaign.

[143]Colonel Nathan Hale of New Hampshire. The number of prisoners claimed by Burgoyne appears to be accurate.

were employed all that day and night in dragging fifty Batteaux over the falls to facilitate the movement of the rest of the first brigade to Fort Anne to dislodge the Enemy there.

July 8th

A report was received from Lt. Colonel Hill[144] commanding the 9th regiment, that the Enemy had been reinforced in the night by a considerable body of fresh Troops, that he could not retire before them with his regiment, but would maintain his ground. The two remaining regiments of the first Brigade under Brigadier Powell were ordered to quicken their march, and upon second intelligence of the Force of the Enemy, and firing being heard, the 20th Regt. was ordered forward, and Major General Phillips with some pieces of artillery was sent to take the Command. A violent storm of rain which lasted the whole day prevented these troops from getting to Fort Anne so soon as was intended; but the delay gave the 9th regiment an opportunity of distinguishing themselves by standing and repulsing an attack of six times their numbers. The enemy finding the position not to be forced in Front endeavoured to surround it, and from the superiority of their numbers that inconvenience was to be apprehended and Lt. Col. Hill therefore found it necessary to change his ground in the heat of Action. So critical an order was executed by the regiment with the greatest steadiness and Bravery. The enemy[,] after an attack of three hours[,] were totally repulsed with great loss. They fled towards Fort Edward setting fire to Fort Anne, but leaving a Saw-mill and block-house in good repair which latter was afterwards possessed by the Kings troops. The 9th regiment acquired during their expedition about thirty Prisoners, some stores and Baggage and the Colours of the second Hampshire Regiment.

The accidents to counterballance these several successes are few. The service has lost an Officer of great Gallantry & experience in Major Grant. The other Officers killed are also to be much regretted. Captain Montgomery of the 9th regiment[,] an Officer of much merit[,] was wounded in the Leg early in the action, and was in the act of being dressed by the Surgeon when the regiment changed ground. Being unable to help himself, he and the Surgeon were taken prisoners. I hear he has been well treated and is in a fair way of recovering at Albany. The wounded Officers and men, in general here are also likely to do well.

[144]Lieutenant Colonel John Hill, 9th Regiment of Foot, previously introduced.

July 9th & 10th

The army much fatigued, many parts of it having wanted their provisions for two days[,] almost the whole [missing] their tents and baggage—assembled in their present position. The right wing occupies the height of Skenesborough in two lines covered on the right flank by Riedesel's Dragoons empotence [i.e., en echelon], the left flank to Wood Creek. The Brunswic troops under M. Genl Reidesel are upon Castleton river with Breymans Corps upon the communication of roads towards Puttney and Rutland. The regiment of Hesse Hanau are at the head of the East Creek to preserve the communication with the Camp at Castleton and secure the bateaux. Brig^{r}. Frazer's Corps is in the Center to move on either wing of the Army.

The remains of the Ticonderoga army are at Fort Edward where they have been joined by considerable corps of fresh troops.[145] Roads are Opening to march to them by fort Anne, and the wood Creek is clearing of fallen trees, sunken Stones, and other obstacles, to give passage to bateaux carrying Artillery, Stores, Provision, and camp equipage &c. These are laborious works but the spirit and zeal of the troops are sufficient to surmount them. In the mean time all possible diligence is using at Ticonderoga to get gun boats, bateaux, and Provision vessels into Lake George. A corps of the Army, will be ordered to penetrate by that route which will afterwards be the route of the Magazines, and a junction of the whole is intended at Fort Edward.

I transmit to your Lordship herewith returns of the killed and wounded, and Lists of such parts of the Artillery, Provisions, and Stores taken from the Enemy as could be collected in so short a time. By a written account found in the Commissary's house at Ticonderoga Six thousand odd hundred Persons were fed from the Magazines the day before the evacuation.[146]

I have the honor to be with the greatest respect
Your Lordship's Most Obedient & Most Humble Servant,
(Signed,)
J: Burgoyne

[145]At this point in the campaign, this claim about American reinforcements was almost certainly not true.

[146]The concluding sentence in this paragraph, "Six thousand odd persons . . . ," is not printed in Burgoyne, *State of the Expedition from Canada*, xxxxvi.

6.16/19

Copy of a Letter from Lieut. Genl. Burgoyne to Lord George Germain, Head Quarters upon Hudson's River near Fort Edward, July 30, 1777 R. [Received] September 26 [1777]

Head Quarters near Fort Edward upon Hudson's river July 30th 1777

My Lord
By my dispatch of the 11th Instant committed to the care of Captain Gardner my Aid de Camp. I had the honor to inform your Lordship of the successful progress which had then been made by the Army under my Command.

Although the continued Retreat of the enemy from one Post to another since that period has prevented any material action, I think the bare date of a Letter from Hudson's river matter of intelligence not to be deferred: and I take this Occasion to give your Lordship the further satisfaction of knowing that the march hither, tho' scarce a day passed without firing[,] was effected without any loss of the regulars. A few wounds only were received by the Indians and Provincials.

The loss of the Enemy including killed and Prisoners, in the several Skirmishes, amount to about three hundred men.

The toil of the march was great, but supported with the utmost alacrity. The Country being a Wilderness in almost every part of the passage, the enemy took the means of Cutting large timber Trees on both sides the road so as to fall across and length ways with the Branches interwoven. The troops had not only layers of these to remove in places where it was impossible to take any other direction, but also they had above forty bridges to construct, and others to repair, one of which was of Log work over a morass two miles in extent.

I was not unapprised that great part of these difficulties might have been avoided by falling back from Skenesborough to Ticonderoga by water in order to take the more commodious Route by Lake George.

But besides wishing to prevent the effect which a retrograde motion often has, to abate the pannick [panic] of an Enemy, I considered that the natural consequence would be a resistance of delay at least, at Fort George; where, as the retreat was open, the enemy could wait securely the preparations of Batteries, or at least a landing in force for the purpose of investment.[147]

The issue has justified my perseverance. The garrison of Fort George in manifest danger of being cutt off by the direct movement from Skenesborough to Hudson's river, took the measure I expected of abandoning the Fort and burning the vessels, thereby leaving the Lake entirely free. A Detachment of the King's troops from Ticonderoga, which I had ordered to be ready for that event, with a great embarkation of provision, passed the lake on the same Day that I took possession of this Communication by Land: and I have the happiness upon the whole to find that the necessaries for continuing the Progress of the Army are more forward in point of time than they could have been by any other means.

The Enemy is at present in force near Saratoga where they profess an intention of standing a Battle, and they have drawn a supply of Artillery from New England for that purpose. The King's troops are employed in bringing forward from Fort George Provisions, bateaux, Artillery, and other materials necessary for proceeding.[148]

I have the honour to be with the greatest respect.
Your Lordships most Obedient and most humble Servant
(Signed)
J. Burgoyne
[To] His Excellency the Lord George German &c. &c. &c.

---

[147]Construction of Fort George, located on the 1755 battlefield at the southern end of Lake George, was begun by General Jeffery Amherst during the 1759 campaign against Fort Ticonderoga. The capture of that fort rendered the location unimportant, and Amherst subsequently halted construction of the fort. Only one stone bastion was completed, which was subsequently converted into a strong redoubt with the construction of barracks, and became known as Fort George. During the 1775–76 campaign Fort George served as an American logistical hub, while during the 1776 campaign it became the designated American smallpox hospital. In the spring and summer of 1777 only a small American garrison occupied it.

[148]For details regarding the movement of the British Royal Artillery down Lake George, and through Fort George to Fort Edward on the Hudson River, refer to Cubbison, *"Artillery never gained more Honour,"* 91–95.

6.16/17

Extract of a Letter from Sir Guy Carleton to Lord George Germain, Quebec, July 9, 1777

Since my last dispatches I have received letters from Niagara, copies of which I think necessary to transmit to your Lordship both as they regard the orders which I have already informed you I had sent for Assembling the Indians of that Neighborhood to be put under the conduct of Lieutenant Colonel St. Leger, and a Corps of Rangers which Colonel Butler has, of himself, formed for the purpose of serving with the Indians.

6.16/17a

Extract of a Letter from Colonel Butler Superintendant [*sic*] of Indian Affairs, [Fort] Niagara, June 15, 1777

Your Excellency's Letters of the 18th and 22nd of May I was honoured with on the 6th instant and immediately in obedience thereto had a meeting with a number of Chiefs[,] Sachems and Warriors of the Six Nations and their Allies then present, and communicated to them your Orders, they expressed great Satisfaction in having an opportunity to show their Friendship to their Father the King in an immediate compliance with his will.

I have sent out Runners and trusty Persons into the Indian Country to collect the Warriors and farther with the advice of the Chiefs assembled here have sent to Mr. Hay[149] at Detroit for a Body of the Western Indians to join their Brothers of the Six Nations on this Expedition, agreeable to mutual Treaties subsisting between them.

[149] Major Jehu Hay (c. 1738–1785), born in Pennsylvania, became an ensign in the 60th Foot (Royal Americans) in 1758, seeing considerable active service during the Seven Years' War. He was stationed at Fort Detroit during the siege resulting from Pontiac's Rebellion, and his diary is a major primary source for that campaign. In 1777 Hay was a half-pay officer serving with the Indian Department at Fort Detroit. He would subsequently be promoted to major and was taken prisoner by George Rogers Clark in the surrender at Vincennes. He ended the war as commandant of Fort Detroit and died there in 1785.

I have the Honour to transmit to your Excellency a List of Officers with their Rank and Pay at the same time beg leave to acquaint you that although from the Nature of the Service I find it requisite to employ a number of other Persons for the good of the Service a List of which is also inclosed, yet I cannot think of recommending them to your Excellency for Commissions or to have Rank[.]

I also transmit to your Excellency a List of a Body of Rangers already raised and in Pay.

6.16/17b

A List of Officers employed in the Indian department, with their Rank and pay

As Captains at 10 Shillings Per day
Peter Ten Broeck
John Johnson
James Wilson
Chas. Reaume
Thos. Butler
As Lieutenants at 4/6 [4 shillings, 6 pence] Sterling Per Diem.
Willm Caldwell
John Powell
John Yost Harcamier [Herkimer]
Lewis Clement
Frederick Yonge
Barent Frey
Andrew Thompson
Wm Ryer Bowin
Geo. McGinnis
Edward Smith, Secretary of the Department with 12 S [shillings] York Currency Per Diem.
Jomes Bennet Indian Commisary of Stores and Provisions at 10 S York Currency Per Diem.
List of persons employed in the Indian Department, as of use with their pay

James Secord at 8 S New York Currency per Diem.
At 6 New York Currency Per Diem.
Philip Frey
Samuel Thompson
John Depue
John Yonge

(Signed)
John Butler

6.16/17c

A List of Persons employ'd as Rangers in the Indian Department[150]

Michael Morris
Thos. Sutton
Geo. Steward
Emanuel Humphrey
Benjamin Davis
Daniel Young
Harmanus House
Jacob Tederick
Yost Patre
Dirk Bell
John Riley
Moses Mounteen
Partial Tarry
Richart —
Peter Danes
Josin Jole
John Secord Junior
David Secord
Silas Secord
John Secord

[150] Note that many of these names are extremely difficult to transcribe.

Solomon Secord
Stephen Secord
Adam Wartman
Jacob Bowman
Henry Seaman
Peter Seaman
Nicholas Phillips
John Phillips
Nicholas Phillips Jr.
Henderson Windeker
John Younger
Jacob English
Joseph Fern
Conrad Sels
Jacob Druner
Redman Parry
Robert Farrington
Joseph Page
Joshua Beebe
Adin Beebe
Jacob Take
Adam Bowman
Charles Encor
Hend Smith
Hend Bowin
Lewis Maybie
John Lord
Levie Green
John Fokes
Frederick Winter
Peter Miller
Abraham Wartiman
Adam Bowsman Junior
Jacob Bowman Junior
Casper Hubert
John Huber

Steph^en Farrington
Hans Oldenikshatt
Geo. Finter
Aug^ust Encar
Nathan^iel Hicks
Charl^es Depue
Peter Secord
John Parks
Thom^as Griffis
Hend. Winter
Jacob Huber
Isaac van Valken Burg
Dacuagne Interpeter
John Murphy Blacksmith

6.16/20

Extract of a Letter from Sir Guy Carleton to Lord George Germain, at Quebec, September 20, 1777

I transmit the Copy of a Letter [File 6.16/21a] which I have received from Lieut. Col. St Leger, giving an Account of a Victory obtained by a part of his Detachment sent by him under the Command of Sir John Johnson with a number of Indians under Col. Butler, over a Body of Rebels, led by a Genl. Herkemer [Herkimer][151] and explaining the reasons, which induced him afterwards to abandon the Siege, which he had began, of Fort Stanwix and to retreat from the Mohawk River. I likewise enclose a Copy transmitted to me by Col. S^t. Leger, of a Letter from Genl. Burgoyne to him; also Copies of Letters I have received from Col. Claus and Butler of the Indian Department [Files 6.16/17a–c, 6.16/20a–f].

Colonel Butler with three principal Chiefs of the five Nation Indians [Iroquois Indians], came down here, being deputed for that purpose, to assure me of the steadiness of their attachment of their readiness still

[151]Brigadier General Nicholas Herkimer, previously introduced.

to undertake anything in their power, for the advantage of His Majesty and their full determination to persevere in the War. Colonel Butler represents to me the expediency of having a Body of Rangers, as in the last War, to serve with the Indians; and proposed to me to raise a Corps properly qualified for that purpose, a part of which he has already engaged and served with him on the late Expedition. I thought the scheme calculated to draw the most Advantage from the Service of the Indians of which the disposition of that People is capable and Colonel Butler having shown himself by his zeal, capacity and Services, worthy of the Trust, I have furnished him with the proper powers to raise a Corps of Rangers for this Service and appointed him Major Commandant of it. A Copy of his beating Orders[152] is herewith inclosed as also a Copy of the Orders which I have given him for the joining as fast as possible the Army under the Command of Lieut. Genl. Burgoyne with his Corps and as large a Body of the Indians of the five Nations as he can collect [File 6.16/20a].

The Domiciled Indians of Canada and those of the upper Country which accompanied Genl. Burgoyne's Army have at different times returned, those of the upper Country alledging the reduced strength [previous two words difficult to transcribe] of their habitations, those of Canada other reasons, which considering that these people are never to be prevailed upon by compulsive means, I did not enter into. But having held a Council with the Chiefs of the upper Indians and ordered them Presents I obtained a Solemn promise that they would return early in the Spring with their Numbers greatly increased and as a pledge they have left some of their young Men to serve thro' the Winter. The Canada Indians have likewise consented to return in considerable Bodies, which they intend to relieve from time to time by which means General Burgoyne's Army, I hope will have large parties of these Indians constantly on Service with him.

---

[152]Official orders issued by the Crown, or the king's authorized representative, providing permission for an appointed officer to recruit a military command; "beating Orders" were so called because they originally permitted an officer to have a drummer beat out a tune to solicit recruits.

6.16/20a

Extract of a Letter from Colonel Butler, [Fort] Ontario, July 28, 1777

I have now the Honor to acquaint your Excellency that on the 13th Instant (two days after the Senecas and 40 of the Western Indians arrived) I left Niagara— In order to spare Provisions I had before Appointed a number of the Seneca Warriors together with many of their Women and Children to meet me at Yrondequat [Irondequoit Bay, now in Ontario Province], where I had promised to deliver them a present of Cloathes and some Provisions to support them in absence of their Husbands; at that Place I waited seven days to deliver them the presents, and give them the Hatchet, which they accepted and promised to make use of it. On the 19th I received from Genl St. Leger orders to send him 150 Indians to act with the King's Troops under his command upon an alert against Fort Stanwix, on the morning of the 20th, I had them ready, and sent off to him under proper Officers whom I flattered myself he would approve Every thing being settled with the Senecas. I left Yrondequat on the 24th and on the 25th arrived at this place, where besides the Indians I brought with me, I found a large party under the direction of Joseph [underline indicates emphasis in original] the Mohawk in consequence of a message I had sent him on the 30th past, besides these I had ordered another large body of the Six Nations to meet me here by way of the Three Rivers; but on my arrival found them stopped there by order of Col. Claus,[153] Upon a review of the whole, I have the Satisfaction to assure your Excellency that the number of Indian Warriors assembled at this place, and the Seneca or Three Rivers cannot fall much short of one thousand. The great resort of those people to this, and every other Place to partake of the King's bounty caused me to present to Col.

[153]Daniel Claus (1727–1787) was the son-in-law of Sir William Johnson, having married his daughter Ann (Nancy) Johnson. Claus had previously served as Johnson's secretary and was intimately familiar with negotiations and relationships between Johnson and Britain's American Indian allies. He is believed to have spoken Mohawk, and he had close relationships with the Mohawk nation. He was appointed superintendent of relations with American Indians, but shortly ran into political difficulties, and was eventually supplanted. During the 1777 campaign he was commissioned by Carleton to serve as the superintendent of the American Indians on St. Leger's campaign. Claus was hampered by personal jealousies and political in-fighting throughout his career. He died in Canada in 1787.

Bolton[154] before I left Niagara another account of 4,011.16.9 Pounds [4,011 pounds, 16 shillings, 9 pence] York Currency for his approbation since when I am informed he has sent it to your Excellency, for your acceptance, I must humbly beg your Excellency will do me the Justice to believe, that in all my Transactions, I have endeavoured to execute your Orders with the greatest Economy in my power; And when your reflect the high value the Indians sett upon their alliance, the tempting Offers the Rebels have frequently made to bring them over to their Interest together with their numerous Women, and Children who will expect to be cloathed in absence of their Husbands, which is my humble Opinion there is no avoiding without disgusting those haughty and tenacious People. When your Excellency has weighed all these Reasons, I flatter myself that you will not think the expence however high, to be useless, or given with too Lavish a hand.

Before I conclude I must beg leave to remind your Excellency, that when I first arrived at Niagara, I found the Six Nation's warriors, and of the two rather inclined to the Rebels. Encouraged by Col. Caldwell,[155] and Capt. Lernwelt[156] and at the same time supported by You, I have spared no pains, nor attention to fix them in the Interests of the King. The pleasure attending my success, I have enjoyed by experiencing your Excellency's approbation of my humble though unwearied endeavours.

[not signed]

---

[154]Lieutenant Colonel Mason Bolton, 8th Regiment of Foot, then commandant of Fort Niagara, which post he assumed in July 1777.

[155]Lieutenant Colonel John Caldwell (?–October 31, 1776) purchased the lieutenant colonelcy of the 8th Regiment of Foot in 1772. He served as commandant of Fort Niagara from 1774 until his death at that fort on October 31, 1776.

[156]Captain Richard Berringer Lernoult, 8th Foot, served during the winter of 1776–77 as the commandant of Fort Niagara and with St. Leger during his campaign upon Fort Stanwix. He subsequently served as commandant of Fort Detroit from 1774 to 1775 and 1778 to 1779 and spent most of the American War of Independence with his regiment at various frontier posts on the Great Lakes. Commissioned into the regiment in 1756, Lernoult served in North America thirteen years until 1784, when he returned to England as a major and left the British army.

6.16/20b

Extract of a Letter from Colonel Butler to Sir Guy Carleton, Camp before Fort Stanwix, August 15, 1777

I have the pleasure to acquaint your Excellency of the Success of His Majesty's Arms against a Detachment of the Rebels on the 6th Inst. Immediately after my arrival here, I was ordered by Brigadier Genl. St. Leger to march with 400 Indians to intercept a Party of the Mohawk River Militia (in number 900) whom he was informed were on their March to throw themselves into this place. On the evening Sir John Johnson with 50 of the Royal New York Regt joined us[;] at 10 oClock the next Morning near the Orisca [Oriskany] field we heard the Rebels in full march with a Convoy of 15 Waggons of Provisions & Stores. We were immediately formed by the Seneka Chiefs, who took the lead in this Action, in concurrence with Sir John Johnson & myself. Sir John was posted on the Road to give the Enemy a Volley as they advanced, myself with the Indians & 20 Rangers were posted to flank them in the Woods: this Disposition was soon after a little altered by the Indians while the Enemy were advancing & when they were near enough threw in a heavy fire on the Rebels, & made a shocking Slaughter among them with their Spears & Hatchets; the Rebels however recovering themselves fell back to a more advantageous Ground & maintained a running fight for about an hour & a half. At length the Indians with the Detachment of the Yorkers & Rangers pursuing their blow, utterly defeated them with the Loss of 500 killed, wounded & taken, many of the latter were conformable to the Indian Custom afterwards killed. Of the New Yorkers, Capt. McDonald was killed, Capt Watts dangerously wounded, & one Subaltern[.] [Of] the Rangers Capts Wilson & Hare killed & one Private wounded.[157]

The Indians suffered much, having 33 killed & 29 wounded; The Senecas alone lost 17 Men, among whom were several of their Chief Warriors & had 16 wounded. During the whole Action the Indians shewed

[157] Captain-Lieutenant Donald John McDonell was commander of the Colonel's Company of the King's Royal Regiment of New York, killed in hand-to-hand fighting at Oriskany. Captain Stephen Watts, Sir John Johnson's brother-in-law, commanded the Light Infantry Company of the same regiment. His leg was amputated as a result of his wounds at Oriskany, although he subsequently purchased a captaincy in the 8th Regiment of Foot. Captain James Wilson and Captain John Hare were officers in the Indian Department and subsequently became company commanders in Butler's Rangers. Watt, *Rebellion in the Mohawk Valley*, 178–179, 185–186.

the greatest Zeal for his Majesty's cause & had they not been a little too precipitate, scarcely a Rebel of the Party had escaped.[158] Most of the leading Rebels are cut off in the Action, so that any further attempt from that Quarter is not to be expected. Capt. Watts of the Royal New Yorkers, whose many amiable Qualities deserved a better fate, lay wounded in this place upon the field, two days before he was found, however it is thought he will recover. I should not do justice to the Indians in general & to the Senecas in particular, was I not to acquaint you that their Behaviour in the Action exceeded any thing I could have expected from them. The Loss the Senecas have sustained will point out to your Excellency how severe a share of it fell to them. The Success of this day will plainly shew the Utility of your Excellency's constant Support of my unwearied Endeavours to conciliate to his Majesty so serviceable a Body of Allies.

6.16/20c

Extract of a Letter from Lieut. Colonel St. Leger to Sir Guy Carleton, [Fort] Oswego, August 27, 1777

A minute detail of every Operation since my leaving La Chine, with the Detachment entrusted to my Care, Your Excellency, will permit me to reserve to a time of less hurry & mortification than the present while I enter into the Interesting Scene before Fort Stanwix, which I invested the 3^{d} of August, having previously pushed forward Lieut. Bird of the King's Regiment [8th Regiment of Foot] with thirty of the King's Troops & two Hundred Indians, under the Direction of Captains Hare & Wilson, and the Chiefs Joseph[159] & Bull,[160] to seize fast hold of the lower Landing Place, and thereby cut off the Enemy's

[158]This description refers to the ambush at Oriskany that was executed before the entirety of the Tryon County Militia was trapped, permitting a substantial portion (approximately one-quarter) of Herkimer's force to escape.

[159]Captain Joseph Brant, a renowned and accomplished Mohawk leader. His sister, Molly Brant, was married to Sir William Johnson, providing him a powerful connection. Brant was well educated; in fact, he had translated (with his friend, Daniel Claus) the Anglican Prayer Book and the Gospel of Mark into Mohawk. He had also traveled to England. He fought as a Mohawk war leader during the St. Leger expedition, and subsequently became a leader of the Mohawk community. Brant has received numerous biographies, the most current being Taylor, *Divided Ground.*

[160]Otherwise unidentified ("Captain Bull" being an extremely common name for an American Indian war leader); possibly he was a Delaware war chief recruited by Joseph Brant for service with the British in 1775 and 1776.

Communication with the Lower Country. This was done with great address by the Lieutenant, though not with the effect I had promised myself, occasioned by the slackness of the Messasagoes. The Brigade of provision Boats & Ammunition I had Intelligence of being arrived & disembarked before this party had taken post.

The 4th & 5th were employed in making Arrangements for opening Wood Creek (which the Enemy with indefatigable labour of One Hundred & fifty Men for fourteen Days had most effectualy choaked up) and the making a temporary Road from pine Ridge upon Fish Creek, sixteen Miles from the Fort, for a present Supply of provision and the transport of our Artillery, the first was effected by the diligence & zeal of Captain Rouville, assisted by Captain Harkimer, of the Indian Department, with one Hundred & ten Men in nine Days; while Lieutenant Lundy, acting as Assistant Quarter Master General, had rendered the Road, in the worst of Weather, sufficiently practicable, to pass the whole Artillery & Stores, with seven Days provision in two Days.[161]

On the 5th in the Evening, Intelligence arrived, by my discovering parties on the Mohawk River, that a Reinforcement of Eight Hundred Militia, conducted by General Herkimer, were on their March to relieve the Garrison, and were actually at that Instant at Oriska [Oriskany], an Indian Settlement twelve Miles from the Fort. The Garrison being apprised of their March by four Men, who were seen enter the Fort in the Morning, through what was thought an impenetrable Swamp, I did not think it prudent to wait for them, and thereby subject myself to be attacked by a Sally from the Garrison in the Rear, while the Reinforcement employed me in Front, I therefore determined to attack them on the March, either openly, or covertly, as Circumstances should offer. At this time, I had not two Hundred & Fifty of the King's Troops in Camp, the various & extensive Operations I was under an absolute Necessity of entering into, having employed the rest; and therefore could not send above Eighty White Men, Rangers & Troops included with the whole Corps of Indians. Sir John Johnson put himself at the Head of this party, and began his March that Evening at 5 o'Clock, and met the Rebel Corps at the same Hour the next Morning: The Impetuousity

[161]Captain Jean-Baptiste-Melchior Hertel de Rouville was the "capitaine" commanding the Company of Canadian Militia assigned to St. Leger's expedition. Lieutenant James Lundy of the Royal Highland Emigrants was St. Leger's quartermaster. Watt, *Rebellion in the Mohawk Valley*, 74–75.

of the Indians is not to be described; on the Sight of the Enemy, forgetting the judicious Disposition formed by Sir John, and agreed to by themselves, which was to suffer the Attack to begin with the Troops in Front, while they should be on both Flank & Rear; they rushed in, hatchet in hand, and thereby gave the Enemy's Rear an Opportunity to escape: in relation to the Victory, it was equally complete, as if the whole had fallen; nay more so, as the two Hundred, who escaped only served to spread the panic wider, but it was not so with the Indians their Loss was great. (I must be understood, Indian Computation, being only about thirty killed and wounded, and in that Number some of their favorite Chiefs, and confidential [*sic*] Warriors were slain.)

On the Enemy's Side almost all their principal Leaders were slain. General Herkimer has since died of his Wounds.[162] It is proper to mention, that the four Men, detached with Intelligence of the March of the Reinforcement set out the Evening before the Action, and consequently the Enemy could have no Account of the Defeat, and were only in possession of the Time appointed for their Arrival; at which, as I suspected the Enemy made a Sally with two Hundred & fifty Men, towards Lieutenant Bird's post, to facilitate the Entrance of the relieving Corps, or bring on a general Engagement, with every Advantage they could wish.[163]

Captain Hoyes was immediately detached to cut in upon their Rear, while they engaged the Lieutenant. Immediately upon the departure of Captain Hoys, I learnt that Lieutenant Bird (misled by the Information of a cowardly Indian that Sir John was pressed) had quitted his Post to march to his Assistance. I marched the Detachment of the King's Regiment in support of Captain Hoyes, by a Road in Sight of the Garrison, which with executive Fire from his party immediately drove the Enemy into the Fort, without any further Advantage than frightening some Squaws, and pilfering the packs of the Warriors, which they left behind them.[164] After this Affair was over, orders were immediately given to complete a two Gun Battery & Mortar Beds, with three strong Redoubts in their Rear,

[162]Brigadier General Herkimer died at his home in the Mohawk Valley on August 16, 1777. The fact that St. Leger had news of his death comparatively rapidly suggests a smoothly functioning military intelligence network in Tryon County on the part of the British.

[163]Lieutenant James Bird of the 8th Regiment of Foot was an extremely experienced officer, having served in Gage's Light Infantry (80th Foot) throughout its existence during the Seven Years' War. Watt, *Rebellion in the Mohawk Valley*, 111.

[164]In fact, the American sortie caused considerable destruction in the Indian and British camp, which badly demoralized the American Indians, particularly when combined with their catastrophic casualties sustained at the Battle of Oriskany.

to enable me, in case of another Attempt to relieve the Garrison, by the Regimented Troops, to march out a larger Body of the King's Troops.

Captain Lernoult was sent with one Hundred & ten Men, to the lower Landing Place, where he established himself with great Judgement & Strength, having an enclosed Battery of a three Pounder opposed to any Sally from the Fort; and another to the side of the Country where a Relief must approach, and the Body of his Camp deeply intrenched and abbatised.[165]

When by the unabating Labour of Officers and Men (the smallness of our Numbers never admitting of a Relief, or above three hours' Cessasation for Sleep or Cooking) the Batteries & Redoubts were finished & new Cheeks and Axletrees made for the Six pounders, those that were sent being reported rotten and unserviceable,[166] it was found that our Cannon had not the least Effect upon the Sod Work of the Fort, and that Our Royals[167] had only the power of teizing [teasing], as a six inch plank was sufficient security for their Powder Magazine as We learnt from the Deserters. At this time Lieutenant Glenie of the Artillery whom I had appointed to act as Assistant Engineer proposed a Conversion of the Royals (if I may use the Expression) into Howitzers; the ingenuity and feasibility of this measure striking me very strongly the business was set about immediately & soon executed—when it was found that nothing prevented their operating with the desired effect, but the distance their Chambers being too small to hold a sufficiency of Powder there was nothing now to be done but to approach the place by sap, to a proper distance that the Ramparts might be brought with their porteé; at the same time

[165]In other words, Lernoult constructed an abatis around his camp. An abatis is an obstacle consisting of felled trees and brush, placed to the front of a fortification to obstruct and delay an enemy attack. Secured to the ground, with branches sharpened, an abatis was intended to slow down the enemy where they are most exposed and vulnerable to friendly fire, much as modern barbed wire would do. A properly constructed abatis was a formidable obstacle; for example, during the British and Provincial assault on the French lines at Ticonderoga in July 1758, an abatis effectively checked the British advance. The British and Provincial soldiers suffered grievous losses while caught within it. Captain Richard B. Lernoult was then with the 8th Regiment of Foot. He was appointed as adjutant general for Governor Haldimand in Canada on August 1, 1779, and served in this position throughout the remainder of the American Revolution.

[166]These are wooden pieces of the gun carriages.

[167]Royal Artillery mortar five and one-half inches in diameter, typically referred to as "Royal Mortars"; howitzers of the same diameter were similarly known as "Royal Howitzers." However, St. Leger carried with him no mortars or howitzers of this size. Rather, he employed the smaller cohorn mortars (4⅖" diameter). Although he creatively placed the cohorn mortar tubes on field carriages (instead of the traditional bed mounts used for mortars) to convert them to howitzers, they were still too small to effectively reduce Fort Stanwix.

all materials were preparing to run a Mine under their most formidable Bastion. In the midst of these operations intelligence was brought in by our Scouts of a second Corps of One thousand Men being on their March[.] The same Zeal no longer animated the Indians; They complained of our thinness of Troops & their former Losses. I immediately called a Council of the Chiefs, encouraged them as much as I could, promised to lead them on myself & bring into the Field three hundred of the best Troops. They listened to this and promised to follow me and agreed that I should reconnoitre the Ground proposed for the Field of Battle the next morning, accompanied by some of their Chief Warriors to settle the plan of Operations. When upon the ground appointed for the Field of Battle, Scouts came in with the Account of the first Number, swelled to two thousand immediately after a third that General Burgoyne's Army was cut to pieces & that Arnold[168] was advancing by rapid and forced Marches with three thousand Men. It was at this moment I began to suspect Cowardice in some and Treason in others; however I returned to Camp not without hopes with the Assistance of my gallant Co-adjutant Sir John Johnson & the influence of the superintendency Colonels Claus and Butler of inducing them to meet the Enemy. A Council according to their Custom was called to know their Resolutions, before the breaking of which I learnt that two hundred were already decamped; in about an hour they insisted that I should retreat, or they would be obliged to abandon me. I had no party to take and a hard party it was to Troops who could do nothing without them, to yield to their Resolves, and therefore proposed to retire at Night, sending on before, my sick, wounded, Artillery &c. down the Wood Creek, covering it by our Line of March.

I now thought it time to call in Captain Lernoult's post, retiring with the Troops in Camp, to the ruined Fort called William, in the Front of the Garrison, not only to wait the Enemy, if they thought proper to sally, but to protect the Boats from the Fury of the Savages; sending forward Captain Hoyes with his Detachment, and one piece of Cannon to the place where Fort Bull stood, to receive the Troops who waited the Arrival of Captain Lernoult.[169] Most of the Boats were escorted that

[168] Major General Benedict Arnold, previously introduced.

[169] Forts Brewerton, William, and Bull were small outposts constructed during the Seven Years' War to provide security on the Wood Creek–Mohawk River portage. Fort Bull had been destroyed in a March 1756 raid by French and Indian forces from Fort de la Presentation at modern Ogdensburg, New York. Forts Brewerton and William, which had been abandoned

night beyond Canada Creek, where no danger was to be apprehended from the Enemy, as the Creek at this place, bending from the Road, has a deep Cedar Swamp between[.] Every Attention was now turned to the Mouth of the Creek, which the Enemy might have possessed themselves of, by a rapid March by the Oneyda Castle: at this place the whole of the little Army arrived by twelve o'Clock at Night, and took post in such a manner, as to have no Fears of anything the Enemy could do: here we remained 'till three o'Clock next Morning, when the Boats which could [underline indicates emphasis in original] come up the Creek arrived, and proceeded across Lake Oneyda to the ruined Fort of Brewerton, where I learnt that some Boats were still labouring down the Creek, after being lightened of the best part of their Freight by the Messagoes. Captain Lernould proposed with a Boat full of Armed Men, to repass the Lake that Night to relieve them from their Labour and supply them with provision. This Transaction does as much Honor to the Humanity as to the Gallantry of this valuable Officer.[170]

In my arrival at the Onandago Falls, I received an Answer to my Letter from General Burgoyne (a Copy of which I have the Honor to transmit to your Excellency) which shewed in the clearest Light the Scene of Treachery that had been practiced upon me; the Messenger had heard indeed, in his way, that they were collecting the same kind of Rabble as before, but that there was not an Enemy within Forty Miles of Fort Stanwix.[171]

Soon after my Arrival here, I was joined by Captain Lernoult with the Men and Boats he had been in search of.

I mean immediately to send off, for the Use of the upper Garrison all the overplus provisions I shall have after keeping a Sufficiency to carry my Detachment down, which I mean to do with every Expedition in my power, the Moment this Business is effected; for which purpose I have ordered here the Snow. The Sloop is already gone from this with its full Lading.

---

at the end of the war, were never anything more than simple dirt and earth field fortifications; and they would certainly have been "ruined" by 1777.

170 The confusion and disorder in the British withdrawal from Fort Stanwix is obvious in this paragraph.

171 Benedict Arnold had employed various ruses as he led a small Continental Army and militia advance to relieve Fort Stanwix. These subterfuges, intended to deceive the Indians in particular regarding the size of his force, proved to be extremely successful.

6.16/20d

Copy of a Letter from Lieut. General Burgoyne to Lieut. Col. St. Leger (no date) In Sir Guy Carleton's of September 28, 1777[172]

Dr Sir

I wrote to you some time since an account of the rapid progress of His Majesty's Arms at Ticonderoga. I apprehend that Letter did not come to hand. Insurmountable difficulties occasioned by the heavy Rains upon the Roads prevented me getting forward; I tried an Expedition to obtain a Supply of Cattle without waiting the Transport of Magazines. It has failed, not without some loss to the Germans. It will now be a fortnight before I can do anything in your favour. It will remain therefore to be considered by you first, whether you can force the place with the Artillery you have; 2^{ndly} If not whether you can remain before it without risk of being cut from your Retreat, 'till I can bring the Enemy to a Battle, or otherwise to assist you. 3^{rdly} If you can reimbark your Artillery, and join me with your Troops by the Route through the Woods to Fort George.[173] I have mentioned these considerations in the Order of Preference I would desire, and a Retreat by Canada, and so to follow me by Ticonderoga is the last.[174]

In case you can effect the Second consideration or any other ways keep footing in the Country, 'till I get possession of the Mouth of the Mohawk, it might be a good measure to leave the Garrison and by forced and rapid Marches to join me; But this must depend upon the good affections of Johnson's Country.

I am D$^{r.}$ Sir yours most faithfully
(signed) J. Burgoyne

---

[172]Obviously written after the Battle of Bennington but before the movement on Albany began in mid-September.

[173]What route Burgoyne is referring to cannot be determined. There was no such route "through the Woods" in 1777 between Fort Stanwix and Fort George at the southern end of Lake George. In fact, there is still no such direct route from Rome, New York, to Lake George Village, New York!

[174]This last option is the one that St. Leger would actually utilize. Following his withdrawal from Fort Stanwix, St. Leger traveled from Oswego across the eastern shore of Lake Ontario, down the St. Lawrence River, past Montreal, then up Lake Champlain, reaching Fort Ticonderoga on September 27, 1777. Too late to participate with Burgoyne's column, he retired to Canada from Fort Ticonderoga and Mount Independence in November 1777. Doblin, *Officer in the Prinz Friedrich Regiment*, 94.

I beg to hear from you as frequently as possible; I have a Copy of this, therefore you need only say, first, second third or last, according to the Consideration you adopt.

N.B. This Letter was not dated. It arrived the 25th [of August or September] at Onandaga Falls.

6.16/20e

Extract of a Letter from Lieut. Colonel St. Leger to Sir Guy Carleton, [Fort] Oswego, August 27, 1777

I have the Honour to inform your Excellency that the accounts we received in Canada concerning Fort Stanwix were the most erroneous that can be conceived[;] instead of the insultable [*sic*] and unfinished work we were taught to expect I found it a respectable Fortress, strongly garrisoned with 700 men and demanding a Train of Artillery we were not masters of, for its speedy subjection— Its form is a kind of Trapezium or four sided Figure with four Bastions freized and picketed without,[175] there is a good ditch with Pickets nipping out a considerable way at the Salient Angles of the Bastions, three Nines, four Sixes, two threes, with a considerable number of wall pieces, were all the Artillery the Enemy made use of during the Siege.

Since I write the above the Hessians are arrived with fifty of their men sick[.] [O]ne fortnight sooner, the Indians cou'd had no plea for their conduct.[176]

[175]St. Leger is referring here to two specific types of fortification. "Freizing" (fraising) refers to sharpened logs incorporated directly into the walls, closely placed so as to prevent infantry from climbing the fortification walls, or using scaling ladders. Thus, an enemy attacking a wall would first have to remove the fraising before they could enter the interior of a fort. The fraising logs were pointed down, so that hand grenades thrown from the ditch would bounce back into the ditch before they detonated, thus harming the attackers. Pickets were large logs, sharpened at the top, and installed as a defensive wall in front of a major fortification. They were well secured into the ground using trenches and buried cross pieces and were usually emplaced at the bottom of ditches to protect them from enemy artillery. Pickets protected a fort from direct enemy assault, serving the same role as an abatis, in that they delayed an enemy assaulting column in front of the major defensive works so that they could be devastated by gunfire. Both pickets and fraising had to be deliberately removed to permit an infantry assault upon a fortification, a dangerous and difficult task under fire. Thus, Fort Stanwix was a formidable fortification, which could not be taken by a simple storming by infantry without appropriate artillery preparation and support, correct tools such as saws and axes, and the risk of heavy casualties.

[176]The meaning of this last sentence cannot be ascertained.

6.16/20f

Extract of a Letter from Danl Claus Esqr., Superintendent on Brigadier St. Leger's Expedition, Oswego, August 28, 1777—To Sir Guy Carleton

I have however the pleasure of assuring your Excellency, that the different Indian Nations I happened to convene since my coming out, have demonstrated the most warm zeal of espousing & acting most heartily in the present cause for the interest of the Crown; and am fully persuaded the 6 Nations & their confederates, are so firmly attached to His Majesty's Interest on the present Crisis, that they will continue so to the end of the contest, to which their late success against the Rebels of Tryon County as well as their pursuing revenge for their lost friends in said Action, will edge them on the more.

As doubtless Brig$^{r.}$ St. Leger has fully given your Excellency a detail of that Affair, as well as thereupon ensued Retreat from Fort Stanwix; I will not incommode you with repetitions, but defer particulars to a personal Interview.

6.16/20g

Copy of Beating Order to John Butler Esqr., appointed Major Commandant of a Corps of Rangers to serve with the Indians In Sir Guy Carleton's of September 20, 1777

Guy Carleton, Knight of the Bath, Captn General & Governor in Chief of the Province of Quebec & Territories depending thereon &c. &c. &c. General and Commander in Chief of his Majesty's Forces in said Province and the Frontiers thereof. &c. &c. &c.

To John Butler Esquire appointed Major Commandant of a Corps of Rangers to serve with the Indians—

By Virtue of the Power and Authority in me vested by the King, I do hereby Authorize & impower you or such Officers as you shall direct, by beat of Drums, or otherwise; forthwith to raise, on the Frontiers of this Province as many able bodied men, of his Majesty's Loyal Subjects, as will form one Company of Rangers to serve with the Indians as occasion shall require, which Company shall consist of a Captain, a first Lieut[t], Second Lieut[t], three Serjeants, three Corporals, & fifty private Men; and when you shall have completed one Company as aforesaid, you are further empowered to raise and form another in like manner, and of like number as the first, and so on until you shall have completed a Number of Companies of Rangers as aforesaid not exceeding in the whole Eight Companies, observing that the first Co. Completed Armed and fit for Service & have passed Muster before such persons as shall be appointed for that purpose; by some one of the Commanding Officers of his Majesty's Troops nearest to where the said Companies so raised shall be at the time, before another be begun to be raised, And of which Eight Companies or such part thereof you shall be able to raise, you shall be Major Commandant, two of the Companies aforesaid (to be composed of People speaking the Indian Language & acquainted with their customs and manner of making war) for their encouragement, shall be paid at the rate of four Shillings New York Currency by the day, non Commissioned Officers in Proportion from the day of their inlisting & the other said Companies to be composed of People well acquainted with the Woods in consideration of the fatigue they are liable to undergo, shall be paid at the Rate of two Shillings New York Currency by the day. Non Commission Officers in proportion, the whole to Cloath & Arm themselves on their own expence, You and the officers so raised, to be paid as is customary to other officers of the like Rank, in his Majesty's Service, And you are carefully to obey and follow such Orders & directions as you shall from time to time receive from me, or the Commander in Chief for the time being, or any other your Superior Officer, According to the rules and discipline of War, in pursuance of the trust hereby reposed in you, Given under my hand and Seal at Arms of Quebec this Fifteenth day of September One thousand Seven hundred and Seventy Seven and in the Seventeenth Year of the Reign of Our Sovereign Lord George the Third by the Grace of God of Great Britain France and Ireland King Defender of the Faith and so forth.

Signed
Guy Carleton
By his Excellencys Command C: Signed [countersigned] C Foy

6.16/20h

Copy of Instructions to Major John Butler, Commandant of a Corps of Rangers to serve with the Indians In Sir Guy Carleton's of September 20, 1777

Guy Carleton, Knight of the Bath, Captain General & Governor in Chief of the Province of Quebec & Territories depending thereon &c. &c. &c. General and Commander in Chief of his Majesty's Forces in said Province and the Frontiers thereof. &c. &c. &c.

To Major John Butler Commandant of a Corps of Rangers to serve with the Indians

Having appointed you to Command a Body of Rangers, which it is expedient, at this time to raise, in order to serve with the Indians, you shall, as soon as Possible, March with such part of the said Rangers, as are already raised, or you shall immediately raise, and as large a Body of the Six Nations, or other Indians, as you can collect, without too much exposing their Country to the incursions of the Rebels, to Join and put yourself under the Command of Lieutenant General Burgoyne, giving him Notice, as expeditiously as possible, of your Approach towards him, and of the Force you bring along with you, and all orders which you shall receive from the said Lieut. General Burgoyne, you are to observe and Obey. Given under my hand at Quebec this fifteenth day of Septem^r One thousand seven hundred and Seventy Seven.

(signed)
Guy Carleton

6.16/21a

Extract of a Letter from Lt. Col. St. Leger to Lieut. Genl. Burgoyne brought through the Woods by an Indian, Before Fort Stanwix, August 11, 1777

After combating the natural difficulties of the River St. Lawrence and the artificial ones the enemy threw into my Way at Wood Creek I invested Fort Stanwix the 3d instant[;] on the 5th I learnt from discovering parties on the Mohawk River that a Body of one thousand Militia were on their March to raise the Siege. On the confirmation of this news I moved a large body of Indians with some troops the same night to try an ambuscade for them on their March. They fell into it. The completed victory was obtained above 400 lay dead on the field amongst the number of whom were almost all the principal Movers of Rebellion in that County. There are six or seven hundred men in the Fort— The Militia will never rally—all that I am to apprehend therefore, that will retard my Progress in joining you, is a reinforcement of what they call their regular troops by the way of Half moon up the Mohawk River. A diversion therefore from your army by that quarter will greatly expedite my junction with either of the Grand Armies.[177]

[177]The Bennington expedition had no effect or influence on affairs at Fort Stanwix, and this letter would be received too late by Burgoyne to have influenced the expedition. By the time that it arrived at Burgoyne's headquarters the Bennington expedition would already have failed, and Burgoyne could not afford to risk any additional soldiers on a diversion on St. Leger's behalf.

6.16/21

Copy of a Letter from Lieut. Genl. Burgoyne to Lord George Germain, Camp nearly opposite to Saratoga, August 20, 1777[178] Rec. October 31 [1777]

Camp nearly Opposite to Saratoga 20th August 1777,

My Lord
In my last Dispatch (a Duplicate of which will be inclosed herewith) I had the honor to inform your Lordship of the proceedings of the Army under my Command to the 30th of July[.]

From that Period to the 15th of August every possible measure was employ'd to bring forward Batteaux, Provision and Ammunition from Fort George to the first Navigable part of Hudson's River; a distance of 18 miles, the roads in some parts steep and in others wanting great repair. Of the Horses furnished by Contracts in Canada not more than a third part was yet arrived.

The delay was not imputable to neglect but to the natural Accidents attending so long and intricate a Combination of Land and Water Carriage. Fifty teams of Oxen which had been collected in the Country through which I had marched were added to assist the Transports but these Resources together were found far inadequate to the purposes of feeding the Army and forming a Magazine at the same time.

Exceeding heavy rains augmented the impediments. It was often necessary to employ ten or twelve Oxen upon a single Batteaux[.] And after the utmost exertions for the fifteen days above stated there were not above four days provisions before hand nor above In Batteaux in the Hudsons River.

Intelligence had reached me that Lt. Col. St. Leger was before Fort Stanwix which was defended. The main Army of the Enemy opposed to me was at Stillwater, a place between Saratoga and the mouth of the Mohawk.

A rapid Movement forward appeared to be of the utmost consequence at this period. The Enemy could not have proceeded up the Mohawk

[178] This letter was printed as Appendix No. 8 in Burgoyne, *State of the Expedition from Canada*, xxxix–xliv.

without putting themselves between two Fires in case L$^{t.}$ Col. S$^{t.}$ Leger should have succeeded, and at best being cut off by my Army from Albany. They must either therefore have stood in Action, have fallen back towards Albany or have passed the Hudson's River in order to secure a Retreat to New England higher up. Which ever of these measures they had taken, so that the King's army had been enabled to advance, Col. S$^{t.}$ Leger's Operations would have been assisted, a Junction with him probably secured and the whole Country of the Mohawk Opened.

To maintain the Communication with Fort George during such a movement so as to be supplied by daily Degrees at a distance continually increasing, was an obvious impossibility. The Army was much too weak to have afforded a Chain of Posts: Escorts for every separate Transport would have been a still greater drain, nor could any have been made so strong as to force their way through such positions as the Enemy might take in one nights march from the White Creek where they had a numerous Militia. Had the Enemy remained superior through fear or Want of comprehending so palpable an advantage the Physical impossibility of being supplied by degrees from Fort George was still in force, because a near necessity of Land Carriage for nine miles arises at Still Water and in the proportion that Carriages had been brought forward to that Place the Transports must have ceased behind.

The alternative therefore was short, either to relinquish the favorable Opportunity of advancing upon the Enemy or to attempt other resources of supply.

It was well known that the Enemys Supplies in Live Cattle from a large Tract of Country passed by the route of Manchester, Arlington and other parts of the Hampshire Grants to Bennington, in order to be occasionally conveyed from thence to the Main Army. A large Depot of Corn and of wheel Carriages was also formed at the same place and the usual Guard was Militia though it varied in numbers from day to day. A Scheme was formed to surprise Bennington. The Possession of the Cattle and Carriages would certainly have enabled the Army to leave their distant Magazines and to have acted with Energy and Dispatch. Success would also have answered many secondary purposes.

Lieut. Col. Baum[179] an Officer well qualified for the undertaking was

[179]Lieutenant Colonel Friedrich Baum, previously introduced.

fixed upon to Command, he had under him two hundred dismounted Dragoons of the Regiment of Reidesel [*sic*], Captain Fraser's Marksmen which were the only British, all the Canadian Volunteers, a Party of the Provincials who perfectly knew the Country[,] an hundred Indians, and two light pieces of Cannon. The whole detachment amounted to about Five hundred Men. The Instructions were positive to keep the regular Corps posted while the light Troops felt their way, and not to incur the danger of being Surrounded or having a Retreat cut off.

In order to facilitate this Operation and to be ready to take advantage of its success, the Army moved up the East shore of Hudson's River, on the 11th [transcription difficult—this may be the 14th] a Bridge was formed of Rafts, over which the advanced Corps passed and encamped at Saratoga. Lieut. Col. Breymans Corps were posted near Batten Kill and upon intelligence from L$^{t.}$ Col. Baum that the Enemy was stronger at Bennington than expected and were aware of his Attack, that Corps consisting of the Brunswick Grenadiers[,] light Infantry and Chasseurs were sent forward to sustain him.

It since appears that Lieut. Col. Baum not having been able to compleat the March undiscovered, was joined at a place called Santoix Mills[180] about four miles short of Bennington, by many people professing themselves to be Loyalists. A Provincial Gentleman of confidence who had been sent with the Detachment as knowing the Country and the Character of Inhabitants was so incautious as to leave at liberty such as took the Oath of allegiance.

His credulity and their profligacy caused the first Misfortune, Col. Baum was induced to proceed without sufficient knowledge of the Ground. His design was betrayed; the men who had taken the Oaths were the first to fire upon him; he was attacked on all sides, he showed great personal Courage, but was overpowered by Numbers.

During this time Lieu$^{t.}$ Col. Breyman was upon the March through a heavy Rain and such were the other impediments stated in that Officers report of bad Roads, tired Horses, difficulty in passing Artillery, Carriages &c. that he was from 8 in the morning of the 15th to 4 in the afternoon of the following Day making about 24 miles, He ingaged[,]

[180]SanCoick or Sancoick Mill, on the Walloomsac River (now North Hoosick, actually about eight miles west of Bennington). Lord, *War over Walloomscoick*, 6–7.

fought gallantly and drove the Enemy from three several Heights, but was too late to succor Col. Baum who was made Prisoner and a Considerable part of his Dragoons were killed or taken.

The failure of Ammunition from the Accidental breaking to pieces of a Tumbril[181] unfortunately obliged L$^{t.}$ Col. Breyman to retire conquering Troops, and to leave behind two pieces of Cannon[182] besides two which had been lost by Lieut. Col. Baum. The Indians made good their Retreat from the first Affair as did Capt. Fraser with part of his Company and many of the Provincials and Canadians. The loss as at present appears amounts to about 400 Men killed and taken in both Actions and twenty six Officers mostly Prisoners, but ones who were disposed in the Woods drop in daily, a correct return shall be transmitted to your Lordship the first Opportunity.

This my Lord is the true State of the Event. I have not dwelt upon Errors because in many instances they were counterbalanced by Spirit.

The enemy will of course find matter of Parade in the Requisition of Four Pieces of Cannon but that apart, they have small cause for Exaltation; their Loss in killed and wounded being more than double to Ours, by the confession of their Prisoners and Deserters and of many Inhabitants who were witness to the Burial of the Dead.[183]

The chief Subject of Regret on our side after that[,] which any loss of gallant Men naturally occasions, is the disappointment of not obtaining live Cattle, and the lapse of time in bringing forward the Magazines.

The heavy work is now nearly completed and a new Bridge of Boats

---

[181]A tumbrel was a two-wheeled cart, twelve feet six inches long and about six feet six inches in overall width. It contained a set of single shafts, such that either a single horse or a team of horses could pull it. The tumbrel held an open bed that was about five feet long by three feet six inches in width with two-foot-tall standing sides to contain working tools. John Muller of Woolwich Academy stated: "The common use of tumbrels is to carry the pioneers and miners tools; but they serve likewise to carry the money of the army." A tumbrel should have been used to carry entrenching tools or supplies, not ammunition. Breymann's own account specifies an ammunition cart; why Burgoyne reports this otherwise in his own account cannot be explained. Muller, *Treatise of Artillery*, 125–143.

[182]Breymann lost two 6-pounder cannon at the Battle of Bennington. Actually British cannon, they were manned by the Hesse-Hanau Company of Artillery. Cubbison, *"Artillery never gained more Honour,"* 96–101.

[183]Needless to say, the Battle of Bennington was regarded by the Americans in 1777, and consistently by historians, to have been a huge victory for the Americans. It directly influenced the course of the campaign. Burgoyne's fortunes never recovered from this defeat.

is thrown over the Hudson's River opposite to Saratoga, the former one of Rafts having been carried away by the swell of Water after the late continual rains. When enabled to move nothing within my scale of Talent shall be left unattempted to fulfill His Majesty's Orders, and I hope circumstances will be such, that my Endeavours may be in some degree assisted by a Cooperation of the Army under Sir William Howe[.]

I have the honor to be &c.
My Lord
(signed)
J. Burgoyne

6.16/22

Translated Copy of a Letter from Baron de Riedesel to Lord George Germain, Camp at Jones Farm, August 28, 1777

My Lord,
I flatter myself that your Excellency deigns still to remember your most obedient Servant, who assuredly serves with Zeal for His Majesty's Service, altho' His Powers are so weak, that he cannot be of such great use as he himself wishes.

The Evacuation of Ticonderoga, getting the day at Huberton, the Capture of Skenesborough, & the Retreat of the Enemy as far as Still Water 22 Miles on this side of Albany, were Successes so rapid, that scarcely could we pursue the Enemy. The want of Carriage greatly retarded the Transport of our Provisions. To remedy this Inconvenience Gen. Burgoyne designed to carry off the considerable Magazine belonging to the Enemy at Bennington, in the hopes of being able to subsist our own Army for a certain time. The Issue of that Expedition was not according to our Wishes.

To prove to your Excellency that neither the troops employed upon that Expedition, nor that the two Commanders were wanting in their Conduct, or acted contrary to Orders, I have the honour to present to your Excellency a brief Relation of that melancholy Affair with the Report & Instructions.

I hope we shall shortly have an Opportunity to repair this Check & that the first News your Excellency will receive from our Army will prove more satisfactory.

Recommending myself to your Excellency's Goodness I have the honour to be &c.
(signed)
Reidesel
Camp near Jones Farm 28th August 1777

6.16/22a

Contents of the Instructions given to Lieut. Colonel Baum with regard to an Expedition which he is to command

The Intention of this Expedition is to dive into the Sentiments of the Inhabitants, to remount the Regiment of Dragoons & to attempt furnishing the Army with Horses, Cattle & Waggons. He was to take the Route of Arlington, Manchester & Rockingham. He was to halt at each of these Places; & from Manchester he was to send a Detachment of Indians & Provincials up Connecticut River, as far as No. 4. From Manchester he was to continue his March to Rockingham, where he was to take Post. The Lieut. Colonel with his Corps of Regular Troops is not to pass beyond Rockingham. He is there to take the most advantageous Situation. All Cattle, Waggons & Horses are to be sent to the Army & driven by Provincials well escorted. When the Service is effected, he is to take the shortest Route by Brattenbourg to Albany, there to join the Body of the Army. Wherever he passes he is to make the Inhabitants believe that the Corps which he commands is the Vanguard of the enemy, which is to take the Route of Boston & that he is to be joined at Spring-field by a Body of Troops from Rhode Island.

In case the Army should not be arrived at Albany so soon as the Lt. Colonel has finished the Business, General Burgoyne will give him Advice & will recall him to the Army, or will give another Route to his Corps.

The Lieut. Colonel must send Intelligence from time to time of his Position & of what he has effected.

Should the Enemy face him with too great a Force Gen$^{l.}$ Burgoyne will not fail to send him the most speedy Succours, or will so take his Measures, that the Enemy shall find themselves between two Fires.[184]

Signed
J. Burgoyne
L$^{t.}$ General

Camp at Fort Edward 7th August 1777.

This in general is the Contents of the Instructions to Lieu$^{t.}$ Col. Baum. The Changes in his Route were made upon the Report of Colonel Skene,[185] who informed General Burgoyne that there was a very considerable Magazine at Bennington & that it would be very easy to surprise & make himself Master of it.

The Lieu$^{t.}$ Colonel was immediately sent from Bratten Kill directly towards Bennington. The Rebels having sent very great Reinforcements to that place, the Lieu$^{t.}$ Col. Could not, absolutely with a handful of Soldiers, resist the Efforts of the Enemy, who had at least ten times his Force.

The unhappy Result is but too well known.

NUMBER OF THE TROOPS EMPLOYED UPON THAT EXPEDITION

Regiment of Dragoons	160
Indians	100
Peter's Corps	150
Provincials & Canadian Volunteers	56
Fraser's Company	50
Total	516.

The Provincials & Canadians not being strong enough General Reidesel added to them 25 Chasseurs & 75 other Soldiers of the Germans.

---

[184] In the event, General Burgoyne's "succours" failed to reach Baum in time, and it was the British expedition that found itself "between two Fires."

[185] Major Philip Skene, previously introduced.

6.16/22b

Account of an Affair which happened near Wallon Creek, August 16, 1777

On the 13th of August, at 8 oClock in the morning, Sir Francis Clarke,[186] aid de Camp to his Excellency Genl. Bourgoyne[,] brought me the order to march immediately with the Corps under my Command, consisting of a Batallion of Grenadiers, one of Chasseurs, one Riffle Company & 2 pieces of Cannon, to the Support of Lt. Colonel Baum.

I marched at 9 o'Clock and on Account of the Scarcity of Carts, I put two Boxes of Ammunition upon the Artillery Carts.[187] Each Soldier Carried 40 Rounds in his Pouch.

The Troops being obliged to ford Battons kill, I was detained a considerable time by it. The number of hills, excessive bad Roads & a continued Rain, impeded our march. So much, that we scarce made ½ english mile in an hour. Each gun & Ammunition Cart was obliged to be dragged up the Hills, one after an other. One Artillery Cart was overturned and with the greatest difficulty was put into a situation to proceed.

All these difficulties delayed us much & not withstanding every means was used and no trouble or labour spared, it was not possible for me to march faster. Our guide lost his way & after a long search in vain, Major Barner was obliged to look out for a Man who put us again in the right road.[188]

Augst. 15th.

All these Accidents prevented me from reaching Cambridge the evening of the 15th & was therefore obliged to halt 7 miles this Side of it, where the Men lay upon their Arms all night. Before I came to the place where I halted I wrote to Lt. Col. Baum, to acquaint him with my coming to his support. Lieut Hannomann[189] went with this Account to

---

186 Sir Francis-Carr Clerke, Burgoyne's aide-de-camp, previously introduced.

187 An ammunition cart was a two-wheeled vehicle with tall sides used by the Royal Artillery to transport spare ammunition. It was about five feet long by three feet six inches in width. According to Muller's *Treatise*: "The roof is covered with oil cloth to prevent dampness from coming to the powder, and each shot locker is divided into four parts by boards of an inch thick, which enter about an inch into the shafts. Each of these carts can stow four barrels of powder only." Muller, *Treatise of Artillery*.

188 Major Bärner commanded the Brunswick Chasseur Battalion on this expedition.

189 Lieutenant Johann Caspar Hanneman, an officer of Bärner's Chasseur Battalion, would subsequently be wounded in the Bennington engagement. Doblin, *Officer in the Prinz Friedrich Regiment*, 103.

Cambridge and from thence to L$^{t.}$ Col. Baum's Post, where he Arrived at 11 oClock at night; I received an answer the next morning.

16th

Early in the morning I marched on, but as the Artillery Horses had had no feed all the day before, and very little during the night, they were so weak as to be scarce able to drag the Cannon, on which Account our march was very slow.

Major Barner with the advanced Guards was obliged to go forward to press horses, which we immediately made use of, and we continued our march as fast as possible, till about 2 miles, on other side of Cambridge, where I halted about ½ an hour to assemble the Troops.

About 2 oClock in the afternoon Colonel Skeene sent me two men, desiring an Officer and 20 Men to take possession of the Mill at Saint Coyss,[190] which the Rebels intended possessing themselves of.

Instead of the Detachment which he asked for I sent a Captain, Glois-senberg[,][191] with the advanced Guard consisting of 60 Grenadiers & Chasseurs & 20 Rifle men.

I followed with the Column, as fast as possible. Upon this march an Ammunition Cart broke down.[192]

At ½ past 4 o'Clock in the afternoon, I reached the Mill, and found the advanced Guard in possession of it, and all quiet.

I must positively declare, that neither during the march, nor even after I reached the Mill I did not hear a single Shot fired, either from small arms or Cannon.

Colonel Skeene was at the Mill, and as he gave me to understand, that the Corps of L$^{t.}$ Colonel Baum, was not above 7 miles from me, I imagined I could not do better, than to push on to his Support. Colonel Skeene was of the same Opinion, and we marched on over the Bridge, near the Mill and savoring to reach Col. Baum, as soon as possible. At this time I knew nothing of his engagement being over. If Col. Skeene

---

[190] Again, SanCoick or Sancoick Mill.

[191] Captain Gottlieb Joachim von Gleissenberg of the Chasseur and Jäger Regiment (Bärner's Battalion) was wounded at Bennington and would subsequently be wounded at Bemis Heights. He would be surrendered at Saratoga and remain in military service in Brunswick, retiring as an Oberst (colonel) in 1801. Doblin, *Officer in the Prinz Friedrich Regiment*, 127.

[192] Refer to Burgoyne's previous account. Here Breymann clearly states that an ammunition cart rather than a tumbrel broke down, which would certainly have caused ammunition problems for the two 6-pounders that accompanied his column.

knew it, I cannot conceive, what his reasons were, for, concealing it from me. If I had known it I certainly should not have engaged the Enemy.

I had scarce passed the bridge 1000 yards, where, I perceived a considerable number of Armed People, some in jackets & some in Shirts, who were endeavoring to gain a height, which was on my left flank.

I showed these people to Col[l.] Skeene who assured me they were Royalists and rode up towards them and called out, but received no Answer, than a discharge of fire Arms. I immediately ordered Major Barner's Battallion to move off towards the heights; the Rifle Company and Grenadiers moved towards the right & then began the attack, and lasted till towards 8 o'Clock.

The Cannon were posted on the road where there was a block house, which the Rebels left as soon as they began to fire upon it. Not withstanding fresh support was constantly coming into them, they were driven from every heights.[193]

The Troops did their duty and every one concerned, did the same. As all the Ammunition was expended and the Cannon Ceased firing nothing was more natural, than to expect the enemy would renew the Attack, which in fact was the Case.

I hastened with a Number of Men towards the Cannon, in order to bring them off. On this Occasion the Men received the most dangerous Wounds, particularly L[t.] Spangenberg[,][194] some Fire workers and some Artillery[men]. The Horses were all killed, and if even one had been alive, it would not have been possible to have moved him.

In order then not to risqué [risk] every thing as I could not return the enemy's Fire, as soon as it was dark, I retired over the bridge, which I broke down, brought off as many of the wounded as I could and in Company with Col[l.] Skene arrived about 12 o'Clock at Cambridge, where, after taking the necessary precautions I remained all night, and the next day the 17th I arrived at the Camp.

---

[193]There was not an actual blockhouse anywhere near this battlefield. Probably what the Germans perceived as such was rather a solid log cabin.

[194]Carl Ditmar Spangenberg, a 2nd lieutenant of the Hesse-Hanau Artillery Company. Spangenberg served throughout the 1776 Valcour Island campaign before participating in the Saratoga Campaign. When Breymann's relief column was assembled, Spangenberg commanded the two British 6-pounders crewed by the Hesse-Hanau Artillery. Lieutenant Spangenberg was severely wounded during the retreat from Bennington, being shot by a rifle or musket ball through the shoulder joint. The wound was so serious that it ended his military service, and he subsequently returned to Germany. Cubbison, *"Artillery never gained more Honour,"* 101.

This is the best Account I can give of this whole Affair. The loss of my Cannon gives me the greatest concern. I did every thing in my power to save them, but the want of Ammunition prevented me, not only from returning the enemy's fire, but even of getting out of it, many lost their lives and limbs & could I have saved my Cannon, I would with pleasure have sacrificed my life, to have effected it.

Signed.
Breymann[,] Lt. Colonel
Translation

6.16/22c

Relation of the Expedition to Bennington In Baron de Riedesel's of August 28, 1777

There being great difficulty in procuring Horses & Carriages to Transport the Baggage & Provisions of the Army; to remedy this great Inconvenience, which retarded the Movement of the Troops, it was determined to send out a Detachment, as soon as expedient, to bring in Horses for the above purpose & to mount the Brunswick Dragoons, if a sufficient Number could be found, the Army being Assembled at Fort Edward, where it must necessarily halt a few days, to Transport the Stores and Provisions over the Carrying Place, and his Excellency L^t. Genl. Burgoyne took this opportunity of Sending out a Detachment under the Command of Lieut^t. Col. Baum who was to have the following Troops with him vizt.

Brunswick Dragoons	150
Capt^t. Frazer's light Company	50
Peters's Provincial Corps[195]	150
Provincial & Canadian Volunteers	56
Indians	100
[Total]	506.

[195]A battalion of Loyalists recruited and commanded by Lieutenant Colonel John Peters, of the Hampshire Grants. This command, always a small battalion and never at full strength, was effectively destroyed at the Battle of Bennington.

Governor Skeen was also sent with this Detachment from whose supposed knowledge of the Country and influence amongst the Inhabitants much was expected.

By Lieut^t. [Colonel] Baum's Instructions (a Copy of which is sent herewith) he was to Proceed by Arlington Manchester &c &c.

August the 9th.

Lieut^t. Col. Baum Marched from Fort Edward with the Dragoons to Fort Miller, where he was to Receive from the Advanced Corps under the Command of Brigr. Genl. Frazer the remainder of the Troops destined to make up his Detachment.

10th

Obliged to halt. The Provincials & Indians intended for him being gone on to Stillwater [underline indicates emphasis in original]. To make up this Deficiency 100 Germans were Ordered from Lieut. Col. Breymann's Corps, to Join Lieut. Col. Baum, some Canadians & Indians also Joined him, but not as many as were first Ordered.

His Excellency Genl. Burgoyne this day changed the Route first intended for the Detachment and Ordered Lieut^t. Col. Baum to March directly to Bennington, Intelligence being Received that the Rebels had a Considerable Magazine there.

11th

Marched & took post at Buten Kill oposite [opposite] Saratoga.

12th

Proceeded to Cambridge, this day, his advanced Guard fell in with and defeated a Party of the Rebels took Eight Prisoners, a Thousand Bushels of Wheat, 150 Bullocks, and Several other Articles, which he sent back to Camp.

Here he was informed that there were from 150 to 18 hundred of the Enemy at Bennington and that they had a very considerable Magazine there besides 2000 Bullocks and 300 Horses.

Encouraged by the Success of his first Attack L^t. Col. Baum proposed to March next day, towards Bennington & dislodge the Enemy from that Post.

August 12th

He sent every day exact Reports of his Progress and Situation to Genl. Burgoyne, with which his Excellency was perfectly satisfied, and approved of his Design, of Attacking Bennington, so soon as Lieut$^{t.}$ Col. Baum was fully informed of the Enemy's numbers and Situation, and that it might be attempted with a prospect of Success & without running any Risque—

13th.

The Detachment Marched & took Post four Miles on this side Bennington.

14th.

L$^{t.}$ Colonel Baum being ready to March of early in the Morning, he was attacked by a Body of 700 Rebels, who after having a few Shot fired at them retired and dispersed.

By some prisoners taken on this Occasion & from some Royalists who came in, L$^{t.}$ Col. Baum was informed that the Enemy were strongly Entrenched at Bennington; that they expected a large Reinforcement from the Rebel Army, and intended to attack him, so soon as the Reinforcement had Joined them.

On receiving this information the L$^{t.}$ Col. properly deferred his intention of Pushing on to Bennington & halted in his Post; sending off an Express to inform Gen$^{l.}$ Burgoyne of his Situation & desiring that some Troops may be ordered to sustain him.

His Report was wrote in such high Spirits that the General was induced to believe, that he asked for a Reinforcement, more to enable him to attack the Enemy, than from any apprehension of his Corps, being in Danger of being Attacked.

Aug. 14th

In consequence of the above Information L$^{t.}$ Col. Breymann was ordered to March with his Corps (the Batt^{n} of Grenadiers; and Barner's Battalion about 500 men) and two Pieces of Cannon to Sustain L$^{t.}$ Col. Baum, and an officer was sent off to inform the Latter that Lieut. Col. Breymann had begun his March early the 15th. The Distance between the two Corps rendered this Reinforcement useless to L$^{t.}$ Col. Baum as he [Breymann] could not get up [in] time enough to Support him [Baum].

Aug$^{t.}$ 15th

Some small Parties were seen near L$^{t.}$ Col. Baum's Post who always retired upon being fired upon.

Accounts were also Received that the Rebels expected every Hour a large Reinforcement from their Army however Lt. Col. Baum being assured, that Breymann's Corps were on the March to Sustain him—determined to maintain his Post, Notwithstanding the Great Number of the Enemy, he took every possible precaution & Posted his Detachment to the Greatest Advantage.[196]

16th.

In the Morning Several Bodies of Men in Arms were observed approaching his Post, Lt. Col. Baum was assured, they were Royalists [underline indicates emphasis in original] but their Numbers increasing he order'd out Parties to Reconoitre & soon perceived that he was Surrounded by the Rebels from Bennington, reinforced by a large Detachment from Mr. Arnold's Army.[197] On a Signal being made by the Rebels about half past ten he was attacked on all sides by superior Numbers; he maintained his Post above two Hours, and often repulsed the Enemy, but finding that his Men had expended all their Ammunition & Lt. Col. Breymann's Corps not yet appearing he was obliged to think of a Retreat with the Dragoons (the Provincials Canadians & Indians being already cut off from him). He twice forced his way thro' the Enemy and was as often Attacked by fresh Troops; as a last resource ["recourse" obviously was meant] he Ordered his Men to draw their Swords, and rush in upon the Enemy where notwithstanding every Effort of Bravery, his Corps overpowered by Superior Numbers, was entirely broke & we know not as yet what has been their Fate—

Seven Dragoons have escaped and Joyned the Army; It is said Lt. Col. Baum is wounded[198] and no doubt numbers of the Officers and men are Killed and Wounded—

The Reports of those who escaped early, are so various and contradictory, that there is no depending upon them.

They all however agree that the Rebels were between three & four thousand strong.

---

[196]In fact, Baum established an extremely poor position and segmented his various commands, such that they could not support each other.

[197]No such American reinforcements ever arrived at Bennington.

[198]Baum was mortally wounded in the battle and died shortly thereafter.

6.16/23

Extract of a Letter from the Honorable Sir William Howe to Lord George Germain, Philadelphia, October 21, 1777 Rec. December 1 [1777]

The Inclosures No. 5, 6, 7, 8 & 9 have been also transmitted to me by Sir Henry Clinton[199] & am sorry to observe by them the very critical Situation of General Burgoyne's Army. He no doubt had success on the 19th September, at the same time, that Action not being decisive, would by leaving him a Number of Wounded to transport, accumulate his Difficulties in proceeding to Albany.

I have reason to believe he had a second Action on the 7th instant, in which by the Enemy's Report they were successful, but this remains extremely doubtful[.] [extract ends, single page only]

6.16/239

Copy of a Letter from Lieut. General Burgoyne to Sir William Howe, Camp at Fort Edward, August 6, 1777, with a Note annexed—received from Sir Henry Clinton, October 7 In Sir William Howe's of October 21, 1777

Sir

I received yesterday the Duplicate of your Letter of the 7 July and shall strictly observe the Contents. My Progress from Skenesborough hither was very laborious through a Country naturally difficult the Roads and Bridges all broken up and in the Face of the Enemy who retired nevertheless from Post to Post with considerable Loss in killed and Prisoners, and without any other Troops engaged on our side than Indians and Provincials and those have suffered no otherwise than in a few wounds.[200] I have had the fullest Satisfaction in the Alacrity of the Army and the Issue has justified my Perseverance in preferring this Route to the

[199] General Sir Henry Clinton, commander of the British army in New York City, previously introduced.

[200] No such loss was sustained by the American forces; Burgoyne is engaging in hyperbole.

retrograde Movement which it would have been to have taken the more commodious one by Ticonderoga and Lake George. The Garrison of Fort George, in danger of being cut off by my movement directly upon the Hudsons River abandoned as I had expected the Fort, and burned the Vessels designed for the Defence of the Lake.[201] The first Embarkation therefore from Ticonderoga which I had ordered to be ready for that Purpose passed the Lake the day I took Possession of this important Communication by Land and the Batteaux which had I taken the other Route must have been destined to the Troops were now employed for the Transport of Part of the Magazines which puts me well forward. I have nevertheless been compelled impatiently but inevitably to give considerable Time to pass Artillery Provisions and bateaux over so long a carrying Place as 14 Miles, with a Small Number of Horses and Carriages respectively for the work. Your Excellency will likewise see the Necessity of fortifying some Posts in so very long a Communication. I hope however to move to Saratoga (where the Enemy is at present posted but making Disposition to retreat) in a few days, but as I have a carrying Place at Fort Miller and another at Stillwater I do not apprehend it will be possible to be in Possession of Albany even supposing the Enemy should not stand a Battle before the 22nd or 23rd. Should the opportunity of any Stroke offer I certainly where I can convey necessary Provision only shall not wait the Carriage of the Tents or any other Baggage. During my Stay here the Indians have done good Service; not a day passed without Prisoners brought in some from Miles behind the Enemys Camp. I have Detachments of seventeen different Nations. There is infinite difficulty to manage them. My Effort has been to keep up their Terror and avoid their Cruelty. I think I have in a great measure Succeeded. They attack very bravely; they Scalp the Dead only; and spare the Inhabitants.[202] I believe the scalp of the famous Partizan Whitcomb who killed Brigadier

[201]There were no American armed vessels on Lake George, only transport bateaux.

[202]The murder and scalping of the young lady Jane McRea, the fiancée of a Loyalist officer with Burgoyne's army, on July 27, 1777, has been widely discussed (and indeed, widely speculated upon) by historians. Numerous historians have suggested that the killing of Miss McRae by Indians of Burgoyne's army proved a great propaganda bonanza for the American cause in the summer and fall of 1777. Her death, which Burgoyne does not mention, suggests either that he was poorly informed of the activities of his American Indian allies, that the incident was considered too minor to be worthy of consideration at British headquarters, or that perhaps Burgoyne was more concerned with his reputation than with telling the truth to Howe. For Jane McRea's murder see Gibbons, "Subtilized into Savages," 88–92.

Gordon last year to be in their Possession.[203] Mr. Arnold professes an inclination to stand an Action, somewhere about Albany. I yet hear nothing of Mr. Washington. St. Leger is, I am assured by intelligence[,] in operation about Fort Stanwix. One Reason of my impatience to gain the Mouth of the Mohawk is to favour him. I hope the difficulties of communicating with your Excellency will soon decrease. I sent a confidential Messenger to you some days ago who I hope arrived safe. The Letter you mention to have been intercepted in a Canteen was not from me nor to you [underline indicates emphasis in original]. It was an Attempt of Material Purpose had it Succeeded without any possible Disadvantage happening from the Discovery.

As I mean Sir Henry Clinton to read this Letter in its Passage I do not write to him separately my best wishes and Affection to him.

I am with every possible Sentiment of Respect and Attachment
Sir
Your most faithful and obedient Servant
Signed
J Burgoyne

Purpose of a Dispatch on or about 20 July 1777.

On the 16th [correct date was July 5] instant the Enemy dislodged from Ticonderoga and were driven on the same day beyond Skenesborough on the Right hand to Huberton on the left with the loss of 128 Pieces of Cannon, all their armed Gallies and Ammunition Military Stores and Provision, to a vast Amount.

---

[203]Lieutenant Benjamin Whitcomb of New Hampshire. As a young man barely of age, Whitcomb had fought with the Provincials and British throughout most of the Seven Years' War in the Lake George/Lake Champlain area. An ardent Patriot, during the 1776 campaign Whitcomb had proved himself to be adept at leading what would today be known as "deep penetration patrols" into the heart of the enemy's country. He was notorious among the British officers for killing Patrick Gordon, lieutenant colonel of the 29th Foot and appointed a brigadier general commanding a brigade of British regulars during service in Canada, in August 1776. The British obtained a good description of Whitcomb, noting of his appearance: "He is between 30 and 40 years of age [Whitcomb was actually 39 years old], to appearance near 6 feet high . . . light brown hair tied behind, rough face . . . he wears a kind of under jacket without sleeves, slash pockets, leather breeches, gray woolen or yard stockings, and shoes. Hat flapped, a gold cord tied round it. He had a firelock, blanket, pouch and powder horn." Whitcomb was not killed during the 1777 campaign, or at any other time by the British, Loyalists, or Indians that he repeatedly fought against. A colorful but sadly neglected figure in the history of the Champlain Valley, Whitcomb has received little attention from historians. An early but still relevant biography is Morris, "Major Whitcomb, Ranger and Partisan Leader," 298–321.

On the two Succeeding days the ascendancy of his Majestys Arms was further established by two separate Actions at distant Places, and against superior Numbers in which the Enemy Loss amounted to above six hundred dead upon the Field above—three times that Number was wounded and one Colonel, seven Captains, ten Subalterns, and near four hundred Prisoners.

Of the Kings troops were killed, one Major, one Captain, three Lieutenants, one Volunteer Lieutenant of Marines, two Serjeants, 41 Rank and File.

Wounded, two Majors, five Captains, ten Lieutenants, one Volunteer, 19 Serjeants[,] 142 Rank and File.

Major Grant of the 24th Regim^{t} was the Field Officer killed.

6.16/23b

Copy of a Note from Lieut. Genl. Burgoyne to Lieut. Genl. Sir Hy [Henry] Clinton, September 23, 1777 Re[ceived] October 5 In Sir William Howe's of October 21, 1777

I have lost the old Cipher, but being sure from the Tenor of your Letter, you meant it to be so read, I have made it out.

An Attack or the Menace of an Attack upon [Fort] Montgomery [on the Hudson River], must be of great Use, as it will draw away a part of this Force and I will follow them close.[204] Do it, my dear Friend, directly.

Yours ever faithfully
J.B.

[204]Fort Montgomery and Fort Clinton, along with a substantial iron chain, obstructed the Hudson River at its intersection with Popolopen Creek. Fort Clinton was south of the creek on high ground; Fort Montgomery was north of Popolopen Creek on high ground. Heavy batteries and a substantial naval force also guarded the river. This was the main American defensive position on the Hudson River from late 1776 through 1777, but the forts were too large to be defended with the available force, and their garrisons were too small to be effective. The forts also contained critical design flaws, such as a single powder magazine for both forts. The forts were seized in an aggressive attack by Sir Henry Clinton on October 6, 1777.

6.16/23c

A Copy of a Letter from Lieut. General Burgoyne to Lieut. Genl. Sir H. Clinton, September 28, 1777, & Received October 5 In Sir William Howe's of October 21, 1777

Sir

The bearer, Capt. Campbell, an officer of Great Merit, and full Confidence, is Charged with an Exact duplicate of my Message to your Excy, dispatched Yesterday by another Officer, I request the most Speedy Answer by Triplicates.

Believe me &c.
(Signed) J. Burgoyne

Copy of an Inclosure received from Lieut[t.] Genl. Sir H. Clinton with the above letter.

Conversation with Capt[n.] Campbell sent by General Burgoyne to me[.]

He said he was desired by Gen[l.] Burgoyne to tell me that the Generals whole Army did not exceed 5000 Men[.] That the Consequences of the Battle on the 19th were the loss of between five and six hundred Men[.]

That the Enemy were within a Mile and a half of him[.] That he knew not their Numbers for certain, but believed them to be twelve or fourteen thousand Men: That there was besides that a considerable Body in his Rear. That he wished to receive my Orders whether he should Attack or retreat, to the Lakes[.]

That he had but Provisions to the 20th of this Month, and that he would not have given up his Communications with Ticonderoga, had he not expected a Cooperating Army at Albany. That he wished to know my Positive Answer as soon as Possible—whether I could open a Communication with Albany, when I should be there, and when there, keep my Communication with New York. That if he did not hear from me by the 12th Instant he should retire.

To which I returned the following Answer by Capt. Campbell—

"That not having received any Instructions from the Commander in Chief relative to the Northern Army, and unacquainted even of his

Intentions concerning the Operations of that Army excepting his wishes that they should get to Albany, Sir H. Clinton cannot presume to give any Orders to Genl Burgoyne[.]

Genl. Burgoyne could not Suppose that Sir H. Clinton had an Idea of Penetrating to Albany with the Small force he mentioned in his last Letter. What he offered in that Letter he has now undertaken; cannot by any means promise himself Success but hopes it will be at any rate Serviceable to Genl. Burgoyne as General Burgoyne Says in his Letter Answering the Offer, that even the Menace of an Attack would be of Use[.]"

6.16/23d

Copy of a Letter from Lieutenant General Sir Henry Clinton to Lieut. Genl. Burgoyne, Fort Montgomery, October 8, 1777[205] In Sir William Howe's of October 21, 1777

Dear Sir

Nous y voila[206] [underline indicates emphasis in original] and nothing now between us but Gates, I sincerely hope this little Success may facilitate Your Operations[.]

In answer to Your Letter of the 28th of Septem^r by C.C. [Captain Campbell; refer to Letter 6.16/23c] I shall only say I cannot presume to order or even advise, for Reasons obvious[.]

I heartily wish You success and am &c.
H.C.

[205]An identical duplicate of this letter was captured from Lieutenant Daniel Taylor, 9th Regiment of Foot, by Brigadier General George Clinton of the New York State Militia at New Windsor, New York, on October 8, concealed in a silver musket ball. *Public Papers of George Clinton*, 413–414.

[206]Translated from the French as "Now here we are." Benjamin K. Bergen and Plauché, "*Voilà voilà*."

6.16/23e

Copy of a Letter from Lieutenant General Burgoyne to Lieut. Genl Sir H. Clinton, September 27, 1777, & Received at Fort Montgomery, October 9, 1777

Sir
Capt. Scott of the 24th Regiment, is intrusted with the fullest Dispatches & Communications, necessary to be known by your Excellency— He is an Officer of Great Merit & intitled to the fullest Confidence.

I request you to return your Orders by Triplicate by Different Routes, Reckoning that your Old Cipher Subsists.

I am &c.
J. Burgoyne

Copy of an Inclosure received from Lieut. Genl. Sir Henry Clinton with the above Letter[.]

Capt. Scott of the 24th Regimt. Arrived on the 9th from Genl Burgoyne said that the Army under the Genl's Command, Amounting to 5000 Men consisted of the following Corps. British 2000[,] Provincials 500[,] Germans 2500.

That the Rebel Army was about 12,000 besides a Body supposed to be above 4,000, that are hovering about. That the Continental Troops alone amount to the Number of Genl. Burgoyne's Army. Both Armies were encamped a few Miles above Stillwater, & the distance at any one place not exceeding a Mile & a half, & in many places not more than half a Mile. The Ground of both Armies very strong, Genl. Burgoyne can remain in his present Position until the 12th or until the 16th should it be certain that the Communication would be open by that time between the Armies of Genl. Clinton & Genl. Burgoyne, If not it will be necessary he should make Good his Retreat to Canada before the Ice sets in.

General Burgoyne begs Sir Henry Clinton will give him an Answer, conveying the plainest & most Positive meaning how he should Act for the good of his Majesty. Whether he should proceed to Albany, or to make good his retreat to Canada[.] He cannot stay longer than the 12th should he be obliged to retire to Canada; nor longer than the 16th

Should he proceed to Albany. He was obliged to give up the Communication between him and the Lakes, on his quitting the Heights of Saratoga[.] [W]as he to get to Albany he does not think he could be supplied with Provisions for the Winter, the Country there & on the Mohawk River, being much drained, unless the Communication is opened between Albany & New York.

In the Action of the 19th Septr. the British Troops acquired great Honor, tho' no material advantage was reaped from it, Night coming on prevented it, The Enemy fought with a good deal of Obstinacy. Our Loss about 530 Mostly British killed & wounded. That of the Enemy about 1200.

Genl. Burgoyne begs Sir H. Clinton will send Duplicates either in Writing, or verbally as soon as Possible—

Genl. Burgoyne thinks he could force his way to Albany, but unless assured that the Communication between that place & New York was kept open, He could not subsist his Army during the Winter—

Sol Feinstone Collection of the American Revolution

Letter from Lieutenant General John Burgoyne to Major General Horatio Gates, [Dovegot House,] October 9, 1777

Lady Harriet Ackland, a Lady of the first distinction by family Rank, and by personal virtue, is under such concern on account of Major Ackland her husband, wounded and a prisoner in your hands, that I cannot refrain from requesting to commit her to your protection.[207]

Whatever general impropriety there may be per our acting in your situation, and avoid to solicit favours, I cannot see the uncommon

[207] Lady Christian Harriet Fox-Strangways Acland (c. 1759–1815), wife of Major John Dyke Acland, commander of the British Grenadier Battalion who was seriously wounded at the Battle of Barber's Wheatfield in October 1777. Lady Acland had requested permission from Burgoyne to travel in a bateaux down the Hudson River to help care for her husband. She was accompanied on this trip by the Anglican Reverend Richard Brudnell, chaplain to the Royal Artillery on this campaign. Major Acland survived his wounds but apparently never fully recovered, dying in England of illness in 1778. Thorp, *Acland Journal*, xv–xxi.

"Lady Harriet Ackland, a Lady of the first distinction by family Rank, and by personal virtue, is under such concern on account of Major Ackland her husband, wounded and a prisoner in your hands, that I cannot refrain from requesting to commit her to your protection." 1857 portrayal of Lady Acland traveling by bateau down the Hudson River to reach her wounded husband following his wounding and capture at the Battle of Barber's Wheatfield. *Courtesy Fort Ticonderoga Museum.*

perseverance in every female grace and exaltation of character of this lady, and her very hard fortune without testifying, that your attention to her will lay me under obligations[.]

I am Sir Your Obedient Servt.
J. Burgoyne
Ocr. 9th 1777

[To] M. Genl. Gates

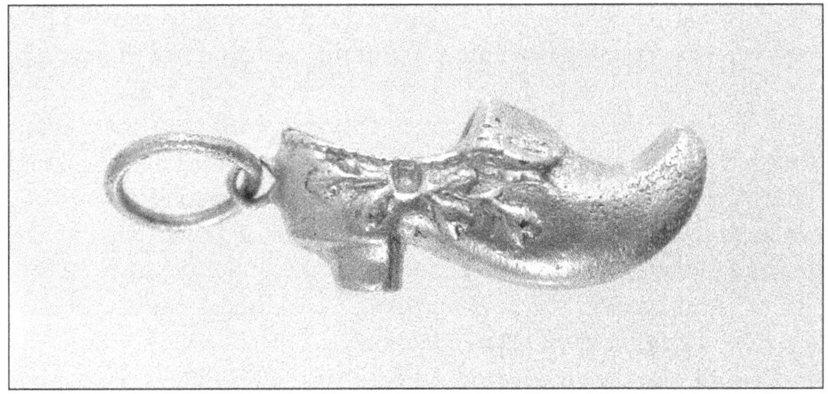

Lady Harriet Acland's watch chain, worn by her Ladyship upon her Hudson River trip. *Courtesy Fort Ticonderoga Museum.*

6.16/24

Copy of a Letter from Lieut. Genl Burgoyne to Lord George Germain, Albany, October 20, 1777[208] Rec. December 15 [1777]

Albany Oct$^{r.}$ 20th 1777.

My Lord,
No possibility of communication with your Lordship having existed since the beginning of September at which time my last dispatches were sent away; I have to Report to your Lordship the Proceedings of the Army under my Command from that Period, a Series of hard toil[,] incessant Effort[,] Stubborn Action 'till disabled in the Collateral Branches of the Army by the Total defection of the Indians; the Desertion or the timidity of the Canadians and Provincials, some individuals excepted; disappointed in the last hope of any timely cooperation from

[208]This letter was printed as Appendix No. 14 in Burgoyne, *State of the Expedition from Canada*, lxxxiii–xcvi. As with his other letters, minor alterations in punctuation, spelling and capitalization are noted. However, no substantive changes, additions or alterations are noted.

other Armies[,] the Regular Troops reduced by losses from the best parts to three thousand five hundred Fighting men, not two thousand of which were British, only three Days Provisions upon Short allowance in Store, Invested by an Army of sixteen thousand Men, and no apparent means of retreat remaining; I called into Council all the Generals, Field officers, and Captains Commanding Corps: and by their unanimous concurrence and advice I was induced to open a Treaty with Major General Gates[.]

Your Lordship will see by the Papers transmitted herewith the disagreeable Prospect which Attended the first Overtures and when the Terms concluded are compared, I trust that the Spirit of the Councils I have mentioned, which under such circumstances dictated instead of Submitting will not be refused a Share of Credit[.][209]

Before I enter upon the detail of these Events I think it a duty of Justice my Lord to take upon myself the Measure of having Passed the Hudson River in Order to force a Passage to Albany[.] I did not think myself authorized to call any Men into Council when the Peremptory Tenor of my Orders and the Season of the Year Admitted no alternative—

Provisions for about thirty days having been brought forward[,] the other necessary Stores prepar'd, and the Bridge of Boats completed, the Army Passed the Hudson's River on the 13th & 14th of September and encamped on the Heights & in the plain of Saratoga, the Enemy being then in the Neighborhood of Still Water—

15th. The whole Army made a movement forward and encamped in a good Position in a Place called Dovogot [Dovegot].

16th. It being found that there were several Bridges to repair[,] that work was begun under Cover of Strong Detachments and the same Opportunity was taken to reconnoitre the Country—

17th. The Army renewed their March[,] repaired other Bridges and encamp'd upon advantageous Ground about four Miles from the Enemy—

18th. The Enemy appear'd in considerable force to Obstruct the further repair of Bridges, and with a view as it was conceived to draw on an Action where the Artillery could not be employed, a small loss was

[209]Precisely what this paragraph means cannot be ascertained, given Burgoyne's extravagant prose.

sustained in Skirmishing but the work of repairing the Bridges was [not] Effected—

19th. The Passages of a Great Ravin [Ravine] & other Roads towards the Enemy having been Reconnoitered, the Army Advanced in the folg [following] order[:]

Brigadier Genl. Frazers Corps Sustained by Lieutt. [Colonel] Breymann's Corps made a Circuit in Order to pass the Ravine commodiously without quitting the Heights, and afterwards to cover the March of the Line to the right, these Corps moved in three Columns and had the Indians, Canadians and Provincials upon their Fronts and Flanks. The British Line led by me in person Passed the Ravin [ravine] in a direct Line South and form'd in Order of Battle as fast as they gain'd the Summit, where they waited to give time to Frazier's Corps to make the Circuit; and to enable the Left Wing and Artillery, which under the Command of Major General Phillips and Major General Reidesel [*sic*] kept the great Road and Meadows near the River in two Columns and had Bridges to Repair to be equally ready to Proceed. The 47th Regimt. Guarded the Batteaux.

The Signal Guns which had been Previously settled to give notice of all the Columns being ready to advance having been fired Between 1 and 2 o'Clock the March continued[.] [T]he Scouts and Flankers of the Column of the British Line were soon fir'd upon from small Parties but with no Effect, after about an hours March the Piquets which made the Advanced Guard of that Column, were attacked in force, and obliged to give ground, but they soon Rallied and were Sustained—[210]

On the first opening of the Wood I formed the Troops; a few Cannon that dislodg'd the Enemy at a House[211] from whence the Piquets had been attacked and Brigadier Genl. Frazer's Corps had arrived with such Precision in Point of time as to be form'd on a very Advantageous Height on the right of the British[.]

[210]The pickets of the British Regular Brigade, comprising primarily the 9th Foot, were very roughly handled at the first fire, being broken and sustaining severe casualties. This regiment had also sustained heavy casualties at Fort Anne, was held in reserve for the remainder of the engagement and did not again participate in the fighting, suggesting that it had not just been "obliged to give ground."

[211]Freeman's small log farmhouse, the only structure in the vicinity of the September 19 engagement.

In the mean time the Enemy not acquainted with the Combination of the March, had moved in great force out of their Intrenchments with a view of turning the Line upon the Right and being check'd by the Position of Brigadier Genl. Frazier Countermarched in Order to direct their great Effort to the left of the British—

From the nature of the Country Movements of this nature however near may be Effected without a Possibility of their being discovered—

About 3 o'Clock the Action began by a very vigorous Attack on the British Line and continued with great obstinacy 'till after Sunset, the Enemy being Continually supplied with fresh Troops, the Stress lay upon the 20th, 21st & 62nd Regiments most parts of which were engaged near four hours without intermission, the 9th had been Order'd early in the day to form in the reserve.[212] The Grenadiers & 24th Regiment were some part of the time brot [brought] into Action as were part of the Light Infantry, and all these Corps charged with their usual Spirit—

The Riflemen and other parts of Breymann's Corps were also of service, but it was not thought advisable to evacuate the Heights where Brigadier Genl Frazier was Posted otherwise than Partially and Occasionally[.][213]

Major Genl Phillips upon first hearing the firing found his way thro' a difficult part of the Wood to the Scene of Action and brot up with him Major Williams and four Pieces of Artillery[214] and from that Moment I stood indebted to that Gallant and Judicious Second for incessant and most material Services, Particularly for restoring the Action in a Point which was critically pressed by a great superiority of Fire and to which he led up the 20th Regiment at the utmost personal hazard[.]

Major Genl Reidesel exerted himself to bring up a part of the left Wing and Arrived in time to Charge the Enemy with regularity and Bravery[.]

[212]Again, the 9th Foot had provided the majority of the pickets that had led the advance but had been shattered by Morgan's initial fire near the Freeman cabin.

[213]Fraser's advance corps was the most important component of the British advance, as it constituted the British maneuver element that was supposed to locate the American left (west) flank; identify appropriate ground where the formidable artillery train could be emplaced, and from which it could effectively drive the American army off Bemis Heights; and hold that ground against American attack while the artillery was being brought up. Burgoyne did not wish to withdraw or dilute Fraser's strength, as that would have abrogated his entire offensive scenario. Cubbison, *"Artillery never gained more Honour,"* 106–108.

[214]The size of these guns is nowhere documented. The author surmises that they were 6-pounders, as these were the lightest and most maneuverable guns in the Artillery Park. Cubbison, *"Artillery never gained more Honour,"* 110.

Just as the Light Closed the Enemy gave Ground on all Sides and left us completely Masters of the Field of Battle with the loss of about five hundred men on their side and as supposed thrice that number Wounded[.]

The darkness preventing a pursuit the prisoners were few—[215]

The behavior of the Officers & Men in General was Exemplary[.] Brigadier Gen[l] Frazer took his Position in the beginning of the day with great Judgment and sustained the Action with constant presence of mind and Vigor. Brig[r] Gen[l] Hamilton was the whole time engaged and Acquitted himself with great honor, activity and good conduct. The Artillery in general was distinguished and the Brigade under Cap[t.] Jones who was Killed in the Action was Conspicuously so.[216]

The Army lay upon their Arms the night of the 19th and the next day took a Position nearly within Cannon Shot of the Enemy fortifying their Right and Extending their left so as to cover the Meadows through which the Great River [i.e., the Hudson] runs, and where their Batteaux and Hospital were placed; the 47th Regiment and the Regiment of Hesse Hanau with a Corps of Provincials Incamped in the Meadows as a further Security—

It was soon found that no Fruits, honor excepted, were attained by the Preceding Victory, the Enemy working with redoubled Ardor to Strengthen their left, their Right was Unattackable already—

On our side it became expedient to Erect Strong Redoubts for the Protection of the Magazines and Hospital, not only against a Sudden Attack but also for their Security in case of a March to Turn the Enemys Flank[.]

21st. A Messenger Arrived from Sir Henry Clinton with a Letter in Cyphers informing me of his intention to attack Fort Montgomery in about 10 Days from the date of his Letter, which was the Tenth Sept[r][.][217] [T]his was the only Messenger of many that I apprehend were

[215]The fact that there were almost no American prisoners suggests the British had not defeated the Americans on the battlefield. The Americans deliberately withdrew from the battlefield, in good order and discipline, carrying most of their wounded with them.

[216]Burgoyne, usually so verbose, barely provides adequate credit for the spectacular and courageous role played in this engagement by Captain Thomas Jones's artillery with the British Regular Brigade, an action among the most honorable and distinguished in the history of the British Royal Artillery. Cubbison, *"Artillery never gained more Honour,"* 108–112.

[217]Clinton attacked Forts Montgomery and Clinton only on October 6, 1777, not September 20 as he originally intended. An attack on September 20 could conceivably have assisted Burgoyne, while the actual attack two weeks later was much too late to provide him any succor.

dispatched by Sir William Howe and him that had reached my Camp since the beginning of August. He was sent back the same Night to inform Sir Henry of my Situation and of the necessity of a Diversion to oblige Genl. Gates to detach from his Army, and my intention to wait favorable Events in that Position if Possible to the 12th October[.]

In the course of the two following days two officers in disguise and other Confidential Persons were dispatch'd by different Routes with Verbal Messages to the same Effect, and I continued fortifying my Camp and Watching the Enemy— whose numbers increased every day—

3^{d} Oct$^{r.}$ I thought it advisable to diminish the Soldiers Rations in order to lengthen out the Provisions, to which measure the Army submitted with the utmost Cheerfulness. The difficulties of a Retreat to Canada were clearly foreseen as was the dilemma[,] sho^{d} [should] the Retreat be effected[,] of leaving at Liberty such an Army as Gen$^{l.}$ Gates to Act ag^{t} [against] Sir Wm Howe.

This consideration operated forcibly to determine me to abide Events as long as Possible, and I reasoned thus, the Expedition I Commanded was Evidently meant at first to be hazarded [and] Circumstances might require it should be devoted [underline indicates emphasis in original]; a critical Junction of M$^{r.}$ Gates' force with M$^{r.}$ Washington might Possibly decide the fate of the War: The failure of my Junction with Sir Henry Clinton, or the loss of my Retreat to Canada would only be a Partial Misfortune.

7th. In this Situation things continued 'till the 7th when no intelligence having been received of the expected Cooperation and four or five days of our Limited Stores in the Camp only remained, it was Judged advisable to make a movement to the Enemy's left, not only to discover Whether there were any Possible means of forcing a Passage, should it be necessary to advance, or of dislodging him for the Convenience of retreat, but also to Cover a Forage of the Army which was in the greatest distress of Account of the Scarcity—[218]

---

[218]Burgoyne's army probably could not have successfully effected a retreat at this point, simply because the animals had been seriously weakened by a lack of forage, and Burgoyne would have been unable to move his full train of artillery, remaining provisions and stores, and hospital still with numerous wounded from the September 19 action. There were several farm fields in Burgoyne's vicinity that were now (in early October) ready for harvest and could provide sufficient forage to feed Burgoyne's livestock, thus permitting him to withdraw safely to Canada.

A Detachment of Fifteen hundred Regular Troops with two 12 pounders[,] two Howitzers, and Six Six pounders were Ordered to move and was Commanded by myself having with me Major Gen$^{l.}$ Phillips[,] Major General Reidesel and Brigadier General Frazer[.] [T]he Guard of the Camp upon the Heights was left to Brigadier Gen^{ls} Hamilton and Specht[.] The Redoubts and the Plain to Brig^{r} General Gall and as the force of the Enemy immediately in their front consisted of more than double their numbers, it was not possible to Augment the Corps that March'd beyond the Numbers above stated[.]

I form'd the Troops within three quarters of a Mile of the Enemies left and Captn Frazer's Rangers with Indians and Provincials had Orders to go by secret Paths in the Woods to gain the Enemies rear and by Shewing themselves there to keep them in Check[.][219]

The further Operations intended were Prevented by a very sudden and rapid Attack of the Enemy on our left where the British Grenadiers were Posted to support the left Wing of the line[,] Major Ackland at the head of them sustained the Attack with great resolution but the Enemys great numbers enabling them in a few Minutes to extend the Attack along the front of the Germans[,] which were immediately on the right of the Grenadiers[,] no part of that Body could be removed to make a Second Line to the Flank where the Stress of the fire lay. The right was at that time unengaged but it was soon observed that the Enemy were marching a large Corps around their Flank to endeavor cutting off their retreat, the Light Infantry and part of the 24th Regiment which were at that Post were therefore Ordered to form a Second Line and to Secure the Return of the Troops into Camp[.] While this Movement was proceeding the Enemy pushed a fresh and Strong reinforcement to renew the Action upon the left, which overpowered by so great a Superiority it gave way, and the Light Infantry & 24th Regiment were obliged to make a quick Movement to save that Point from being entirely carried, in doing which Brig^{r} Genl Fraser was mortally wounded—

The Danger to which the Lines were Exposed becoming at this Moment of the most Serious nature, Orders were given to Major Genl

[219] This movement was made in the direction of Saratoga Lake several miles to the west of the American lines. This diversion failed completely, as there is no evidence that Fraser's marksmen had any effect whatsoever on the American response to Burgoyne's advance.

Phillips and Reidesel to cover the Retreat while such Troops as were most ready for the purpose returned for the defense of them, the Troops retreated hard Pressed but in good Order, They were obliged to leave Six Pieces of Cannon all the Horses having been killed and most of the Artillery Men who had behav'd as usual with the utmost Bravery under the Command of Major Williams being either killed or wounded—

The Troops had Scarcely entered the Camp when it was Storm'd with great fury, the Enemy rushing to the Lines under a Severe fire of Grape Shot and Small Arms, the Post of the Light Infantry under Lord Balcarres, Assisted by some of the Line who threw themselves by Order into those Intrenchments, was defended with great Spirit, and the Enemy led on by Gen$^{l.}$ Arnold was finally repulsed and the Genl wounded, but unhappily the Intrenchments of the German reserve Commanded by Lieut$^{n.}$ Col. Breymann who was killed were carried, and altho' Ordered to be Recovered they never were so, and the Enemy by that Misfortune Gain'd an Opening on Our Right & Rear. The Night put an End to the Action.

Under the disadvantages thus Apparent in our Situation the Army was Ordered to quit the present Position during the Night and take Post upon the Heights above the Hospital. Thus by an entire Change of Front to reduce the Enemy to form a new disposition.[220] This Movement was Effected with Great Order & without Loss, tho' all the Artillery and Camp were removed at the same time the Army continued offering Battle to the Enemy in their new Position the whole day of the 8th—

8th. Intelligence was now Received that the Enemy were Marching to turn the right [Burgoyne's right or east flank], and no means could prevent that Measure but retiring towards Saratoga, the Army began the Move at 9 O'Clock at Night. Major General Reidesel commanding the Van Guard and Major Genl Phillips the Rear.

This Retreat, tho' within Musquet Shot of the Enemy, and encumbered with all the Baggage of the Army was made without loss; but a very heavy Rain & the difficulties of Guarding the Batteaux which contain'd All the Provisions, occasioned delays which prevented the Army reaching Saratoga 'till the Night of the 9th, and the Artillery could not pass the Fords of the Fish Kill 'till the Morning of the 10th—

[220] Such a "change of front" is more properly described in universal military terminology as a "retreat."

At Our Arrival near Saratoga a Corps of the Enemy between five and six hundred were discovered throwing up Intrenchments on the Heights, but retired over a ford of the Hudsons River at our Approach and join'd a Body posted to oppose our Passage there[.]

It was Judged proper to send a Detachment of Artificers under a Strong Escort to Repair the Bridges and open a Road to Fort Edward; the 47th Regiment[,] Capt. Frasers Marksmen & Mackeys Provincials were Ordered for that service, but the Enemy appearing on the Heights of the Fish Kill were in great force and makg [making] a disposition to pass and give us Battle, the 47th Regiment and Fraser's Marksmen were Recalled, the Provincials left to cover the Workmen at the first Bridge, run away upon a very Slight Attack of a Small Party of the Enemy, and left the Artificers to escape as they could without a Possibility of their performing any Work[.]

During these different Movements the Batteaux with Provisions were frequently fir'd upon from the opposite side of the River, some of them were lost and Several men were Killed and Wounded in those which remain'd[.]

11th. Attacks upon the Batteaux were continued sevl [several] were taken and retaken; but their situation being much nearer to the main Force of the Enemy than to ours it was found impossible to Secure the Provisions any otherwise than by Landing them and carrying them upon the Hill; this was Effected under fire and with great difficulty—

The Possible means of further Retreat were now considered in Councils of War, Compos'd of the General Officers, minutes of which will be transmitted to your Lordship[.]

The only one, that seem'd at all Practicable was by a Night March to Gain Fort Edward with the Troops carrying their Provisions upon their Backs, the impossibility of repairing Bridges putting a Conveyance of Artillery & Carriages out of the question and it was proposed to force the Ford at Fort Edward or the Ford above it[.]

Before this Attempt could be made Scouts returned with Intelligence that the Enemy were Entrench'd opposite those Fords & Possessed a Camp in force on the High Ground between Fort Edward and Fort George with Cannon, they had also Parties down the whole Shore to watch our motions and Posts so near to Us upon our own side of the Water as must prevent the Army moving a Single Mile undiscovered.

The Bulk of the Enemy Army was Hourly Joined by new Corps of Militia & Volunteers & their Numbers together amounted to Sixteen thousand Men[.]

Their Position, which extended three parts in four of a Circle Round us, was from the nature of the Ground, unattackable on all parts—

In this situation the Army took the best Position Possible and fortified waiting 'till the 13th at Night in the Anxious hope of Succor from our Friends or the next desirable expectation, an Attack from our Enemies—

During this time the Men lay continually upon their Arms and were Cannonaded in every part; Even Rifle Shot and Grape Shot came into all parts of the Line tho' without any considerable Effect—

At this Period an Exact Account of the Provisions was taken & the circumstances stated in the opening of this Letter became Compleat[.]

The Council of War was extended to all the Field Officers & Captains commanding Corps of the Army, and the Convention inclosed herewith ensued[,] a Transaction which I am sure was unavoidable; and which I trust in that Situation will be esteem'd honorable[.]

After the Execution of the Treaty Genl. Gates drew together the Force that had surrounded my Position, and I had the Consolation to have as many witnesses as I have Men under my Command of its amounting to the Numbers mentioned above[.]

During the Events Stated above an Attempt was made against Ticonderoga by an Army Assembled under Major Genl. Lincoln who found means to March with a considerable Corps from Hubberton undiscovered, while another Column of his Force Passed the Mountains between Skenesborough and Lake George; and on the Morning of the 18th of September a Sudden and Genl Attack was made upon the Carrying place at Lake George[,] Sugar Hill [Mount Defiance,] Ticonderoga and Mount Independence. The Sea Officer commanding the Arm'd Sloop Stationed to defend the carrying place as also some of the Officers Commanding at the Posts of Sugar Hill & at the Portage were surprized and a considerable part of four Companies of the 53rd Regimt were made Prisoners[.] A Blockhouse commanded by Lieutt. Lord of the 53rd Regimt was the only Post on that side that had time to make Use of their Arms, and they made a brave defence 'till Cannon taken from the Surprized Vessel was brot against them—

After stating and lamenting so fatal a want of Vigilance I have to inform your Lordship of the Satisfactory events which followed[:]

The Enemy having twice Summoned Brig^{r} Genl Powell and Received Such Answers as became a Gallant officer entrusted with so important a Post, and having tried during the Course of four days Several attacks, and being repulsed in all[,] retreated without having done any considerable damage[.]

Brig^{r} Genl Powell from whose Report to me I extract this Relation gives great Commendations to the Regiment of Prince Frederick & the other Troops stationed at Mount Independence, the Brigadier also mentions with great applause the behavior of Cap$^{t.}$ Taylor of the 21st Regiment who was accidentally there on his Road to the Army from the Hospital & L$^{t.}$ Beecroft of 24th Reg$^{t.}$ who with the Artificers in Arms defended an Important Battery—

On the 24th Septr the Enemy Enabled by the Capture of the Gun Boats & Batteaux which they had made after the Surprize of the Sloop to embark upon Lake George attacked Diamond Island in two Divisions[.]

Capt$^{n.}$ Aubrey[221] and two Companies of the 47th Regim^{t} had been posted at that Island from the time the Army Passed the Hudsons River as a better Situation for the Security of the Stores, At the South End of Lake George; than Fort George which is on the Continent, and not tenable against Artillery and Numbers. The Enemy were Repulsed by Cap$^{t.}$ Aubrey with Great Loss & pursued by the Gun Boats under his Command to the East Shore, where two of their Principal Vessels were retaken together with all the Cannon; they had just time to set fire to the other Batteaux and retreated over the Mountains[.]

I beg leave to refer your Lordship for further particulars to my Aid de Cap Lord Petersham, and I humbly take Occasion to recommend to his Majesty's notice, that Nobleman, as one endowed with Qualities

---

[221] Captain Thomas Aubrey was a highly experienced British officer, having joined the 9th Foot in 1762. He commanded a company of the 47th Foot at the Battle of Bunker Hill in June 1775. His successful defense of Diamond Island earned Captain Aubrey considerable recognition. He eventually rose to major, and from 1788 he remained on the half-pay list as a captain. He died in retirement in London in 1814. Rogers, *Hadden's Journal and Orderly Books*, 321–323. For the successful defense of Diamond Island, refer to Nelson, "Battle of Diamond Island," 36–53; Clarke, ed., "Colonel John Brown's Expedition," 284–293; and DeCosta, *Fight at Diamond Island*. For a more modern secondary account, see Cubbison, *"Artillery never gained more Honour,"* 132–133.

to do important Services to his Country in every Station to which his Birth may lead, In this late Campaign in particular his Behavior has been such as to entitle him to the fullest applause and I am confident his Merit will be thought a Sufficient ground for Preferment tho' deprived of the Eclat and sort of Claim which generally attends the delivery of fortunate dispatches[.][222]

I have only to add my Lord a Genl Report of the Killed and Wounded[.] I do not give it as Correct the hurry of the time and the Separation of the Corps having rendered it impossible to make it so, the British officers have bled profusely and Most honorably all who have fallen were valuable but the extensive merits which marked the Publick & private Character of Brigadier General Fraser will long remain upon the Memory of this Army and make his Loss a Subject of particular Regret; those who remain unwounded have been equally forward and the General officers from the mode of Fighting, have been more exposed than in other Services— Among the rest I have had my escapes— It depends upon the Sentence his Majesty shall pass upon my Conduct upon the Judgement of my profession, and of the Impartial and respectable parts of my Country, whether I am to esteem them Blessings or Misfortunes—

I have the honor to be with the greatest respect
Yr [Your] Lordships Most Obedt & Most Humble Servt
J. Burgoyne
P.S.
The above in an Exact duplicate of the dispatch sent by Lord Petersham[,] Capt. Craigg of the 47th Regiment who has the charge of it,[223] is an officer of Great Merit; and is particularly worthy of Notice for having Served with unabated Zeal and Activity thro' this laborious Campaign notwithstanding a wound thro' his Arm which he received at Hubbarton—

---

[222]Lord Petersham, the 3rd Earl of Harrington (1753–1829), came from a long distinguished military line. Early in 1776, as a captain of the Grenadier Company of the 29th Foot, he traveled to Canada with the large British relief column. From July 12, 1777, he served as an aide-de-camp to Burgoyne. An extensive biographical sketch is in Rogers, *Hadden's Journal and Orderly Books*, 367–372.

[223]Captain James Craig, previously introduced, was severely wounded at Hubbardton and subsequently served in Burgoyne's headquarters during his convalescence.

6.16/24a

Copy of a Note from Lieut. Genl. Burgoyne to Major Genl Gates and his answer. In Lt. Genl. Burgoyne's of October 20, 1777

October 13th 1777

Lieut. Gen. Burgoyne is desirous of sending a Field Officer with a Message to Major Genl Gates upon a Matter of high moment to both Armies. He requests to be informed at what Hour Genl gates will receive him tomorrow Morning.

Major General Gates Answer

Major Genl. Gates will receive a Field Officer from Lt. Genl. Burgoyne at the advanced Post of the Army of the United States at Ten o'Clock tomorrow morning from whence he will be conducted to Head Quarters.

Camp at Saratoga
9 o'Clock P.M.
13 October 1777

6.16/24b

Copy of A Message from Lieut. Genl Burgoyne to Major Genl Gates, by Major Kingston In Lieut. Genl. Burgoyne's of October 20, 1777[224]

Major Kingston delivered the following Message to Major General Gates Octr. 14 1777.

After having fought you twice Lieutt. Genl. Burgoyne has waited some days in his present Position determined to try a third conflict against any force you could bring to attack him.

He is apprized of the superiority of your Numbers and the disposition of your Troops to impede his Supplies and render his retreat a Scene of Carnage on both sides. In this Situation he is impelled by humanity

[224] This letter was printed in Burgoyne, *State of the Expedition from Canada*, cii–ciii. Aside from minor variations in spelling, punctuation, and capitalization, this letter has not been modified in Burgoyne's defense.

and thinks himself justified by established principles and precedents of State, and of War, to spare the lives of brave men upon honourable terms; Should Major Genl. Gates be inclined to treat upon that Idea Genl. Burgoyne would propose a cessation of Arms during the time necessary to communicate the preliminary terms by which in any extremity he and his Army mean to abide.

6.16/24c

Copy of Major Genl. Gates's Proposals & of Lieut. General Burgoyne's Answer Incl. [in] Genl. Burgoyne's of October 20, 1777[225]

Major Genl Gates's Proposal

1st. Genl. Burgoyne's Army being exceedingly reduced by retreated Defeats by desertion Sickness &c. their Provisions exhausted their military Horses, Tents and Baggage taken or destroyed their retreat cut off and their Camp invested they can only be allowed to surrender Prisoners of War.

[Answer:] Lieut. General Burgoyne's Army however reduced will never admit that their retreat is cut off while they have Arms in their hands.

2nd. The Officers and Soldiers may keep the Baggage belonging to them. The Generals of the United States never permit Individuals to be pillaged.

[Answer: None, implying acceptance].

3rd. The troops under his Excellency General Burgoyne will be conducted by the most convenient Route to New England marching by easy Marches and Sufficiently provided for by the way.

[Answer:] This Article is answered by Genl. Burgoyne's first Proposal which is here annexed.

4th. The Officers will be admitted on Parole, may wear their side Arms and will be treated with the Liberality customary in Europe, so long as they by proper behavior, continue to deserve it[,] but those who are

[225] This letter was printed in Burgoyne, *State of the Expedition from Canada*, ciii–civ. Again, aside from minor variations, Burgoyne did not alter this letter.

apprehended having broke their Parole as some British Officers have done must expect to be close confined.

[Answer:] There being no Officer in this Army under or capable of being under the description of breaking Parole[,] this Article needs no answer.

5th. All Public Stores, Artillery, Arms, Ammunition, Carriages, Horses &c. &c. must be delivered to Commissaries appointed to receive them.

[Answer:] All Public Stores may be delivered—Arms excepted.

6th. These terms being agreed to and signed The troops under his Excellency Genl. Burgoyne's Command may be drawn up in their Encampments where they will be ordered to Ground their Arms and may thereupon be marched to the River side to be passed over in their way towards Bennington.[226]

[Answer:] This Article inadmissible in any extremity sooner than this Army will consent to ground their Arms in their Encampments they will rush on the Enemy determined to take no Quarter.

7th. A Cessation of Arms to continue till Sunset to receive General Burgoyne's answer.

Signed
Horatio Gates
Camp at Saratoga October 14[,] 1777.

6.16/24d

Copy of Second Message from Lieut. Genl. Burgoyne to Major Genl Gates by Major Kingston[227] Incl. [in] Genl. Burgoyne's of October 20, 1777

Major Kingston met the Adjutant General of Major General Gates's Army October 14th at Sun Set and delivered the following Message.

[226]An army that had been forced to surrender after an honorable resistance would expect to march out of its works to yield, thus indicating that it still held its own works and was still capable of a defense. By permitting Gates to occupy his works and permitting the surrender of his troops within their own works, Burgoyne would be admitting that he was no longer capable of maintaining an effective defense, and had been defeated. Such an admission would have obviously proven false Burgoyne's delusion that he was entering into a "convention" instead of being forced to surrender, so he adamantly rejected this article.

[227]This letter was printed in Burgoyne, *State of the Expedition from Canada*, xiv, in substantially the same form.

If General Gates does not mean to recede from the sixth Article the Treaty ends at once.

The Army will to a Man proceed to any Act of Desperation rather than submit to that Article.

The Cessation of Arms ends this Evening.

6.16/24e

Copy of Lieut. General Burgoyne's Proposal &c. [and] of Major General Gates's Answer, In Lieut. Genl. Burgoyne's of October 20, 1777

Lieut^t^ Genl. Burgoyne's Proposal

The annexed answers being given to Major General Gates's Proposal it remained for Lieut^t.^ Genl. Burgoyne and the Army under his Command to state the following preliminary Articles on their part.

1st The Troops to march out of their Camp with the Honours of War and the Artillery of the Intrenchments which will be left as hereafter may be regulated.

Major Genl Gates's Answers.

The troops to march out of their Camp with the Honours of War and the Artillery of the Intrenchments to the verge of the River where the old Fort stood where their Arms and Artillery must be left.

2nd A free Passage to be granted to this Army to Great Britain upon Condition of not serving again in North America during the present Contest and a proper Port to be assigned for the Entry of Transports to receive the troops wherever Genl Howe shall so order.

Agreed to for the Port of Boston.

3rd Should any Cartel take place by which this Army or any part of it may be exchanged the foregoing Article to be void as far as such Exchange shall be made.

Agreed.

4th All Officers to retain their Carriages[,] Bat Horses, and other Cattle and no Baggage to be molested or searched, the Lieut^t.^ General giving his Honour that there are no Public Stores Secreted therein[.]

Major General Gates will of course take the necessary measures for the security of this Article.

Agreed.

5th Upon the March the Officers are not to be separated from their men, and in quarters, the Officers shall be lodged according to Rank and are not to be hindered from assembling their men for Roll Calling and other necessary purposes of Regularity.

Agreed to as far as Circumstances will admit.

6th There are various Corps in this army composed of Sailors, Batteau Men, Artificers, Drivers, Independent Companies and followers of the Army and it is expected that those Persons of whatever Country shall be included in the fullest sense and utmost extent of the above Articles and comprehended in every Aspect as British Subjects.[228]

Agreed to in the fullest Extent.

7th All Canadians and Persons belonging to the Establishment in Canada to be permitted to return there.

Agreed.

8th Passports to be immediately granted for three Officers not exceeding the Rank of Captain who shall be appointed by General Burgoyne to carry dispatches to Sir William Howe, Sir Guy Carleton and to Great Britain by the way of New York and the Public Faith to be engaged that the dispatches are not to be opened.[229]

Agreed.

9th The foregoing Articles are to be considered only as Preliminaries for framing a treaty in the course of which others may arise to be considered by both Parties for which Purpose it is proposed that two Officers of each Army shall meet and report their Deliberations to their respective Generals.

This Capitulation to be finished by two o'Clock this day and the Troops March from their Encampments at five and be in readiness to move towards Boston tomorrow morning.

10th Lieut. General Burgoyne will send his D. A. [Deputy Adjutant]

228This article specifically protected any American Loyalists serving in or accompanying Burgoyne's army from any possible reprisals by American Patriots.

229Captain Alexander Fraser of the 34th Foot, commander of the Company of Select Marksmen, served this role for the dispatches carried from Burgoyne to Sir Guy Carleton.

General to receive Major General Gates's Answer tomorrow Morning at 10 o'Clock

Complied with[.]

Signed Horatio Gates
Saratoga 15 Octr. 1777

6.16/24f

Copy of third Message from Lieut. Genl. Burgoyne to Major Genl Gates by Major Kingston In Lieut. Genl. Burgoyne's of October 20, 1777

The eighth & first Preliminary Articles of Lieutenant General Burgoyne's Proposals and the 2^d^[,] 3rd and 4th of those of Major General Gates of yesterday being agreed to the foundation of the proposed treaty is out of dispute. But the several Subordinate Articles and Regulations necessarily springing from these Preliminaries and requiring explanation and Precision between the Parties before a Definitive Treaty can be safely executed, a longer time that that mentioned by Genl. Gates in his answer to the 9th article becomes indispensably necessary. Lieut^t.^ Genl. Burgoyne is willing to appoint two Officers immediately to meet two others from Major General Gates to propound, discuss and settle those subordinate Articles in order that the treaty in due form may be executed as soon as possible.[230]

Signed
Jno Burgoyne
Camp at Saratoga Octr. 15th 1777
Major Kingston has authority to settle the Place for the meeting of the Officers proposed.
Settled by Major Kingston on the Ground where Mr. Schuylers House stood.

---

[230]It is difficult from the flowery language of Burgoyne to ascertain what he was actually attempting to gain from this correspondence. Conceivably, it was simply a delaying ploy on his part to win some additional time for Clinton's advance to change the deplorable military and tactical circumstances that he was facing.

6.16/24g

Copy of Message from Lieut. Genl. Burgoyne to Major Gen Gates In Lieut. Genl. Burgoyne's of October 20, 1777

In the Course of the Night Lieutenant General Burgoyne has received intelligence that a considerable force has been detached from the Army under the Command of Major General Gates during the course of the Negotiations of the Treaty depending between them; Lieutenant General Burgoyne conceives this if true to be not only a Violation of the Cessation of Arms but Subversive of the Principles on which the Treaty originated, viz$^{t.}$ A great superiority of Numbers in General Gates's Army. Lieutenant General Burgoyne therefore requires that two Officers on his Part be permitted to see that the strength of the Forces now opposed to him is Such as will convince him that no such Detachments have been made, and that the Same principle of Superiority on which the Treaty first began still exists.[231]

16 October.

6.16.24h

Copy of Articles of Convention between Lieut. Genl. Burgoyne & Major Gen. Gates[232] In Lt. Genl. Burgoyne's of October 20, 1777

Articles of Convention between Lieut. General Burgoyne and Major General Gates.

1st. The Troops under Lieut. Gen$^{l.}$ Burgoyne to march out of their Camp with the Honours of War, and the Artillery of the Intrenchments, to the Verge of the River, where the Old Fort Stood; where the Arms

[231]This appears to be nothing more than a clever ruse on Burgoyne's part to gain intelligence regarding the American army, which he was utterly unable to obtain in any other manner.

[232]The final negotiated and signed articles under which Burgoyne surrendered to Gates.

and Artillery are to be left. The Arms to be piled by word of Command from their own Officers.

2nd. A free passage to be granted to the Army under Lieut. General Burgoyne to great Britain on condition of not serving again in North America during the present Contest and the Port of Boston is assigned for the entry of Transports to receive the Troops, whenever General Howe shall so order.[233]

3rd. Should any Cartel take place by which the Army under Gen$^{\text{l.}}$ Burgoyne, or any part of it, may be exchanged, the foregoing Article to be void as far as such exchange shall be made[.]

4th. The Army under Lieu$^{\text{t.}}$ General Burgoyne to march to Massachusetts Bay, by the easiest[,] most expeditious and Convenient Route and to be quartered in[,] near or as Convenient as possible to Boston that the March of the Troops may not be delay'd, when Transports arrive to receive them.

5th The Troops to be supplied on their March and during their being in Quarters with Provisions by Major General Gates's Orders at the same rate of Rations as the Troops of his own Army, and if possible the Officers Horses and Cattle are to be supplied with forage at the usual Rates.

6th. All Officers to retain their Carriages[,] Bat Horses and other Cattle and Baggage [not] to be molested or searched. Lieut. Gen$^{\text{l.}}$ Burgoyne giving his Honor that there are no Public Stores secreted therein. Major General Gates will of course take the necessary measures for the due performance of this Article; should any carriages be wanted during the march for the Transportation of Officers Baggage, they are if possible to be supplied by the Country at the usual Rates.

7th. Upon the march and during the time the Army shall remain in Quarters in the Massachusetts Bay, the Officers are not as far as Circumstances will admit to be separated from their men. The Officers are to be quartered according to Rank, and are not to be hindered from assembling their men for Roll Callings and other necessary purposes of Regularity.

8th. All Corps whatever of General Burgoyne's Army, whether composed of Sailors, Batteau Men[,] Artificers, Drivers, Independent

[233] This was the most contentious of the Articles, as Burgoyne's army could simply replace other British soldiers in Great Britain or the European continent, who could then be transferred to North America.

Companies and followers of the Army of whatever Country shall be included in the fullest sense and utmost extent of the above Articles and comprehended in every respect as British Subjects.

9th. All Canadians and Persons belonging to the Canadian Establishment, consisting of Sailors, Batteau Men, Artificers, Drivers[,] Independent Companies and any other followers of the Army who come under no particular description, are to be permitted to return there, they are to be conducted immediately by the shortest Route to the first British post on Lake George[,] are to be supplied with Provisions in the same manner as the other Troops and are to be bound by the same Condition of not serving during the present contest in North America.

10th. Passports to be immediately granted for three Officers not exceeding the Rank of Captains who shall be appointed by Lieut. Genl. Burgoyne to carry Dispatches to Sir William Howe[,] Sir Guy Carleton, and to great Britain, by the way of New York[,] and Major General Gates engages the public Faith that these Dispatches shall not be opened— These Officers are to set out immediately, after receiving their Dispatches, and are to travel the shortest Route and in the most expeditious Manner.

11th. During the stay of the Troops in the Massachusetts Bay the Officers are to be admitted on Parole, and are to be permitted to wear their side Arms.

12th. Should the Army under Lieut. General Burgoyne find it necessary to send for their cloathing and other Baggage from Canada they are to be permitted to do it in the most [expeditious] manner and the necessary Passports granted for that purpose.

13th. These Articles are to be mutually signed and exchanged tomorrow morning at Nine O'Clock and the Troops under Lieutenant General Burgoyne are to march out of their Intrenchments at three O'Clock in the Afternoon.

Camp at Saratoga 16th October 1777.
Horatio Gates, Major General
(True Copy)

To prevent any doubts that might arise from Lieut. General Burgoyne's name not being mentioned in the above Treaty Major General Gates hereby declares that he is understood to be comprehended in it as fully as if his name had been specifically mentioned.[234]

Horatio Gates.

6.14/24i

Copy of the Minutes of a Council of War held on the Heights of Saratoga on October 12, 13, 14, & 15, 1777. In Lieut. Genl. Burgoyne's of October 20, 1777

Minutes of a Council of War held on the heights of Saratoga October 12th 1777.[235]

Present[:]
Lieut. Genl. Burgoyne
Major Genl. Phillips
Major Genl. Riedesel
Brigr Genl Hamilon[.]

The Lieutenant General States to the Council the present Situation of Affairs.

The Enemy in force according to the best intelligence he can obtain to the amount of upwards of fourteen thousand men and a considerable quantity of Artillery, are on this side the Fish Kill, and threaten an attack; On the other side the Hudson's River between this Army and Fort Edward is another Army of the Enemy, the numbers unknown, but one Corps which there has been an opportunity of observing is reported to be about fifteen hundred men they have likewise Cannon on the other side the Hudson's River and they have a Bridge below Saratoga Church by which the two Armies can communicate[.]

The Batteaux of the Army have been destroyed, and no means appear of making a Bridge over the Hudsons River, were it even practicable from the position of the Enemy[.]

---

234 Why Gates inserted this final paragraph at the end of the Articles cannot be ascertained.

235 This letter was printed as Appendix No. 15 in Burgoyne, *State of the Expedition from Canada*, xcviii–cii. As per the other letters that Burgoyne utilized, Burgoyne used this letter in an unaltered state, except for minor variations of punctuation, capitalization and spelling.

The only means of Retreat therefore, are by the Ford at Fort Edward, or taking the Mountains in order to pass the River higher up by Rafts, or by another Ford which is reported [underline indicates emphasis in original] to be practicable with difficulty or by keeping the Mountains to pass the head of Hudsons River and continue to the westward of Lake George all the way to Ticonderoga, it is true this last passage was never made but by Indians or very small Bodies of Men.

In order to pass Cannon or any Wheel Carriages, from hence to Fort Edward, some Bridges must be repaired under fire of the enemy from the opposite side of the River and the principal Bridge will be a Work of fourteen or fifteen hours; there is no good position for the Army to take to sustain that Work, and if there were the time stated as necessary would give the Enemy on the other side the Hudsons River an Opportunity to take post on the strong ground about Fort Edward or to dispute the Ford while General Gates's Army followed the Rear.

The Intelligence from the lower part of Hudsons River is founded upon the concurrent reports of Prisoners and Deserts who say it was the news in the Enemy's Camp that Fort Montgomery was taken and one man a friend to Government, who arrived yesterday and mentions some particulars of the manner which it was taken.

The Provisions of the Army may hold out to the 20th there is neither Rum nor Spruce Beer[.] Having committed this State of Facts to the consideration of the Council the General requires their Sentiments on the following Propositions.

1st. To wait in the present position an attack from the enemy or the chance of favorable Events.

2nd. To attack the Enemy[.]

3rd. To retreat[,] repairing the Bridges as the Army moves[,] for the Artillery[,] in order to force the passage of the Ford.

4th. To retreat by night leaving the Artillery and the baggage, and should it be found impracticable to force the Passage with musquetry to attempt the Upper Ford or the passage round Lake George.

5th. In case the Enemy by extending to their left leave their rear open[,] to march rapidly for Albany.

Upon the first proposition Resolved that the Situation would grow worse by delay, that the Provisions now in Stores is not more than sufficient for the retreat should impediments intervene or a Circuit of Country become necessary and as the Enemy did not attack, when the ground was unfortified, it is not probable they will do it now, as they have a better game to Play.

The second unadvisable and Desperate, there being no possibility of reconnoitering the Enemy's position and his great Superiority of numbers Known.

The third impracticable.

The Fifth thought worthy of consideration by the Lieutenant General[,] Major Gen$^{l.}$ Phillips and Brig$^{r.}$ General Hamilton but the position of the Enemy yet gives no open for it.

Resolved that the fourth proposition is the only resource [recourse], and that to Effect it, the utmost secrecy and silence is to be observed, and the Troops are to be put in motion from the right in the still part of the night without any change in the Disposition.

N.B. It depended upon the Delivery of six Days provision in due time, and upon the return of Scouts who had been sent forward; to examine by what route the Army could probably move the first four [underline indicates emphasis in original] miles undiscovered whither the Plan should take place on that day or on the morrow.

The Scouts on their return reported, that the Enemy's position on our right [i.e., to the north] was such, and they had so many small parties out, that it would be impossible to move without our march being immediately Discovered.

Minutes and Proceedings of a Council of War, consisting of all the General Officers and Field Officers and Captains commanding Corps on the Heights of Saratoga Octob^{r} 13th 1777.[236]

The Lieutenant General having explained the situation of Affairs as in the preceeding Council, with the Additional Intelligence that the Enemy was intrenched at the Fords at Fort Edward and likewise occupied the strong position on the Pine Plains between Fort George and Fort Edward; Expressed his readiness to undertake at their head any enterprise of Difficulty or hazard, that should appear to them within the Compass of their Strength or Spirit. He added that he had reason to

[236]This letter was printed in Appendix No. 15 in Burgoyne, *State of the Expedition from Canada*, ci–cii, in a nearly identical form. There is no break in the manuscript above this heading.

believe a Capitulation had been on the Contemplation of some, perhaps of all, who knew the real Situation of things, that upon a circumstance of such consequences to National and personal honor, he thought it a duty to his Country, and to himself, to extend his Council beyond the usual limits; that the assembly present; might justly be esteemed a full Representation of the Army, and that he should think himself unjustifiable in taking any step in so serious a matter, without such a concurrenc of sentiment as should make a Treaty the act of the Army as well as that of the General.

The First Question therefore he desired them to Decide, was, whether an Army of 3500 fighting men and well provided with Artillery were justifiable upon the Principles of National Dignity and Military honor in capitulating in any possible Situation?

Resolved Nem. Con.[237] in the Affirmative.

Quest. 2nd: Is the present situation of that nature?

Resolved Nem. Con. That the present Situation justifies a Capitulation upon honourable terms.

The Lieutenant Genl. Then Drew up the Message Marked N$^{o.}$ 2 in the papers relative to the Negotiation, and laid it before the Council [Letter 6.16/24d]. It was unanimously approved and upon that foundation the Treaty open'd[.]

Octob. 14th. Major Kingston having delivered the Message mark'd N$^{o.}$ 2 returned with the proposals marked N$^{o.}$ 3 [Letter 6.16/24e] and the Council of War being Assembled again, the Lieutenant General laid them before it, when it was Resolved unanimously to reject the 6th Article and not to admit of it in ay Extremity whatever[.] The Lieut. Gen$^{l.}$ Then laid before the Council the answer to Major Gen$^{l.}$ Gates's proposals as marked in the same paper, together with his own preliminary proposals which were unanimously approved of.

Octob. 15. The Council being assembled again Major Gen$^{l.}$ Gates['s] answers to Lieut$^{t.}$ Gen$^{l.}$ Burgoyne's proposals were laid before them, whereupon it was resolved that they were satisfactory and a sufficient Ground for proceeding to a Definitive Treaty.

---

[237] Meaning "of one mind; without dissent."

Lloyd W. Smith Collection, Reel 8, Frame 28

Letter from Lieutenant General John Burgoyne to Major General William Heath, Cambridge, November 18, 1777

Cambridge, November 18th, 1777

Sir

The inclement season advancing fast, the cold the soldiers endure by the exposure & construction of the Barracks being already extreme, it becomes an object of the greatest concern with me to provide for their relief. I therefore request you, Sir, as I am persuaded your disposition will interest you in my application, to order enquiry to be made in what quantity & at what price blanketing, or warm mittens, or cloth proper to make soldiers leggings, can be purchased in Boston.

From what I have been able to gather in conversation, I apprehend much expectation cannot be placed upon any of these supplies in Boston at present, I therefore as the next resource [recourse] desire your protection to forward the letter inclosed to Genl. Pigott at Rhode Island by express, & to grant such passports as my secure the expeditious conveyance of such materials as can be furnished there at the present, or be afterwards transported thither from New York.

I confide, Sir, to your honour not to make publick unnecessarily what I have written to Genl. Pigott concerning the fate of the army & of myself. At the same time if there is a sentence or a word that upon perusal you shall think improper to let pass I will change or efface it—my only views are to remove misrepresentations that my effort may occasion, & to secure the conveyance for my letter. I request the messenger may be of your own ordering & I will readily pay the expence that may best insure his quick return.

I shall have to beg the same sort of favour of you in a few days to pass an open letter to Sir Willm Howe.

I have the honor to be
Sir
Your obedient Servant
J: Burgoyne
[To] M. Genl. Heath

Lloyd W. Smith Collection, Reel 8, Frame 28

Letter from Lieutenant General John Burgoyne to Mr. David Geddes, Assistant Pay Master General, Cambridge, Massachusetts, March 6, 1778

Cambridge 6th March 1778

Sir,
Whereas there are some Sailors and Artificers belonging to the different Departments in Canada that were taken prisoners before the Convention and are now on board the Guard Ship in the Harbour of Boston, in great distress, you will therefore Pay each of them some Money on Account of their Pay, from time to time while they remain there; for which the Representatives of the different Departments they belong to are to Account to you.

I am Sir
Your Humble Servant
J Burgoyne
Lt: Genl:
To
Mr. David Geddes
A. Pay Mr. General

Haldimand Papers, File 21834

Letter from Lieutenant General John Burgoyne to General Frederick Haldimand, Cambridge, Massachusetts, April 4, 1778

Cambridge, April 4, 1778

Sir
I beg leave to recommend to your notice & protection as a valuable officer, Capt. Willoc who will have the honour to present you this letter.[238]

I take the same occasion to congratulate your Excellency upon your appointment in Canada where I trust this will find you in safety & health.

I have the honour to be with great respect
Sir
Your most Obedient Humble Servant
J Burgoyne
[To] His Excy Genl Haldimand

Haldimand Papers, File 21834

Letter from Lieutenant General John Burgoyne to Sir Guy Carleton, Cambridge, Massachusetts, April 4, 1778

Cambridge April 4, 1778

Sir
The embarkation of the troops of this army being suspended I am to request your Excellency to order the Cloathing, men's necessaries, officers baggage & all other articles, arms & accoutrements excepted, to be Shipped for the Port of Boston. A passport will be sent herewith for the safe conduct of the vessel.

[238]Captain Willoc was a captain of the Grenadier Company of the 8th Regiment of Foot. He had been detailed to serve as an assistant to German general Riedesel and served on his staff throughout the Valcour Island and Saratoga campaigns. Presumably, he must have spoken fluent German. Riedesel noted that he was "an officer of talent, and full of zeal for the service." Rogers, *Hadden's Journal and Orderly Books*, 177.

This letter will be delivered by Capt. Willoc who I beg leave to recommend as a valuable officer. A duplicate will be dispatched by a flag of truce by him.[239]

I have the honour to be with great respect
Your Excellency's Most Obedient Humble Servant
J. Burgoyne[240]

Haldimand Papers, File 21834

Letter from Lieutenant Colonel Phillip Skene to Sir Guy Carleton, Cambridge, Massachusetts, April 16, 1778

Cambridge the 16th of April 1778

Sir
I take this, the first opportunity of paying my respects on paper, the assurances that I had of being exchanged for a Mr. Fell, induced me to take this Route, in order to be as Early as General Burgoyne in Europe. Things are since Changed, and I am here, waiting in hopes of returning to my family in Canada, the place of my distination, by the Genls Convention[.] Before he went away, in justice to my Son,[241] for Rank promised, he [Lieutenant General John Burgoyne] gave the following testimony[:]

> "Governor Skene, wishing to have from my hand a testimony of his Son's behaviour during the late Campaign, I think it due to justice to assure all those whom it may concern, that he distinguished himself very particularly by diligence, address, and bravery, and I warmly recommend him as an Officer of great promise, to the Service, and Worthy of higher rank that he now holds. Given at Cambridge, April 4th 1778. J Burgoyne, Lt Genl."

239 Captain Willoc traveled by way of Halifax to Quebec, under "flag of truce" on an American or British vessel.

240 Upon successfully reaching Quebec, Captain Willoc delivered this request to Carleton. The army's baggage was subsequently shipped to the Convention Army, although it did not arrive until the spring of 1779.

241 Lieutenant Andrew Skene of the 43rd Regiment of Foot and only son of Philip Skene. Lieutenant Skene served throughout the Saratoga Campaign with the Company of Select Marksmen. Strach, "Exploits of Captain Alexander Fraser," 91–98.

Lieut Skene is in the prime for rank which if Missed, he will never regain, and altho' he is of the Eldest in General Howe's Army being of Oc^{r} 1762 by your recommendation, and is Serving and doing his duty as well with you Sir, in Canada (yet I fear) he will be deemed Absent, and neglected, to the Southward in point of his preferment. The Corps of the Canadian department flatter themselves, that an Exchange may take place to return them to their Corps, by returning Americans to their Number, Lieut Rotton would be as happy as I should expect to be, in that case.[242] We are in good Health and learn Philosophy. I have the Honor to be

With the Highest sense of Gratitude
Your Excellencys most faithful and obedient humble Servant
Philip Skene
His Excellency Sir Guy Carleton &c &c &c

Lloyd W. Smith Collection, Reel 8, Frame 28

Letter from Lieutenant General John Burgoyne to Mr. Henry Laurens, President of the Congress, Cambridge, Massachusetts, February 11, 1778

Cambridge 11th February 1778

Sir,
Should the first Letter which my Aide de Camp will have the honour to deliver you fail in the intended effect of restoring the Convention in Saratoga to its original Force & if the Congress adhere to their Resolves of the 8th of January, I become subject to the Dilemma of sacrificing probably my Life & certainly much nearer Interests, or to accept a Passport for England, should the Congress think proper to grant it, as a matter of Indulgence.

---

[242]John Rotten was a nephew of Sir Guy Carleton, his mother being Carleton's sister, Catherine Rotten. As an ensign of the 47th Foot (Carleton's Regiment), he had inadvertently landed near Philadelphia in August 1775, not knowing that hostilities had commenced, and was taken prisoner by the Americans. He was promoted to lieutenant on July 10, 1776. He remained prisoner through at least August 1776. Exchanged, he then served with the 47th Regiment of Foot throughout the Saratoga Campaign, having the misfortune of being again surrendered by the Convention at Saratoga. Rogers, *Hadden's Journal and Orderly Books*, 213–214.

Principle & Duty require me to avow that I did conceive the Cause of my King and Country to be involved, or the great Question upon the Point of public Faith to be committed by my Concession, these personal Sacrifices should be made; But conscious that a Request founded upon individual & private Concerns cannot be prejudicial to the political Interest or Intentions of Great Britain, & persuaded that a Compliance with them can as little effect the same Considerations in America, I address myself to you, Sir, as the Channel which I conceive to be most proper to lay before the Congress the following representations & Application for Relief.

My Health, to which the Climate of America was always adverse, has lately declined by more than ordinary Degrees. The Symptoms of a Complaint I have been subject to before, & to which the Bath Waters have been found the only Remedy, are daily increasing, and it is the Opinion of my Physician, as well as my own, that my Life, under God,—depends in great Measure upon that Resource.

Accounts with the Treasury of Great Britain, to great Extent, and of a very complicated nature, lie open by reason of my Absence, and my Death before they are settled might occasion much Embarrassment, and great Injury to my relations and Friends.

These Circumstances apply to the general Principles of justice and Humanity; another yet remains for generous Consideration. By my Detention in this Country I am deprived of every possible means to give an account of my Actions, and my Character stands—exposed, after an intricate and unsuccessful Campaign, to all the Aspersions and extraneous Interpretations that the malevolent, the prejudiced, or the misinformed may choose to cast upon it.

Such Hardships of Situation, where considered severally or collectively, will, I trust, carry a Weight,—that no Ardour of Hostility or other Circumstances of these unhappy Times can oppose.—

In this confidence & conscious of the favor that I have repeatedly shown to Officers of the Continental Troops upon far less urgent Exigencies, I ask of the Congress leave for myself, the Officers of my Family, whose name & Ranks are transmitted herewith, & my Servants, to return to England by Rhode island, New York, or any other expeditious Route the Congress shall appoint.

I am ready to renew my Obligations, if thought necessary, to all the Stipulations of the Convention of Saratoga, & scorning to withdraw myself upon less Reasons than Life and Honor from any possible Lot of my Profession, I am willing to give further Parole that should the Suspension of Embarkation be by any means prolonged beyond the time apprehended I will return to American upon demand of the Congress, & Due notice given, redeliver my Person into their Power, & abide the common fate of my Brethren in this Army.

I am &c.
Signed
J Burgoyne[,] L$^{t.}$ Gen$^{l.}$
To the Honble Henry Laurens
President of the Congress

Lloyd W. Smith Collection, Reel 8, Frame 28

Resolution of Continental Congress, York, Pennsylvania, March 3, 1778, issuing Parole to Lieutenant General John Burgoyne

In Congress, March 3^{d} 1778

The Committee, to whom was referr'd the Letter No. 2, from Lieutenant General Burgoyne Feb. 11th with a paper inclosed brought in a Report, which was taken into Consideration Whereupon

Resolved,

That Lieutenant General Burgoyne on account of his Ill State of Health have Leave to embark for England, by Rhode Island, or any more expeditious Route, with the Officers of his Family & his Servants, that General Heath furnish the necessary Passports, accepting a Parole from Lieutenant General Burgoyne, Lieutenant Colonel Kingston & Doctor Wood "that should the Embarkation of the Troops of the Convention of Saratoga be by any means prolonged beyond the Time apprehended, those Officers will return to America upon Demand and due Notice given and will redeliver themselves into the Power of Congress unless regularly exchanged.

Conclusions

As an independent commander, John Burgoyne demonstrated considerable military acumen in Portugal late in the Seven Years' War. He displayed dynamic, aggressive, self-confident leadership that garnered a significant victory for British arms. In the ensuing years, Burgoyne gained a reputation at the gaming tables of Europe and London, where he derived great pleasure from the excitement and risk offered by a gamut of games of skill, fortune, and chance. At the same time, as a member of Parliament representing the interests of the monarchy, he achieved political prominence. At the onset of the American rebellion, he possessed proven leadership skills and political reliability and was still youthful enough to retain the health, vigor, and energy required to sustain the demands imposed by a stressful senior military leadership position.

Dispatched to Boston in 1775, Burgoyne contributed almost nothing to the defense of that city against the American blockade. Still, it afforded him at least a modicum of experience with military and civil affairs in North America. Most important, he observed the Battle of Bunker Hill, seeing firsthand the Americans' propensity to expedite the construction of formidable defenses, and the talents of even raw American militia fighting with grim fortitude behind such fortifications.

Returning to Canada the next year, Burgoyne accomplished little throughout the 1776 military campaign. However, he clearly fostered mutual respect, confidence, and admiration between the officers and other ranks of the British army in that colony. He forged close personal relationships with senior officers such as Governor-General Carleton, Major General Riedesel, and Major General Phillips. Burgoyne also gained considerable knowledge of the full range of logistical, transportation, and topographical considerations of Canada and the Lake Champlain area. In view of his wife's death while he was overseas, the absence of prospects for active service against the American defenders of Ticonderoga, and his poor health, Burgoyne returned from Canada for four months.

Although historians have made much of Burgoyne's influence on the formulation of the 1777 campaign during his sojourn in England, the decision to entrust an expedition from Canada against Albany to Burgoyne had already been made in London. Burgoyne clearly contributed to the enhancement of the British government's plans for that campaign. Most significantly, he successfully advanced his concept of a strong column dispatched from Canada up the St. Lawrence River and Lake Ontario against the Mohawk River valley, as a diversion to the main advance on Lake Champlain. Burgoyne was clearly influenced by Sir John Johnson, who was convinced of overwhelming Loyalist fervor along the Mohawk that could be exploited by a British incursion. However, the dilution of strength necessary to facilitate such an expedition provided no real advantage to Burgoyne, and the additional combat power could have made an important contribution to his column in its advance toward Albany.

Arriving in Quebec the first week of May 1777, Burgoyne spent the first five weeks of the campaign, through mid-June, performing critical organizational and administrative steps in necessary preparation. The expedition against the Mohawk Valley to be commanded by Lieutenant Colonel Barry St. Leger, in particular, proved to be a considerable distraction as no previous arrangements to facilitate such a movement had been put in place. The numerous papers included herein regarding this column document the effort necessary to dispatch St. Leger's expedition. Burgoyne's efforts during this five-week period, well documented in these papers, appear to have been active, energetic, carefully considered, and well advised.

Between mid-June and mid-July, Burgoyne displayed the full breadth of his talents and abilities in maneuvering his army against the American bulwarks of Fort Ticonderoga and Mount Independence. Although his planned efforts against Mount Independence on his left (east) flank were frustrated by the vagaries of terrain, Burgoyne's maneuvers on his right (west) flank were conducted with skill and aplomb. In short order, without particular difficulties and while sustaining almost no casualties, Burgoyne defeated the American garrison and drove it south. His pursuit of the retreating Americans on Lake Champlain and on the military road from Mount Independence was swift and vigorous.

However, ominously, while his tactical pursuit was flawless, his logistical arrangements to sustain these twin pursuing columns was woefully inadequate. And although Burgoyne aggressively pushed the pursuit and obtained a significant victory at Skenesboro on July 6, in sustained combat at Hubbardton and Fort Anne his pursuing columns were rebuffed through desperate and determined fighting on the part of the American rear guards. Although Burgoyne's victorious reports to London were ebullient and exuded confidence, General Fraser's advance guard and Colonel Hill's 9th Regiment of Foot had sustained heavy casualties among their irreplaceable British regulars.

From mid-July to mid-September, Burgoyne's resolution appears to have first faltered and then vanished in the face of the demanding logistical and transportation requirements of the campaign. His memorandums prepared in England that winter had been exhaustive in their evaluation of movements upon Lake Champlain, but proved inadequate for his movements south of that body of water and Lake George to Albany. It appears as if Burgoyne believed that, once he reached the Hudson River and initiated his penultimate movement against Albany, his success was preordained. Unfortunately for the British, slowly but steadily during these two months, all of Burgoyne's initiative and energies deteriorated as columns of overloaded carts and wagons ponderously slogged their way south along narrow, rutted, muddy country lanes. Burgoyne could scarcely have imagined this reality while safely ensconced in a warm, comfortable drawing room during a London winter. In the two months spent at Skenesboro and Fort Edward, it became all too apparent that a dashing cavalry officer such as Burgoyne was ill prepared, either intellectually or emotionally, for the tedious, grinding, and monotonous logistical and transportation work that campaigns in North America demanded.

When he finally resumed his approach south on the Hudson River in mid-September, Burgoyne's constrained logistics and supply trains dictated an aggressive and swift advance, precisely the type of schedule at which he had previously excelled years before in Portugal, and mere weeks ago along the shores of Lake Champlain. Instead, Burgoyne's maneuvers became halting and slow, featuring a single day's dilatory movement followed by one to two days' pause. Burgoyne's leadership on the field of battle at Freeman's Farm remained resolute and courageous in the face of considerable danger and adversity, but by the next morning it was apparent that he lacked the combat and logistical power to force passage to his objective. A resolute Burgoyne, the man who carefully evaluated the odds at the gaming tables of Europe, would have recognized that any further advance was impossible, and that his army's energies would be better expended establishing strong permanent garrisons on Lake George and Lake Champlain from which an advance upon Albany could be facilitated the next campaign season.

Instead, Burgoyne seemed frozen, hesitant, and tentative. He remained static in his entrenchments above the Hudson River while the aggressive Americans swarmed to his front, flanks, and around his rear. Burgoyne surrendered the initiative, lost control of the battle space to his front, and simultaneously surrendered his freedom of maneuver. He remained fixed in place, his sole activity during these three critical weeks being to send desperate entreaties to his friend Sir Henry Clinton for succor, while his army continuously and inexorably consumed scarce rations. Following the engagement at Freeman's Farm, Burgoyne behaved like a beaten man. Although the evidence is regrettably scarce, Burgoyne's plaintive pleas to Clinton reflect his growing desperation and absence of resolution and strongly intimate that Burgoyne himself recognized that he had been personally defeated. When Burgoyne finally moved on October 7 in his ill-fated and poorly considered reconnaissance in force, it was too little too late, and the Continental Army had little difficulty shattering it within a few brief hours' combat.

Burgoyne's withdrawal to the north again lacked resolve and commitment. By this moment in the campaign, he was a broken man. Even when a courageous reconnaissance by one of his regimental commanders revealed that the road to Canada remained open, Burgoyne lacked the will to immediately exploit the vulnerability in the noose that the Americans were at that moment drawing tightly around him. The American commanders did not permit this opening to remain for long, and from the moment it was closed, Burgoyne's capitulation was inevitable.

The Convention of Saratoga provided the impetus that France's political leaders required to openly declare their support of the United Colonies and was of great import to the French monarchy. The French resumed their quest to achieve revenge for the great defeat that their nation had sustained in the Seven Years' War. Burgoyne's surrender also eliminated one of Britain's few, and with the French entry into the war, virtually irreplaceable, armies of maneuver. Burgoyne's Convention permanently removed any strategic British offensive capability from Canada, though Britain sent relatively small raids against the frontiers of the American colonies throughout the remainder of the war. While these infrequent raids were violent and destructive, and greatly feared by families living on the American frontier, Britain never again had the capacity to launch a major attack, in force, from Canada against New York. With French military and logistical support flowing into American ports, Continental Army commander General George Washington was enabled to concentrate his small but committed force against a single British threat, considerably simplifying his strategic calculations.

These papers reveal the story of Lieutenant General John Burgoyne in the 1777 Saratoga Campaign. They demonstrate his influence in the organization and planning of the campaign; through his early brilliant leadership upon Lake Champlain; through his gradual deterioration during the two-month time frame during which tactical maneuvers ceased and logistical and transportation considerations became paramount; and culminating in his loss of will and resolve in a month west of the Hudson River, locked in combat with an American army that blocked his path south.

John Burgoyne remains one of the most fascinating soldiers of the American War of Independence. His early military accomplishments, his elopement with a lady of nobility over an affair of the heart, his enjoyment of the gaming tables of London and the Continent, his success as a playwright, his participation in the London social scene, his relationships with the leading politicians of England including King George III and Lord George Germain, together render him an intriguing historical figure. These papers document not only Burgoyne's contributions to and participation in the 1777 Saratoga Campaign, but also the information upon which he formulated his actions and decisions that would profoundly influence the development of three great nations—France, Great Britain, and the United States.

Appendix
Calendar of the Papers

RECORD	DESCRIPTION	REMARKS
U.S. Military Academy Archives	Letter from Maj. Gen. John Burgoyne to Lord Stanley, Boston, June 25, 1775	Printed copy also at Massachusetts Historical Society, Boston
File 17:24, Henry Clinton Papers	Letter from Maj. Gen. John Burgoyne to Maj. Gen. Henry Clinton, Fort Chambly, Canada, July 7, 1776	
6.16/1	Extract of a Letter from Lord George Germain to Sir William Howe, Whitehall, August 22, 1776	
6.16/2	Extract of a Letter from Lord George Germain to Sir Guy Carleton, Whitehall, August 22, 1776	This letter was printed as Appendix No. 2 in Burgoyne, *State of the Expedition from Canada*, ii–iii.
[No file #]	Letter from Maj. Gen. William Phillips to Maj. Gen. Jonathan Burgoyne, Fort Crown Point, October 23, 1776	DeFonblanque, *Political and military episodes*, 218–221.
File 18:47a, Henry Clinton Papers	Letter from Maj. Gen. John Burgoyne to Maj. Gen. Henry Clinton, Quebec, November 7, 1776	
6.16/3	Extract of a Letter from Sir William Howe to Lord George Germain, New York, November 28, 1776	

6.16/4	Copy of a Letter from General Burgoyne to Lord George Germain, Hartford Street [London], January 1, 1777	This letter was printed as Appendix No. 1 in Burgoyne, *State of the Expedition from Canada*, i–ii.
6.16/6	Memorandum of General Carleton relative to the next Campaign communicated to Lieutenant General Burgoyne	
6.16/7	Copy of a Letter from Maj. Gen. William Phillips to General Carleton, St. John's, November 9, 1776	The original letter is in the George Germain Papers, William L. Clement Library, University of Michigan, Ann Arbor. An edited transcription of a portion of the original letter has been previously provided in Cubbison, *"Artillery never gained more Honour,"* 62–63.
6.16/8	"Orders for Winter Quarters, For the British Troops in Canada," as ordered by Governor Guy Carleton, November 1, 1776	
6.29/3	Copy of Extract of a Letter from His Excellency Gen. Guy Carleton, November 25, 1776	Shortage of Rum in Canada, Winter 1776–1777

RECORD	DESCRIPTION	REMARKS
6.16/5	"Memorandums & Observations related to the Service in Canada, submitted to Lord George Germain" by Lt. Gen. John Burgoyne	
6.16/9	"Thoughts for conducting the War from the Side of Canada" by Lt. Gen. John Burgoyne	This letter was printed as Appendix No. 3 in Burgoyne, *State of the Expedition from Canada*, iii–xii.
File 20:34, Henry Clinton Papers	Letter from Maj. Gen. John Burgoyne to Capt. Philemon Pownell, Royal Navy, March 2, 1777	
6.16/10	Extract of a Letter from Lord George Germain to General Sir Guy Carleton, Whitehall, March 26, 1777	This letter was printed as Appendix No. 4 in Burgoyne, *State of the Expedition from Canada*, xii–xvii.
6.16/11	Extract of a Letter from Sir William Howe to Lord George German, New York, April 2, 1777	
6.16/11a	Copy of a Letter from Sir William Howe to Gen. Sir Guy Carleton, New York, April 5, 1777	
6.16/12	Extract of a Letter from Sir Guy Carleton to Lord George Germain, Quebec, May 9, 1777	

6.16/13	Extract of a Letter from Sir Guy Carleton to Lord George Germain, Quebec, June 26, 1777	
6.16/13a	Copy of a Letter from Sir Guy Carleton to Lieutenant General Burgoyne, Montreal, June 10, 1777	
6.16/14	Extract of a Letter from Sir William Howe to Lord George Germain, New York, June 5, 1777	
6.16/15	Extract of a Letter from Lieutenant General Burgoyne to Lord George Germain, Camp on the River Bouquet near Lake Champlain, June 22, 1777	
6.16/15a	"Substance of the Speech of Lieutenant General Burgoyne to the Indians in Congress at the Camp upon the River Bouquet June 21, 1777, And their Answer"	This letter was printed as Appendix No. 6 in Burgoyne, *State of the Expedition from Canada*, xxi–xxv.
6.16/15b	"Copy of Manifesto issued by Lieutenant General J. Burgoyne"	
[No file #]	General Orders issued by Lt. Gen. John Burgoyne, June 30, 1777	
6.5/6	Monthly General Returns of the British Troops, Canada, May 1, 1777	
6.5/7	General Monthly Returns of the German Troops, Canada, May 1, 1777	

RECORD	DESCRIPTION	REMARKS
6.16/16	Letter from Sir William Howe to Lord George Germain, New York, July 15, 1777	
6.16/16a	Copy of a Letter from Lt. Gen. John Burgoyne to Sir William Howe, before Ticonderoga, July 2, 1777	
6.5/5	Return of the Additional Companies, Quebec, July 1, 1777	
6.5/4	Monthly General Return of the Army in Canada, October 1, 1777	
6.24	Correspondence of Sir Guy Carleton relating to Lt. Gen. John Burgoyne's Expedition	List of correspondence, contained in Carleton's letter to Lord George Germain, June 26, 1777 (6.16/13)
6.24/1	Extract of a Letter from Sir Guy Carleton to Lord George Germain, Quebec, May 20, 1777	
6.24/2	Copy of a Letter from Sir Guy Carleton to Maj. Gen. William Phillips, Quebec, April 8, 1777	
6.24/3	Copy of a Letter from Sir Guy Carleton to Maj. Gen. William Phillips, Quebec, May 12, 1777	

6.24/4	Copy of Orders for the Troops to serve under Lt. Gen. John Burgoyne	
6.24/5	Copy of a Letter from Captain Foy, to Lt. Col. Barry St. Leger, Quebec, May 12, 1777	
6.24/6	Copy of a Circular Letter for the Militia Colonels and Commissaries of Canadian Transport	The original of this letter is in French.
6.24/7	Copy of a Letter from Captain Foy to Capt. Alexander Fraser, Assistant Superintendent of Indian Affairs, Quebec, May 13, 1777	
6.24/8	Copy of a Letter from Sir Guy Carleton to Lt. Gen. John Burgoyne, Quebec, May 19, 1777	
6.24/9	Copy of a Letter from Sir Guy Carleton to Lieutenant Colonel Bolton of the 8th Regiment, Quebec, May 18, 1777	
6.24/10	Copy of a Letter from Sir Guy Carleton to the Officer commanding at Oswegatchie, Quebec, May 18, 1777	
6.24/11	Copy of a Letter from Sir Guy Carleton to Col. John Butler, Quebec, May 18, 1777	
6.24/12	Copy of a Letter from Captain Foy to Captain Mackey, Quebec, May 19, 1777	

RECORD	DESCRIPTION	REMARKS
6.24/13	Extract of a Letter from Lt. Gen. John Burgoyne to Sir Guy Carleton, Montreal, May 26, 1777	
6.24/14	Proposed Disposition of the Hospital for the Service in Canada	
6.24/15	List of the Staff Proposed for the Expedition under Lt. Gen. John Burgoyne	
6.24/16	Copy of a Letter from Lt. Col. Barry St. Leger to Lt. Gen. John Burgoyne, May 15, 1777	
6.24/17	Extract of a Letter from Sir Guy Carleton to Lt. Gen. John Burgoyne, Quebec, May 29, 1777	
6.24/18	Extract of a Letter from Sir Guy Carleton to Lt. Gen. John Burgoyne, Quebec, May 28,1777	
6.24/19	Extract of a Letter from Sir Guy Carleton to Lieutenant Governor Cramahé, Montreal, June 9, 1777	
6.24/20	Copy of a Letter from Lt. Gen. John Burgoyne to Sir Guy Carleton, Montreal, June 7, 1777	
6.24/21	Proposal for furnishing Horses, Carriages and Drivers for the Service of the Army under the Command of Lt. Gen. John Burgoyne	

6.24/22	Proposals for furnishing Horses & Drivers for the Service of the Artillery on the Expedition under Lt. Gen. John Burgoyne	
6.24/23	Copy of a Letter from Sir Guy Carleton to Lt. Gen. John Burgoyne, Montreal, June 7, 1777	
6.24/24	Extract of a Letter from the Secretary at War to Sir Guy Carleton, August 17, 1776	
6.24/25	Extract of a Letter from the Secretary at War to Sir Guy Carleton, March 25, 1777	
6.24/26	Copy of a Letter from Captain Foy to Lt. Col. Barry St. Leger, Montreal, June 10, 1777	
6.24/27	Copy of a Letter from Sir Guy Carleton to Lt. Gen. John Burgoyne, St. Johns, June 13, 1777	
6.24/28	Copy of a Letter from Lt. Gen. John Burgoyne to Sir Guy Carleton, St. John's, June 15, 1777	
6.24/29	Copy of a Letter from Sir Guy Carleton to Lt. Gen. John Burgoyne, Montreal, June 17, 1777	
6.24/30	Copy of a Letter from Maj. Gen. William Phillips to Sir Guy Carleton, St. Johns, June 17, 1777	

RECORD	DESCRIPTION	REMARKS
6.24/31	Copy of a Letter from Maj. Gen. William Phillips to Sir Guy Carleton, St. Johns, June 17, 1777	
6.24/32	Copy of a Letter from Sir Guy Carleton to Maj. Gen. William Phillips, Montreal, June 18, 1777	
6.24/33	Copy of Orders, Montreal, June 18, 1777	
6.24/34	Copy of a Letter from Maj. Gen. William Phillips to Sir Guy Carleton, St. John's, June 19, 1777	
6.24/35	Copy of a Letter from Sir Guy Carleton to Maj. Gen. William Phillips, Quebec, June 26, 1777	
6.24/36	Copy of a Letter from Sir Guy Carleton to Lt. Gen. John Burgoyne, Quebec, June 26, 1777	
6.16/18	Copy of a Letter from Lieutenant General Burgoyne to Lord George Germain, Head Quarters Skenesboro House, July 11, 1777	Contains accounts of fall of Fort Ticonderoga, Battle of Hubbardton, and Battle of Fort Anne; also contains British Army Headquarters Journal for July 1–10, 1777; this letter was printed as Appendix No. 7 in Burgoyne, *State of the Expedition from Canada*, xxv–xxxvi.

6.16/19	Copy of a Letter from Lt. Gen. John Burgoyne to Lord George Germain, Head Quarters upon Hudson's River near Fort Edward, July 30, 1777	
6.16/17	Extract of a Letter from Sir Guy Carleton to Lord George Germain, Quebec, July 9, 1777	
6.16/17a	Extract of a Letter from Colonel Butler, Superintendent of Indian Affairs, Fort Niagara, June 15, 1777	Early muster rolls for Butler's Rangers
6.16/17b	"A List of Officers employed in the Indian department, with their Rank and pay" submitted by Col. John Butler	
6.16/17c	"A List of Persons employ'd as Rangers in the Indian Department" provided by Col. John Butler	
6.16/20	Extract of a Letter from Sir Guy Carleton to Lord George Germain, Quebec, September 20, 1777	
6.16/20a	Extract of a Letter from Col. John Butler, Fort Ontario, July 28, 1777	
6.16/20b	Extract of a Letter from Col. John Butler to Sir Guy Carleton, Camp before Fort Stanwix, August 15, 1777	Includes account of the Battle of Oriskany

RECORD	DESCRIPTION	REMARKS
6.16/20c	Extract of a Letter from Lt. Col. Barry St. Leger to Sir Guy Carleton, Oswego, August 27, 1777	Includes account of the entire Fort Stanwix Campaign, including the Battle of Oriskany
6.16/20d	Copy of Lt. Gen. John Burgoyne's Letter to Lt. Col. Barry St. Leger, n.d.	Letter not dated, sometime late August to mid-September 1777
6.16/20e	Extract of a Letter from Lt. Col. Barry St. Leger to Sir Guy Carleton, Oswego, August 27, 1777	Contains description of Fort Stanwix
6.16/20f	Extract of a Letter from Daniel Claus, Superintendent of Indian Affairs, to Sir Guy Carleton, Oswego, August 28, 1777	
6.16/20g	"Copy of Beating Order to John Butler, appointed Major Commandant of a Corps of Rangers to serve with the Indians"	
6.16/20h	"Copy of Instructions to Major John Butler Commandant of a Corps of Rangers to serve with the Indians, in Sir Guy Carleton's of 20th September 1777"	
6.16/21a	Extract of a Letter from Lt. Col. Barry St. Leger to Lt. Gen. John Burgoyne, before Fort Stanwix, August 11, 1777	

6.16/21	Copy of a Letter from Lt. Gen. John Burgoyne to Lord George Germain, Camp nearly opposite to Saratoga, August 20, 1777	This letter was printed as Appendix No. 8 in Burgoyne, *State of the Expedition from Canada*, xxxix–xliv. It contains detailed information on the Bennington expedition, plus forwarded supporting correspondence and documentation.
6.16/22	Translated Copy of a Letter from Baron de Riedesel to Lord George Germain, Camp at Jones Farm, August 28, 1777	
6.16/22a	"Contents of the Instructions Given to Lieutenant Colonel Baum with Regard to an Expedition which he is to Command"	Orders to Lieutenant Colonel Baum for the Bennington expedition; reprinted in various sources; e.g., "General Burgoyne's Instructions to Baum," 12–14.
6.16/22b	"Account of an Affair which happened near Wallon Creek, August 16, 1777"	Description of the Battle of Bennington, Breymann's relief column
6.16/22c	"Relation of the Expedition to Bennington, in Baron de Riedesel's of 28th August 1777"	Description of the Battle of Bennington, Baum's detachment

RECORD	DESCRIPTION	REMARKS
6.16/23	Extract of a Letter from the Honorable Sir William Howe to Lord George Germain, Philadelphia, October 21, 1777	
6.16/23a	Copy of a Letter from Lt. Gen. John Burgoyne to Sir William Howe, Camp at Fort Edward, August 6, 1777, "with a Note annexed-received from Sir Henry Clinton 7 October"	
6.16/23b	Copy of a Note from Lt. Gen. John Burgoyne to Lt. Gen. Sir Henry Clinton, September 23, 1777	
6.16/23c	Copy of a Letter from Lt. Gen. John Burgoyne to Lt. Gen. Sir Henry Clinton, September 28, 1777	
6.16/23d	Copy of a Letter from Lt. Gen. Sir Henry Clinton to Lt. Gen. John Burgoyne, Fort Montgomery, October 8, 1777	An identical duplicate copy (captured by Americans at New Windsor on October 10) is contained in *Public Papers of George Clinton*, 413–414.
6.16/23e	Copy of a Letter from Lt. Gen. John Burgoyne to Lt. Gen. Sir Henry Clinton, September 27, 1777	
Sol Feinstone Collection	Letter from Lt. Gen. John Burgoyne to Maj. Gen. Horatio Gates, [Dovegot House,] October 9, 1777	

6.16/24a	Copy of a Note from Lt. Gen. John Burgoyne to Maj. Gen. Horatio Gates and his answer, October 13, 1777	
6.16/24b	Copy of a Message from Lt. Gen. John Burgoyne to Maj. Gen. Horatio Gates, by Major Kingston, October 14, 1777	This letter was printed in Burgoyne, *State of the Expedition from Canada*, cii–ciii.
6.16/24c	Copy of Maj. Gen. Horatio Gates's Proposals & of Lt. Gen. John Burgoyne's Answer, October 14, 1777	This letter was printed in Burgoyne, *State of the Expedition from Canada*, ciii–civ.
6.16/24d	Copy of Second Message from Lt. Gen. John Burgoyne to Maj. Gen. Horatio Gates by Major Kingston, October 14, 1777	This letter was printed in Burgoyne, *State of the Expedition from Canada*, xiv.
6.16/24e	Copy of Lt. Gen. John Burgoyne's Proposal, and of Maj. Gen. Horatio Gates's Answer, October 15, 1777	
6.16/24f	Copy of third Message from Lt. Gen. John Burgoyne to Maj. Gen. Horatio Gates by Major Kingston, October 15, 1777	
6.16/24g	Copy of Message from Lt. Gen. John Burgoyne to Maj. Gen. Horatio Gates, October 16, 1777	

RECORD	DESCRIPTION	REMARKS
6.16/24h	Copy of Articles of Convention between Lt. Gen. John Burgoyne & Maj. Gen. Horatio Gates, October 16, 1777	Articles of Convention under which Burgoyne's army surrendered at Saratoga on October 17, 1777
6.16/24i	Copy of the Minutes of a Council of War held on the Heights of Saratoga, October 12–15, 1777	This letter was printed as Appendix No. 15 in Burgoyne, *State of the Expedition from Canada*, xcviii–ci; ci–cii.
Lloyd W. Smith Collection, Reel 8, Frame 28	Letter from Lt. Gen. John Burgoyne to Maj. Gen. William Heath, Cambridge, February 11, 1778	Supplies for Convention Army
Lloyd W. Smith Collection, Reel 8, Frame 28	Letter from Lt. Gen. John Burgoyne to Mr. David Geddes, Assistant Pay Master General, Cambridge, March 6, 1778	Authorizes payments to British prisoners in Boston Harbor
Haldimand Papers, File 21834	Letter from Lt. Gen. John Burgoyne to Gen. Frederick Haldimand, Cambridge, April 4, 1778	Recommendation for Captain Willoc
Haldimand Papers, File 21834	Letter from Lt. Gen. John Burgoyne to Sir Guy Carleton, Cambridge, April 4, 1778	Requests shipment of army's baggage from Canada

Haldimand Papers, File 21834	Letter from Lt. Col. Phillip Skene to Sir Guy Carleton, Cambridge, April 16, 1778	Includes testimony from Lt. Gen. John Burgoyne on behalf of Lieutenant Colonel Skene's son, for conduct during Saratoga Campaign
Lloyd W. Smith Collection, Reel 8, Frame 28	Letter from Lt. Gen. John Burgoyne to Mr. Henry Laurens, President of the Congress, Cambridge, February 11, 1778	Requests parole
Lloyd W. Smith Collection, Reel 8, Frame 28	Resolution of Continental Congress, York, Pennsylvania, March 3, 1778, issuing Parole to Lt. Gen. John Burgoyne	

Bibliography

The core of these papers was gathered by Lieutenant General John Burgoyne in support of his defense during the 1779 parliamentary investigations into his conduct of the Saratoga Campaign of 1777. The originals of these papers are located in the Parliamentary Archives, House of Parliament, London. Other key Burgoyne papers are located in the Sir Henry Clinton Papers and Lord George Germain Papers, William L. Clement Library, University of Michigan, Ann Arbor; and in the Sir Frederick Haldimand Papers, British Library (microfilm copies at the David Library of the American Revolution, Washington Crossing, Pennsylvania; and the University of Toronto Library, Toronto, Ontario).

Primary Sources

Alexander, David E., ed. "Diary of Captain Benjamin Warren." *Journal of American History* 3, no. 2 (1909): 201–216.

Arndt, Karl J. R. "New Hampshire and the Battle of Bennington: Colonel Baum's Mission and Bennington Defeat as Reported by a German Officer." *Historical New Hampshire* 32 (Winter 1977): 198–227.

Atkinson, C. T., ed. "Some Evidence for Burgoyne's Expedition." *Journal of the Society for Army Historical Research* 26 (1948): 132–142.

Barker, Thomas M. "The Battles of Saratoga and the Kinderhook Tea Party: The Campaign Diary of a Junior Officer of Baron Riedesel's Musketeer Regiment in the 1777 British Invasion of New York." *Journal of the Johannes Schwalm Historical Association* 9 (2006): 25–48.

Baxter, James Phinney, ed. *The British Invasion from the North: Digby's Journal of the Campaigns of Generals Carleton and Burgoyne from Canada, 1776–1777*. 1887; reprint, New York: DaCapo Press, 1970.

Benians, E. A, ed. *A Journal by Thomas Hughes*. Cambridge: Cambridge University Press, 1947.

Boardman, Oliver. "Journal of Oliver Boardman of Middletown, 1777, Burgoyne's Surrender." *Collections of the Connecticut Historical Society* 7 (Hartford, 1899): 223–327.

Boyle, Joseph Lee, ed. "From Saratoga to Valley Forge: The Diary of Lieutenant Samuel Armstrong." *The Pennsylvania Magazine of History and Biography* 121, no. 3 (July 1997): 237–270.

Bradford, S. Sydney, ed. "Lord Francis Napier's Journal of the Burgoyne Campaign." *Maryland Historical Magazine* 57, no. 4 (December 1962): 285–333.

Brown, Lloyd A., and Howard H. Peckham, eds. *Revolutionary War Journals of Henry Dearborn, 1775–1783*. Chicago: The Caxton Club, 1939.

Burgoyne, Bruce E., trans. and ed. *George Pausch's Journal and Reports of the Campaign in America*. Bowie, Md.: Heritage Books, 2003.

———. *Hesse-Hanau Order Books, A Diary, and Rosters*. Bowie, Md.: Heritage Books, 2003.

Burgoyne, Lieutenant General John. "Letter to Lord Stanley, Boston, June 25, 1775 on Battle of Bunker Hill." Special Collections and Archives, Jefferson Hall, U.S. Military Academy, West Point, N.Y.

———. "Letter to Lord Stanley, Boston, June 25, 1775 on Battle of Bunker Hill." Boston: Massachusetts Historical Society, www.masshist.org/bh/burgoyne.html (accessed August 15, 2011).

———. "Letter to Major General Horatio Gates, [Dovegot House,] October 9, 1777." Sol Feinstone Collection of the American Revolution, David Library of the American Revolution, Washington Crossing, Penn.

———. *A State of the Expedition from Canada*. London: J. Almon, 1780; reprint, New York: The New York Times & Arno Press, 1969.

Chambers, Captain William, Royal Navy. *Atlas of Lake Champlain, 1779–1780*. Montpelier and Bennington: Vermont Heritage Press and Vermont Historical Society, 1984.

Clarke, William Butler, ed. "Colonel John Brown's Expedition Against Ticonderoga and Diamond Island, 1777." *New England Historic Genealogical Society* (October 1920), 284–293.

Clement, Justin, ed. *Orderly Book, 47th Regiment of Foot, Ticonderoga to Saratoga*. N.p., n.d.

———. *Orderly Book of the 47th Regiment Grenadier Company, Major Acland's Grenadier Battalion, June 7, 1777–July 3, 1777*. N.p., n.d.

———. *The Orderly Book of the Royal Regiment of Artillery May 8, 1776 through June 29, 1777*. N.p., n.d.

Clinton, Governor George. *Public Papers of George Clinton*. New York and Albany: Synkoop, Hallenbeck, & Crawford, State Printers, 1889. Vol. 1, *Military, 1775–1777*.

Davies, K. G., ed. *Documents of the American Revolution, 1770–1783*. Vol. 14. Shannon: Irish University Press, 1972.

Doblin, Helga G., trans. *The American Revolution, Garrison Life in French Canada and New York, Journal of an Officer in the Prinz Friedrich Regiment, 1776–1783*. New York: Greenwood Press, 1993.

———. *An Eyewitness Account of the American Revolution and New England Life, The Journal of J. F. Wasmus, German Company Surgeon, 1776–1783*. New York: Greenwood Press, 1990.

———. *The Specht Journal, A Military Journal of the Burgoyne Campaign*. New York: Greenwood Press, 1995.

Gabriel, Michal P., ed., and S. Pascale Vergereau-Dewey, trans. *Quebec during the American Invasion, 1775–1776: The Journal of Francois Baby, Gabriel Taschereau, & Jenkin Williams*. East Lansing: Michigan State University Press, 2005.

"General Burgoyne's Instructions to Lieutenant Colonel Friedrich Baum for the Ill-fated Expedition at Bennington, Vermont, 1777." *New York Historical Society Quarterly Bulletin* 3, no. 1 (April 1919): 12–14.

Houlding, J. A., and G. Kenneth Yates, eds. "Corporal Fox's Memoir of Service, 1766–1783: Quebec, Saratoga, and the Convention Army." *Journal of the Society for Army Historical Research* 68 (Autumn 1990): 146–168.

Jackman, Sydney, ed. *With Burgoyne from Quebec: An Account of the Life at Quebec and of the Famous Battle at Saratoga, by Thomas Anburey*. Toronto: Macmillan of Canada, 1963.

Kingsley, Ronald F., ed. "Letters to Lord Polwarth from Sir Francis-Carr Clerke, Aide-de-Camp to General John Burgoyne." *New York History* 79 (1998): 393–424.

Lamb, Sergeant R. *An Original and Authentic Journal of Occurrences during the Late American War, from Its Commencement to the Year 1783*. Dublin: Wilkinson & Courtney, 1809; reprint, New York: Arno Press, 1968.

Maguire, J. Robert, ed. "Dr. Robert Knox's Account of the Battle of Valcour Island, October 11–13, 1776." *Vermont History* 46, no. 3 (Summer 1978): 141–150.

M'Alpine, John. *Genuine Narratives and Concise Memoirs of Some of the Most Interesting Exploits and Singular Adventures of J. M'Alpine, a Native Highlander, from the Time of his Emigration from Scotland to America in 1773, during the long period of his faithful attachment to . . . the British Armies under the command of the Generals Carleton and Burgoyne . . . till December 1779*. 1780; reprint, Greenock, Scotland: Black Pennell Press, 1985.

McAdam, E. L., Jr., and George Milne, eds., *Johnson's Dictionary: A Modern Selection*. New York: Pantheon Books, 1963.

Muller, John. *A Treatise of Artillery*. 1757, 1780; reprint, Alexandria Bay, N.Y., and Bloomfield, Ont.: Museum Restoration Service, 1977.

O'Callaghan, E. B., ed. *Orderly Book of Lieutenant General John Burgoyne*. Albany, N.Y.: J. Munsell, 1860.

Phillips, Major General William. "Extracts from the Brigade Orders of Major General Phillips in Canada, 1776–1777." Courtesy of the Royal Artillery Historical Trust, Woolwich, London.

Riedesel, Baroness von. "Baroness Von Riedesel, Her Revolutionary Journal." In Hugh F. Rankin, ed., *Narratives of The American Revolution*. 1827; reprint, Chicago: Lakeside Press, 1976, 289–427.

Rogers, Brevet Brigadier General Horatio, U.S. Army Volunteers, ed. *Hadden's Journal and Orderly Books: A Journal Kept in Canada and Upon Burgoyne's Campaign in 1776 and 1777 by Lieutenant James M. Hadden, Royal Artillery.* 1884; reprint, Boston: Gregg Press, 1972.

A Society of Gentlemen in Scotland. *Encyclopaedia Britannica, or a Dictionary of Arts and Sciences.* 3 vols. Edinburgh: A. Bell and C. Macfarquhar, 1768–1771.

Squier, Frank, ed. "Diary of Ephraim Squier." *Magazine of American History* 2, no. 11 (November 1878): 685–694.

Stanley, George F. G., ed. *For Want of a Horse.* Sackville, New Brunswick: Tribune Press, 1961.

Stone, William L., ed. *Journal of Captain Pausch Chief of the Hanau Artillery during the Burgoyne Campaign.* Albany, N.Y.: Joel Munsell's Sons, 1886.

———. *Memoirs, Letters and Journals of Major General Riedesel.* 2 vols. Albany, N.Y., 1861.

Thorp, Jennifer D., ed. *The Acland Journal: Lady Harriet Acland and the American War.* Hampshire County Council, 1994.

Treat, Robert. "Journal of Robert Treat, Captain Isaac Treats Company of Light Horse under the Command of Major Hide." Revolutionary War Soldiers Pension Files, National Archives and Records Administration, Washington, D.C., Pension File M804, Roll 2411, 984–996.

Tulloch, Lida C., ed. "An Eye-Witness of Burgoyne's Surrender." *Magazine of American History* 29 (March 1893): 279–280.

Williamson, John. *A Treatise on Military Finance.* London: T. Egerton, 1782.

Secondary Sources

Bentley, Harriet A. *The Old Military Road from Fort Edward to Lake George, 1755.* Glens Falls, N.Y.: Bullard Press, 1927.

Bergen, Benjamin K., and Madelaine C. Plauché. "*Voilà voilà*: Extensions of Deictic Constructions in French." University of California, Berkeley. www.icsi.berkeley.edu/~bbergen/CSDL4paper.PDF (accessed September 9, 2008).

Billias, George A., ed. *George Washington's Generals.* New York: William Morrow and Company, 1964.

———, ed. *George Washington's Opponents: British Generals and Admirals in the American Revolution.* New York: William Morrow and Company, 1969.

———. "Horatio Gates: Professional Soldier." In Billias, *George Washington's Generals*, 79–108.

———. "John Burgoyne: Ambitious General." In Billias, *George Washington's Opponents*, 142–192.

Bowler, R. Arthur. "Sir Guy Carleton and the Campaign of 1776 in Canada." *Canadian Historical Review* 55, no. 2 (June 1974): 131–140.

Bradley, A. G. *Sir Guy Carleton (Lord Dorchester)*. Toronto, University of Toronto Press, 1966.

Brisebois, Michel. "Books from General Wolfe's Library at the National Library of Canada." *National Library News* 28, no. 2 (February 1996). http://epe.lac-bac.gc.ca/100/202/301/nlnews/nlnews-h/1996/02/2802e-15.htm (accessed December 5, 2007).

Browne, G. P. "Guy Carleton, 1st Baron of Dorchester." In *Dictionary of Canadian Biography*. Toronto: University of Toronto Press, 1966–1994, 5:141–155.

Buchanan, Brenda J., ed. *Gunpowder, Explosives and the State: A Technological History*. Burlington, Vt., and Aldershot, England: Ashgate Publishing, 2000.

Burt, A. L. *Guy Carleton, Lord Dorchester, 1724–1804*. Ottawa: Canadian Historical Association,1955.

———. "The Quarrel Between Germain and Carleton: An Inverted Story." *Canadian Historical Review* 11, no. 3 (September 1930): 202–222.

Caruana, Adrian. "Sir Thomas Blomefield and the Blomefield System of Ordnance." *Arms Collecting* 21, no. 3 (August 1983): 95–100.

Clark, Jane. "The Command of the Canadian Army for the Campaign of 1777." *Canadian Historical Review* 10 (1929): 129–135.

———. "Responsibility for the Failure of the Burgoyne Campaign." *American Historical Review* 35, no. 3 (April 1930): 542–559.

Clement, Justin, and Douglas R. Cubbison. "The British and German Artillery Gunboats at the Battle of Valcour Island." *Society for the Journal of Army Historical Studies* 85, no. 343 (Autumn 2007): 247–256.

Cubbison, Douglas R. *The American Northern Theater Army in 1776: The Ruin and Reconstruction of the Continental Force*. Jefferson, N.C.: McFarland Publishers, 2009.

———. *"The Artillery never gained more Honour": The British Royal Artillery in the 1776 Valcour island and 1777 Saratoga Campaigns*. Fleischmanns, N.Y.: Purple Mountain Press, 2008.

———. "'Eight Pence a Day': The Pay of the Private British Soldier during the War for American Independence." *The Petit Guerre: Newsletter of Captain Fraser's Company of Select Marksmen, British Brigade and Brigade of the American Revolution* (Winter 2004). www.csmid.com.

———. *Historic Structures Report: The Redoubts of West Point*. West Point, N.Y.: U.S. Military Academy, January 2004.

Davis, Robert P. *"Where a Man Can Go": Major General William Phillips, British Royal Artillery, 1731–1781*. Westport, Conn.: Greenwood Press, 1999.

DeCosta, B. F. *The Fight at Diamond Island, Lake George*. New York: J. Sabin & Sons, 1972.

DeFonblanque, Edward B. *Political and military episodes in the latter half of the eighteenth century; Derived from the life and correspondence of the Right Hon. John*

Burgoyne, general, statesman, dramatist. London: Macmillan and Company, 1876.

Drake, Samuel Adams. *Burgoyne's Invasion of 1777*. Boston: Lee and Shepard, 1889.

Edgar, Gregory T. "Burgoyne's Fatal Mistake." *Patriots of the American Revolution* 3, no. 3 (May–June 2010): 6–10.

Gadue, Colonel Michael R. "Lieutenant Colonel Friedrich S. Baum, Officer Commanding the Bennington Expedition: A Figure Little Known to History." *The Hessians: Journal of the Johannes Schwalm Historical Association* 11 (2008): 37–54.

Geddes, David. "'David Geddes, Who You Pronounced A Dunce': Some Notes on the Military Career of the Paymaster to General Burgoyne's Army, 1777–1781." *Bulletin of the Fort Ticonderoga Museum* 15, no. 6 (1997): 425–476.

Gibbons, Luke. "Subtilized into Savages: Edmund Burke, Progress, and Primitivism." *South Atlantic Quarterly* 100, no. 1 (Winter 2001): 83–109.

Glover, Michael. *General Burgoyne in Canada and America*. London: Gordon & Cremonesi, 1976.

Hanson, Lee, and Dick Ping Hsu. *Casemates and Cannonballs, Archaeological Investigations at Fort Stanwix, Rome, New York*. Washington: U.S. Department of the Interior, 1975.

Hargeaves, Reginald. "Burgoyne and America's Destiny." *American Heritage* 7, no. 4 (June 1956): 4–7, 83–85.

Hargrove, Richard J. "General John Burgoyne, 1722–1777." PhD diss., Duke University, 1971.

Howson, Gerald. *Burgoyne of Saratoga*. New York: Times Books, 1979.

Hudleston, F.J. *Gentleman Johnny Burgoyne: Misadventures of an English General in the Revolution*. Indianapolis: Bobbs-Merrill Company, 1927.

Kingsley, Ronald F., Harvey Alexander, and Eric Schnitzer. "German Auxiliaries Project: The Incursion to Mount Independence, the Burgoyne Campaign, July 1777, Part I: Investigation of the Landing and Encampment." *Journal of the Johannes Schwalm Historical Association* 8 (2005): 28–41

———. "German Auxiliaries Project: The Incursion to Mount Independence, the Burgoyne Campaign, July 1777, Part II: The Advance Against Mount Independence." *Journal of the Johannes Schwalm Historical Association* 9 (2006): 53–72.

Kopperman, Paul. "The Numbers Game: Health Issues in the Army that Burgoyne Led to Saratoga." *New York History* 88, no. 3 (2007). www.historycooperative.org/journals/nyh/88.3/kopperman.html (accessed April 7, 2008).

Leroy, Perry E. "Sir Guy Carleton as a Military Leader During the American Invasion and Repulse in Canada, 1775–1776." PhD diss., Ohio State University, 1960.

Lewis, Paul. *The Man Who Lost America: A Biography of Gentleman Johnny Burgoyne.* New York: Dial Press, 1973.

Lord, Philip, Jr. *War over Walloomscoick: Land Use and Settlement Pattern on the Bennington Battlefield—1777.* Albany: New York State Museum, 1989.

Lunt, James. *John Burgoyne of Saratoga.* New York and London: Harcourt Brace Jovanovich, 1975.

Luzader, John F. *Saratoga: A Military History of the Decisive Campaign of the American Revolution.* New York and El Dorado Hills, Calif.: Savas Beatie, 2008.

"Major General Sir Thomas Blomefield, Bt., R.A." http://web.ukonline.co.uk/ewh.bryan/blom-2.html (accessed January 4, 2006).

Martin, James Kirby. *Benedict Arnold, Revolutionary Hero: An American Warrior Reconsidered* (New York: New York University Press, 1997.

Mintz, Max M. *The Generals of Saratoga, John Burgoyne & Horatio Gates.* New Haven and London: Yale University Press, 1990.

Morris, George F. "Major Whitcomb, Ranger and Partisan Leader in the Revolution." *Proceedings of the New Hampshire Historical Society* (Concord) 4 (1899–1905), Part III: 298–321.

Morrissey, Brendan. *Saratoga 1777: Turning Point of a Revolution.* Oxford: Osprey Publishing, 2000.

Morton, Doris Begor. *Philip Skene of Skenesborough.* Granville, N.Y.: Grastorf Press, 1959.

Nelson, Paul D. *General Horatio Gates: A Biography.* Baton Rouge: Louisiana State University Press, 1976.

———. *General Sir Guy Carleton, Lord Dorchester: Soldier-Statesman of Early British Canada.* Madison, N.J., and London: Fairleigh Dickinson University Press, 2000.

Nelson, Peter. "The Battle of Diamond Island." *Proceedings of the New York State Historical Association* 20 (1922): 36–53.

Nickerson, Hoffman. *The Turning Point of the Revolution; or, Burgoyne in America.* 2 vols. 1928; reprint, Port Washington, N.Y.: Kennikat Press, 1967.

Patterson, Samuel W. *Horatio Gates: Defender of American Liberties.* New York: Columbia University Press, 1941.

Randall, Willard S. *Benedict Arnold, Patriot and Traitor.* New York: William Morrow and Company, 1990.

Reynolds, Paul R. *Guy Carleton: A Biography.* Toronto: Gage Publishing, 1980.

Risch, Erna. *Quartermaster Support of the Army: A History of the Corps, 1775–1939.* Washington, D.C.: Center of Military History, U.S. Army, 1989.

Smith, Paul H. "Sir Guy Carleton: Soldier Statesman." In Billias, *George Washington's Opponents,* 103–141.

Speelman, Patrick J. *Henry Lloyd and the Military Enlightenment of Eighteenth-Century Europe*. Westport, Conn.: Greenwood Press, 2002.

Stitt, Edward W., Jr. "Horatio Gates." *Bulletin of the Fort Ticonderoga Museum* 9, no. 2 (Winter 1953): 93–115.

Stone, William L. *The Campaign of Lieutenant General John Burgoyne and the Expedition of Lieutenant Colonel Barry St. Leger*. Albany, N.Y.: Joel Munsell, 1877.

Strach, Stephen G. *An Episode in the History of the Schuyler Mansion: The Visit of Lieutenant General John Burgoyne, October 18–27, 1777*. Albany, N.Y.: Friends of the Schuyler Mansion, 1982; rev. ed., 2002.

———. "A Memoir of the Exploits of Captain Alexander Fraser and His Company of British Marksmen, 1776–1777." *Journal of the Society for Army Historical Research* 63 (1985): 91–98.

Taylor, Alan. *The Divided Ground: Indians, Settlers and the Northern Borderland of the American Revolution*. New York: Alfred A. Knopf, 2006.

Underwood, Wynn. "Indian and Tory Raids on the Otter Valley, 1777–1782." *Vermont Quarterly* 15 (October 1947): 195–221.

Wallace, Willard W. "Benedict Arnold: Traitorous Patriot." In Billias, *George Washington's Generals*, 163–192.

———. *Traitorous Hero: The Life and Fortunes of Benedict Arnold*. New York: Harper & Brothers, 1954.

Ward, Christopher. *The War of the Revolution*. 2 vols. New York: The Macmillan Company, 1952.

Watt, Gavin K. *Rebellion in the Mohawk Valley: The St. Leger Expedition of 1777*. Toronto: Dundurn Press, 2002.

Wickman, Donald H. "Built with Spirit, Deserted in Darkness: The American Occupation of Mount Independence, 1776–1777." Master's thesis, University of Vermont, 1993.

Willcox, William B. "Too Many Cooks: British Planning before Saratoga." *Journal of British Studies* 2, no. 1 (November 1962): 56–90.

Williams, John. "The Battle of Hubbardton: The American Rebels Stem the Tide." Vermont Division of Historic Preservation, 1988 (accessed online June 30, 2002).

Wilson, Barry K. *Benedict Arnold: A Traitor in our Midst*. Montreal and Kingston, Ont.: McGill-Queen's University Press, 2001.

Wright, Colonel John W. "Sieges and Customs of War at the Opening of the Eighteenth Century." *American Historical Review* 39, no. 4 (July 1934): 629–644.

Index